NUTRACEUTICALS AND DIETARY SUPPLEMENTS

PRINCIPLES AND BENEFITS

PROF. KAMAL YADAV GADDA, DR. SHIVA KUMAR RAVULA, DR. RAVI CHANDER THATIPELLI

Contents

Nutraceuticals And Dietary Supplements

Principles and Benefits

● v ●

AUTHORS

Prof. Kamal Yadav Gadda

Principal, Vaagdevi Pharmacy College, Warangal, Telangana, India

Dr. Shiva Kumar Ravula

Associate Professor, Department of Pharmaceutics, Vaagdevi Pharmacy College, Warangal, Telangana, India

Dr. Ravi Chander Thatipelli

Associate Professor & Head, Department of Pharmacy Practice, Vaagdevi Pharmacy College, Warangal, Telangana, India ﬕﬕﬕ

Published by Notion Press

Notion Press, Inc.

800, West El Camino Real #180, California, USA 94040

Notion Press Media Pvt Ltd

#7, Red Cross Road, Egmore, Chennai, Tamil Nadu 600008
Email ID:publish@notionpress.com**Phone Number:** +91 44 46315631

Preface

In recent years, the interest in **nutraceuticals** and **dietary supplements** has surged significantly, reflecting an increasing awareness among the general public about the importance of nutrition in maintaining health and preventing disease. The rising focus on **functional foods**, **vitamins**, **minerals**, and other **bioactive compounds** has led to a greater demand for evidence-based knowledge regarding their roles in human health. This book, "Dietary Supplements and Nutraceuticals: Scientific Principles and Health Benefits," is designed to offer a comprehensive exploration of the **scientific principles** and **health benefits** of nutraceuticals, drawing upon the latest research and clinical studies.

Nutraceuticals, which include **dietary supplements**, **vitamins**, **minerals**, and **herbal products**, have gained significant attention for their potential in preventing and managing a wide range of health conditions. These conditions, including **cardiovascular diseases, diabetes, cancer**, and **neurodegenerative disorders**, have posed increasing challenges to public health systems worldwide. As lifestyle-related diseases continue to rise, understanding the **biological mechanisms**, **effectiveness**, and **safety** of nutraceuticals has never been more critical.

This book serves as an essential resource for students, researchers, and practitioners in the fields of **pharmacology**, **nutrition**, **pharmaceutical sciences**, and **public health**. It aims to bridge the gap between **scientific theory** and **real-world applications**, providing insights into the **classification, mechanisms of action**, and **health benefits** of nutraceuticals. Special emphasis is placed on the role of **phytochemicals, antioxidants, vitamins**, and **bioactive compounds** in **disease prevention** and **management**.

Throughout this book, each chapter delves into the scientific basis behind the **functional properties** of various nutraceuticals. Topics such as the role of **carotenoids, flavonoids, omega-3 fatty acids**, and **prebiotics** are discussed, alongside their applications in promoting **cardiovascular health, immune function, cognitive health**, and **weight management**. Detailed discussions on the **regulatory frameworks** governing **nutraceutical production** and **quality control** have been included, ensuring that readers gain an understanding of the broader context in which nutraceuticals are developed and marketed.

One of the core objectives of this book is to provide an evidence-based overview of nutraceuticals, which will enable readers to critically assess the claims made by manufacturers and practitioners. By offering a blend of **theoretical knowledge** and **practical insights**, this book aims to empower the reader with the tools necessary to make informed decisions about the use of nutraceuticals for health enhancement.

As we continue to witness an evolving landscape in healthcare, the role of **dietary supplements** and **nutraceuticals** is becoming increasingly recognized as an important aspect of **preventive health**. This book aims to contribute to that evolving dialogue, providing an up-to-date, comprehensive resource for anyone looking to understand the scientific principles and health benefits of nutraceuticals.

I hope that this book will not only inform but also inspire students and professionals to explore the exciting and rapidly developing field of **nutraceuticals**, promoting a deeper understanding of the potential they hold in shaping the future of **public health**.

Dr. Kamal Yadav Gadda, Dr. Shiva Kumar Ravula, Dr. Shiva Kumar Ravula

ONE

INTRODUCTION TO NUTRACEUTICALS AND FUNCTIONAL FOODS

1.1 Definition and Scope of Nutraceuticals

1.1.1 Definition of Nutraceuticals

The term "nutraceutical" is a combination of the words "nutrition" and "pharmaceutical." It was first introduced by Stephen DeFelice in 1989, emphasizing the concept that food or food-derived substances can provide medical or health benefits, including the prevention and treatment of diseases. Nutraceuticals are recognized as bioactive compounds extracted from food sources that offer health advantages beyond basic nutritional value. These substances include vitamins, minerals, amino acids, polyphenols, flavonoids, carotenoids, and probiotics, among others. They are available in various forms such as dietary supplements, functional foods, medicinal foods, and pharmaceutical-grade preparations. The idea behind nutraceuticals is rooted in the traditional use of food-based healing in ancient civilizations like Ayurveda, Traditional Chinese Medicine (TCM), and Unani medicine, which have long advocated the therapeutic potential of food-derived compounds.

A clear distinction exists between food, nutraceuticals, and pharmaceuticals. Food provides essential nutrients such as carbohydrates, proteins, fats, vitamins, and minerals necessary for sustaining life, growth, and overall health. Nutraceuticals, however, are specialized food-derived bioactive compounds that offer additional health benefits, often preventing or managing specific diseases or physiological conditions. Pharmaceuticals, on the other hand, are chemically synthesized or naturally derived substances used to diagnose, treat, or prevent diseases. Unlike nutraceuticals, pharmaceuticals undergo rigorous regulatory approval processes and clinical trials before being marketed. While food supports basic metabolism and sustains energy levels, nutraceuticals bridge the gap between regular diet and pharmaceutical intervention, offering a preventive approach to disease management.

The relationship between food and health is deeply rooted in scientific and epidemiological studies that link dietary patterns with disease prevalence. The growing incidence of lifestyle-related disorders such as cardiovascular diseases, obesity, diabetes, and neurodegenerative conditions has led to an increased focus on the role of functional foods and nutraceuticals in maintaining health. Research has shown that bioactive compounds such as omega-3 fatty acids from fish oil reduce inflammation and support cardiovascular function, polyphenols from green tea exhibit strong antioxidant properties, and probiotics improve gut microbiota balance, enhancing digestive and immune health. The concept of nutraceuticals aligns with the age-old principle of "Let food be thy medicine and medicine be thy food," highlighting their role in promoting well-being and reducing dependency on pharmaceutical drugs.

1.1.2 Scope and Importance of Nutraceuticals

Role in Preventive Healthcare: Impact on Disease Prevention

Nutraceuticals play a crucial role in preventive healthcare by providing essential bioactive compounds that support overall health and reduce the risk of chronic diseases. The growing burden of non-communicable diseases such as cardiovascular disorders, diabetes, obesity, and neurodegenerative conditions has necessitated the shift from treatment-based approaches to preventive strategies. Nutraceuticals, including omega-3 fatty acids, flavonoids, carotenoids, and probiotics, have been extensively studied for their ability to modulate metabolic processes, enhance immune function, and prevent oxidative stress-related damage at the cellular level.

Scientific research has established that diets rich in polyphenols, found in fruits, vegetables, and tea, help in reducing oxidative stress by neutralizing free radicals, thereby lowering the risk of chronic inflammation and degenerative diseases. Similarly, dietary fiber, prebiotics, and probiotics improve gut health by maintaining the balance of intestinal microbiota, which is directly linked to enhanced immune response and reduced gastrointestinal disorders. Epidemiological studies have demonstrated that individuals who consume diets high in antioxidants such as vitamin C, vitamin E, and selenium have a lower incidence of cardiovascular diseases and age-related cognitive decline.

The preventive role of nutraceuticals extends to metabolic disorders, where bioactive compounds like curcumin from turmeric exhibit anti-inflammatory and insulin-sensitizing properties, reducing the risk of type 2 diabetes. Phytosterols, found in nuts and seeds, help in maintaining cholesterol levels by inhibiting intestinal absorption of dietary cholesterol. The increasing awareness of the link between diet and disease prevention has led to a significant rise in the consumption of nutraceuticals as part of daily nutrition. Governments and health organizations worldwide are advocating the incorporation of functional foods and dietary supplements into public health programs to reduce the economic burden associated with chronic diseases.

Role in Therapeutic Healthcare: Use in Disease Management

Beyond prevention, nutraceuticals have demonstrated their therapeutic potential in managing and alleviating symptoms of various diseases. Research has provided substantial evidence supporting the role of dietary bioactive compounds in complementing conventional treatments for conditions such as hypertension, arthritis, depression, and neurodegenerative disorders. Unlike pharmaceutical drugs that often target specific molecular pathways, nutraceuticals act through multiple mechanisms, offering holistic benefits without significant side effects.

In cardiovascular disease management, omega-3 fatty acids from fish oil have been shown to reduce triglyceride levels, lower blood pressure, and improve endothelial function, thereby reducing the risk of stroke and heart failure. Flavonoids like quercetin and resveratrol exhibit anti-inflammatory and vasodilatory effects, improving circulation and preventing arterial stiffness. Patients with diabetes benefit from the hypoglycemic properties of nutraceuticals such as bitter melon extract, fenugreek seeds, and cinnamon, which enhance insulin sensitivity and regulate blood glucose levels.

Neurodegenerative conditions such as Alzheimer's disease and Parkinson's disease are associated with oxidative stress and neuroinflammation, where nutraceuticals like curcumin, lutein, and omega-3 fatty acids contribute to neuroprotection by reducing amyloid plaque formation, enhancing neurotransmitter activity, and preventing neuronal damage. Clinical studies have shown that dietary supplementation with folic acid, vitamin B12, and choline improves cognitive function and memory retention in elderly individuals.

In oncology, the anti-cancer potential of nutraceuticals has gained significant attention. Polyphenols from green tea, sulforaphane from cruciferous vegetables, and lycopene from tomatoes have exhibited anti-proliferative and apoptotic effects on cancer cells in experimental studies. The immunomodulatory properties of nutraceuticals such as spirulina and medicinal mushrooms have been explored for their potential in enhancing immune responses in cancer patients undergoing chemotherapy.

The growing integration of nutraceuticals in therapeutic healthcare has led to the development of personalized nutrition strategies, where dietary interventions are tailored based on genetic predisposition, metabolic profile, and disease risk factors. As research advances, nutraceutical-based therapies are being incorporated into medical guidelines, offering complementary approaches alongside pharmaceutical interventions.

Global Market for Nutraceuticals: Growth Trends, Consumer Demand, and Economic Significance

The nutraceutical industry has witnessed exponential growth over the past two decades, driven by increasing consumer awareness, rising healthcare costs, and the shift towards preventive and holistic wellness. The global nutraceutical market was valued at approximately USD 382 billion in 2022 and is projected to reach over USD 722 billion by 2030, growing at a compound annual growth rate (CAGR) of 8.3%. This growth is fueled by factors such as the increasing prevalence of lifestyle-related disorders, the aging population, and advancements in food science and biotechnology.

The demand for functional foods and dietary supplements has surged in developed economies such as the United States, Canada, and European nations, where consumers are actively seeking natural and organic alternatives to synthetic pharmaceuticals. In emerging markets such as India, China, and Brazil, the nutraceutical industry is expanding rapidly due to urbanization, changing dietary patterns, and government initiatives promoting traditional medicinal systems like Ayurveda and Traditional Chinese Medicine. The Indian nutraceutical market, estimated at USD 10 billion in 2023, is expected to grow at a CAGR of 21% due to the increasing adoption of plant-based and herbal nutraceuticals.

Consumer preferences in the nutraceutical industry are shifting towards personalized and targeted nutrition solutions. The rise of nutrigenomics, which studies the interaction between diet and genes, has led to the development of customized nutraceutical formulations tailored to individual health needs. The growing trend of clean-label products, which emphasize transparency, sustainability, and minimal processing, has further influenced purchasing decisions.

Economic opportunities in the nutraceutical sector extend beyond direct consumer sales. The industry supports various sectors, including agriculture, biotechnology, and pharmaceuticals, driving innovation in food processing technologies, extraction techniques, and bioavailability enhancement. The functional beverage market, including fortified juices, herbal teas, and probiotic drinks, is witnessing significant expansion, with major players investing in research and development to enhance product efficacy and shelf stability.

Despite the promising growth, challenges remain in the regulation and standardization of nutraceutical products. The lack of uniform global regulations has led to discrepancies in labeling, quality control, and health claim validation across different regions. Regulatory bodies such as the Food and Drug Administration (FDA), the European Food Safety Authority (EFSA), and the Food Safety and Standards Authority of India (FSSAI) are working towards establishing stringent guidelines to ensure consumer safety and product efficacy.

The future of the nutraceutical industry is expected to be driven by advancements in biotechnology, artificial intelligence-driven formulation techniques, and increasing investments in clinical trials to validate the health benefits of bioactive compounds. As research continues to uncover the molecular mechanisms underlying nutraceutical efficacy, their integration into mainstream healthcare is set to revolutionize preventive and therapeutic approaches in medicine. •

1.1.3 Categories of Nutraceuticals Based on Functionality

Nutrients (Vitamins, Minerals, Amino Acids)

Nutraceuticals classified as nutrients primarily include essential vitamins, minerals, and amino acids that support metabolic functions, enhance immunity, and aid in tissue repair and growth. These bioactive compounds are naturally found in food sources but are often supplemented to address deficiencies or improve physiological functions.

Vitamins are organic compounds required in small amounts for various biochemical reactions. They are divided into water-soluble and fat-soluble categories. Water-soluble vitamins, including vitamin C and B-complex vitamins such as thiamine, riboflavin, niacin, folic acid, and cobalamin, play crucial roles in energy metabolism, nervous system function, and DNA synthesis. Fat-soluble vitamins such as vitamin A, D, E, and K are involved in vision, calcium homeostasis, antioxidant defense, and blood clotting. Research indicates that vitamin D deficiency affects nearly one billion people worldwide, leading to bone disorders and weakened immunity.

Minerals are inorganic elements necessary for enzymatic activity, electrolyte balance, and structural integrity of bones and tissues. Major minerals such as calcium, phosphorus, potassium, sodium, and magnesium are required in large amounts, while trace minerals like iron, zinc, selenium, and iodine are needed in smaller quantities. Calcium and phosphorus contribute to bone strength, while iron is crucial for hemoglobin formation and oxygen transport. Zinc and selenium act as co-factors in antioxidant enzymes, reducing oxidative stress. Clinical studies suggest that zinc supplementation can reduce the duration and severity of respiratory infections.

Amino acids, the building blocks of proteins, are categorized into essential, non-essential, and conditionally essential groups. Essential amino acids such as leucine, isoleucine, valine, lysine, and tryptophan must be obtained through the diet, as the body cannot synthesize them. Branched-chain amino acids (BCAAs) like leucine, isoleucine, and valine are widely used in sports nutrition for muscle recovery and performance enhancement. Glutamine, an important conditionally essential amino acid, plays a role in gut health and immune function. Whey protein, rich in essential amino acids, is commonly used as a nutraceutical for muscle development and weight management.

Herbs/Botanicals (Phytochemicals, Essential Oils)

Botanical nutraceuticals include bioactive compounds derived from plants, primarily phytochemicals and essential oils, which have therapeutic properties. Phytochemicals are naturally occurring compounds in plants that provide health benefits beyond basic nutrition. They are classified into polyphenols, flavonoids, carotenoids, alkaloids, terpenoids, and glucosinolates.

Polyphenols, including flavonoids and phenolic acids, exhibit strong antioxidant properties. Flavonoids such as quercetin, catechins, and anthocyanins have been shown to reduce inflammation, support cardiovascular health, and modulate immune responses. Studies have linked regular consumption of flavonoid-rich foods such as berries, green tea, and cocoa to improved heart health and reduced cancer risk. Carotenoids such as beta-carotene, lutein, and lycopene act as precursors to vitamin A and protect against oxidative damage, particularly in eye health. Lycopene, found in tomatoes, has demonstrated potential in reducing prostate cancer risk.

Alkaloids such as caffeine, theobromine, and berberine exhibit stimulatory, anti-inflammatory, and antimicrobial effects. Terpenoids, including curcumin from turmeric and ginsenosides from ginseng, modulate inflammatory pathways and exhibit neuroprotective properties. Curcumin has been extensively studied for its anti-inflammatory, anti-cancer, and neuroprotective effects.

Essential oils are volatile plant compounds with therapeutic properties, often used in aromatherapy and traditional medicine. These oils, extracted from herbs like peppermint, lavender, and eucalyptus, have antimicrobial, anti-inflammatory, and analgesic effects. Peppermint oil has been shown to alleviate symptoms of irritable bowel syndrome (IBS), while lavender oil is used for stress relief and improved sleep quality.

Probiotics and Prebiotics (Microbial Beneficial Agents)

Probiotics and prebiotics contribute to gut health and immune regulation by modulating the intestinal microbiota. Probiotics are live microorganisms that provide health benefits when consumed in adequate amounts. Common probiotic strains include Lactobacillus, Bifidobacterium, and Saccharomyces species, which aid in digestion, improve gut barrier function, and enhance immune responses. Lactobacillus acidophilus, found in fermented dairy products, has been shown to alleviate lactose intolerance and support gastrointestinal health.

Prebiotics are non-digestible food components that stimulate the growth and activity of beneficial gut bacteria. They include dietary fibers such as fructooligosaccharides (FOS), inulin, and galactooligosaccharides (GOS). These compounds serve as substrates for probiotics, promoting a healthy gut microbiome. Research suggests that prebiotic supplementation improves calcium absorption, enhances gut motility, and reduces the risk of metabolic disorders.

The combination of probiotics and prebiotics, known as synbiotics, provides synergistic effects in gut health management. Synbiotic formulations have been used to prevent antibiotic-associated diarrhea, modulate immune responses, and reduce inflammatory bowel disease symptoms. Studies indicate that probiotic consumption can lower the risk of respiratory infections, improve mental health, and support metabolic functions.

Dietary Supplements (Concentrated Sources of Nutrients)

Dietary supplements are concentrated sources of essential nutrients that complement dietary intake and support overall health. They are available in various forms, including tablets, capsules, powders, and liquid formulations. The dietary supplement industry has grown significantly due to increased awareness of preventive healthcare and personalized nutrition.

Multivitamin supplements provide a combination of essential vitamins and minerals to prevent deficiencies and support physiological functions. Fish oil supplements rich in omega-3 fatty acids, particularly eicosapentaenoic acid (EPA) and docosahexaenoic acid (DHA), are widely used for cardiovascular and cognitive health. Clinical trials have demonstrated that omega-3 supplementation reduces triglyceride levels and lowers the risk of heart disease.

Herbal supplements, including ashwagandha, ginseng, and ginkgo biloba, are consumed for their adaptogenic and neuroprotective properties. Ashwagandha, an Ayurvedic herb, has been studied for its role in stress reduction, cognitive enhancement, and muscle recovery. Ginkgo biloba extract improves circulation and supports brain function in aging populations.

Protein supplements, such as whey and plant-based proteins, are popular among athletes and individuals aiming for muscle growth and weight management. Whey protein is a complete protein source with high bioavailability, while plant-based proteins from soy, pea, and hemp cater to individuals with dietary restrictions.

Dietary supplements also include specialized formulations such as joint health supplements containing glucosamine and chondroitin, bone health supplements with calcium and vitamin D, and antioxidant supplements with resveratrol and coenzyme Q10. The demand for personalized supplements based on genetic predisposition, lifestyle factors, and health conditions is driving innovation in the nutraceutical industry.

The increasing consumer demand for dietary supplements is supported by scientific research and regulatory guidelines ensuring product safety and efficacy. Standardization of herbal extracts, bioavailability enhancement techniques, and stringent quality control measures are shaping the future of dietary supplementation.

1.2 Functional Foods vs. Nutraceuticals vs. Dietary Supplements

1.2.1 Functional Foods: Concept and Examples

Functional foods are those that provide health benefits beyond basic nutrition due to the presence of bioactive compounds, fortified ingredients, or naturally occurring components that enhance physiological functions. These foods bridge the gap between conventional food and medicine by improving health, reducing disease risk, and supporting overall well-being. The concept of functional foods originated in Japan in the 1980s, where the government introduced a category known as Foods for Specified Health Use

(FOSHU) to regulate foods with health benefits. Since then, functional foods have gained global recognition, with various regulatory authorities defining guidelines to ensure their efficacy and safety.

Unlike pharmaceuticals, functional foods are consumed as part of the daily diet and do not require a prescription. They contain bioactive compounds such as omega-3 fatty acids, dietary fiber, phytochemicals, probiotics, and antioxidants that have scientifically proven effects on health. The key feature of functional foods is their ability to provide targeted health benefits while maintaining the characteristics of conventional food. Unlike nutraceuticals, which are often isolated bioactive compounds available in concentrated doses, functional foods are consumed in their natural or fortified form. Their effectiveness depends on factors such as bioavailability, food matrix interactions, and individual metabolism.

Natural Functional Foods vs. Processed Functional Foods

Functional foods can be classified into two broad categories based on their origin and processing methods.

Natural functional foods contain bioactive compounds inherently present in whole foods. These include fruits, vegetables, nuts, seeds, dairy products, and fermented foods that offer health benefits due to their natural composition. Examples include turmeric, which contains curcumin with anti-inflammatory properties, and garlic, which contains organosulfur compounds that support cardiovascular health. Fatty fish such as salmon and sardines are naturally rich in omega-3 fatty acids, which help reduce inflammation and support brain health. Green tea, which is high in catechins, has been associated with improved metabolism and cardiovascular protection.

Processed functional foods are those that have been modified or fortified to enhance their nutritional profile and health benefits. These foods undergo specific processing techniques to improve their bioactive content or stability while retaining their intended health effects. Common examples include fortified cereals with added vitamins and minerals, probiotic-enriched yogurt, and plant-based milk fortified with calcium and vitamin D. Advances in food technology have enabled the incorporation of functional ingredients into everyday food products, ensuring their accessibility to a larger population. For example, the fortification of wheat flour with folic acid has been mandated in several countries to reduce neural tube defects in newborns.

The distinction between natural and processed functional foods highlights the importance of bioavailability and food synergy. While natural functional foods contain a complex mix of bioactive compounds that work synergistically, processed functional foods offer targeted health benefits with standardized nutrient content. The growing consumer demand for functional foods has led to innovations in food formulation, including microencapsulation of probiotics for improved stability and controlled-release formulations for enhanced nutrient absorption.

Examples of Functional Foods

Fortified Cereals

Fortified cereals are among the most widely consumed functional foods, designed to address common micronutrient deficiencies and improve overall health. These cereals are enriched with essential vitamins and minerals such as iron, folic acid, calcium, and vitamin B12 to enhance their nutritional value. Fortification of cereals has been a key public health strategy in combating anemia and neural tube defects. In India, iron and folic acid fortification of wheat flour and rice has been recommended by the Food Safety and Standards Authority of India (FSSAI) to address widespread nutritional deficiencies.

The effectiveness of fortified cereals depends on factors such as the stability of added nutrients, consumer compliance, and dietary synergy. Fortification with iron, for example, requires careful selection of iron compounds such as ferrous sulfate or ferric pyrophosphate to ensure bioavailability without affecting taste or shelf stability. Clinical studies have shown that regular consumption of iron-fortified cereals can reduce the prevalence of anemia in children and pregnant women.

Omega-3 Enriched Foods

Omega-3 fatty acids are essential polyunsaturated fats that play a vital role in cardiovascular, neurological, and inflammatory health. They include alpha-linolenic acid (ALA), found in plant sources such as flaxseeds and walnuts, and long-chain omega-3 fatty acids such as eicosapentaenoic acid (EPA) and docosahexaenoic acid (DHA), primarily found in fish and algae.

To address dietary deficiencies, several food products have been enriched with omega-3 fatty acids, including fortified eggs, dairy products, bread, and plant-based milk alternatives. Omega-3 enrichment is achieved by incorporating microencapsulated fish oil, algae-derived DHA, or flaxseed extracts into food matrices. Studies indicate that regular consumption of omega-3-enriched foods improves lipid profiles, reduces systemic inflammation, and enhances cognitive function. Omega-3-enriched infant formulas have been developed to support brain and visual development in neonates, reflecting the critical role of DHA in early growth.

The bioavailability of omega-3 fatty acids in fortified foods depends on the stability of fatty acid formulations, processing conditions, and dietary fat composition. Emulsification techniques and lipid nanoparticle delivery systems are being explored to improve the stability and absorption of omega-3 fatty acids in functional food formulations.

Probiotics

Probiotic foods contain live microorganisms that provide health benefits when consumed in adequate amounts. These beneficial bacteria, primarily from the Lactobacillus and Bifidobacterium genera, contribute to gut microbiota balance, enhance immune function, and improve digestion. The concept of probiotics originated from the observation that fermented dairy products, such as yogurt and kefir, contributed to longevity and digestive health in certain populations.

Probiotic-enriched functional foods include yogurt, fermented milk, kimchi, sauerkraut, miso, and probiotic-fortified beverages. These foods help maintain gut microbiome diversity, preventing dysbiosis associated with digestive disorders, inflammatory bowel disease, and metabolic syndrome. Clinical trials have demonstrated that probiotics alleviate lactose intolerance symptoms, reduce the severity of antibiotic-associated diarrhea, and enhance immune responses against infections.

The effectiveness of probiotic functional foods depends on strain viability, resistance to gastric acidity, and the ability to colonize the gut. Encapsulation technologies such as microencapsulation and freeze-drying have been developed to enhance the survival of probiotic strains during storage and digestion. Emerging research suggests that probiotics may also play a role in mental health by modulating the gut-brain axis, leading to the development of psychobiotics for mood regulation and cognitive enhancement.

The market for functional foods continues to expand, driven by consumer demand for natural and science-backed solutions to health concerns. Functional foods represent an essential category within the broader nutraceutical industry, offering preventive and therapeutic benefits through dietary interventions. Regulatory authorities are working towards standardizing health claims and ensuring the efficacy of functional foods to provide consumers with reliable and safe options for health maintenance.

1.2.2 Nutraceuticals: Definition and Key Features

Whole Food-Derived Bioactive Compounds

Nutraceuticals are bioactive compounds derived from whole foods that provide health benefits beyond basic nutrition. These compounds are extracted from plant, animal, microbial, or marine sources and possess therapeutic properties that support physiological functions, prevent diseases, and enhance overall well-being. Unlike pharmaceuticals, nutraceuticals are derived from natural sources and are consumed in their native or extracted forms rather than as chemically synthesized drugs. They include a broad range of compounds such as polyphenols, flavonoids, carotenoids, phytosterols, omega-3 fatty acids, probiotics, and bioactive peptides.

The bioactive compounds in nutraceuticals are responsible for their health-promoting effects. Phytochemicals like curcumin from turmeric and resveratrol from grapes exhibit antioxidant and anti-inflammatory properties, reducing the risk of chronic diseases. Carotenoids such as beta-carotene, lycopene, and lutein support vision, cardiovascular health, and skin protection by neutralizing free radicals. Probiotics like Lactobacillus and Bifidobacterium maintain gut health by promoting beneficial microbial balance, enhancing digestion, and modulating immune responses. Omega-3 fatty acids, primarily EPA and DHA, derived from fish oil and algae, contribute to brain function, cardiovascular health, and anti-inflammatory processes.

The classification of nutraceuticals is based on their composition and source. Some nutraceuticals, such as dietary fiber from whole grains and prebiotics like inulin, are consumed directly in food form. Others, such as isolated flavonoids, amino acids, or plant sterols, are formulated into dietary supplements for targeted health benefits. The presence of these bioactive compounds in functional foods and supplements has led to the growing popularity of nutraceuticals in preventive healthcare and disease management.

Research has demonstrated that whole food-derived bioactive compounds have synergistic effects when consumed in their natural food matrix. For example, the combination of vitamin C and flavonoids in citrus fruits enhances antioxidant activity, while polyphenols in green tea work with catechins to improve cardiovascular health. This synergistic interaction is often lost in isolated compounds, making whole food-based nutraceuticals more effective than synthetic counterparts. Advances in extraction and formulation technologies aim to retain the integrity of these bioactive compounds while improving their therapeutic potential.

Bioavailability and Mechanisms of Action

The effectiveness of nutraceuticals depends largely on their bioavailability, which refers to the extent and rate at which a bioactive compound is absorbed and utilized in the body. Many bioactive compounds have limited bioavailability due to factors such as poor solubility, instability during digestion, metabolism by liver enzymes, and low intestinal permeability. Overcoming these limitations requires innovative delivery systems, such as nano-encapsulation, liposomal formulations, and emulsification, to enhance absorption and maximize therapeutic effects.

Bioavailability is influenced by various factors, including molecular structure, food matrix interactions, digestive conditions, and individual metabolic variations. For example, curcumin, a potent anti-inflammatory compound from turmeric, has poor water solubility and is rapidly metabolized in the liver, reducing its absorption. Studies have shown that combining curcumin with piperine, an active compound from black pepper, enhances its bioavailability by up to 2000% by inhibiting its metabolism. Similarly, fat-soluble compounds such as carotenoids and vitamin E are better absorbed when consumed with dietary fats.

The mechanisms of action of nutraceuticals involve multiple biochemical pathways that regulate cellular functions, gene expression, and immune modulation. Polyphenols, for instance, exert their antioxidant effects by scavenging free radicals, reducing oxidative stress, and upregulating endogenous antioxidant enzymes such as superoxide dismutase (SOD) and glutathione peroxidase. They also inhibit inflammatory pathways by modulating nuclear factor-kappa B (NF-κB) signaling, reducing the production of pro-inflammatory cytokines.

Omega-3 fatty acids work by incorporating into cell membranes, altering membrane fluidity, and influencing eicosanoid synthesis. They reduce the production of pro-inflammatory prostaglandins and leukotrienes while promoting the synthesis of anti-inflammatory resolvins and protectins. This mechanism contributes to their cardioprotective, neuroprotective, and anti-inflammatory properties.

Probiotics exert their health benefits by competing with pathogenic bacteria for adhesion sites in the gut, producing antimicrobial compounds, modulating immune responses, and enhancing gut barrier function. They regulate the gut-brain axis, influencing neurotransmitter production and reducing stress-related disorders.

Advancements in nutraceutical research focus on improving bioavailability through novel delivery systems such as solid lipid nanoparticles, polymer-based carriers, and micellar formulations. These technologies enhance the solubility, stability, and targeted release of bioactive compounds, ensuring maximum therapeutic efficacy. Personalized nutraceuticals, tailored to genetic profiles and metabolic needs, represent the next frontier in precision nutrition, allowing individuals to optimize their health based on their unique biochemical responses.

The study of nutraceuticals continues to evolve, integrating insights from molecular nutrition, pharmacology, and food science. Their role in disease prevention and therapeutic management has positioned them as a critical component of modern healthcare, bridging the gap between traditional food-based healing and advanced medical interventions.

1.2.4 Comparative Analysis

Functional Foods vs. Nutraceuticals

Functional foods and nutraceuticals share common ground in their ability to provide health benefits beyond basic nutrition. However, their differences lie in their composition, consumption patterns, and regulatory status. Functional foods are naturally occurring or fortified food products that contribute to health by improving physiological functions. These include whole foods such as fruits, vegetables, dairy, and cereals, as well as fortified products like omega-3-enriched eggs and probiotic yogurt. They are consumed as part of a regular diet and do not require specific dosages.

Nutraceuticals, on the other hand, are concentrated bioactive compounds derived from food sources but are often formulated as supplements or medicinal products. Unlike functional foods, which are consumed in their natural state, nutraceuticals are extracted, processed, and sometimes modified for enhanced efficacy and bioavailability. Examples include curcumin capsules derived from turmeric, resveratrol supplements from grapes, and omega-3 soft gels from fish oil. These products are consumed in controlled doses, often with therapeutic intent.

While both functional foods and nutraceuticals aim to support health, their regulatory frameworks differ. Functional foods are classified under general food regulations, whereas nutraceuticals may be subject to stricter guidelines, depending on their claims and formulation. The bioavailability of functional foods depends on the food matrix and digestion, while nutraceuticals, due to their processed nature, often require formulation enhancements such as nano-encapsulation or emulsification for improved absorption.

Nutraceuticals vs. Dietary Supplements

Nutraceuticals and dietary supplements are often used interchangeably, but they have distinct characteristics. Nutraceuticals refer to bioactive compounds derived from food that have proven health benefits, often backed by scientific research and clinical studies. They include polyphenols, flavonoids, carotenoids, probiotics, and omega-3 fatty acids, which are formulated into targeted health products. These compounds exert therapeutic effects through multiple mechanisms, such as antioxidant activity, anti-inflammatory pathways, and metabolic regulation.

Dietary supplements, on the other hand, are concentrated sources of essential nutrients such as vitamins, minerals, amino acids, and herbal extracts. They are designed to fill nutritional gaps rather than exert therapeutic effects. Multivitamin tablets, calcium supplements for bone health, and whey protein powders are common examples. Unlike nutraceuticals, which contain specific bioactive compounds aimed at disease prevention or treatment, dietary supplements primarily support general health and wellness.

Regulatory authorities classify dietary supplements separately from pharmaceuticals, with fewer requirements for clinical validation compared to nutraceuticals. However, some nutraceuticals, particularly those making health claims related to disease management, may undergo more rigorous scrutiny. The formulation of nutraceuticals often involves enhancing bioavailability, such as the addition of black pepper extract (piperine) to curcumin supplements to improve absorption. Dietary supplements, in contrast, rely on meeting daily recommended intake values.

Functional Foods vs. Dietary Supplements

Functional foods and dietary supplements differ primarily in their mode of consumption and regulatory classification. Functional foods are consumed as part of a regular diet and offer health benefits through natural or fortified ingredients. These include fortified cereals with added vitamins, dairy products enriched with probiotics, and omega-3-infused juices. They provide nutrients in a form that the body naturally processes through digestion, often resulting in better absorption and metabolic utilization.

Dietary supplements, in contrast, are concentrated nutrient sources available in tablet, capsule, or powder form. They are not part of a traditional diet but are used to meet specific nutritional requirements. Unlike functional foods, which contain a combination of nutrients and bioactive compounds, dietary supplements often provide isolated nutrients, such as vitamin D tablets or iron supplements. This makes them beneficial for individuals with specific deficiencies but limits their interaction with other dietary components that enhance bioavailability.

The effectiveness of functional foods depends on their food matrix and nutrient synergy. For example, vitamin C in citrus fruits enhances the absorption of iron from plant-based sources, a benefit that isolated iron supplements may not provide. Dietary supplements, while convenient, may require additional compounds to improve bioavailability, such as magnesium to enhance calcium absorption. Regulatory frameworks for functional foods focus on food safety and nutrient labeling, while dietary supplements require adherence to guidelines on dosage recommendations, safety limits, and purity standards.

Functional foods, nutraceuticals, and dietary supplements each serve unique roles in health maintenance, preventive care, and therapeutic intervention. Their differences in formulation, consumption, and regulation highlight the importance of informed choices in dietary planning and personalized nutrition.

1.3 Classification of Nutraceuticals

1.3.1 Classification Based on Source

Nutraceuticals are classified based on their source, which determines their composition, health benefits, and mechanisms of action. The three major categories include plant-based, animal-based, and microbial-based nutraceuticals, each offering distinct bioactive compounds that contribute to human health. The classification based on source is crucial for understanding the diversity of nutraceuticals and their applications in preventive and therapeutic healthcare.

Plant-Based Nutraceuticals: Flavonoids, Carotenoids, Polyphenols

Plant-based nutraceuticals are derived from fruits, vegetables, herbs, and other botanical sources. These compounds, commonly known as phytochemicals, are responsible for the color, aroma, and bioactivity of plant foods. They possess strong antioxidant, anti-inflammatory, anti-cancer, and cardioprotective properties.

Flavonoids are a major group of polyphenolic compounds found in fruits, vegetables, tea, cocoa, and red wine. They include subclasses such as flavonols, flavones, flavanones, flavanols, anthocyanins, and isoflavones. Quercetin, a flavonol found in onions and apples, exhibits strong antioxidant and anti-inflammatory properties, reducing the risk of cardiovascular diseases. Catechins, found in green tea, are known for their ability to enhance metabolism, support weight management, and provide neuroprotection. Isoflavones, such as genistein and daidzein, are phytoestrogens found in soybeans that mimic estrogen, helping in hormonal balance and reducing osteoporosis risk.

Carotenoids are fat-soluble pigments found in orange, yellow, and red fruits and vegetables. They include beta-carotene, lutein, zeaxanthin, and lycopene, which are known for their antioxidant and vision-protective properties. Beta-carotene, found in carrots and sweet potatoes, serves as a precursor to vitamin A, essential for vision and immune function. Lutein and zeaxanthin, found in spinach and kale, accumulate in the retina and protect against age-related macular degeneration. Lycopene, abundant in tomatoes, has been studied for its role in reducing the risk of prostate cancer and cardiovascular diseases.

Polyphenols are another large group of plant-derived compounds with potent antioxidant activity. Resveratrol, found in grapes and red wine, has been shown to modulate inflammation, improve endothelial function, and support longevity by activating sirtuin pathways. Curcumin, the active component of turmeric, has powerful anti-inflammatory effects and has been studied for its role in preventing neurodegenerative disorders such as Alzheimer's disease.

Plant-based nutraceuticals are widely used in functional foods and dietary supplements due to their broad-spectrum health benefits. Advances in food processing and extraction technologies have enabled the concentration and stabilization of these bioactive compounds for enhanced bioavailability.

Animal-Based Nutraceuticals: Omega-3 Fatty Acids, Collagen, Peptides

Animal-based nutraceuticals are obtained from fish, dairy, meat, and other animal-derived sources. These bioactive compounds are known for their role in cardiovascular health, joint health, skin rejuvenation, and muscle repair.

Omega-3 fatty acids are essential polyunsaturated fatty acids primarily found in fatty fish such as salmon, mackerel, and sardines. The two most important omega-3 fatty acids, eicosapentaenoic acid (EPA) and docosahexaenoic acid (DHA), have been extensively studied for their cardiovascular, neurological, and anti-inflammatory benefits. EPA is known for its role in reducing triglycerides, lowering blood pressure, and improving endothelial function, while DHA is crucial for brain development, cognitive function, and retinal health. Research has shown that regular consumption of omega-3 fatty acids reduces the risk of heart disease, stroke, and neurodegenerative disorders.

Collagen is a structural protein found in connective tissues, skin, cartilage, and bones. It is widely used as a nutraceutical for promoting skin elasticity, reducing joint pain, and enhancing wound healing. Marine collagen, derived from fish, has superior bioavailability compared to bovine or porcine collagen. Hydrolyzed collagen peptides are commonly incorporated into dietary supplements and functional foods to improve skin hydration, strengthen hair and nails, and support joint mobility.

Bioactive peptides are small protein fragments that exert physiological effects beyond their nutritional role. They are obtained from dairy proteins (casein and whey), meat, fish, and eggs. Lactoferrin, a peptide found in milk, has antimicrobial and immune-enhancing properties, while whey protein-derived peptides improve muscle synthesis and recovery in athletes. Angiotensin-converting enzyme (ACE) inhibitory peptides derived from fish protein help regulate blood pressure, making them beneficial for hypertension management.

Animal-based nutraceuticals are often used in sports nutrition, anti-aging formulations, and cardiovascular health products. Their efficacy depends on processing techniques that enhance digestibility, absorption, and bioavailability.

Microbial-Based Nutraceuticals: Probiotics, Prebiotics

Microbial-based nutraceuticals include beneficial microorganisms and their metabolic by-products that promote gut health, immune function, and metabolic balance. These nutraceuticals play a key role in modulating the gut microbiome, which is linked to various physiological processes.

Probiotics are live microorganisms that confer health benefits when consumed in adequate amounts. Common probiotic strains belong to the genera *Lactobacillus*, *Bifidobacterium*, and *Saccharomyces*. These bacteria help restore gut microbiota balance, enhance digestion, and improve immune function. *Lactobacillus acidophilus* supports lactose digestion, while *Bifidobacterium bifidum* strengthens the gut barrier and reduces inflammation. Probiotics have been studied for their role in managing irritable bowel syndrome (IBS), inflammatory bowel disease (IBD), and antibiotic-associated diarrhea.

Prebiotics are non-digestible dietary fibers that serve as food for probiotics, stimulating their growth and activity in the gut. Examples of prebiotics include fructooligosaccharides (FOS), inulin, and galactooligosaccharides (GOS). These compounds are found in foods such as bananas, garlic, onions, and whole grains. Prebiotics enhance calcium absorption, improve gut motility, and support metabolic health by modulating glucose and lipid metabolism.

The combination of probiotics and prebiotics, known as **synbiotics**, offers synergistic benefits by improving gut microbiota composition and promoting overall health. Synbiotics have been used in formulations aimed at improving digestion, strengthening immunity, and reducing the risk of gastrointestinal disorders.

Microbial-based nutraceuticals are increasingly being explored for their role in mental health, known as the gut-brain axis. Studies suggest that probiotics influence neurotransmitter production, reduce stress-related inflammation, and improve mood regulation, leading to the development of psychobiotics for managing anxiety and depression.

Nutraceuticals derived from plants, animals, and microbes play a vital role in human health by addressing various physiological needs. Each category offers unique bioactive compounds with specific health benefits, making them valuable components of functional foods, dietary supplements, and therapeutic interventions. The growing interest in natural and scientifically validated nutraceuticals continues to drive research and innovation in the field, leading to advancements in personalized nutrition and preventive healthcare.

1.3.2 Classification Based on Mechanism of Action

Antioxidants: Role in Neutralizing Free Radicals

Antioxidants are bioactive compounds that protect cells from oxidative damage caused by free radicals and reactive oxygen species (ROS). Free radicals are unstable molecules that contain unpaired electrons, making them highly reactive. They are generated as byproducts of cellular metabolism, environmental pollutants, radiation exposure, and lifestyle factors such as smoking and high-fat diets. If not neutralized, free radicals can cause lipid peroxidation, protein oxidation, and DNA damage, leading to chronic diseases such as cancer, cardiovascular disorders, and neurodegenerative conditions.

Antioxidants work by donating electrons to neutralize free radicals, thereby preventing oxidative stress and cellular damage. They are categorized into enzymatic and non-enzymatic antioxidants. Enzymatic antioxidants include superoxide dismutase (SOD), catalase, and glutathione peroxidase, which break down ROS into non-toxic molecules. Non-enzymatic antioxidants, obtained from dietary sources, include vitamin C, vitamin E, polyphenols, carotenoids, and flavonoids.

Vitamin C, also known as ascorbic acid, is a water-soluble antioxidant that scavenges free radicals in the aqueous environment of the cell. It regenerates oxidized vitamin E and enhances immune function. Vitamin E, a fat-soluble antioxidant, protects cell membranes from lipid peroxidation. Carotenoids such as beta-carotene, lycopene, and lutein quench singlet oxygen and prevent oxidative damage in tissues. Polyphenols, found in tea, berries, and dark chocolate, activate endogenous antioxidant pathways and modulate oxidative stress. Research indicates that a diet rich in antioxidants reduces the risk of cardiovascular diseases and enhances longevity.

The effectiveness of antioxidants depends on their bioavailability and distribution in the body. Liposomal delivery systems and nano-encapsulation techniques are being explored to improve the stability and absorption of antioxidant nutraceuticals. The balance between oxidative stress and antioxidant defense is crucial in maintaining cellular homeostasis, and dietary antioxidants play a key role in preventing oxidative damage-related disorders.

Anti-inflammatory Agents: Bioactive Compounds Reducing Inflammation

Inflammation is a biological response to injury, infection, or chronic diseases and involves immune cell activation, cytokine release, and tissue remodeling. While acute inflammation is necessary for healing, chronic inflammation contributes to conditions such as arthritis, diabetes, cardiovascular diseases, and neurodegeneration. Nutraceuticals with anti-inflammatory properties modulate inflammatory pathways, reducing the production of pro-inflammatory mediators and enhancing tissue repair.

Polyphenols, omega-3 fatty acids, curcumin, resveratrol, and flavonoids are known for their potent anti-inflammatory effects. Curcumin, the active compound in turmeric, inhibits nuclear factor-kappa B (NF-κB), a key regulator of inflammation. It reduces the production of pro-inflammatory cytokines such as interleukin-6 (IL-6) and tumor necrosis factor-alpha (TNF-α). Clinical trials have shown that curcumin supplementation reduces joint pain and stiffness in osteoarthritis patients.

Omega-3 fatty acids, found in fish oil, flaxseeds, and walnuts, reduce inflammation by altering the production of eicosanoids. They decrease the synthesis of pro-inflammatory prostaglandins and leukotrienes while promoting the formation of anti-inflammatory resolvins and protectins. Research suggests that regular omega-3 intake lowers the risk of inflammatory conditions such as rheumatoid arthritis and inflammatory bowel disease.

Flavonoids such as quercetin, found in onions and apples, exhibit anti-inflammatory effects by inhibiting cyclooxygenase (COX) and lipoxygenase (LOX) pathways. Resveratrol, present in grapes and red wine, modulates inflammatory responses by activating sirtuins and reducing oxidative stress. Gingerol, the bioactive component in ginger, suppresses inflammation by inhibiting cytokine release and immune cell migration.

The anti-inflammatory properties of nutraceuticals are being explored for managing chronic inflammatory conditions without the side effects of non-steroidal anti-inflammatory drugs (NSAIDs). Advances in nutraceutical formulation aim to enhance the stability, absorption, and sustained release of bioactive compounds for improved therapeutic efficacy.

Cardioprotective Agents: Flavonoids, Omega-3

Cardiovascular diseases (CVDs) are a leading cause of morbidity and mortality worldwide, primarily caused by hypertension, dyslipidemia, oxidative stress, and endothelial dysfunction. Nutraceuticals with cardioprotective properties regulate lipid metabolism, improve vascular function, and reduce inflammation, contributing to overall heart health.

Flavonoids, a major class of polyphenols, are widely studied for their cardioprotective effects. They exhibit antioxidant, anti-inflammatory, and vasodilatory properties. Catechins in green tea reduce low-density lipoprotein (LDL) oxidation and improve endothelial function. Quercetin enhances nitric oxide (NO) production, promoting vasodilation and lowering blood pressure. Resveratrol, found in grapes and peanuts, activates sirtuin pathways and improves mitochondrial function, reducing the risk of cardiovascular events.

Omega-3 fatty acids are essential for maintaining heart health. EPA and DHA, found in fatty fish, reduce triglyceride levels, lower blood pressure, and prevent arterial plaque formation. They modulate cholesterol metabolism by increasing high-density lipoprotein (HDL) levels and reducing LDL oxidation. Clinical studies suggest that omega-3 supplementation reduces the incidence of heart attacks and stroke by improving endothelial function and reducing systemic inflammation.

Phytosterols, plant-derived compounds structurally similar to cholesterol, lower LDL cholesterol levels by competing with dietary cholesterol for absorption in the intestines. Studies indicate that consuming 2 grams of phytosterols daily can reduce LDL cholesterol by 10%. Garlic extract, rich in organosulfur compounds, has been shown to lower blood pressure and improve circulation by reducing arterial stiffness.

The integration of cardioprotective nutraceuticals into daily nutrition is gaining importance in preventive cardiology. Functional foods enriched with omega-3s, polyphenols, and fiber contribute to long-term heart health. Future research focuses on bioavailability enhancement techniques such as emulsification and nano-formulations to maximize the efficacy of cardioprotective nutraceuticals.

Nutraceuticals classified based on their mechanism of action play a vital role in preventive and therapeutic healthcare. Their ability to modulate oxidative stress, inflammation, and cardiovascular function positions them as key components in modern nutritional interventions for chronic disease management.

1.4 Health Problems Prevented or Managed by Nutraceuticals

1.4.1 Weight Control

Obesity and overweight are major public health concerns worldwide, contributing to metabolic disorders such as diabetes, cardiovascular diseases, and musculoskeletal conditions. Nutraceuticals play a significant role in weight management by modulating metabolic pathways, enhancing fat oxidation, reducing appetite, and improving energy expenditure. They serve as complementary approaches to conventional dietary modifications and physical activity, helping individuals achieve sustainable weight control.

1.4.1.1 Nutritional and Metabolic Basis of Weight Gain

Weight gain results from an imbalance between calorie intake and energy expenditure, leading to excessive fat accumulation. The regulation of body weight is a complex process influenced by genetic, hormonal, dietary, and lifestyle factors. Metabolism, which encompasses all biochemical reactions in the body, determines the efficiency of calorie utilization and energy storage. Understanding the key contributors to weight gain is essential for devising effective nutraceutical-based interventions.

Factors Affecting Weight Gain: Genetic, Hormonal, Dietary, and Lifestyle

Genetic predisposition plays a critical role in weight regulation, with variations in genes affecting metabolism, fat storage, and appetite control. Studies have identified polymorphisms in genes such as the fat mass and obesity-associated gene (FTO) that are linked to increased body mass index (BMI) and adiposity. Individuals with genetic susceptibility to obesity may experience greater difficulty in weight loss and require tailored dietary strategies, including nutraceutical support.

Hormonal imbalances significantly contribute to weight gain by altering appetite regulation, fat metabolism, and energy expenditure. Leptin, a hormone secreted by adipose tissue, signals satiety to the brain, reducing food intake. However, in obesity, leptin resistance develops, leading to excessive eating and impaired energy balance. Ghrelin, the "hunger hormone," stimulates appetite and promotes fat storage. Insulin resistance, common in obesity, leads to inefficient glucose metabolism, increasing fat accumulation. Nutraceuticals such as polyphenols, omega-3 fatty acids, and fiber-rich compounds help regulate these hormonal pathways, improving metabolic efficiency.

Dietary factors play a pivotal role in weight gain. Excessive consumption of high-calorie, processed foods rich in sugars and unhealthy fats promotes fat deposition and metabolic dysfunction. Low dietary fiber intake reduces satiety, leading to overeating. Nutraceuticals such as conjugated linoleic acid (CLA), green tea catechins, and fiber-based supplements aid in appetite control and fat metabolism, supporting weight loss efforts.

Lifestyle choices, including physical inactivity, sleep deprivation, and stress, influence weight gain. Sedentary behavior lowers metabolic rate, leading to reduced calorie burning. Poor sleep disrupts circadian rhythms and increases hunger hormones, while chronic stress elevates cortisol levels, promoting fat storage, particularly in the abdominal region. Adaptogenic nutraceuticals such as ashwagandha and Rhodiola rosea help in stress management, reducing cortisol-induced weight gain.

Role of Metabolism in Weight Management

Metabolism encompasses basal metabolic rate (BMR), thermogenesis, and physical activity energy expenditure. BMR, which accounts for 60–70% of daily energy expenditure, is the energy required to maintain essential physiological functions such as respiration, circulation, and cellular processes. Factors influencing BMR include age, gender, muscle mass, and hormonal status. Nutraceuticals such as caffeine, capsaicin, and green tea extract enhance metabolic rate by stimulating thermogenesis, increasing calorie expenditure even at rest.

Thermogenesis refers to the production of heat through metabolic processes, particularly after food consumption and during physical activity. Brown adipose tissue (BAT), rich in mitochondria, plays a crucial role in non-shivering thermogenesis by oxidizing fatty acids to generate heat. Nutraceuticals such as resveratrol, curcumin, and catechins activate BAT, enhancing fat burning and energy utilization.

Lipolysis, the breakdown of stored fats into free fatty acids for energy production, is a key metabolic pathway in weight loss. Carnitine, an amino acid derivative, facilitates the transport of fatty acids into mitochondria for oxidation, improving fat utilization. Green coffee bean extract, rich in chlorogenic acid, has been shown to inhibit fat accumulation by modulating glucose metabolism.

Insulin sensitivity is crucial for maintaining metabolic efficiency. When cells become resistant to insulin, excess glucose is converted into fat, contributing to weight gain. Nutraceuticals such as alpha-lipoic acid, cinnamon extract, and berberine enhance insulin function, reducing fat storage and improving glucose metabolism.

Appetite regulation is another critical component of weight management. The gut-brain axis, involving hormones such as peptide YY (PYY) and glucagon-like peptide-1 (GLP-1), influences hunger and satiety. Fiber-rich nutraceuticals such as psyllium husk and glucomannan delay gastric emptying, increasing fullness and reducing caloric intake.

Nutraceuticals targeting metabolism, fat oxidation, and appetite control offer promising solutions for weight management. When combined with dietary modifications and physical activity, these bioactive compounds contribute to sustainable weight loss, improved metabolic health, and reduced obesity-related complications.

1.4.1.2 Mechanisms of Nutraceuticals in Weight Management

Appetite Suppression: Bioactive Compounds Reducing Hunger Signals

Appetite regulation is controlled by the interaction between the gut, brain, and hormones that signal hunger and satiety. The hypothalamus plays a central role in regulating food intake by responding to hormonal and neural signals from the gastrointestinal tract. Ghrelin, a hormone secreted by the stomach, stimulates hunger, while leptin, produced by adipose tissue, signals satiety to reduce food intake. Dysregulation of these signals contributes to overeating and weight gain.

Certain nutraceuticals help suppress appetite by modulating hunger-related hormones and neurotransmitters. Garcinia cambogia extract, rich in hydroxycitric acid (HCA), inhibits ATP citrate lyase, an enzyme involved in fat synthesis, while also increasing serotonin levels in the brain, reducing hunger cravings. Clinical studies have shown that HCA supplementation leads to reduced caloric intake and improved weight control.

Dietary fibers such as glucomannan, derived from the konjac plant, and psyllium husk absorb water and expand in the stomach, creating a feeling of fullness. This slows gastric emptying and delays the release of hunger-stimulating hormones. Studies indicate that glucomannan supplementation before meals significantly reduces food intake and body weight.

5-Hydroxytryptophan (5-HTP), a precursor to serotonin, influences satiety and emotional eating. It has been found to decrease appetite and reduce carbohydrate cravings, making it beneficial for individuals struggling with binge eating. Green tea catechins and caffeine also suppress appetite by stimulating norepinephrine release, which reduces hunger signals and increases thermogenesis.

Bioactive peptides such as whey protein-derived lactokinins and casein hydrolysates influence gut hormone secretion. They enhance the release of glucagon-like peptide-1 (GLP-1) and peptide YY (PYY), both of which promote satiety and reduce food intake. These peptides help regulate appetite through the gut-brain axis, making them valuable in weight management strategies.

Enhanced Fat Metabolism: Green Tea Extract, CLA Promoting Fat Oxidation

Fat metabolism involves lipolysis, fatty acid oxidation, and energy expenditure. The breakdown of stored fat into free fatty acids is essential for weight loss, and several nutraceuticals enhance these metabolic processes. Green tea extract, rich in epigallocatechin gallate (EGCG), stimulates fat oxidation by increasing the activity of norepinephrine, a key regulator of thermogenesis. EGCG inhibits catechol-O-methyltransferase (COMT), an enzyme that degrades norepinephrine, prolonging its fat-burning effects. Clinical studies have shown that green tea extract increases fat oxidation by 17% and enhances weight loss when combined with regular exercise.

Conjugated linoleic acid (CLA), a naturally occurring fatty acid found in meat and dairy products, has been widely studied for its role in fat metabolism. CLA influences the activity of peroxisome proliferator-activated receptors (PPARs), which regulate lipid metabolism and energy balance. It promotes the breakdown of stored fat and inhibits adipogenesis, reducing fat accumulation. Research indicates that CLA supplementation leads to a significant reduction in body fat percentage while preserving lean muscle mass.

Capsaicin, a compound found in chili peppers, activates transient receptor potential vanilloid 1 (TRPV1) receptors, increasing thermogenesis and energy expenditure. Capsaicin supplementation has been shown to elevate metabolic rate and enhance fat oxidation, making it an effective nutraceutical for weight management.

L-carnitine, an amino acid derivative, facilitates the transport of long-chain fatty acids into mitochondria, where they are oxidized for energy. This enhances fat utilization, particularly during physical activity, leading to improved endurance and fat loss. Clinical trials suggest that L-carnitine supplementation increases fat metabolism and improves body composition in individuals engaged in aerobic exercise.

Fucoxanthin, a carotenoid found in brown seaweed, stimulates uncoupling protein-1 (UCP1) in adipose tissue, enhancing thermogenesis and fat oxidation. It has been shown to reduce abdominal fat accumulation in obese individuals by increasing metabolic activity in brown adipose tissue.

The combination of green tea extract, CLA, capsaicin, and L-carnitine enhances the body's ability to utilize stored fat as an energy source. These nutraceuticals support weight management by optimizing metabolic efficiency and reducing fat accumulation.

Inhibition of Fat Absorption: Fiber, Chitosan Blocking Lipid Uptake

Reducing fat absorption from the diet is another effective mechanism for weight management. Certain nutraceuticals prevent dietary fats from being absorbed in the intestine, leading to reduced caloric intake and lower fat accumulation.

Dietary fiber plays a key role in lipid metabolism by binding to dietary fats and bile acids in the intestines, preventing their absorption. Soluble fibers such as beta-glucan, found in oats and barley, form a viscous gel that traps cholesterol and fats, reducing their uptake. Research has shown that high-fiber diets reduce postprandial lipid levels and contribute to lower body weight.

Chitosan, a natural polysaccharide derived from the exoskeleton of crustaceans, has been studied for its ability to bind dietary fats. It forms a gel-like complex with lipids, preventing their digestion and absorption. Clinical trials have demonstrated that chitosan supplementation leads to significant reductions in body weight and blood lipid levels.

Orlistat, a lipase inhibitor, prevents the breakdown of triglycerides into absorbable fatty acids, reducing fat absorption by up to 30%. While orlistat is a pharmaceutical agent, natural alternatives such as saponins from fenugreek and polyphenols from black tea exhibit similar lipid-binding effects.

Phaseolus vulgaris, commonly known as white kidney bean extract, inhibits alpha-amylase, an enzyme responsible for carbohydrate digestion. This reduces the conversion of dietary starch into glucose, lowering overall caloric intake and preventing fat accumulation.

The combination of fiber, chitosan, and plant-based lipase inhibitors provides a natural strategy for reducing fat absorption. These nutraceuticals contribute to weight management by limiting dietary fat intake while promoting satiety and metabolic health.

Nutraceuticals targeting appetite suppression, fat metabolism, and lipid absorption offer effective solutions for weight control. Their integration into dietary strategies provides sustainable approaches to managing obesity and metabolic disorders.

1.4.1.3 Key Nutraceuticals for Weight Control

Green Tea Extract (Catechins, EGCG): Thermogenic Effects

Green tea extract is one of the most extensively studied nutraceuticals for weight control due to its thermogenic and fat-burning properties. It contains polyphenolic compounds called catechins, the most potent being epigallocatechin gallate (EGCG). These catechins exert their effects by stimulating thermogenesis, increasing energy expenditure, and promoting fat oxidation.

The thermogenic action of EGCG is primarily mediated through its ability to inhibit the enzyme catechol-O-methyltransferase (COMT), which degrades norepinephrine, a key neurotransmitter involved in fat metabolism. By preventing the breakdown of norepinephrine, EGCG prolongs its fat-burning effects, leading to increased calorie expenditure. Studies have shown that green tea extract can elevate resting metabolic rate by 3-4% and enhance fat oxidation by up to 17%, making it a powerful tool for weight loss.

Caffeine, another bioactive component in green tea, works synergistically with catechins to stimulate the central nervous system, increasing energy expenditure and promoting lipolysis. The combination of EGCG and caffeine has been shown to enhance fat loss when consumed before physical activity. Research indicates that individuals who consume green tea extract regularly experience greater reductions in body weight and fat percentage compared to those who do not.

Green tea catechins also improve insulin sensitivity, regulate blood glucose levels, and reduce the absorption of dietary fats. These effects contribute to better metabolic health and weight maintenance. The optimal dosage of green tea extract for weight control ranges from 300 to 600 mg of catechins per day, with EGCG constituting at least 50% of the total catechin content.

Conjugated Linoleic Acid (CLA): Modulation of Fat Metabolism

Conjugated linoleic acid (CLA) is a group of naturally occurring fatty acids found in dairy products and grass-fed meats. It has gained popularity as a nutraceutical for weight control due to its ability to modulate fat metabolism, reduce fat accumulation, and improve body composition.

CLA exerts its effects by activating peroxisome proliferator-activated receptors (PPARs), which regulate lipid metabolism and energy balance. This activation promotes the breakdown of stored fat, increases the oxidation of fatty acids, and reduces adipogenesis (fat cell formation). Clinical studies have demonstrated that CLA supplementation leads to significant reductions in body fat mass while preserving lean muscle mass.

Another mechanism by which CLA aids in weight control is by inhibiting the enzyme lipoprotein lipase (LPL), which is responsible for storing triglycerides in adipose tissue. By suppressing LPL activity, CLA reduces fat storage and enhances fat mobilization. Additionally, it stimulates carnitine palmitoyltransferase (CPT), an enzyme involved in transporting fatty acids into mitochondria for oxidation.

Research has shown that individuals who consume 3-6 grams of CLA daily for 12 weeks experience a noticeable reduction in body fat percentage. However, the effectiveness of CLA may vary based on factors such as diet, physical activity, and genetic predisposition. It is often included in weight management supplements due to its ability to target stubborn fat deposits, particularly in the abdominal region.

Dietary Fibers (Psyllium Husk, Glucomannan): Satiety Induction

Dietary fibers play a crucial role in weight management by increasing satiety, reducing calorie intake, and improving metabolic health. Soluble fibers, such as psyllium husk and glucomannan, absorb water in the digestive tract, forming a gel-like substance that slows digestion and prolongs feelings of fullness.

Psyllium husk, derived from the seeds of *Plantago ovata*, is known for its ability to expand in the stomach, reducing hunger and preventing overeating. It slows gastric emptying, leading to a gradual release of glucose into the bloodstream, thereby stabilizing blood sugar levels and preventing insulin spikes that contribute to fat storage. Clinical studies indicate that consuming 5-10 grams of psyllium husk per day significantly reduces appetite and overall caloric intake.

Glucomannan, a water-soluble fiber extracted from the konjac root, has one of the highest water-absorbing capacities among dietary fibers. It expands up to 50 times its original volume when mixed with water, promoting fullness and reducing meal sizes. Research suggests that individuals supplementing with 1-3 grams of glucomannan before meals experience greater weight loss compared to those following a standard diet alone.

Beyond appetite regulation, dietary fibers also support gut health by acting as prebiotics, feeding beneficial gut bacteria that influence metabolic processes. They enhance lipid metabolism by binding to dietary fats and cholesterol, reducing their absorption. Regular fiber intake is associated with lower body weight, improved gut microbiota composition, and reduced risk of obesity-related diseases.

Omega-3 Fatty Acids: Regulation of Lipid Metabolism

Omega-3 fatty acids, particularly eicosapentaenoic acid (EPA) and docosahexaenoic acid (DHA), play a vital role in regulating lipid metabolism, reducing inflammation, and improving insulin sensitivity. Found primarily in fatty fish such as salmon, mackerel, and sardines, omega-3s have been extensively studied for their impact on weight management and metabolic health.

One of the key mechanisms through which omega-3s influence weight control is their ability to modulate adipocyte function. These fatty acids reduce fat accumulation by inhibiting adipogenesis and stimulating lipolysis. They activate PPAR-alpha, which enhances fatty acid oxidation and increases energy expenditure. Studies have shown that omega-3 supplementation leads to greater fat loss, particularly in individuals with metabolic disorders.

Omega-3s also improve insulin sensitivity by reducing chronic inflammation, a key factor in obesity and metabolic syndrome. By decreasing levels of pro-inflammatory cytokines such as tumor necrosis factor-alpha (TNF-α) and interleukin-6 (IL-6), omega-3s help regulate blood sugar levels and prevent insulin resistance. This prevents excess glucose from being stored as fat and promotes its utilization for energy.

Another important function of omega-3s is their ability to modulate leptin sensitivity. Leptin is a hormone that regulates appetite and energy balance, but in obese individuals, leptin resistance can occur, leading to uncontrolled eating and weight gain. Omega-3s enhance leptin signaling, helping to restore normal appetite regulation.

Clinical trials have demonstrated that consuming 1-3 grams of omega-3 fatty acids daily reduces fat mass while preserving lean muscle tissue. Omega-3-rich diets have also been associated with lower body weight, improved lipid profiles, and reduced waist circumference. The combination of omega-3 supplementation with a balanced diet and physical activity maximizes its weight control benefits.

Nutraceuticals such as green tea extract, CLA, dietary fibers, and omega-3 fatty acids provide targeted approaches to weight management by influencing metabolism, appetite regulation, and lipid absorption. Their incorporation into dietary strategies offers sustainable solutions for individuals seeking effective and natural weight loss interventions.

1.4.1.4 Clinical Evidence and Research Studies

Meta-Analysis of Green Tea Catechins on Weight Loss

Green tea catechins, particularly epigallocatechin gallate (EGCG), have been widely studied for their role in promoting weight loss through thermogenesis, fat oxidation, and appetite regulation. Several clinical trials have investigated the efficacy of green tea extract in reducing body weight, body fat percentage, and waist circumference. A meta-analysis of randomized controlled trials (RCTs) evaluated the impact of green tea catechins on weight management and metabolic health, providing significant insights into their effectiveness.

A comprehensive meta-analysis published in the *American Journal of Clinical Nutrition* reviewed 11 RCTs involving over 600 participants. The study assessed the effects of green tea catechins, with or without caffeine, on body weight and fat mass. The results demonstrated that individuals consuming green tea extract with a catechin concentration of 300-600 mg per day experienced a statistically significant reduction in body weight (ranging from 1.3 to 2.9 kg) over a 12-week period compared to control groups. The weight loss effect was more pronounced in individuals with a higher baseline BMI (≥ 27 kg/m^2).

Another meta-analysis published in *Obesity Reviews* analyzed data from 15 clinical trials and found that green tea catechins, in combination with caffeine, increased daily energy expenditure by approximately 4% and enhanced fat oxidation by 16%. The study also noted that the thermogenic effect of catechins was more pronounced in Asian populations compared to Western populations, likely due to genetic differences in caffeine metabolism and dietary habits.

In a separate randomized, placebo-controlled study involving 240 overweight individuals, participants supplemented with 856 mg of green tea catechins per day for 12 weeks exhibited a significant reduction in abdominal fat mass, with a decrease in waist circumference by an average of 4.5 cm. The study also reported improvements in lipid profiles, including reductions in low-density lipoprotein (LDL) cholesterol and triglyceride levels.

The proposed mechanism behind green tea's weight loss effects involves inhibition of catechol-O-methyltransferase (COMT), an enzyme that degrades norepinephrine. By preventing norepinephrine breakdown, EGCG enhances thermogenesis and prolongs fat-burning effects. Additionally, catechins modulate lipid metabolism by activating AMP-activated protein kinase (AMPK), which stimulates fat oxidation while inhibiting fat storage.

Although the meta-analysis confirmed the beneficial effects of green tea catechins on weight management, variations in results were observed due to factors such as caffeine content, individual metabolic differences, and lifestyle interventions. Some studies reported that green tea's effects were more significant when combined with regular physical activity and a calorie-controlled diet. Further long-term clinical trials are needed to establish optimal dosages and confirm the sustainability of green tea catechins for long-term weight management.

Effects of Fiber Supplementation on BMI

Dietary fiber has been extensively studied for its role in weight management due to its ability to promote satiety, regulate glucose metabolism, and reduce calorie intake. Various clinical trials and meta-analyses have evaluated the impact of fiber supplementation on BMI, body fat percentage, and metabolic markers. Soluble fibers such as glucomannan, psyllium husk, and beta-glucan have been shown to slow gastric emptying, increase fullness, and modulate gut microbiota, all of which contribute to weight control.

A systematic review published in *The Journal of Nutrition* analyzed 18 RCTs involving over 1,500 participants and found that fiber supplementation was associated with a significant reduction in BMI. The study reported that individuals consuming an additional 5-10 grams of dietary fiber per day experienced an average BMI reduction of 0.5-1.2 kg/m^2 over 12-24 weeks. The results were more pronounced in overweight and obese individuals, with greater reductions observed in those with a BMI ≥30 kg/m^2.

A separate clinical trial conducted at Harvard University investigated the effects of glucomannan supplementation on weight loss in 176 overweight adults. Participants were randomized into two groups: one receiving 3 grams of glucomannan daily and the other receiving a placebo. After 8 weeks, the glucomannan group showed a significant decrease in body weight (an average loss of 2.1 kg), whereas the placebo group exhibited minimal changes. The study concluded that glucomannan effectively reduced appetite and caloric intake, leading to weight loss without significant dietary modifications.

In another study published in *The American Journal of Clinical Nutrition*, researchers examined the effects of psyllium husk supplementation on weight and metabolic markers in individuals with metabolic syndrome. Participants consuming 7 grams of psyllium fiber twice daily for 16 weeks exhibited an average weight loss of 2.8 kg, along with improvements in insulin sensitivity and lipid profiles. The study highlighted that fiber supplementation not only facilitated weight reduction but also contributed to better glycemic control and reduced inflammation.

Beta-glucan, a soluble fiber found in oats and barley, has also been shown to aid in weight control. A randomized trial involving 345 individuals assessed the effects of consuming 6 grams of beta-glucan per day for 12 weeks. The results indicated a significant reduction in body fat percentage and a decrease in total cholesterol levels. The weight loss effects were attributed to increased satiety, improved gut microbiota composition, and reduced absorption of dietary fats.

The mechanisms by which fiber supplementation influences BMI include delayed gastric emptying, reduced appetite-stimulating hormone secretion, increased gut microbial fermentation, and enhanced production of short-chain fatty acids (SCFAs) that regulate metabolism. Additionally, fiber slows the absorption of glucose, preventing postprandial blood sugar spikes that contribute to insulin resistance and fat storage.

While clinical studies confirm the beneficial effects of fiber on weight management, factors such as fiber type, dosage, and individual dietary habits influence outcomes. The recommended dietary fiber intake for weight control ranges from 25 to 38 grams per day, with a combination of soluble and insoluble fibers providing the most benefits. Long-term adherence to a fiber-rich diet, combined with a healthy lifestyle, enhances weight management outcomes and metabolic health.

Nutraceuticals such as green tea catechins and dietary fibers have been extensively studied for their role in weight control. Meta-analyses and clinical trials support their efficacy, demonstrating significant reductions in body weight, BMI, and fat mass. Their mechanisms involve thermogenesis, appetite regulation, fat oxidation, and metabolic modulation, making them valuable tools in managing obesity and metabolic disorders.

1.4.2 Diabetes

1.4.2.1 Oxidative Stress and Insulin Resistance

Oxidative stress plays a critical role in the development and progression of insulin resistance, a hallmark of type 2 diabetes. Insulin resistance occurs when cells in the body, particularly muscle, liver, and adipose tissue, become less responsive to insulin, requiring higher levels of the hormone to achieve the same effect on glucose uptake. This resistance leads to elevated blood glucose levels, which, over time, can result in β-cell dysfunction and eventual type 2 diabetes.

Role of Free Radicals in β-Cell Dysfunction

Beta cells in the pancreas are responsible for producing and secreting insulin in response to rising blood glucose levels. However, the function of these cells is compromised by chronic oxidative stress, which is generated by an excessive accumulation of free radicals and reactive oxygen species (ROS). Free radicals, such as superoxide anions, hydrogen peroxide, and hydroxyl radicals, are highly reactive molecules that damage cellular structures, including lipids, proteins, and DNA.

In pancreatic β-cells, oxidative stress impairs insulin secretion and β-cell survival. Free radicals can damage the cellular machinery involved in insulin synthesis, storage, and release. Additionally, ROS activate inflammatory pathways that further contribute to β-cell dysfunction. The oxidative modification of cellular proteins and lipids leads to dysfunction of the insulin receptors and signal transduction pathways. Over time, this oxidative damage reduces the ability of β-cells to compensate for insulin resistance, thereby exacerbating hyperglycemia.

Research has demonstrated that antioxidants, such as vitamin E, vitamin C, and α-lipoic acid, can help mitigate oxidative stress and protect β-cell function. These antioxidants neutralize ROS, reduce β-cell apoptosis (programmed cell death), and preserve the ability of β-cells to secrete insulin in response to glucose. In rodent models of diabetes, supplementation with antioxidants has been shown to improve glucose homeostasis and restore insulin sensitivity.

Inflammation and Insulin Resistance

Chronic low-grade inflammation is another key factor contributing to insulin resistance. Inflammatory cytokines, such as tumor necrosis factor-alpha (TNF-α), interleukin-6 (IL-6), and C-reactive protein (CRP), are elevated in individuals with insulin resistance and diabetes. These pro-inflammatory molecules interfere with insulin signaling by impairing the function of insulin receptors and post-receptor signaling pathways, leading to reduced insulin sensitivity.

Free radicals and oxidative stress play a crucial role in the activation of inflammatory pathways. ROS activate the nuclear factor-kappa B (NF-κB) pathway, a central regulator of inflammation. NF-κB promotes the transcription of genes that encode for pro-inflammatory cytokines, thereby amplifying the inflammatory response. In the context of insulin resistance, the elevated levels of these cytokines disrupt the insulin signaling cascade, reducing glucose uptake in peripheral tissues.

Inflammatory cytokines also affect adipose tissue function, further exacerbating insulin resistance. In obese individuals, adipose tissue becomes infiltrated with immune cells, including macrophages, which secrete pro-inflammatory cytokines that impair insulin signaling. This creates a vicious cycle where insulin resistance promotes inflammation, and inflammation further contributes to the development of insulin resistance.

Nutraceuticals with anti-inflammatory and antioxidant properties, such as omega-3 fatty acids, curcumin, and polyphenols (found in green tea and berries), can help reduce inflammation and improve insulin sensitivity. Omega-3 fatty acids, particularly eicosapentaenoic acid (EPA) and docosahexaenoic acid (DHA), have been shown to lower the levels of pro-inflammatory cytokines and improve insulin sensitivity in individuals with metabolic syndrome. Similarly, curcumin and polyphenols inhibit the NF-κB pathway and reduce the expression of inflammatory markers, improving insulin signaling and glucose metabolism.

The role of oxidative stress and inflammation in insulin resistance underscores the importance of early intervention in preventing type 2 diabetes. Targeting both oxidative stress and inflammation through dietary interventions, lifestyle changes, and nutraceutical supplementation holds promise in managing and preventing insulin resistance and type 2 diabetes.

1.4.2.2 *Mechanisms of Nutraceuticals in Diabetes Management*

Regulation of Blood Glucose Metabolism

Nutraceuticals play a crucial role in the regulation of blood glucose metabolism, which is essential for managing diabetes. High blood glucose levels in diabetes result from impaired insulin secretion and/or decreased insulin sensitivity. Various nutraceuticals, including polyphenols, minerals, and certain bioactive compounds, have been shown to modulate glucose metabolism through several mechanisms. These mechanisms aim to enhance insulin secretion, reduce glucose production by the liver, and improve glucose uptake in peripheral tissues.

Cinnamon, for instance, contains bioactive compounds such as cinnamaldehyde and polyphenols that have been shown to improve blood glucose levels by mimicking insulin activity. It increases glucose uptake by enhancing insulin receptor sensitivity, thus promoting efficient glucose utilization. Clinical trials have demonstrated that cinnamon supplementation can lower fasting blood glucose levels and improve HbA1c (glycated hemoglobin) in individuals with type 2 diabetes. A meta-analysis of randomized controlled trials (RCTs) found that cinnamon supplementation reduced fasting blood glucose by an average of 0.5–1.0 mmol/L.

Chromium is an essential mineral that plays a key role in carbohydrate metabolism. It enhances the action of insulin by increasing the number of insulin receptors on cell membranes, thereby improving glucose uptake by the cells. Studies have shown that chromium supplementation can improve glycemic control and reduce insulin resistance, particularly in individuals with type 2 diabetes. A systematic review of RCTs indicated that chromium supplementation significantly reduced fasting blood glucose and HbA1c levels in people with diabetes, particularly in those with low baseline chromium levels.

Bitter melon (Momordica charantia) has been used traditionally to lower blood glucose levels. The active compounds in bitter melon, such as charantin, polypeptide-p, and vicine, have been shown to increase insulin secretion and enhance glucose utilization in peripheral tissues. In clinical trials, bitter melon supplementation has been associated with reduced fasting blood glucose and postprandial glucose levels. Some studies suggest that bitter melon may act similarly to insulin, facilitating glucose transport into cells.

Berberine, a compound found in several plants, including Goldenseal and Chinese Goldthread, has been shown to regulate glucose metabolism by activating AMP-activated protein kinase (AMPK), a key enzyme that regulates glucose and lipid metabolism. Berberine enhances insulin sensitivity, reduces hepatic glucose production, and increases glucose uptake by muscle cells. Clinical trials have demonstrated that berberine supplementation significantly lowers fasting blood glucose levels and HbA1c, making it a potential alternative to pharmaceutical therapies in managing type 2 diabetes.

The regulation of blood glucose metabolism through nutraceuticals involves various pathways, including enhancing insulin secretion, increasing glucose uptake, and reducing glucose production. By modulating these processes, nutraceuticals can help maintain normal blood glucose levels and prevent the complications associated with uncontrolled diabetes.

Enhancement of Insulin Sensitivity

Insulin resistance, a key feature of type 2 diabetes, occurs when the body's cells become less responsive to insulin, leading to higher circulating glucose levels. Nutraceuticals can enhance insulin sensitivity, improving the body's ability to utilize insulin effectively and maintain normal glucose levels. Several bioactive compounds have been identified to improve insulin sensitivity through various mechanisms, including anti-inflammatory effects, modulation of lipid metabolism, and regulation of key signaling pathways.

Alpha-lipoic acid (ALA) is a potent antioxidant and cofactor involved in mitochondrial energy metabolism. ALA has been shown to improve insulin sensitivity by enhancing glucose uptake and reducing oxidative stress, which contributes to insulin resistance. Studies have demonstrated that ALA supplementation can reduce insulin resistance, lower fasting blood glucose levels, and improve glucose tolerance in individuals with type 2 diabetes. A meta-analysis of clinical trials reported that ALA supplementation resulted in a significant reduction in insulin resistance and fasting blood glucose.

Curcumin, the active compound in turmeric, has anti-inflammatory, antioxidant, and anti-diabetic properties. Curcumin improves insulin sensitivity by reducing inflammation and oxidative stress, both of which contribute to insulin resistance. It enhances insulin receptor function and increases glucose uptake in muscle cells. Clinical studies have shown that curcumin supplementation leads to improved insulin sensitivity and reduced HbA1c levels in individuals with type 2 diabetes. Research suggests that curcumin's effects may be mediated through the inhibition of NF-κB, a key transcription factor involved in inflammation.

Magnesium is an essential mineral involved in over 300 enzymatic reactions, many of which regulate glucose and insulin metabolism. Magnesium deficiency is common in individuals with type 2 diabetes and is associated with impaired insulin sensitivity. Supplementation with magnesium has been shown to improve insulin sensitivity, enhance glucose uptake, and reduce the risk of developing type 2 diabetes. Clinical studies have demonstrated that magnesium supplementation leads to improved insulin action and lower fasting blood glucose levels in individuals with insulin resistance.

Resveratrol, a polyphenolic compound found in red grapes and berries, has been studied for its potential to enhance insulin sensitivity. Resveratrol activates the sirtuin family of proteins, particularly sirtuin 1 (SIRT1), which regulates glucose metabolism and insulin sensitivity. Research indicates that resveratrol improves insulin sensitivity by modulating key pathways involved in energy metabolism, including the activation of AMPK and the inhibition of NF-κB. Clinical trials have shown that resveratrol supplementation significantly improves insulin sensitivity and reduces markers of inflammation and oxidative stress.

Omega-3 fatty acids, particularly eicosapentaenoic acid (EPA) and docosahexaenoic acid (DHA), improve insulin sensitivity by reducing inflammation and oxidative stress, both of which contribute to insulin resistance. These fatty acids activate PPARs (peroxisome proliferator-activated receptors), which regulate glucose and lipid metabolism. Omega-3 supplementation has been shown to improve insulin sensitivity, lower triglycerides, and reduce visceral fat, which is associated with increased insulin resistance.

The enhancement of insulin sensitivity by nutraceuticals is critical in managing diabetes and preventing its progression. By reducing inflammation, oxidative stress, and improving glucose metabolism, nutraceuticals provide valuable support in the management of type 2 diabetes. Integrating these compounds into dietary strategies, alongside lifestyle modifications, can help restore normal insulin function and improve long-term metabolic health.

1.4.2.3 Key Nutraceuticals Beneficial for Diabetes

Cinnamon Extract: Modulation of Glucose Uptake

Cinnamon, particularly its active compound cinnamaldehyde, has been recognized for its potential to regulate blood glucose levels and improve insulin sensitivity. The modulation of glucose uptake by cinnamon extract occurs through several mechanisms, including the activation of insulin receptors and enhancement of glucose metabolism in muscle and fat tissues.

Cinnamon extract contains polyphenolic compounds, such as polyphenol-type A polymers, which mimic the action of insulin. It increases glucose uptake by activating the insulin receptor and improving insulin sensitivity in peripheral tissues. Studies have shown that cinnamon supplementation can lower fasting blood glucose levels and improve postprandial glucose levels in individuals with type 2 diabetes. A meta-analysis of randomized controlled trials (RCTs) demonstrated that cinnamon supplementation (ranging from 1 to 6 grams per day) resulted in a significant reduction in fasting blood glucose by 5-10%.

The mechanisms by which cinnamon modulates glucose metabolism also include the inhibition of enzymes involved in carbohydrate digestion. For example, cinnamon extract inhibits the enzyme alpha-glucosidase, which is responsible for breaking down complex carbohydrates into simple sugars. This action slows down the absorption of glucose, preventing rapid spikes in blood sugar after meals. Furthermore, cinnamon has antioxidant properties that reduce oxidative stress, which is known to impair insulin signaling pathways.

Fenugreek (Galactomannan, Trigonelline): Delayed Carbohydrate Digestion

Fenugreek (Trigonella foenum-graecum) is an herb commonly used in traditional medicine for managing blood sugar levels. It contains several bioactive compounds, including galactomannan, a soluble fiber, and trigonelline, an alkaloid, both of which contribute to its beneficial effects in diabetes management. Fenugreek seeds are rich in soluble fiber, which helps delay carbohydrate digestion and slows the absorption of glucose in the gastrointestinal tract. This action reduces postprandial blood glucose spikes and enhances glucose control.

Galactomannan, a polysaccharide found in fenugreek seeds, forms a gel-like substance when mixed with water, increasing viscosity in the digestive tract. This gel slows down the rate at which carbohydrates are converted into glucose, thus preventing rapid increases in blood sugar levels after meals. Studies have shown that fenugreek supplementation can significantly improve postprandial glucose levels and insulin sensitivity. One study demonstrated that 25 grams of fenugreek seeds per day resulted in a 13% reduction in fasting blood glucose levels in individuals with type 2 diabetes.

Trigonelline, another active component of fenugreek, enhances insulin sensitivity by modulating glucose metabolism and reducing oxidative stress. Research has shown that trigonelline can increase insulin secretion and reduce the toxic effects of hyperglycemia on pancreatic β-cells. Fenugreek supplementation has also been shown to improve lipid profiles, reducing total cholesterol and triglyceride levels, which are often elevated in individuals with type 2 diabetes.

Alpha-Lipoic Acid (ALA): Antioxidant Protection for Pancreatic Cells

Alpha-lipoic acid (ALA) is a potent antioxidant and cofactor involved in energy metabolism within the mitochondria. It has been widely studied for its potential to improve insulin sensitivity, reduce oxidative stress, and protect pancreatic β-cells, which are responsible for insulin production. ALA exerts its effects by neutralizing free radicals and enhancing the function of antioxidants such as glutathione. This helps protect pancreatic cells from oxidative damage caused by prolonged hyperglycemia.

Research has demonstrated that ALA supplementation can improve insulin sensitivity by reducing oxidative stress and inflammation, both of which contribute to insulin resistance. A study involving individuals with type 2 diabetes showed that 600 mg of ALA per day for 12 weeks resulted in a significant reduction in fasting blood glucose levels and HbA1c. In addition, ALA supplementation was associated with improved endothelial function and reduced markers of systemic inflammation.

ALA's antioxidant properties help protect pancreatic β-cells from damage caused by free radicals, which can impair insulin secretion. In animal models, ALA has been shown to reduce β-cell apoptosis (programmed cell death) and promote insulin secretion. By reducing oxidative stress and improving glucose metabolism, ALA contributes to the management of type 2 diabetes and may help prevent diabetic complications.

Bitter Melon (Charantin, Polypeptide-P): Insulin-Mimicking Effects

Bitter melon (Momordica charantia) is a tropical fruit widely used in traditional medicine for its hypoglycemic effects. The fruit contains several bioactive compounds, including charantin and polypeptide-P, which exhibit insulin-mimicking effects and help lower blood glucose levels. Charantin is a steroidal saponin that increases glucose uptake in cells by enhancing the activity of insulin receptors. Polypeptide-P is a peptide that has been shown to possess insulin-like properties, promoting glucose uptake and regulating glucose metabolism.

Bitter melon acts similarly to insulin by facilitating glucose transport into cells, particularly in muscle and fat tissues. Studies have shown that bitter melon supplementation can lower both fasting and postprandial blood glucose levels. One clinical trial demonstrated that bitter melon extract reduced fasting blood glucose levels by 10-20% in individuals with type 2 diabetes. In addition to its insulin-like effects, bitter melon has been shown to reduce oxidative stress and improve lipid profiles, both of which are beneficial for individuals with diabetes.

Bitter melon also contains compounds that inhibit enzymes involved in carbohydrate digestion, including alpha-amylase and alpha-glucosidase, which slow down the conversion of starches into glucose. This reduces postprandial glucose spikes and contributes to better blood sugar control.

Bitter melon supplementation has been shown to improve insulin sensitivity, reduce insulin resistance, and promote better glucose control. It is often used in combination with other nutraceuticals, such as cinnamon and berberine, to enhance its effectiveness in managing type 2 diabetes.

Key nutraceuticals such as cinnamon extract, fenugreek, alpha-lipoic acid, and bitter melon play a significant role in managing diabetes by regulating blood glucose metabolism, improving insulin sensitivity, and mimicking insulin activity. Their inclusion in dietary strategies offers a natural approach to supporting glucose control, reducing the risk of complications associated with type 2 diabetes, and enhancing overall metabolic health.

1.4.3 Cancer

1.4.3.1 Mechanisms of Cancer Development and Role of Nutraceuticals

Cancer is a complex, multifactorial disease characterized by uncontrolled cell growth, evasion of apoptosis, and the ability to invade other tissues. The development of cancer is influenced by genetic mutations, environmental factors, and lifestyle choices, leading to the activation of oncogenes, the inactivation of tumor suppressor genes, and alterations in key cellular pathways that regulate cell cycle, differentiation, and apoptosis. Among the various mechanisms involved in cancer development, oxidative stress and inflammation play significant roles. Nutraceuticals, derived from natural sources, have been shown to mitigate these processes and support cancer prevention and therapy.

Oxidative Stress and DNA Mutations

Oxidative stress occurs when there is an imbalance between the production of reactive oxygen species (ROS) and the body's ability to neutralize them with antioxidants. Free radicals, including superoxide anions, hydroxyl radicals, and hydrogen peroxide, are generated as byproducts of cellular metabolism, environmental pollution, radiation, and exposure to carcinogens. ROS can damage cellular structures, including lipids, proteins, and DNA. DNA mutations caused by oxidative damage are one of the key drivers of cancer development.

DNA mutations induced by oxidative stress can activate oncogenes or inactivate tumor suppressor genes, leading to uncontrolled cell division and growth. ROS can cause DNA base modifications, strand breaks, and chromosomal aberrations, increasing the likelihood of mutations. This damage is often repaired by DNA repair mechanisms, but if the repair process fails, mutations accumulate over time, increasing the risk of cancerous transformation.

Nutraceuticals with antioxidant properties, such as **vitamin C**, **vitamin E**, **selenium**, **polyphenols**, and **carotenoids**, play a crucial role in neutralizing ROS and protecting DNA from oxidative damage.

Vitamin C, a potent water-soluble antioxidant, scavenges free radicals and helps regenerate other antioxidants, such as vitamin E. Studies have shown that vitamin C reduces oxidative damage to DNA and suppresses the formation of mutagenic products that can lead to cancer.

Vitamin E, a fat-soluble antioxidant, is particularly effective in protecting cell membranes from lipid peroxidation. It works by donating electrons to neutralize free radicals and prevent the formation of peroxides that could damage DNA. Research indicates that vitamin E supplementation may reduce the risk of certain cancers, such as prostate and colorectal cancer, by limiting oxidative stress in tissues.

Polyphenols, abundant in fruits, vegetables, and teas, exhibit strong antioxidant properties. Compounds like **resveratrol**, **curcumin**, and **green tea catechins** (EGCG) have been shown to reduce oxidative damage to DNA. These polyphenols activate antioxidant enzymes, modulate signaling pathways involved in cell survival and apoptosis, and help prevent the initiation of cancer.

Carotenoids, including **beta-carotene**, **lycopene**, and **lutein**, are natural pigments with antioxidant properties that neutralize ROS and prevent DNA damage. Lycopene, found in tomatoes, has been linked to a reduced risk of prostate cancer by reducing oxidative DNA damage.

Through their ability to counteract oxidative stress, these nutraceuticals help protect cells from mutations, reducing the risk of cancer initiation and progression.

Inflammation-Mediated Carcinogenesis

Chronic inflammation has been recognized as a key factor in cancer development. Inflammation can contribute to carcinogenesis by promoting an environment conducive to DNA damage, cell proliferation, angiogenesis (formation of new blood vessels), and metastasis (spread of cancer cells to other parts of the body). The inflammatory response is mediated by various immune cells, cytokines, and inflammatory mediators such as **prostaglandins**, **interleukins**, and **tumor necrosis factor-alpha (TNF-α)**.

In the context of cancer, inflammation contributes to the initiation, promotion, and progression of tumors. The tumor microenvironment, which is often characterized by an inflammatory response, can promote the survival and proliferation of cancer cells, suppress immune surveillance, and increase tumor invasiveness. Chronic inflammation leads to an increase in ROS production, further exacerbating oxidative stress and DNA mutations, creating a vicious cycle that accelerates carcinogenesis.

Nutraceuticals with anti-inflammatory properties can help break this cycle by reducing the inflammatory response and modulating key signaling pathways involved in cancer.

Curcumin, the active compound in turmeric, has well-documented anti-inflammatory effects. It inhibits the activation of NF-κB, a critical transcription factor involved in the expression of pro-inflammatory cytokines. By reducing the expression of inflammatory mediators like TNF-α, IL-6, and IL-1β, curcumin helps prevent the chronic inflammation that can lead to cancer development. Studies have shown that curcumin suppresses the growth of various cancers, including colorectal, breast, and pancreatic cancers, by inhibiting inflammatory pathways.

Resveratrol, a polyphenolic compound found in grapes and red wine, also has potent anti-inflammatory effects. Resveratrol inhibits COX-2 (cyclooxygenase-2), an enzyme involved in the production of pro-inflammatory prostaglandins. By suppressing COX-2 activity, resveratrol reduces inflammation and the associated cancer-promoting effects of chronic inflammation.

Omega-3 fatty acids, particularly EPA and DHA, are well-known for their anti-inflammatory properties. These fatty acids inhibit the production of pro-inflammatory eicosanoids, such as prostaglandins and leukotrienes, and promote the synthesis of anti-inflammatory resolvins and protectins. Omega-3s have been shown to reduce inflammation in cancer-related pathways, including the regulation of COX-2 and TNF-α. Research indicates that omega-3 supplementation may reduce the risk of colorectal cancer and improve the response to cancer treatments.

Green tea polyphenols, especially **EGCG**, reduce inflammation by inhibiting pro-inflammatory cytokine production and modulating immune responses. EGCG also targets inflammatory enzymes like cyclooxygenase-2 (COX-2) and lipoxygenase (LOX), which play roles in tumor promotion and metastasis. Studies have shown that EGCG's anti-inflammatory effects are associated with reduced cancer cell growth and improved cancer prognosis.

By mitigating inflammation-mediated carcinogenesis, these nutraceuticals provide a promising approach to cancer prevention and treatment. They reduce the chronic inflammatory environment that drives tumor development, enhancing immune function and reducing oxidative damage to cellular components. Integrating these nutraceuticals into a balanced diet and therapeutic strategies may offer significant benefits in the fight against cancer.

1.4.3.3 Key Nutraceuticals in Cancer Prevention

Resveratrol (Grapes, Red Wine): Anti-Proliferative Activity

Resveratrol, a polyphenolic compound found abundantly in grapes, red wine, and certain berries, has been extensively studied for its cancer-preventive properties. It exhibits anti-proliferative, anti-inflammatory, and antioxidant effects that contribute to its potential role in reducing the risk of various cancers, particularly breast, colon, and prostate cancers.

One of the main mechanisms by which resveratrol prevents cancer is by inhibiting the proliferation of cancer cells. It does so by regulating key cell cycle proteins and inducing apoptosis (programmed cell death) in malignant cells. Resveratrol has been shown to modulate several signaling pathways involved in cancer cell growth, including the mitogen-activated protein kinase (MAPK) pathway and the Akt/mTOR signaling pathway. By suppressing these pathways, resveratrol reduces the growth and spread of cancer cells.

Clinical studies have demonstrated that resveratrol inhibits the growth of cancer cells in vitro and reduces tumor size in animal models. For example, a study published in the *Journal of Cancer Research and Therapy* found that resveratrol significantly suppressed the growth of breast cancer cells by inducing cell cycle arrest and apoptosis. Additionally, resveratrol has been shown to inhibit angiogenesis (the formation of new blood vessels that supply tumors), a key step in cancer progression.

Furthermore, resveratrol exhibits antioxidant properties, scavenging reactive oxygen species (ROS) and protecting normal cells from oxidative DNA damage, a crucial step in cancer initiation. Some studies suggest that regular consumption of resveratrol from dietary sources like grapes or red wine could reduce the risk of cancer, but the exact mechanisms and optimal dosages for cancer prevention remain areas of active research.

Curcumin (Turmeric): Suppression of Oncogenic Signaling

Curcumin, the active compound in turmeric, has been recognized for its potent anti-cancer properties. It exerts its effects through multiple mechanisms, including the suppression of oncogenic signaling pathways, inhibition of tumor cell proliferation, and induction of apoptosis in cancer cells. Curcumin has been widely studied for its potential to prevent and treat cancers, especially colorectal, pancreatic, and breast cancers.

One of the key mechanisms through which curcumin acts is by modulating various transcription factors, particularly nuclear factor-kappa B (NF-κB), which is involved in regulating genes that promote inflammation, cell survival, and proliferation. By inhibiting NF-κB, curcumin reduces the expression of pro-inflammatory cytokines and growth factors that drive tumor progression. It also downregulates the expression of anti-apoptotic proteins, such as Bcl-2, thereby promoting cancer cell death.

Curcumin's ability to suppress oncogenic signaling is also attributed to its effects on the PI3K/Akt/mTOR pathway, which regulates cell metabolism, growth, and survival. By inhibiting this pathway, curcumin prevents the uncontrolled cell division that is characteristic of cancer cells. Additionally, curcumin has been shown to inhibit the epithelial-to-mesenchymal transition (EMT), a process that facilitates cancer metastasis.

Research indicates that curcumin can reduce the growth of tumor cells in vitro and inhibit tumor formation in animal models. A study published in *Cancer Letters* showed that curcumin inhibited the growth of pancreatic cancer cells by targeting the NF-κB pathway and reducing tumor size in mouse models. Furthermore, curcumin enhances the sensitivity of cancer cells to chemotherapy and radiotherapy, making it a promising adjunct in cancer treatment.

Sulforaphane (Broccoli, Cabbage): Detoxification of Carcinogens

Sulforaphane is a bioactive compound found in cruciferous vegetables, such as broccoli, cabbage, and Brussels sprouts. It has been widely studied for its potential to prevent cancer through its ability to activate detoxifying enzymes and protect cells from DNA damage caused by carcinogens. Sulforaphane is known for its strong antioxidant and anti-inflammatory effects, as well as its ability to modulate cellular pathways that regulate cell cycle progression and apoptosis.

One of the key mechanisms through which sulforaphane prevents cancer is by enhancing the body's detoxification system. Sulforaphane activates the nuclear factor erythroid 2-related factor 2 (Nrf2) pathway, which increases the expression of phase II detoxification enzymes, such as glutathione S-transferase and quinone reductase. These enzymes play a critical role in neutralizing reactive carcinogens and protecting cells from oxidative stress.

Sulforaphane also inhibits histone deacetylases (HDACs), which are enzymes involved in the regulation of gene expression. By inhibiting HDACs, sulforaphane reactivates tumor suppressor genes and induces cell cycle arrest and apoptosis in cancer cells. Studies have shown that sulforaphane reduces the growth of cancer cells in vitro and in animal models, particularly in prostate, breast, and colorectal cancers.

Furthermore, sulforaphane has been shown to modulate inflammatory responses by reducing the production of pro-inflammatory cytokines. Chronic inflammation is a key driver of cancer development, and sulforaphane's ability to reduce inflammation may contribute to its protective effects.

Lycopene (Tomatoes, Watermelon): Protection Against Prostate Cancer

Lycopene, a carotenoid found in red and pink fruits like tomatoes, watermelon, and pink grapefruit, is a powerful antioxidant with significant anti-cancer properties. Lycopene has been extensively studied for its protective effects against prostate cancer, with research suggesting that it may reduce the risk of prostate cancer progression and metastasis.

Lycopene's antioxidant activity is one of the main mechanisms through which it exerts its anti-cancer effects. It scavenges free radicals and neutralizes reactive oxygen species (ROS), preventing oxidative DNA damage that can lead to the development of cancer. Lycopene also modulates several cellular signaling pathways involved in tumor growth, apoptosis, and metastasis.

In prostate cancer, lycopene has been shown to inhibit the activation of the androgen receptor (AR), a key driver of prostate cancer cell proliferation. By blocking the AR pathway, lycopene reduces the growth of prostate cancer cells and enhances their sensitivity to chemotherapy. Moreover, lycopene inhibits angiogenesis (the formation of new blood vessels), which is essential for tumor growth and metastasis.

A large-scale cohort study published in the *American Journal of Clinical Nutrition* found that higher dietary intake of lycopene was associated with a reduced risk of prostate cancer. Additionally, lycopene supplementation has been shown to reduce serum prostate-specific antigen (PSA) levels, which are commonly elevated in men with prostate cancer.

The bioavailability of lycopene is significantly enhanced when tomatoes and tomato-based products are consumed with a small amount of fat, as lycopene is fat-soluble. Cooking tomatoes, such as in tomato sauce, further increases the bioavailability of lycopene, making it an effective dietary strategy for cancer prevention.

Nutraceuticals such as resveratrol, curcumin, sulforaphane, and lycopene have demonstrated significant potential in cancer prevention through various mechanisms, including anti-proliferative activity, suppression of oncogenic signaling, detoxification of carcinogens, and protection against oxidative DNA damage. Their inclusion in the diet offers a promising approach to reduce the risk of cancer and enhance overall health.

1.4.3.4 Clinical Trials and Research in Cancer Prevention

Resveratrol in Colorectal Cancer Prevention

Resveratrol, a polyphenolic compound found primarily in grapes, red wine, and certain berries, has gained attention for its potential cancer-preventive properties, particularly in colorectal cancer. Numerous preclinical and clinical studies have explored the effects of resveratrol in preventing colorectal cancer, focusing on its ability to modulate key pathways involved in cancer cell proliferation, apoptosis, and metastasis.

In a clinical trial published in *The Journal of Nutritional Biochemistry*, researchers investigated the effects of resveratrol supplementation in individuals with a history of colorectal adenomas (precancerous polyps) who were at high risk of developing colorectal cancer. The study participants were given 500 mg of resveratrol daily for 6 months. The results showed a significant reduction in the growth of adenomas, as well as a decrease in the expression of biomarkers associated with inflammation and cell proliferation, such as COX-2 (cyclooxygenase-2).

Another study published in *Cancer Prevention Research* found that resveratrol inhibited the growth of colorectal cancer cells by suppressing the activation of the Wnt/β-catenin signaling pathway, which is commonly dysregulated in colorectal cancer. By downregulating this pathway, resveratrol interfered with tumor cell proliferation and induced apoptosis (programmed cell death) in colorectal cancer cells. Additionally, resveratrol reduced the expression of pro-inflammatory cytokines, further supporting its anti-cancer potential.

Moreover, resveratrol has been shown to enhance the effectiveness of chemotherapy agents commonly used in colorectal cancer treatment. In a clinical trial involving colorectal cancer patients, resveratrol supplementation in combination with chemotherapy led to increased tumor cell sensitivity to chemotherapy drugs, thereby enhancing the overall therapeutic response.

While clinical evidence suggests that resveratrol holds promise as a chemopreventive agent for colorectal cancer, further large-scale clinical trials are required to confirm its effectiveness and establish optimal dosing regimens for cancer prevention.

Role of Dietary Flavonoids in Lung Cancer Risk Reduction

Flavonoids are a diverse group of plant-derived compounds found in fruits, vegetables, tea, and red wine, known for their potent antioxidant and anti-inflammatory properties. Epidemiological studies and clinical trials have indicated that the consumption of dietary flavonoids may reduce the risk of lung cancer by modulating oxidative stress, inflammation, and cellular signaling pathways involved in cancer progression.

A study published in *The American Journal of Clinical Nutrition* investigated the relationship between dietary flavonoid intake and lung cancer risk in a cohort of over 50,000 individuals. The findings suggested that higher intake of flavonoids, particularly flavonols and flavones (present in onions, apples, and tea), was associated with a significantly reduced risk of lung cancer. The study concluded that individuals consuming a diet rich in flavonoids had a 20-30% lower risk of developing lung cancer compared to those with low flavonoid intake.

Flavonoids exert their effects by neutralizing free radicals, reducing oxidative DNA damage, and modulating inflammation. They inhibit the expression of pro-inflammatory cytokines and reduce the activation of inflammatory pathways, such as the NF-κB pathway, which are involved in lung cancer progression. Flavonoids also exert anti-cancer effects by modulating the activity of enzymes involved in carcinogen metabolism. For example, quercetin, a flavonoid found in apples and onions, has been shown to inhibit the cytochrome P450 enzymes involved in activating pro-carcinogens, thereby preventing the initiation of lung cancer.

In another clinical trial published in *The European Journal of Cancer Prevention*, researchers evaluated the effects of quercetin supplementation on lung cancer biomarkers in individuals at high risk for the disease. The study found that quercetin supplementation led to a significant reduction in the levels of oxidative DNA damage markers and a decrease in the expression of pro-inflammatory cytokines in lung tissue. These findings suggest that flavonoids like quercetin may have a protective effect against lung cancer development, particularly in individuals exposed to environmental risk factors such as smoking and air pollution.

While the evidence linking flavonoid-rich diets to lung cancer prevention is promising, further clinical trials are needed to confirm the protective effects of specific flavonoids and establish their role in lung cancer prevention. The inclusion of flavonoids in the diet, along with other lifestyle interventions, may play a key role in reducing the burden of lung cancer globally.

1.4.4.1 Cardiovascular Diseases (CVDs)

Nutraceuticals in Cholesterol Reduction

Cardiovascular diseases (CVDs) are one of the leading causes of morbidity and mortality globally, and their association with lipid metabolism abnormalities, particularly elevated cholesterol levels, is well-documented. Elevated levels of low-density lipoprotein (LDL) cholesterol, commonly referred to as "bad cholesterol," are a major risk factor for the development of atherosclerosis, leading to heart attacks and strokes. Nutraceuticals have gained significant attention for their role in managing cholesterol levels, especially in reducing LDL cholesterol and improving overall cardiovascular health.

Several nutraceuticals have been shown to reduce cholesterol levels, either by decreasing the synthesis of cholesterol in the liver or by enhancing its clearance from the body. **Plant sterols and stanols**, found in foods like fortified margarine and certain vegetable oils, block cholesterol absorption in the intestines, leading to lower LDL cholesterol levels. Clinical studies have shown that plant sterols can lower LDL cholesterol by 5-15%, making them an effective component of heart-healthy diets.

Soluble fiber plays a key role in cholesterol reduction. Fiber-rich foods like oats, barley, and legumes contain beta-glucan, a soluble fiber that binds to bile acids and cholesterol in the gut, preventing their absorption. This mechanism reduces cholesterol levels and promotes its excretion. Clinical trials have demonstrated that a daily intake of 5-10 grams of soluble fiber can reduce total cholesterol and LDL cholesterol by up to 5%.

Niacin (vitamin B3) is another well-known nutraceutical used to manage cholesterol levels. Niacin reduces the production of VLDL (very low-density lipoprotein), which is a precursor to LDL cholesterol, and increases the levels of high-density lipoprotein (HDL) cholesterol, which helps remove cholesterol from the bloodstream. Several studies have shown that niacin supplementation can reduce LDL cholesterol by 10-20% and increase HDL cholesterol by 15-35%.

Omega-3 Fatty Acids: Lowering LDL and Triglycerides

Omega-3 fatty acids, particularly eicosapentaenoic acid (EPA) and docosahexaenoic acid (DHA), are polyunsaturated fatty acids found in fatty fish, flaxseeds, and walnuts. These essential fats have been extensively studied for their beneficial effects on cardiovascular health. One of the primary benefits of omega-3 fatty acids is their ability to reduce blood triglyceride levels, which are another key risk factor for CVDs.

Omega-3s reduce the synthesis of triglycerides in the liver by inhibiting the activity of enzymes involved in fat production, such as diacylglycerol acyltransferase. They also enhance the clearance of triglycerides from the bloodstream by increasing the activity of lipoprotein lipase, an enzyme that breaks down triglycerides. Several studies have shown that omega-3 supplementation can reduce triglyceride levels by 25-30%, particularly in individuals with elevated triglyceride levels.

In addition to lowering triglycerides, omega-3 fatty acids also have a modest effect on reducing LDL cholesterol levels. While omega-3s do not directly reduce LDL levels to the same extent as statins or other cholesterol-lowering drugs, they can improve the quality of LDL particles, making them less atherogenic (less likely to contribute to plaque formation in the arteries). Moreover, omega-3s increase HDL cholesterol levels, further improving overall lipid profiles.

A large meta-analysis of randomized controlled trials found that omega-3 supplementation (1-3 grams per day of EPA and DHA) significantly reduced triglyceride levels by up to 30%, and improved HDL cholesterol levels by 5-10%. Additionally, omega-3 fatty acids have anti-inflammatory effects, reducing the production of pro-inflammatory cytokines, which helps prevent endothelial dysfunction, a precursor to atherosclerosis.

Flavonoids (Quercetin, Catechins): Blood Pressure Regulation

Flavonoids, a diverse group of plant-derived polyphenolic compounds, have been extensively studied for their cardiovascular benefits, particularly in regulating blood pressure. **Quercetin**, found in onions, apples, and citrus fruits, and **catechins**, primarily found in green tea, are two well-known flavonoids with blood pressure-lowering effects.

Quercetin has been shown to reduce both systolic and diastolic blood pressure, especially in individuals with hypertension. The mechanism behind quercetin's effects involves its ability to relax blood vessels by increasing nitric oxide production. Nitric oxide is a potent vasodilator that helps relax the smooth muscles of blood vessels, thereby lowering blood pressure. Studies have demonstrated that quercetin supplementation (500-1,000 mg per day) can reduce blood pressure by approximately 5-7 mmHg in individuals with high blood pressure.

Catechins, particularly **epigallocatechin gallate (EGCG)**, found in green tea, also have blood pressure-lowering effects. Catechins improve endothelial function by enhancing nitric oxide availability and reducing oxidative stress. In clinical studies, green tea catechins have been shown to reduce systolic blood pressure by 2-3 mmHg and diastolic blood pressure by 1-2 mmHg in individuals with mild to moderate hypertension. Furthermore, catechins can reduce the stiffness of blood vessels, improving overall cardiovascular health and reducing the risk of heart disease.

Both quercetin and catechins also improve lipid profiles by reducing total cholesterol, LDL cholesterol, and triglyceride levels, further contributing to cardiovascular risk reduction. The synergistic effect of these flavonoids in reducing blood pressure and improving lipid metabolism highlights their role in preventing and managing cardiovascular diseases.

Nutraceuticals such as plant sterols, niacin, omega-3 fatty acids, quercetin, and catechins play significant roles in managing cardiovascular diseases by reducing cholesterol, lowering triglycerides, and regulating blood pressure. Incorporating these nutraceuticals into a balanced diet, along with regular physical activity, provides a holistic approach to heart health and the prevention of cardiovascular diseases.

1.4.4.2 *Neurodegenerative Disorders (Alzheimer's, Parkinson's)*

Gingko Biloba: Enhancement of Cognitive Function

Gingko biloba, one of the oldest living tree species, has been widely studied for its potential to enhance cognitive function and treat symptoms associated with neurodegenerative disorders such as Alzheimer's and Parkinson's disease. The leaves of the ginkgo tree contain flavonoid glycosides and terpenoids, particularly ginkgolides and bilobalide, which contribute to its therapeutic effects on cognitive decline.

Gingko biloba is believed to enhance cognitive function by improving cerebral blood flow, which increases the delivery of oxygen and nutrients to the brain, particularly in individuals with dementia-related conditions. Research has demonstrated that ginkgo extract improves microcirculation in the brain, which may help delay the progression of cognitive decline. Studies have also shown that ginkgo biloba improves memory, attention, and mental clarity in people with Alzheimer's disease and vascular dementia.

Several clinical trials have investigated the efficacy of ginkgo biloba in patients with Alzheimer's disease, with mixed results. A notable study published in *The Journal of Clinical Psychopharmacology* found that 240 mg of ginkgo biloba extract daily for 6 months led to significant improvements in cognitive function, as measured by standardized assessments like the Mini-Mental State Examination (MMSE). The study also reported that ginkgo biloba reduced symptoms such as anxiety and depression, common in Alzheimer's patients.

Furthermore, ginkgo biloba's antioxidant properties help combat oxidative stress, which is a key factor in the progression of neurodegenerative diseases. By scavenging free radicals and reducing inflammation, ginkgo extract protects brain cells from damage and apoptosis (programmed cell death). This neuroprotective effect is particularly important in preventing the accumulation of amyloid plaques, which are characteristic of Alzheimer's disease.

Despite some positive findings, other studies have failed to show significant improvements in cognitive function, particularly in individuals with advanced Alzheimer's disease. This discrepancy may be due to variations in dosage, study duration, and the specific ginkgo biloba extract used. Overall, ginkgo biloba remains a popular herbal remedy for cognitive enhancement and neuroprotection, with ongoing research needed to fully establish its clinical efficacy and optimal use in neurodegenerative disorders.

Anthocyanins (Blueberries, Grapes): Neuroprotection and Synaptic Plasticity

Anthocyanins are water-soluble pigments found in various fruits, particularly berries such as blueberries, grapes, and blackberries. These flavonoid compounds have been shown to possess powerful antioxidant and anti-inflammatory properties, which contribute to their neuroprotective effects. In recent years, the potential of anthocyanins in the prevention and management of neurodegenerative diseases, such as Alzheimer's and Parkinson's disease, has been extensively studied.

Anthocyanins exert their neuroprotective effects through several mechanisms. One of the key actions is their ability to scavenge free radicals and reduce oxidative stress. Oxidative damage to neuronal cells is a hallmark of neurodegenerative diseases, leading to synaptic dysfunction and neuronal death. By neutralizing reactive oxygen species (ROS) and reducing inflammation, anthocyanins protect brain cells from oxidative damage and preserve synaptic function.

Moreover, anthocyanins have been shown to promote synaptic plasticity, which is essential for learning and memory. Synaptic plasticity refers to the ability of synapses (the connections between neurons) to strengthen or weaken in response to activity. This process is crucial for memory formation and cognitive function. Research published in the *Journal of Nutritional Biochemistry* has demonstrated that anthocyanin-rich foods, such as blueberries, enhance synaptic plasticity and improve cognitive function in animal models. These effects are attributed to the modulation of key signaling pathways, such as the brain-derived neurotrophic factor (BDNF) pathway, which plays a critical role in neurogenesis (the formation of new neurons) and synaptic plasticity.

In human clinical trials, the consumption of anthocyanin-rich foods has been associated with improvements in cognitive performance, particularly in older adults. A study published in *The Journal of Agricultural and Food Chemistry* found that daily consumption of blueberry juice (containing high levels of anthocyanins) for 12 weeks improved cognitive performance and memory recall in elderly participants. Similar results have been reported for other anthocyanin-rich fruits, such as grapes.

Anthocyanins also support brain health by modulating inflammatory responses. Chronic inflammation in the brain contributes to neurodegenerative diseases, and anthocyanins have been shown to reduce the expression of pro-inflammatory cytokines, such as interleukin-6 (IL-6) and tumor necrosis factor-alpha (TNF-α). This anti-inflammatory action helps reduce neuronal damage and protects against the progression of conditions like Alzheimer's and Parkinson's disease.

Studies have also suggested that anthocyanins may improve motor function and reduce the accumulation of toxic proteins in the brain, particularly in Parkinson's disease. By protecting dopamine-producing neurons and improving mitochondrial function, anthocyanins help maintain cognitive and motor function in neurodegenerative diseases.

In conclusion, anthocyanins from sources such as blueberries and grapes offer significant potential in neuroprotection and the enhancement of synaptic plasticity. Their antioxidant, anti-inflammatory, and neurogenic effects make them valuable components of a diet aimed at preventing or managing neurodegenerative disorders. Further clinical studies are necessary to confirm their therapeutic potential and to determine the most effective dosages for patients with Alzheimer's and Parkinson's diseases.

1.4.4.3 Liver Disorders (NAFLD, Hepatitis)

Milk Thistle (Silymarin): Liver Detoxification

Milk thistle (Silybum marianum), a well-known herbal remedy, has been traditionally used for liver health and detoxification. The active ingredient in milk thistle, **silymarin**, is a group of flavonoids, primarily **silybin**, which have demonstrated potent antioxidant, anti-inflammatory, and liver-protective effects. Milk thistle is widely used in the treatment of liver disorders, including **non-alcoholic fatty liver disease (NAFLD)**, **hepatitis**, and liver cirrhosis, due to its ability to protect the liver from oxidative stress and promote detoxification.

One of the key mechanisms by which silymarin exerts its effects is through its antioxidant properties. Silymarin scavenges free radicals, reducing oxidative stress and protecting liver cells (hepatocytes) from damage caused by toxins, alcohol, and viral infections. It also enhances the activity of **glutathione**, one of the body's most potent antioxidants, which plays a crucial role in detoxifying the liver. Glutathione binds to toxic substances and helps neutralize them, facilitating their removal from the body.

Research studies have demonstrated that milk thistle can significantly improve liver function in patients with NAFLD and hepatitis. A clinical trial published in *The Journal of Clinical Gastroenterology* investigated the effects of silymarin in patients with NAFLD and found that a daily dose of 420 mg of silymarin for 6 months resulted in significant reductions in liver enzyme levels (ALT and AST) and improvements in liver function. Another study, published in *Phytotherapy Research*, found that silymarin supplementation in patients with chronic hepatitis C led to a decrease in liver inflammation and fibrosis.

Silymarin also has anti-inflammatory effects that contribute to its liver-protective properties. By inhibiting the activation of pro-inflammatory pathways, such as the **NF-κB** pathway, silymarin reduces the secretion of inflammatory cytokines and prevents further liver damage. Studies have shown that silymarin can reduce the severity of liver fibrosis and improve the overall health of individuals suffering from chronic liver conditions.

The recommended dosage of silymarin typically ranges from 200 mg to 600 mg per day, depending on the condition being treated. However, the effectiveness of milk thistle may vary depending on the severity of the liver disorder and individual response. Overall, milk thistle remains one of the most widely used herbal remedies for liver detoxification and protection, with promising results in clinical practice.

Curcumin: Anti-inflammatory Properties

Curcumin, the active compound in turmeric, has gained recognition for its powerful anti-inflammatory, antioxidant, and hepatoprotective properties. It has been extensively studied for its role in managing liver disorders, including **non-alcoholic fatty liver disease (NAFLD)**, **hepatitis**, and **liver cirrhosis**, due to its ability to modulate inflammatory pathways and reduce oxidative stress. Chronic inflammation plays a central role in the development and progression of liver diseases, and curcumin's ability to reduce inflammation makes it an effective nutraceutical for liver health.

Curcumin exerts its anti-inflammatory effects by inhibiting the activation of several pro-inflammatory pathways, most notably the **NF-κB pathway**, which is a key regulator of inflammation. By blocking the NF-κB signaling pathway, curcumin reduces the expression of pro-inflammatory cytokines such as **TNF-α**, **IL-6**, and **IL-1β**, which contribute to liver injury and fibrosis. In a study published in *Phytotherapy Research*, curcumin was shown to reduce the levels of these inflammatory markers in patients with hepatitis and liver fibrosis, suggesting its potential to modulate the inflammatory response in the liver.

In addition to its anti-inflammatory effects, curcumin also acts as a potent antioxidant. It scavenges free radicals and reduces oxidative stress in liver cells, which is a key factor in the pathogenesis of liver diseases. Curcumin's antioxidant properties help protect hepatocytes from damage and promote the regeneration of liver tissue. In a study published in *The Journal of Nutritional Biochemistry*, curcumin supplementation was shown to reduce oxidative stress markers and improve liver function in animal models of liver injury.

Curcumin also enhances the detoxification process in the liver by stimulating the activity of detoxifying enzymes such as **glutathione S-transferase** and **quinone reductase**, which neutralize toxic substances and facilitate their elimination from the body. This detoxification process is particularly important for individuals with liver conditions, as the liver plays a central role in metabolizing and detoxifying harmful compounds.

The therapeutic dose of curcumin used in clinical trials ranges from 500 mg to 2 grams per day, often combined with black pepper extract (piperine) to enhance bioavailability. Despite its low bioavailability, curcumin supplementation has shown promising results in improving liver function and reducing liver inflammation. However, further clinical studies are needed to determine the optimal dosage and long-term safety of curcumin for the management of liver disorders.

In conclusion, curcumin's anti-inflammatory and antioxidant properties make it a valuable nutraceutical in the prevention and treatment of liver disorders. By modulating inflammatory pathways, reducing oxidative stress, and enhancing liver detoxification, curcumin provides comprehensive support for liver health. It is often used in combination with other treatments and lifestyle interventions for the management of liver conditions like NAFLD and hepatitis.

1.4.4.4 Osteoarthritis and Joint Health

Glucosamine and Chondroitin: Joint Cartilage Protection

Glucosamine and chondroitin are two widely used nutraceuticals that support joint health and are commonly employed in the management of osteoarthritis (OA), a degenerative joint disease characterized by the breakdown of joint cartilage. Cartilage is a key tissue that provides cushioning and flexibility to the joints, and its degradation leads to pain, stiffness, and reduced mobility in individuals with OA.

Glucosamine is an amino sugar that plays an essential role in the synthesis of glycosaminoglycans, which are components of cartilage. It is believed to stimulate the production of cartilage-forming cells and help maintain the structural integrity of cartilage. Clinical studies have shown that glucosamine supplementation can help slow the progression of cartilage degradation in OA and provide relief from joint pain and stiffness.

One of the most widely studied forms of glucosamine is **glucosamine sulfate**, which has demonstrated significant efficacy in reducing symptoms of OA, particularly in the knee and hip joints.

In a meta-analysis published in *The Lancet* of 10 randomized controlled trials (RCTs), glucosamine sulfate was shown to reduce pain and improve joint function in individuals with knee OA. The study also indicated that glucosamine supplementation could slow the narrowing of the joint space, a sign of cartilage loss. The dosage used in these studies ranged from 1,500 mg per day, with significant improvements observed in pain reduction and physical function.

Chondroitin is a naturally occurring glycosaminoglycan found in cartilage. It works by attracting water to the cartilage, providing it with more elasticity and helping to cushion the joints. Chondroitin also has anti-inflammatory properties, which further aid in reducing joint swelling and pain. In several clinical trials, chondroitin supplementation has been shown to improve joint mobility, decrease pain, and protect against cartilage breakdown.

A large, well-known clinical trial, the *GAIT study* (Glucosamine/ chondroitin Arthritis Intervention Trial), examined the effects of glucosamine and chondroitin in patients with knee OA. The results showed that chondroitin supplementation at a dose of 1,200 mg per day led to improvements in knee pain and function, particularly in individuals with moderate to severe pain. When used together with glucosamine, the combination showed enhanced efficacy in alleviating symptoms compared to a placebo.

The combination of glucosamine and chondroitin has become a widely recommended supplement for people with osteoarthritis, as it has shown promise in reducing inflammation, slowing cartilage degradation, and improving joint function.

Collagen Peptides: Strengthening of Connective Tissues

Collagen is a major structural protein found in connective tissues, including cartilage, tendons, ligaments, and skin. It plays a critical role in maintaining the strength and elasticity of joints and connective tissues. Collagen peptides, which are derived from hydrolyzed collagen, have been gaining recognition as effective nutraceuticals for joint health, particularly in the prevention and treatment of osteoarthritis and other joint-related disorders.

Collagen peptides contain smaller protein fragments that are easily absorbed and utilized by the body. When ingested, collagen peptides stimulate the synthesis of collagen and other extracellular matrix components in cartilage, promoting joint repair and maintaining the structural integrity of the joints. Studies have shown that collagen peptides can help reduce joint pain, improve joint function, and even repair cartilage in individuals with osteoarthritis.

A clinical study published in *Current Medical Research and Opinion* examined the effects of collagen peptide supplementation (10 grams per day) in individuals with knee OA. The study found that after 6 months of supplementation, participants reported significant reductions in joint pain and stiffness, as well as improvements in overall joint function. The study also observed a significant increase in the collagen content of the cartilage, suggesting that collagen peptides help regenerate and maintain cartilage tissue.

Another study in *Osteoarthritis and Cartilage* showed that collagen peptides reduced the levels of inflammatory markers, such as **C-reactive protein (CRP)** and **interleukin-6 (IL-6)**, in individuals with osteoarthritis, further supporting the anti-inflammatory properties of collagen. Collagen peptides have also been shown to increase joint mobility and reduce morning stiffness, making them an effective intervention for individuals with OA-related symptoms.

The recommended dosage of collagen peptides typically ranges from 5 to 15 grams per day, with the most significant effects observed after 3 to 6 months of supplementation. Collagen peptides are generally well-tolerated, with few side effects, making them an attractive option for individuals seeking to manage joint health naturally.

Collagen peptides have also been studied for their role in improving bone density and strength, as collagen is a key component of bone tissue. In addition to joint health, collagen supplementation has shown potential benefits for individuals with osteoporosis, making it a versatile nutraceutical for overall musculoskeletal health.

TWO

NUTRACEUTICALS FROM NATURAL SOURCES AND THEIR HEALTH BENEFITS

2.1 Spirulina: Composition, Marker Compounds, and Benefits

2.1.1 Introduction to Spirulina

Definition and Classification

Spirulina is a type of blue-green algae that is classified as cyanobacteria. Its scientific name is *Arthrospira platensis*, though it is commonly referred to as spirulina. This microalga grows in both fresh and saltwater and is widely known for its nutritional value and health benefits. Spirulina is considered a superfood due to its rich nutrient profile, which includes proteins, essential fatty acids, vitamins, and minerals. It is commonly consumed in powdered or tablet form as a dietary supplement.

Spirulina belongs to the cyanobacteria group of microorganisms, which are considered one of the oldest forms of life on Earth. It thrives in alkaline, warm water bodies, particularly in tropical and subtropical regions. The alga is typically harvested from freshwater lakes and ponds, but it is also cultivated under controlled conditions in aquaculture facilities. Spirulina's natural blue-green pigment is derived from the presence of two primary pigments: **phycocyanin** (which gives the algae its blue-green color) and **chlorophyll** (responsible for its green color).

History and Origin of Spirulina Use in Human Diet

Spirulina has a long history of use in the human diet, dating back to ancient civilizations. It was traditionally harvested from lakes in Africa and Mexico, where it was consumed by indigenous peoples. The Aztecs in Central America, for instance, are known to have used spirulina as a source of food. They would harvest it from Lake Texcoco in Mexico, where it was a natural component of the lake's ecosystem. They dried the algae and consumed it in the form of cakes.

In Africa, particularly in regions near Lake Chad, spirulina has been used by local populations for centuries. It was traditionally harvested and consumed by people in Chad, where it is still part of their diet today, often in the form of dried spirulina powder. The benefits of spirulina became more widely recognized in the 20th century, leading to its adoption as a global supplement for boosting nutrition.

Spirulina gained international attention in the 1940s when French scientist **Dr. Jean Léonard** conducted research into its nutritional value, further establishing it as a health-promoting food. It was later recognized by the United Nations as a potential solution to food shortages due to its rich nutrient profile and ease of cultivation.

Cultivation and Sustainable Production

The cultivation of spirulina is an environmentally friendly process. It requires warm temperatures (30-35°C) and alkaline water (pH between 8-11) to thrive. Spirulina is typically grown in large ponds or raceway systems, which are shallow, open-air tanks designed for algae cultivation. These systems allow for the optimal growth conditions for spirulina and also provide a sustainable method of production.

In terms of sustainability, spirulina production has several advantages over traditional crops. It requires significantly less land, water, and energy compared to conventional agriculture. Spirulina cultivation also does not require pesticides or herbicides, making it an environmentally friendly process.

Many commercial spirulina farms today use closed-loop systems, where the water is continuously recycled, and nutrients are controlled to optimize algae growth. This method reduces the risk of contamination and ensures the consistency of the final product. The sustainable nature of spirulina production makes it a viable option for meeting global nutritional demands, especially in areas where food security is a concern.

2.1.2 Composition and Nutritional Profile

Macronutrient Composition
Protein Content and Amino Acid Profile
Spirulina is renowned for its high protein content, containing approximately 60-70% protein by dry weight. This makes it one of the most protein-dense foods available. The protein in spirulina is of high biological value and contains all the essential amino acids, making it a complete protein source. The amino acid profile of spirulina includes **glutamic acid**, **aspartic acid**, **leucine**, **lysine**, and **phenylalanine**, which are essential for muscle repair, immune function, and overall health. Spirulina's amino acid profile is similar to that of eggs and soy, making it an excellent plant-based protein source.

Carbohydrates and Dietary Fiber
Spirulina contains approximately 15-20% carbohydrates by dry weight, primarily in the form of polysaccharides. The carbohydrate content in spirulina includes simple sugars like glucose and fructose, as well as complex carbohydrates, such as glycogen. Spirulina also contains dietary fiber, which aids in digestion and promotes gut health. Fiber in spirulina is thought to be beneficial for reducing the risk of cardiovascular diseases by lowering cholesterol levels and improving bowel regularity.

Healthy Fats, Including Omega-3 Fatty Acids
Spirulina is also rich in healthy fats, constituting about 5-7% of its total weight. The primary fats in spirulina are polyunsaturated fatty acids, including **omega-3 fatty acids** (especially **alpha-linolenic acid or ALA**) and **omega-6 fatty acids** (primarily **linoleic acid**). Omega-3 fatty acids are essential for brain health, reducing inflammation, and supporting cardiovascular function. A diet rich in omega-3s has been associated with a decreased risk of chronic diseases such as heart disease, arthritis, and cognitive decline. Spirulina also contains **gamma-linolenic acid (GLA)**, a beneficial omega-6 fatty acid that supports immune function and acts as an anti-inflammatory agent.

Micronutrient Composition

Vitamins

Spirulina is an excellent source of several important vitamins. It contains high levels of **B-complex vitamins**, including **B1 (thiamine)**, **B2 (riboflavin)**, **B3 (niacin)**, **B6**, **B12**, and **folic acid**. These vitamins play crucial roles in energy production, metabolism, and red blood cell formation. Spirulina is particularly noted for its B12 content, which is important for nerve function and the formation of DNA. However, the form of B12 in spirulina is debated regarding its bioavailability to humans, as it is not always in the active form.

Spirulina is also a good source of **Vitamin E**, an antioxidant that helps protect cells from oxidative damage, and **Vitamin A**, which supports immune function, skin health, and vision. Additionally, spirulina contains small amounts of **Vitamin K**, which is essential for blood clotting and bone health.

Minerals

Spirulina is rich in essential minerals, including **iron, calcium, magnesium,** and **zinc**. Iron is crucial for oxygen transport in the blood and the formation of red blood cells. The bioavailability of iron from spirulina is enhanced when consumed with vitamin C-rich foods. Spirulina contains non-heme iron, which is commonly found in plant-based foods.

Calcium and magnesium, both important for bone health, are present in spirulina in substantial amounts. Magnesium also plays a role in energy production and muscle function, while calcium is vital for maintaining bone density and preventing osteoporosis. Spirulina's zinc content supports immune function, wound healing, and protein synthesis.

In addition to these, spirulina contains trace minerals like **potassium, phosphorus, selenium,** and **manganese**, which are involved in various enzymatic processes and overall cellular function. These micronutrients contribute to the overall health benefits of spirulina, including its anti-inflammatory, immune-boosting, and antioxidant properties.

2.1.3 Bioactive Marker Compounds and Their Functions

Phycocyanin – Antioxidant and Anti-inflammatory Properties

Phycocyanin is a blue pigment protein found in spirulina, which is responsible for its characteristic blue-green color. This bioactive compound has garnered attention for its potent antioxidant and anti-inflammatory properties. As a powerful antioxidant, phycocyanin neutralizes free radicals, thus protecting cells from oxidative stress, which is a key contributor to aging, inflammation, and chronic diseases, including cardiovascular and neurodegenerative disorders.

Research has demonstrated that phycocyanin's antioxidant effects are largely due to its ability to scavenge reactive oxygen species (ROS) and reduce lipid peroxidation. In addition to its antioxidant activity, phycocyanin exhibits anti-inflammatory effects by inhibiting the activity of cyclooxygenase (COX) enzymes and reducing the production of pro-inflammatory cytokines like TNF-α and IL-6. This makes phycocyanin useful in managing inflammatory conditions, such as arthritis, and preventing inflammation-related diseases.

In a study published in the *Journal of Agricultural and Food Chemistry*, phycocyanin supplementation was shown to significantly reduce oxidative stress and inflammation markers in animals with induced inflammatory conditions. Additionally, clinical trials have found that phycocyanin can be effective in lowering the levels of inflammatory markers in individuals with conditions like asthma and rheumatoid arthritis, further supporting its therapeutic potential.

Gamma-Linolenic Acid (GLA) – Lipid Metabolism and Cardiovascular Benefits

Gamma-linolenic acid (GLA) is an omega-6 polyunsaturated fatty acid found in spirulina, as well as in other sources such as evening primrose oil, borage oil, and black currant seed oil. GLA plays an important role in lipid metabolism and has several cardiovascular benefits. It is metabolized into **dihomo-γ-linolenic acid (DGLA)**, which subsequently leads to the production of prostaglandins, signaling molecules that regulate various physiological processes, including inflammation and blood flow.

GLA is beneficial for cardiovascular health because it helps reduce inflammation, a major contributor to heart disease. It has been shown to lower triglycerides, reduce LDL cholesterol levels, and increase HDL cholesterol, all of which contribute to improved heart health. Several studies have suggested that GLA supplementation can significantly reduce the risk factors associated with cardiovascular disease.

A clinical trial published in *The American Journal of Clinical Nutrition* showed that GLA supplementation led to a reduction in total cholesterol and LDL cholesterol levels, as well as improved blood vessel function in patients with high cholesterol. Moreover, GLA has been shown to reduce blood pressure by improving endothelial function and promoting vasodilation (the widening of blood vessels).

GLA also has anti-inflammatory effects, which contribute to its cardiovascular benefits by reducing the inflammation of blood vessels that can lead to atherosclerosis (hardening of the arteries). It is important to note that while GLA has beneficial effects on lipid metabolism and inflammation, it should be consumed in balance with omega-3 fatty acids, as excessive intake of omega-6 fatty acids can lead to an imbalance that promotes inflammation.

Chlorophyll – Detoxification and Immune-Boosting Effects

Chlorophyll is the green pigment found in spirulina that is responsible for photosynthesis in plants. In addition to its role in plant metabolism, chlorophyll possesses several health-promoting properties. It has strong detoxifying effects, helping to remove toxins from the body by binding to heavy metals, environmental pollutants, and carcinogens, which then facilitates their elimination through the urinary system.

Chlorophyll's detoxification properties are particularly beneficial for the liver, the body's primary detoxifying organ. By promoting the excretion of toxins, chlorophyll helps to protect the liver from oxidative stress and damage. Studies have shown that chlorophyll can reduce liver enzyme levels and improve overall liver function. In a study published in *The Journal of Medicinal Food*, chlorophyll supplementation was found to reduce liver damage caused by toxic chemicals, supporting its role in detoxification.

Additionally, chlorophyll has immune-boosting effects due to its ability to increase the production of red and white blood cells, which are crucial for immune function and oxygen transport. Chlorophyll also exhibits antimicrobial properties, further enhancing the body's ability to fight infections. Research suggests that chlorophyll can stimulate the production of **interferon**, an immune system protein that plays a key role in antiviral defense.

Polysaccharides – Immunomodulatory Activities

Polysaccharides are complex carbohydrates found in spirulina that have significant immunomodulatory effects. These bioactive compounds are primarily responsible for enhancing the immune system's ability to fight infections and maintain overall health. Spirulina's polysaccharides, including **phycocyanin** and **spirodextrins**, have been shown to activate the immune system by stimulating the production of immune cells, such as **macrophages** and **natural killer (NK) cells**, which are essential for detecting and destroying pathogens.

Polysaccharides in spirulina work by enhancing the activity of macrophages, which are key players in the immune response, helping to identify and eliminate foreign invaders like bacteria and viruses. These polysaccharides also help regulate the production of cytokines, signaling molecules that are involved in immune cell communication. By modulating the balance of cytokines, spirulina's polysaccharides ensure a well-coordinated immune response.

Several studies have demonstrated the immunomodulatory effects of spirulina. In a study published in *The International Journal of Immunopathology and Pharmacology*, spirulina supplementation was shown to significantly increase the activity of macrophages and NK cells in individuals with compromised immune systems. Furthermore, spirulina's polysaccharides have been shown to enhance vaccine efficacy by stimulating a stronger immune response.

The immunomodulatory properties of spirulina's polysaccharides make it a valuable nutraceutical for improving immune function, particularly in individuals with weakened immunity or those at risk of infections. Regular consumption of spirulina can help support the body's natural defenses and reduce the incidence of infections and diseases.

2.1.4 Health Benefits of Spirulina

Enhancement of Immune System Function

Spirulina has been shown to significantly enhance immune system function due to its rich array of bioactive compounds, including polysaccharides, phycocyanin, and essential vitamins and minerals. Polysaccharides, in particular, are known to stimulate the immune response by activating immune cells such as macrophages and natural killer (NK) cells, both of which play crucial roles in identifying and eliminating pathogens. These immune cells act as the first line of defense, detecting harmful microorganisms and cancer cells, and initiating an immune response.

Several studies have shown that spirulina supplementation can improve immune function in both healthy individuals and those with weakened immune systems. In a study published in the *Journal of Medicinal Food*, spirulina supplementation was shown to significantly enhance NK cell activity and increase the levels of antibodies in the blood, thereby boosting the body's ability to fight infections. Similarly, another study in *The International Journal of Immunopathology and Pharmacology* found that spirulina improved immune responses in elderly individuals, suggesting its potential for boosting immunity in aging populations.

Additionally, spirulina's ability to modulate the production of cytokines—signaling molecules that regulate immune responses—further supports its role in immune enhancement. By balancing pro-inflammatory and anti-inflammatory cytokines, spirulina helps prevent excessive inflammation, which can lead to autoimmune diseases and chronic health issues.

Antioxidant and Anti-inflammatory Effects

Spirulina is rich in antioxidants, including phycocyanin, carotenoids, and vitamin E, which help to combat oxidative stress in the body. Oxidative stress occurs when there is an imbalance between free radicals and antioxidants, leading to damage of cellular components such as DNA, lipids, and proteins. This damage is associated with various chronic diseases, including cardiovascular disease, diabetes, and cancer. Spirulina's antioxidant compounds neutralize free radicals, reducing oxidative stress and thereby preventing cell damage.

Phycocyanin, the blue pigment in spirulina, is particularly noted for its powerful antioxidant properties. Studies have demonstrated that phycocyanin scavenges reactive oxygen species (ROS) and inhibits the formation of lipid peroxides, thus protecting cells from oxidative damage. Additionally, spirulina has anti-inflammatory effects that complement its antioxidant actions. Phycocyanin has been shown to reduce the production of pro-inflammatory cytokines like TNF-α and IL-6, which play key roles in inflammatory processes that contribute to chronic diseases such as arthritis and cardiovascular disease.

The anti-inflammatory effects of spirulina are also attributed to its ability to inhibit the activation of inflammatory pathways such as NF-κB (nuclear factor kappa-light-chain-enhancer of activated B cells). NF-κB regulates the expression of genes involved in inflammation, and by suppressing its activity, spirulina can help reduce chronic inflammation, thus lowering the risk of inflammatory diseases.

Role in Cardiovascular Health and Cholesterol Reduction

Spirulina has demonstrated promising effects on cardiovascular health, primarily through its ability to reduce cholesterol levels, lower blood pressure, and improve lipid profiles. One of the key benefits of spirulina is its ability to reduce **LDL (low-density lipoprotein)** cholesterol, also known as "bad" cholesterol, while increasing **HDL (high-density lipoprotein)** cholesterol, known as "good" cholesterol.

A study published in the *Journal of Nutritional Biochemistry* examined the effects of spirulina supplementation (1–2 grams per day) on lipid profiles in individuals with hyperlipidemia (elevated cholesterol levels). The results showed a significant reduction in LDL cholesterol and total cholesterol levels, along with an increase in HDL cholesterol. Spirulina was also shown to reduce triglyceride levels by up to 30%, providing additional support for heart health.

Spirulina's antioxidant properties play a critical role in improving cardiovascular function by reducing oxidative stress and preventing the oxidation of LDL cholesterol. Oxidized LDL is more likely to contribute to the formation of plaque in the arteries, leading to atherosclerosis (hardening of the arteries). By reducing oxidative damage, spirulina helps maintain healthy blood vessels and reduces the risk of cardiovascular diseases.

Additionally, spirulina has been shown to have a beneficial effect on blood pressure. Several studies suggest that spirulina supplementation can reduce systolic and diastolic blood pressure by improving endothelial function, which is responsible for the regulation of blood vessel dilation.

Potential in Weight Management and Obesity Control

Spirulina has also been studied for its potential role in weight management and the prevention of obesity. Due to its high protein content and nutrient density, spirulina helps increase satiety (the feeling of fullness) and can reduce overall calorie intake. Spirulina's rich amino acid profile, including essential amino acids like leucine, which plays a role in muscle protein synthesis, may also contribute to maintaining lean body mass while reducing fat mass.

A study published in *The Journal of Medicinal Food* found that supplementation with spirulina led to significant weight loss and reduced fat mass in obese individuals. The study participants were given 6 grams of spirulina daily for 12 weeks, and the results showed a marked reduction in body weight, waist circumference, and fat percentage. This effect is thought to be due to spirulina's ability to regulate lipid metabolism, reduce adipogenesis (formation of fat cells), and increase fat oxidation.

Moreover, spirulina's high fiber content contributes to weight control by improving digestion and promoting gut health. Fiber slows down the absorption of sugars and fats, reducing spikes in blood sugar and insulin levels after meals, and improving overall metabolic health.

Anti-cancer Potential Through Modulation of Oxidative Stress

Spirulina's antioxidant and anti-inflammatory properties extend to its potential role in cancer prevention. Oxidative stress and inflammation are well-established contributors to cancer development, and spirulina's ability to modulate these processes makes it a promising nutraceutical in the fight against cancer.

Phycocyanin, a major component of spirulina, has been shown to exhibit anti-cancer properties by reducing oxidative damage to DNA and preventing the formation of cancer-causing mutations. In vitro studies have demonstrated that phycocyanin inhibits the growth of cancer cells, induces apoptosis (programmed cell death), and prevents the metastasis of cancer cells.

Furthermore, spirulina has been shown to enhance the body's detoxification mechanisms by stimulating the production of enzymes involved in detoxifying carcinogens. **Polysaccharides** in spirulina also enhance immune function, helping the body to recognize and eliminate abnormal cells before they can develop into cancer.

Clinical studies on spirulina's role in cancer prevention are ongoing, with promising results in animal models and preliminary human trials. Studies have shown that spirulina may help prevent cancers of the digestive system, such as colorectal and liver cancers, by reducing oxidative damage, modulating inflammatory pathways, and supporting immune function.

2.1.5 Clinical Studies on Spirulina

Research on Spirulina in Oxidative Stress-Related Diseases

Oxidative stress is a key factor in the pathogenesis of many chronic diseases, including cardiovascular diseases, neurodegenerative disorders, and cancer. Spirulina, with its rich antioxidant profile, has been the subject of numerous clinical studies exploring its potential in mitigating oxidative stress and preventing related diseases.

Several clinical studies have demonstrated the ability of spirulina to reduce oxidative stress markers and improve antioxidant status in individuals with oxidative stress-related diseases. In a study published in *The American Journal of Clinical Nutrition*, spirulina supplementation (1-2 grams per day) significantly reduced serum malondialdehyde (MDA) levels, a marker of lipid peroxidation, in individuals with hyperlipidemia. The study also found an increase in the levels of **superoxide dismutase (SOD)**, a key endogenous antioxidant enzyme, suggesting that spirulina helps improve the body's antioxidant defense mechanisms.

In a clinical trial involving patients with **chronic obstructive pulmonary disease (COPD)**, a condition associated with oxidative stress, spirulina supplementation (2 grams per day for 8 weeks) led to significant improvements in **lung function** and **blood antioxidant levels**. The study found that spirulina reduced oxidative damage to lung tissue and helped increase the activity of antioxidant enzymes like **glutathione peroxidase** and **catalase**. These findings suggest that spirulina could be beneficial in managing diseases linked to oxidative stress, such as COPD, asthma, and even cardiovascular diseases.

Spirulina's effects on oxidative stress have also been studied in neurodegenerative diseases. A study published in *Neurochemical Research* explored the effects of spirulina on **Parkinson's disease** and found that supplementation reduced oxidative damage in the brain and improved the function of dopaminergic neurons. The researchers noted that spirulina's antioxidants, particularly **phycocyanin**, contributed to these protective effects by neutralizing ROS and reducing inflammation in the brain.

Studies on Spirulina's Role in Managing Metabolic Syndrome and Diabetes

Metabolic syndrome is a cluster of conditions, including **abdominal obesity**, **high blood pressure**, **elevated blood sugar**, and **abnormal cholesterol levels**, which increase the risk of heart disease, stroke, and diabetes. Diabetes, particularly type 2 diabetes, is closely linked to metabolic syndrome, and effective management is crucial for reducing the risk of complications. Spirulina has been studied for its role in managing metabolic syndrome and diabetes due to its effects on lipid metabolism, blood glucose levels, and inflammation.

In a clinical trial published in *The Journal of Nutritional Biochemistry*, spirulina supplementation (2 grams per day for 8 weeks) was shown to significantly reduce **blood glucose levels** in individuals with type 2 diabetes. The study found that spirulina not only lowered fasting blood glucose but also improved **insulin sensitivity**, a key factor in managing diabetes. The researchers attributed these effects to spirulina's antioxidant properties, which help reduce oxidative stress-induced insulin resistance.

Another clinical study in *The Journal of Medicinal Food* investigated the impact of spirulina supplementation on individuals with **metabolic syndrome**. The study involved 100 participants who received 1 gram of spirulina per day for 12 weeks. The results showed a significant reduction in **blood pressure**, **cholesterol**, and **triglyceride levels**, with improvements in **lipid profiles** and **blood sugar regulation**. This study highlights spirulina's potential to improve multiple components of metabolic syndrome, including lipid metabolism and blood sugar levels, suggesting its value in preventing diabetes and cardiovascular diseases.

Furthermore, a study published in *Diabetes & Metabolic Syndrome: Clinical Research & Reviews* demonstrated that spirulina supplementation (1 gram per day) helped reduce **abdominal fat** in individuals with type 2 diabetes, a key feature of metabolic syndrome. The researchers noted that spirulina's ability to regulate lipid metabolism, coupled with its anti-inflammatory and antioxidant effects, contributed to these improvements.

Spirulina's role in improving **insulin sensitivity** and reducing **inflammation** is critical in the management of metabolic syndrome and diabetes. Chronic inflammation and oxidative stress play a significant role in the development of insulin resistance and the progression of diabetes. Spirulina's ability to modulate inflammatory pathways and improve antioxidant status makes it a promising adjunct to traditional diabetes therapies.

2.2 Soybean: Isoflavones, Phytoestrogens, and Health Effects

2.2.1 Introduction to Soybean as a Functional Food

Origin and Historical Consumption Patterns

Soybean (*Glycine max*) is native to East Asia and has been cultivated for thousands of years, with its use in human diets dating back to at least 1100 BCE in China. It was originally domesticated from wild soybeans found in China and later spread to other parts of Asia, including Japan and Korea. Over time, soybean became an integral part of the traditional Asian diet, providing a rich source of plant-based protein, especially for populations with limited access to animal-based proteins.

Historically, soybeans were used in a variety of forms, including whole beans, soybean sprouts, and soy milk, as well as fermented products such as **tempeh** and **miso.** In China, soybeans were primarily grown as a rotation crop for enhancing soil fertility, but over time, they became a major food source. During the Tang Dynasty (618-907 AD), soybeans were first fermented to create products like **soy sauce** and **tofu**, which remain staples in Asian cuisine today.

Soybean consumption spread globally over the past century, particularly after the recognition of its high protein and health benefits. In the 20th century, soybean became a significant crop in Western countries, especially in the United States, where it is used not only as food but also as animal feed and a source of oil. In recent decades, interest in soybeans as a functional food has grown due to their nutritional properties, particularly their rich content of **iso-flavones**, which are classified as phytoestrogens and are believed to have health-promoting effects.

Today, soybeans are consumed in various forms around the world, from whole beans to processed products like tofu, tempeh, soy milk, soy protein isolates, and soy oil. They are recognized for their significant role in plant-based diets, particularly among vegetarians and vegans. Soybeans are also a major component in the production of **soy-based functional foods**, which are marketed as beneficial for health conditions such as heart disease, osteoporosis, and hormone-related disorders.

Processing Methods (Fermented vs. Non-fermented Soy Products)

Soybeans undergo various processing methods to improve their digestibility, nutritional content, and taste. These methods can be broadly categorized into fermented and non-fermented products, each offering different health benefits.

Fermented Soy Products:

Fermentation is an ancient technique used to enhance the nutritional value and digestibility of soybeans. The fermentation process involves the breakdown of soybeans by beneficial microorganisms, which helps reduce the presence of antinutritional factors like **phytates** (which interfere with mineral absorption) and **protease inhibitors** (which can hinder protein digestion). Fermented soy products are also rich in **probiotics**, which support gut health by promoting the growth of beneficial bacteria.

Common fermented soy products include **tempeh, miso, natto,** and **soy sauce. Tempeh** is a fermented soy cake, typically consumed in Indonesia, that is made by fermenting whole soybeans with the fungus **Rhizopus oligosporus**. It is rich in protein, fiber, vitamins, and minerals, and is considered easier to digest than unfermented soybeans. **Miso**, a fermented paste made from soybeans, is widely used in Japanese cuisine, particularly in soups and sauces. It is known for its rich umami flavor and probiotic content. **Natto**, a traditional Japanese dish, consists of fermented soybeans and is known for its strong flavor and sticky texture. It is particularly rich in **vitamin K2**, a form of vitamin K important for bone health. **Soy sauce**, another fermented soy product, is commonly used as a condiment in various Asian cuisines.

Fermented soy products are particularly valued for their potential health benefits. They are easier to digest than non-fermented products and contain beneficial microorganisms that can improve gut health. Fermentation also enhances the bioavailability of nutrients, making it easier for the body to absorb essential vitamins and minerals.

Non-fermented Soy Products:

Non-fermented soy products are widely consumed and include items like **tofu, soy milk, soy protein isolates,** and **soy flour**. These products are typically made by processing soybeans through methods such as boiling, grinding, and extracting. Non-fermented soy products do not have the probiotic content of fermented soy, but they are still rich in nutrients, including protein, fiber, and essential fatty acids.

Tofu is made by curdling soy milk with a coagulant and pressing the resulting curds to form blocks. It is a versatile ingredient used in a variety of dishes and is a significant source of plant-based protein. **Soy milk**, made by soaking and blending soybeans, is a popular dairy alternative and is rich in protein, vitamins, and minerals. **Soy protein isolates** are refined forms of soy protein used in food processing and as meat substitutes, particularly in vegetarian and vegan diets. **Soy flour** is made by grinding defatted soybeans and is used in baking and as a thickening agent.

Non-fermented soy products, particularly tofu and soy milk, have become mainstream in Western diets due to their health benefits, such as being heart-healthy, high in protein, and lactose-free. However, non-fermented soy products may not offer the same gut health benefits as fermented products, since they lack the probiotics and enhanced nutrient absorption properties that come with fermentation.

2.2.2 Nutritional Composition and Bioactive Compounds

Macronutrients

Protein and Amino Acid Profile

Soybeans are one of the richest plant-based sources of protein, offering approximately 36-40% protein by weight. This makes them a highly valuable food for vegetarians and vegans seeking plant-based alternatives to animal proteins. The protein in soybeans is considered a **complete protein**, as it contains all nine essential amino acids required by the human body.

The amino acid profile of soy protein is similar to that of animal protein, providing essential amino acids such as **leucine, valine, tryptophan**, and **lysine**. Of these, **leucine** plays a crucial role in muscle protein synthesis, making soy protein an excellent option for muscle maintenance and repair. The protein in soy is also well-digested and absorbed, providing an effective source of amino acids for the body.

Soy protein is not only rich in essential amino acids but also contains non-essential amino acids, such as **glutamine, proline**, and **glutamic acid,** which support immune function, gut health, and neurological health.

Lipids, Including Omega-6 Fatty Acids

Soybeans are a good source of healthy fats, containing approximately 18-20% fat by weight, much of which is unsaturated. The fat content is primarily made up of **polyunsaturated fatty acids**, particularly **omega-6 fatty acids**, with **linoleic acid** being the most prevalent. Omega-6 fatty acids play a critical role in maintaining cell membrane integrity, supporting immune function, and promoting healthy skin.

Soybean oil, extracted from the seeds, is commonly used in cooking and food processing due to its favorable fatty acid composition. While omega-6 fatty acids are essential for human health, they must be balanced with omega-3 fatty acids to maintain optimal health. A high omega-6 to omega-3 ratio has been associated with increased inflammation in the body, which is why it is important to balance the intake of omega-6-rich foods with omega-3 sources like flaxseeds and fatty fish.

Soybeans also contain **omega-9 fatty acids**, particularly **oleic acid**, which is known for its heart-healthy effects, helping to reduce LDL cholesterol and support overall cardiovascular health.

Micronutrients

Vitamins

Soybeans are rich in several essential vitamins, making them a valuable addition to a balanced diet. Key vitamins found in soybeans include:

- **Folate** (Vitamin B9): Soybeans are a significant source of folate, providing about 280 micrograms per 100 grams. Folate is essential for DNA synthesis, cell division, and the prevention of neural tube defects during pregnancy. It also plays a role in red blood cell formation and the reduction of homocysteine levels, which is important for cardiovascular health.
- **Vitamin K**: Soybeans contain a considerable amount of vitamin K, with about 15 micrograms per 100 grams. Vitamin K is crucial for blood clotting and bone health, as it helps regulate the activity of proteins that are involved in calcium metabolism. Adequate intake of vitamin K has been linked to improved bone density and reduced risk of fractures, particularly in postmenopausal women.

- **Riboflavin** (Vitamin B2): Soybeans provide around 0.2-0.3 mg of riboflavin per 100 grams. Riboflavin is vital for energy production, skin health, and the maintenance of normal vision. It also helps in the metabolism of fats, proteins, and carbohydrates, converting them into energy.

These vitamins work synergistically to support metabolic functions, boost immunity, and promote overall health.

Minerals

Soybeans are a rich source of several essential minerals, contributing significantly to the intake of:

- **Calcium**: Soybeans contain about 277 mg of calcium per 100 grams, which is essential for bone health, muscle function, nerve transmission, and blood clotting. The calcium content in soybeans is particularly beneficial for individuals who avoid dairy products. Additionally, some soy products, such as tofu and soy milk, are often fortified with calcium, further enhancing their bone-strengthening properties.
- **Magnesium**: Soybeans provide around 280 mg of magnesium per 100 grams. Magnesium plays a key role in muscle and nerve function, blood sugar regulation, and bone health. It also supports enzyme activity involved in protein synthesis and energy production. Magnesium deficiency is commonly linked to increased risks of cardiovascular diseases, osteoporosis, and migraines.
- **Iron**: Soybeans are an excellent source of non-heme iron, offering around 15 mg per 100 grams. Iron is essential for the production of hemoglobin, which carries oxygen in the blood. It also plays a critical role in energy production and immune function. The non-heme form of iron found in soybeans is less readily absorbed than heme iron from animal products, but its absorption can be enhanced when consumed with vitamin C-rich foods.

Isoflavones as Phytoestrogens

Soybeans are particularly known for their content of **isoflavones**, which are a type of phytoestrogen—plant compounds that mimic the action of estrogen in the body. Isoflavones are thought to offer several health benefits, particularly in hormone-related conditions, such as menopause, osteoporosis, and certain types of cancer. The primary isoflavones found in soybeans include **genistein, daidzein,** and **glycitein.**

Genistein

Genistein is the most abundant and biologically active isoflavone in soybeans. It has been shown to have strong antioxidant properties and is believed to have a protective effect against certain types of cancer, including breast and prostate cancer. Genistein works by binding to estrogen receptors, helping to modulate estrogenic activity in the body. Research has also suggested that genistein may help regulate **blood glucose levels**, reduce **cholesterol**, and improve **bone health**, making it beneficial for individuals with metabolic syndrome and osteoporosis.

Daidzein

Daidzein is another major isoflavone in soybeans, and it is metabolized into **equol** by certain gut bacteria, which has potent estrogenic effects. Daidzein has been linked to several health benefits, including **cardiovascular protection** by reducing cholesterol levels and **improving blood pressure.** Studies have also shown that daidzein may have neuroprotective effects, particularly in the prevention of cognitive decline associated with aging. Additionally, it may help alleviate some symptoms of **menopause**, such as hot flashes, by modulating estrogen activity.

Glycitein

Glycitein is the least abundant isoflavone in soybeans but is still significant in terms of its potential health effects. Like genistein and daidzein, glycitein has antioxidant and anti-inflammatory properties. It has been shown to reduce oxidative stress and inflammation in various tissues, making it beneficial for managing conditions like **cardiovascular diseases, arthritis**, and **type 2 diabetes.** Glycitein may also contribute to the overall anticancer effects of soy by inhibiting cancer cell proliferation and inducing apoptosis (cell death) in cancer cells

2.2.3 Health Benefits of Soybean and Isoflavones

Hormonal Balance and Menopause Symptom Relief

Soybeans are particularly well-known for their content of **isoflavones**, plant-derived compounds that function as phytoestrogens, which means they can mimic the effects of estrogen in the body. Isoflavones, particularly **genistein**, **daidzein**, and **glycitein**, have a profound impact on hormonal balance, making soy a beneficial food for women experiencing menopause. Menopause leads to a decrease in estrogen levels, causing symptoms such as hot flashes, night sweats, and mood swings.

Numerous studies have shown that soy isoflavones can alleviate these symptoms by binding to estrogen receptors and exerting mild estrogen-like effects in the body. A study published in *Menopause* found that daily consumption of 50 mg of isoflavones significantly reduced the frequency and severity of hot flashes in postmenopausal women. Additionally, a meta-analysis of clinical trials indicated that soy isoflavones help manage other menopause-related symptoms, such as sleep disturbances and vaginal dryness, contributing to an improvement in quality of life for women undergoing this transition.

Moreover, soy isoflavones may help to mitigate the risk of osteoporosis in postmenopausal women, a condition often linked to the decrease in estrogen levels. The estrogen-like activity of isoflavones has been shown to support bone density and strength, making soy beneficial for managing menopausal symptoms and preventing long-term complications like osteoporosis.

Cardiovascular Benefits and Cholesterol Management

Soybeans are also recognized for their cardiovascular benefits, particularly in cholesterol management. The protein content in soybeans, combined with their high fiber, low saturated fat, and beneficial fatty acid composition, makes them heart-healthy food. Research has consistently shown that replacing animal-based protein sources with soy protein helps to lower LDL (bad cholesterol) and increase HDL (good cholesterol).

Several clinical studies have confirmed the cholesterol-lowering effects of soy protein. A meta-analysis published in the *American Journal of Clinical Nutrition* reviewed studies on soy protein and found that consuming 25 grams of soy protein per day resulted in a 5–10% reduction in LDL cholesterol. This reduction is significant as high LDL cholesterol is a major risk factor for heart disease.

In addition to lowering cholesterol, soybeans and soy isoflavones have been shown to help lower **blood pressure** and improve endothelial function, which is important for overall heart health. Studies have found that consuming soy protein, particularly in the form of soy milk or tofu, helps reduce both systolic and diastolic blood pressure. These effects are thought to be due to the action of isoflavones, which help improve vascular health by enhancing blood vessel dilation and reducing vascular stiffness.

Cancer Prevention Mechanisms (Breast and Prostate Cancer)

Soy isoflavones have shown promise in cancer prevention, particularly in hormone-related cancers such as breast and prostate cancer. The estrogen-like effects of soy isoflavones may help modulate the activity of estrogen receptors, reducing the risk of estrogen-dependent cancers.

Breast Cancer

Soy consumption has been linked to a reduced risk of breast cancer, particularly in women who consume soy regularly in early life. Isoflavones, especially **genistein**, can bind to estrogen receptors on cells and exert protective effects against cancer cell growth. Research published in *Cancer Epidemiology, Biomarkers & Prevention* suggests that women who consume soy foods during adolescence or early adulthood have a lower risk of developing breast cancer later in life. Isoflavones in soy may inhibit the growth of **estrogen receptor-positive (ER+)** breast cancer cells by interfering with the pathways involved in tumor growth.

Additionally, soy isoflavones have been shown to enhance the effectiveness of certain chemotherapy drugs in treating breast cancer by promoting the apoptotic (cell death) pathway in cancerous cells. Some studies suggest that the anti-cancer potential of soy is enhanced when combined with other natural compounds, such as those found in cruciferous vegetables like broccoli.

Prostate Cancer

Similar to breast cancer, prostate cancer has been linked to the hormone testosterone and its more active form, **dihydrotestosterone (DHT)**. Soy isoflavones, particularly **genistein**, may have protective effects against prostate cancer by inhibiting the activity of enzymes involved in the production of DHT and reducing the growth of prostate cancer cells.

In clinical studies, consumption of soy foods has been shown to decrease the risk of prostate cancer and reduce the proliferation of prostate cancer cells. A study in *The Journal of Urology* demonstrated that men who consumed soy protein had a lower incidence of prostate cancer and a slower progression of existing prostate tumors. Genistein has been shown to inhibit the growth of prostate cancer cells by regulating the cell cycle and inducing apoptosis.

Bone Health and Osteoporosis Prevention

Isoflavones, particularly **genistein**, in soybeans have been found to support bone health by mimicking the effects of estrogen, which plays a critical role in maintaining bone density. Estrogen deficiency, as seen in postmenopausal women, is a major risk factor for osteoporosis, a condition characterized by the weakening of bones and an increased risk of fractures.

Soy isoflavones help to protect against bone loss by increasing bone mineral density and improving the balance between bone formation and resorption. Studies have shown that soy isoflavones can help prevent bone loss in postmenopausal women by stimulating the activity of bone-building cells called **osteoblasts** and inhibiting the activity of bone-resorbing cells called **osteoclasts**.

A study published in *The Journal of Nutrition* showed that daily consumption of 40 mg of soy isoflavones led to a significant improvement in bone mineral density in postmenopausal women, compared to a placebo. Other research has indicated that the intake of soy isoflavones may help reduce the risk of fractures in elderly women, further supporting their role in maintaining bone health.

2.2.4 Clinical Studies and Meta-Analyses

2.4.4 Clinical Research and Pharmacological Studies

Garlic and Cardiovascular Risk Reduction

Garlic has long been studied for its potential to reduce **cardiovascular risk** factors such as **high blood pressure, high cholesterol**, and **atherosclerosis**. Numerous clinical studies and pharmacological trials have investigated the effects of garlic on various aspects of cardiovascular health, and the results consistently demonstrate its beneficial impact.

One of the most prominent areas of research has focused on garlic's ability to **lower blood pressure**. A meta-analysis published in *The Journal of Clinical Hypertension* reviewed 16 randomized controlled trials (RCTs) involving over **900 participants**. The study found that garlic supplementation, particularly in the form of **garlic extract** or **aged garlic** (with dosages ranging from **600 mg to 1,500 mg per day**), resulted in a significant reduction in both **systolic** and **diastolic blood pressure**. On average, systolic blood pressure decreased by **5–8 mmHg**, and diastolic blood pressure decreased by **2–5 mmHg** in hypertensive individuals, which is clinically relevant in reducing the risk of heart disease and stroke.

Another well-known study published in *The American Journal of Clinical Nutrition* examined the effects of **garlic powder tablets** (containing **1,200 mg of garlic powder per day**) on **cholesterol levels**. The research showed that regular garlic supplementation led to a **7% reduction in total cholesterol** and a **10% reduction in LDL cholesterol** (the "bad" cholesterol). Garlic also increased **HDL cholesterol** (the "good" cholesterol) by **2–3%**. This lipid-modulating effect helps in reducing the formation of plaque in the arteries, thereby lowering the risk of **atherosclerosis**, a condition that can lead to heart attacks and strokes.

In addition to its effects on blood pressure and cholesterol, garlic has been shown to **improve endothelial function**, which is critical for maintaining healthy blood vessels. A study published in *Circulation* found that garlic supplementation improved the flexibility and health of arteries, which helps regulate blood flow and prevent **arterial stiffness**. The researchers concluded that regular garlic consumption could be an effective preventive measure against cardiovascular diseases.

Furthermore, garlic has been found to have **antiplatelet** properties, which help reduce the risk of **blood clot formation**. A study in *Thrombosis Research* showed that garlic extract inhibited platelet aggregation, which is essential in preventing conditions like **deep vein thrombosis** and **pulmonary embolism**.

Meta-analysis on Garlic's Impact on Immune Function

Garlic has been shown to have a significant impact on **immune function**, and several meta-analyses have evaluated its effects in this area. The immune-boosting properties of garlic are largely attributed to its **sulfur**

compounds, such as **allicin**, which enhance the activity of immune cells, including **macrophages**, **natural killer cells**, and **T lymphocytes**. These cells play critical roles in the body's defense against infections, tumors, and other diseases.

One meta-analysis published in *The Journal of Nutrition* reviewed the effects of garlic supplementation on **immune system markers** in both healthy individuals and those with compromised immune function. The analysis included **19 studies** with a total of **over 2,000 participants**. The results showed that garlic supplementation significantly increased the levels of **interferon** and **interleukins**, proteins that help regulate immune responses and enhance the body's ability to fight off infections. The study also found that garlic consumption reduced the incidence of **upper respiratory tract infections** and helped reduce the severity and duration of cold symptoms.

A study in *The American Journal of Clinical Nutrition* investigated the impact of **aged garlic extract** on **immune function** in elderly individuals. The trial showed that **daily supplementation with 2.4 grams of aged garlic extract** for **12 weeks** resulted in a significant improvement in **immune cell function**, particularly in terms of **natural killer cell activity**. These findings suggest that garlic supplementation may help strengthen the immune system, particularly in older adults who are more vulnerable to infections.

Additionally, several studies have highlighted the **antimicrobial properties** of garlic, particularly its ability to fight bacterial, viral, and fungal infections. The antimicrobial effects of garlic have been well-documented in vitro, with research showing that **allicin** inhibits the growth of a wide range of pathogens, including **E. coli, Staphylococcus aureus**, and the **common cold virus**. A meta-analysis published in *Phytomedicine* showed that garlic supplementation was associated with a reduced risk of **flu** and **cold-related illnesses**, providing further evidence of its immune-enhancing effects.

Garlic's ability to enhance immune function and prevent infections is thought to be due to its **antioxidant** and **anti-inflammatory** properties. By reducing oxidative stress and inflammation, garlic helps to maintain immune system balance, which is essential for optimal immune responses.

In conclusion, the body of clinical research and meta-analyses strongly supports garlic's beneficial effects on cardiovascular health, particularly in reducing blood pressure, cholesterol, and atherosclerosis risk. Additionally, garlic's immune-boosting and antimicrobial properties make it an effective natural remedy for enhancing the body's defense mechanisms, improving overall immune function, and preventing infections. The active sulfur compounds, particularly **allicin**, are key to these health benefits, making garlic a valuable nutraceutical for supporting heart health and immune function.

2.2.4 Clinical Studies and Meta-Analyses

Studies on Soy Isoflavones in Postmenopausal Health

Soy isoflavones have been the subject of numerous clinical studies, particularly in the context of postmenopausal health. As women undergo menopause, the decline in estrogen levels often leads to symptoms such as hot flashes, mood swings, and an increased risk of conditions like osteoporosis and cardiovascular disease. Soy isoflavones, being plant-based phytoestrogens, have been studied for their potential to alleviate these symptoms and improve overall health in postmenopausal women.

One of the most significant studies on this topic is the **ISOFEM** trial, a large, randomized, controlled trial that investigated the effects of soy isoflavone supplementation in postmenopausal women. The study found that taking **54 mg** of soy isoflavones daily for **12 weeks** resulted in a significant reduction in the frequency and severity of hot flashes, a common symptom of menopause. In addition to the reduction in vasomotor symptoms, the study also reported improved sleep quality and decreased anxiety levels in participants taking soy isoflavones compared to the placebo group.

A **meta-analysis** published in *Maturitas* evaluated the effects of soy isoflavones on **bone mineral density (BMD)** and **osteoporosis** in postmenopausal women. This analysis included data from 17 randomized controlled trials (RCTs) and found that soy isoflavones led to a modest but significant improvement in BMD, suggesting their potential for preventing bone loss in postmenopausal women. The dosage of isoflavones in these studies ranged from **40 mg to 100 mg** daily, and the supplementation duration varied from **6 months to 2 years**. These findings are important for women at risk of developing osteoporosis after menopause.

Another study, published in the *Journal of Clinical Endocrinology &* *Metabolism*, focused on the effects of soy isoflavones on cardiovascular health in postmenopausal women. The study showed that supplementation with **60 mg** of soy isoflavones daily for **6 months** significantly reduced LDL cholesterol levels and improved endothelial function, a key factor in cardiovascular health. The study also noted improvements in arterial stiffness, which is an important marker of heart disease risk.

Soy Protein and Cholesterol Reduction: Clinical Trials

Soy protein has long been recognized for its ability to reduce cholesterol levels and improve cardiovascular health. Several clinical trials and meta-analyses have examined the cholesterol-lowering effects of soy protein, with consistent findings supporting its benefits in reducing **LDL cholesterol** and increasing **HDL cholesterol.**

One of the key studies in this area is the **Meta-analysis of Soy Protein and Cholesterol**, published in *The American Journal of Clinical Nutrition.* This analysis included 38 studies and found that the consumption of **25 grams of soy protein per day** led to a **9-10% reduction in LDL cholesterol** and a **5-6% reduction in total cholesterol.** The results were significant across various populations, including those with normal cholesterol levels and those with hyperlipidemia. The study also noted that the cholesterol-lowering effects of soy protein were more pronounced in individuals with higher baseline cholesterol levels.

In addition to its effects on LDL cholesterol, soy protein has also been shown to increase HDL cholesterol, which is associated with a reduced risk of cardiovascular disease. A randomized controlled trial published in *Circulation* investigated the effects of soy protein supplementation on **HDL cholesterol** and found that daily consumption of **40 grams** of soy protein significantly increased HDL levels in individuals with elevated cholesterol. The study concluded that soy protein could be an effective dietary intervention for improving lipid profiles and reducing heart disease risk.

Another clinical trial published in *The Journal of Nutrition* examined the effects of soy protein on **triglyceride levels** in individuals with **type 2 diabetes.** The trial found that a diet rich in soy protein reduced triglyceride levels by **10-15%**, contributing to improved lipid profiles and better overall metabolic health. The study also found that soy protein was effective in lowering **blood pressure**, particularly systolic blood pressure, making it beneficial for individuals with hypertension, a common comorbidity in diabetes.

These findings are important for individuals looking to manage cholesterol levels and reduce their risk of cardiovascular disease. The cholesterol-lowering effects of soy protein are thought to result from its unique composition of amino acids and the presence of bioactive compounds such as isoflavones, which may enhance lipid metabolism and reduce fat accumulation.

2.3 Ginseng: Bioactive Compounds and Medicinal Properties

2.3.1 Introduction to Ginseng and Its Traditional Uses

Types of Ginseng: Asian Ginseng, American Ginseng, Siberian Ginseng

Ginseng is a well-known herb used for centuries in traditional medicine, particularly in Asian countries. The term "ginseng" refers to several plant species, each with distinct medicinal properties and uses. The most common types of ginseng are **Asian ginseng** (*Panax ginseng*), **American ginseng** (*Panax quinquefolius*), and **Siberian ginseng** (*Eleutherococcus senticosus*). Although these plants are related, they differ in their origins, chemical composition, and therapeutic effects.

- **Asian Ginseng** (*Panax ginseng*): Asian ginseng, also called **Korean ginseng,** is the most widely studied and used type of ginseng. It has been a staple in Chinese, Korean, and other East Asian traditional medicines for over 2,000 years. The root of Asian ginseng is considered to have adaptogenic properties, meaning it helps the body resist physical, chemical, and biological stressors. **Panax ginseng** is often used to improve overall vitality, boost energy, enhance cognitive function, and support the immune system.
- **American Ginseng** (*Panax quinquefolius*): Native to North America, American ginseng is often considered to have a milder effect than its Asian counterpart. It is typically used to enhance relaxation, reduce stress, and support overall well-being. It has been historically used by Native American populations for its medicinal properties, including to enhance stamina and alleviate fatigue. American ginseng is often considered cooler in nature, making it suitable for individuals who may find the stimulating effects of Asian ginseng too strong.
- **Siberian Ginseng** (*Eleutherococcus senticosus*): Despite its name, Siberian ginseng is not a true ginseng but rather belongs to a different genus.

It has a similar adaptogenic profile and has been used in traditional Russian and Chinese medicine for thousands of years. Siberian ginseng is believed to enhance endurance, improve mental clarity, and protect against stress. Unlike Asian and American ginseng, Siberian ginseng does not contain **ginsenosides**, the primary bioactive compounds in true ginseng species, but instead contains other compounds like **eleutherosides**, which contribute to its medicinal properties.

Each type of ginseng has its unique characteristics and is used to address specific health concerns. Asian ginseng is typically more stimulating, while American ginseng and Siberian ginseng are often used for calming and balancing effects.

Traditional Medicinal Applications in Chinese and Korean Medicine

Ginseng has played a prominent role in traditional Chinese and Korean medicine for centuries. In **Traditional Chinese Medicine (TCM)**, ginseng is classified as a tonic herb, used to **revitalize the body**, improve **Qi** (the vital life force), and restore balance to the body's energy systems. It is commonly used to treat fatigue, improve concentration, boost immune function, and promote longevity. In TCM, ginseng is believed to be particularly beneficial for individuals who experience weakness or depletion of energy due to chronic illness or stress.

Ginseng is often used in combination with other herbs in **herbal formulas**, such as **Ba Zhen Tang** and **Shi Quan Da Bu Tang**, to treat conditions like **fatigue**, **low libido**, and **chronic stress**. In TCM, ginseng is thought to have a warming effect, which is why it is often recommended for individuals who suffer from **coldness** or **weakness** in the body.

In **Korean traditional medicine**, ginseng is revered as a "king of herbs" and is considered an essential remedy for promoting longevity and enhancing physical strength. Korean ginseng, in particular, is associated with **yin-yang balance** and is believed to help harmonize the body's internal systems. It has a long history of use for treating **mental exhaustion, immunity issues**, and **digestive problems.**

In both Chinese and Korean medicine, ginseng is considered to have **adaptogenic** properties, meaning it helps the body adapt to various stressors, including physical, emotional, and environmental challenges. Ginseng is often recommended for improving **mental clarity**, supporting **cognitive function**, and increasing **physical stamina.**

Some traditional uses of ginseng in Chinese and Korean medicine include:

- **Enhancing physical endurance** and reducing fatigue
- **Improving memory and concentration**, particularly in older adults
- **Boosting the immune system**, making it effective in preventing colds and flu
- **Restoring sexual function** and improving libido
- **Balancing blood sugar** levels, especially in those with diabetes
- **Treating digestive disorders**, such as bloating and indigestion

Ginseng is typically consumed in various forms, including **powdered root**, **teas**, **tinctures**, and **capsules**, depending on the tradition and health needs. It is also commonly used in **ginseng extracts** or as part of **herbal tonics** that target overall wellness and vitality.

2.3.2 Key Bioactive Compounds in Ginseng

Ginsenosides and Their Pharmacological Effects

Ginsenosides are the primary bioactive compounds found in ginseng, especially in *Panax ginseng* and *Panax quinquefolius*. These saponins are responsible for many of ginseng's pharmacological effects, which include enhancing energy, improving cognitive function, and providing adaptogenic properties. There are over 30 different ginsenosides identified in ginseng, with the most commonly studied being **Rb1**, **Rb2**, **Rg1**, and **Rg3**.

- **Ginsenoside Rb1** is considered one of the most prominent ginsenosides and is primarily responsible for the **adaptogenic** and **anti-fatigue** properties of ginseng. It works by enhancing blood circulation and improving oxygen utilization in the body. Studies have shown that ginsenoside Rb1 helps alleviate fatigue by increasing the activity of **mitochondrial enzymes** and improving the efficiency of cellular energy production. This makes it beneficial in treating conditions related to chronic fatigue syndrome.
- **Ginsenoside Rg1** is known for its **neuroprotective** effects. It has been shown to improve cognitive function and memory by enhancing

synaptic plasticity and reducing neuroinflammation. It also promotes the release of acetylcholine, a neurotransmitter essential for learning and memory. Due to these properties, ginsenoside Rg1 is often studied for its potential to prevent or treat neurodegenerative diseases like **Alzheimer's** and **Parkinson's disease.**

- **Ginsenoside Rg3** has been found to have **anticancer** properties, particularly in inhibiting the growth of **lung** and **breast cancer cells**. It induces apoptosis (programmed cell death) in cancer cells by regulating **p53** gene expression and inhibiting the activity of oncogenes. Rg3 has also been shown to improve the effectiveness of chemotherapy treatments in certain types of cancer.

Polysaccharides and Peptides

In addition to ginsenosides, ginseng contains other bioactive compounds, including **polysaccharides** and **peptides**, which contribute to its medicinal properties.

Polysaccharides, such as **ginsan**, are large carbohydrate molecules that are known for their **immune-boosting** effects. These compounds have been shown to stimulate the activity of **macrophages**, **natural killer cells**, and **dendritic cells**, which play critical roles in the body's immune response. Polysaccharides in ginseng have been linked to improved resistance against infections, particularly viral and bacterial infections.

A study published in *The Journal of Ethnopharmacology* demonstrated that ginseng polysaccharides could increase the production of **interleukins**, which are important for the activation of immune cells. These compounds also help reduce inflammation, making them useful in managing conditions like **arthritis** and **inflammatory bowel diseases.**

Peptides found in ginseng, such as **ginseng peptide A** and **ginseng peptide B**, have been shown to exhibit **antioxidant** and **anti-inflammatory** properties. These peptides work by scavenging free radicals, thus protecting cells from oxidative damage. They also inhibit the production of inflammatory mediators, such as **prostaglandins** and **cytokines**, which are involved in chronic inflammatory processes. Research has shown that ginseng peptides can help reduce inflammation in conditions such as **rheumatoid arthritis** and **allergic reactions.**

Vitamins and Minerals

Ginseng is also rich in several essential **vitamins** and **minerals**, which contribute to its health-promoting effects. The mineral content of ginseng includes **potassium, calcium, iron**, and **magnesium**, all of which play key roles in maintaining overall health.

- **Potassium** is vital for maintaining **electrolyte balance, nerve function**, and **muscle contraction**. It helps regulate blood pressure and supports the normal functioning of the cardiovascular system.
- **Calcium** is essential for **bone health**, nerve signaling, and muscle function. Ginseng's calcium content helps support healthy bones, especially in older adults.
- **Iron** is necessary for the production of **hemoglobin**, the protein in red blood cells that carries oxygen throughout the body. Iron deficiency can lead to **anemia**, a condition characterized by fatigue and weakness, which ginseng can help alleviate by providing a source of bioavailable iron.
- **Magnesium** is involved in over 300 biochemical reactions in the body, including the regulation of **blood sugar** levels, **blood pressure**, and **muscle function**. It also helps reduce **stress** and supports a healthy immune system.

In addition to these minerals, ginseng contains several **B vitamins**, including **B1 (thiamine), B2 (riboflavin), B3 (niacin)**, and **B6**, which are important for energy metabolism and the proper functioning of the nervous system. These vitamins help convert food into energy and support the production of neurotransmitters essential for cognitive function.

2.3.3 Health Benefits of Ginseng

Cognitive Enhancement and Neuroprotection

Ginseng is widely known for its ability to improve cognitive function and provide neuroprotection. The bioactive compounds in ginseng, particularly **ginsenosides**, have been shown to enhance memory, concentration, and overall mental clarity. This has made ginseng a popular supplement for individuals experiencing cognitive decline or those looking to improve their brain function.

One of the most studied ginsenosides in terms of cognitive enhancement is **ginsenoside Rg1**. Research published in *Neurochemical Research* has demonstrated that ginsenoside Rg1 promotes **synaptic plasticity**, which is crucial for learning and memory. It enhances the formation of connections between nerve cells, which supports improved cognitive function. Ginsenoside Rg1 is also believed to increase the release of acetylcholine, a neurotransmitter essential for memory and learning.

Additionally, ginseng has neuroprotective properties that help shield the brain from age-related degeneration. Studies have shown that ginsenosides can reduce **oxidative stress** in the brain, which is a major contributor to **neurodegenerative diseases** like Alzheimer's and Parkinson's disease. Ginseng's antioxidant properties help reduce the damage caused by **free radicals**, thereby protecting neurons from degeneration. Research has shown that ginseng supplementation can reduce the accumulation of **beta-amyloid plaques**, a hallmark of Alzheimer's disease.

Ginseng also helps to increase **blood circulation** to the brain, which can further enhance cognitive function. This increased circulation provides the brain with more oxygen and nutrients, supporting overall mental clarity and focus. These neuroprotective and cognitive-enhancing effects make ginseng an effective herbal remedy for improving brain health and preventing cognitive decline with aging.

Anti-inflammatory and Immune-boosting Properties

Ginseng has powerful **anti-inflammatory** and **immune-boosting** properties, which contribute to its ability to promote overall health and fight disease. The bioactive compounds in ginseng, particularly **ginsenosides** and **polysaccharides**, have been shown to regulate the immune system by stimulating the activity of key immune cells such as **macrophages**, **natural killer cells**, and **T-cells**. These cells are essential for the body's defense against infections and harmful pathogens.

Ginseng has been shown to reduce the production of **pro-inflammatory cytokines** like **TNF-α** (tumor necrosis factor-alpha) and **IL-6** (interleukin-6), which are involved in chronic inflammation and autoimmune diseases. By modulating the immune response and reducing inflammation, ginseng helps to protect the body from inflammation-related diseases, such as **rheumatoid arthritis, asthma**, and **inflammatory bowel disease.**

The **polysaccharides** in ginseng have been found to act as immunomodulators, promoting the activation and regulation of immune cells. A study published in *The Journal of Immunology* found that ginseng polysaccharides enhanced the production of **interferons**, proteins that are crucial in antiviral responses. Ginseng supplementation has also been shown to improve **immune response** to infections like the common cold, reducing the severity and duration of symptoms.

These anti-inflammatory and immune-boosting effects make ginseng a beneficial herb for managing chronic inflammatory conditions, improving immune function, and enhancing the body's ability to fight infections.

Role in Energy Metabolism and Anti-fatigue Effects

Ginseng is widely used as an **adaptogen**, helping the body to adapt to physical and mental stress. One of its primary benefits is its role in **energy metabolism** and its ability to combat fatigue. Ginseng enhances energy levels by improving mitochondrial function, which is responsible for producing the energy molecules (ATP) necessary for cellular activity.

A study published in *The American Journal of Chinese Medicine* demonstrated that ginseng supplementation significantly reduced fatigue and improved endurance in individuals with chronic fatigue syndrome. The study found that daily supplementation of **200 mg** of ginseng root extract improved physical performance and reduced perceived levels of fatigue.

The **ginsenosides** in ginseng play a central role in energy production by increasing **adrenal gland activity**, which helps the body produce more energy during times of stress. Ginseng has been shown to stimulate the **adrenal cortex**, promoting the release of **cortisol**, the body's primary stress hormone, which helps regulate energy levels.

Additionally, ginseng has been found to improve exercise performance by increasing **oxygen uptake** and enhancing **muscle oxygenation** during physical activity. This makes it a popular supplement among athletes and those looking to improve physical endurance. Ginseng is also commonly used to improve mental alertness and concentration, contributing to reduced fatigue during both physical and cognitive tasks.

2.4 Garlic: Sulfur Compounds, Antioxidant, and Cardiovascular Benefits

2.4.1 Introduction to Garlic as a Nutraceutical

Historical and Cultural Significance

Garlic (*Allium sativum*) has a rich history of use in both culinary and medicinal practices across various cultures. It has been cultivated for over 5,000 years, with records of its use dating back to ancient Egypt, where it was not only a staple in the diet but also revered for its therapeutic properties. The Egyptians believed that garlic was a powerful medicinal herb, using it to treat ailments like respiratory issues, digestive problems, and even to enhance strength and stamina among laborers building the pyramids.

In **ancient Greece**, garlic was used to improve physical performance, particularly by athletes who consumed it to boost endurance. The renowned physician **Hippocrates** included garlic in his treatments for a variety of health problems, including **digestive issues, infections**, and **respiratory ailments**. Garlic's use continued through Roman and medieval times, where it was also believed to possess **protective properties** against evil spirits and disease.

In **Chinese traditional medicine**, garlic has long been used for its **warming** and **detoxifying effects**. It is considered effective for improving digestion, treating infections, and enhancing immunity. Similarly, in **Indian Ayurvedic medicine**, garlic is recognized for its ability to balance the body's **doshas** (bioenergy forces) and is commonly used for its **digestive, cardioprotective**, and **immune-boosting** properties.

In modern times, garlic is not only a key ingredient in global cuisines but has also been extensively researched for its health benefits, particularly for its **antioxidant, antimicrobial**, and **cardiovascular** effects. Garlic has been embraced as a **nutraceutical**, a food that offers health benefits beyond basic nutrition, and is commonly available in the form of fresh bulbs, powdered supplements, and extracts.

Modern Dietary Applications

Garlic continues to be an essential component of many culinary traditions, used to add flavor and aroma to a wide range of dishes. It is particularly common in Mediterranean, Middle Eastern, and Asian cuisines, where it is used both raw and cooked.

Beyond its culinary use, garlic is also widely used as a dietary supplement due to its **health-promoting properties**. It is available in various forms, including **garlic powder, garlic oil, aged garlic extracts**, and **garlic tablets**. Garlic supplements are commonly marketed for their ability to improve **cardiovascular health, lower cholesterol levels, enhance immune function**, and provide **antioxidant protection.**

Garlic's versatility makes it easy to incorporate into a wide variety of meals, from soups and salads to roasted meats and stir-fries. Additionally, garlic is often used as a natural remedy in the form of **garlic-infused oils** or **garlic teas** to treat conditions like **cold and flu**, **high blood pressure**, and **digestive disorders.**

2.4.2 Active Sulfur Compounds in Garlic

Garlic's medicinal properties are primarily attributed to its **sulfur-containing compounds**, which are released when the garlic is crushed or chopped. The two most studied sulfur compounds in garlic are **allicin** and **diallyl sulfides**, both of which are responsible for its therapeutic effects.

Allicin – Antimicrobial and Cardiovascular Properties

Allicin is one of the most well-known and bioactive compounds found in garlic. It is formed when **alliin**, a sulfur-containing amino acid, is converted into allicin through the action of an enzyme called **alliinase**, which is activated when garlic is chopped or crushed. Allicin is known for its strong **antimicrobial properties**, which make it effective against a wide range of **bacteria**, **viruses**, and **fungi.**

Allicin has been shown to inhibit the growth of pathogenic bacteria like **E. coli**, **Salmonella**, and **Staphylococcus aureus**, and has been used as a natural remedy to fight infections. Research published in *The Journal of Antimicrobial Chemotherapy* found that allicin effectively reduced the bacterial load in infected wounds and could even help treat respiratory infections such as the **common cold.**

Apart from its antimicrobial effects, allicin has **cardioprotective** benefits. Studies have demonstrated that allicin can help reduce **blood pressure, cholesterol levels**, and improve overall **heart health.** In one study published in *The Journal of Nutrition*, participants who took a daily dose of garlic extract containing allicin showed significant reductions in **systolic** and **diastolic blood pressure.** Allicin also helps in the reduction of **LDL cholesterol** and **triglyceride levels**, both of which are risk factors for cardiovascular diseases.

Allicin's ability to improve **blood vessel function** and **enhance circulation** also contributes to its **cardiovascular benefits**, making it an important compound for supporting heart health and preventing the development of conditions such as **atherosclerosis.**

Diallyl Sulfides and Trisulfides – Antioxidant and Detoxifying Effects

Another important group of sulfur compounds in garlic are **diallyl sulfides** and **diallyl trisulfides**. These compounds are responsible for garlic's **antioxidant** and **detoxifying effects.** Research has shown that diallyl sulfides have the ability to neutralize **free radicals** and reduce **oxidative stress**, which plays a significant role in aging and the development of chronic diseases like **cancer, heart disease**, and **diabetes.**

Diallyl trisulfides, another sulfur-containing compound in garlic, have been found to have **anti-inflammatory** and **detoxifying** properties. Studies have shown that these compounds can help support **liver detoxification** processes by promoting the activity of enzymes involved in the elimination of **toxins** from the body. A study published in *The Journal of Nutritional Biochemistry* demonstrated that diallyl trisulfides could increase the production of **phase II detoxifying enzymes** such as **glutathione-S-transferase**, which are crucial in protecting the liver from oxidative damage.

These sulfur compounds also exhibit **anti-cancer properties**, particularly in reducing the growth of **tumor cells**. A study in *Cancer Prevention Research* found that diallyl trisulfides inhibited the growth of **breast cancer cells** by inducing apoptosis (programmed cell death) and reducing tumor proliferation. The compounds are believed to achieve this by modulating **gene expression** involved in cell growth and survival.

In summary, garlic's health benefits are largely attributed to its rich content of active sulfur compounds, particularly **allicin, diallyl sulfides,** and **diallyl trisulfides.** These compounds provide **antimicrobial, cardioprotective, antioxidant**, and **detoxifying** effects, making garlic an important nutraceutical for maintaining overall health, preventing infections, supporting heart health, and reducing the risk of chronic diseases such as **cancer, diabetes**, and **cardiovascular disease.**

2.4.3 Health Benefits of Garlic

Blood Pressure Reduction and Cardiovascular Protection

Garlic has long been recognized for its ability to improve heart health and reduce blood pressure. Numerous clinical studies and trials have demonstrated that garlic can be an effective natural remedy for **hypertension**, which is a key risk factor for **cardiovascular diseases** such as heart attack and stroke. The **active sulfur compounds** in garlic, particularly **allicin**, are primarily responsible for its **blood pressure-lowering effects.**

A study published in *The Journal of Clinical Hypertension* found that daily consumption of **600–1,500 mg** of garlic extract for **12 weeks** resulted in a significant reduction in both **systolic** and **diastolic blood pressure** in individuals with high blood pressure. The blood pressure reduction was observed in both **systolic** (by approximately 8-10 mmHg) and **diastolic** (by approximately 5-7 mmHg) measurements. The study attributed these effects to the ability of garlic to **relax blood vessels**, improve **blood flow**, and enhance the **bioavailability of nitric oxide**, a molecule that plays a key role in vasodilation (the widening of blood vessels).

Furthermore, garlic has been found to have **cardioprotective effects**. Research has demonstrated that garlic supplementation can lower **LDL cholesterol** (bad cholesterol) levels, **increase HDL cholesterol** (good cholesterol), and **reduce triglycerides**, all of which contribute to overall cardiovascular health. A meta-analysis published in *The American Journal of Clinical Nutrition* examined 26 studies on garlic and found that garlic intake led to a **7% reduction in total cholesterol** and a **10% reduction in LDL cholesterol** in participants. These findings suggest that garlic can play a vital role in reducing the risk of **atherosclerosis, stroke**, and **heart attack** by improving lipid profiles and vascular health.

Immune System Enhancement and Antimicrobial Effects

Garlic is well-known for its **immune-boosting properties** and has been used for centuries to fight infections and support overall immune function. The **antimicrobial effects** of garlic are primarily attributed to **allicin**, which has been shown to possess **antiviral**, **antibacterial**, **antifungal**, and **antiprotozoal** properties. Garlic has been used to combat a wide variety of infections, from the common cold to more serious conditions like **respiratory infections** and **gastrointestinal infections**.

A study published in *The Journal of Nutrition* found that individuals who took garlic supplements regularly had a significantly lower incidence of **colds** and **flu-like illnesses**. Garlic was found to stimulate the activity of **white blood cells**, such as **macrophages** and **natural killer cells**, which play a crucial role in the body's defense against pathogens. Additionally, garlic's ability to increase **interferon** production enhances the immune system's antiviral defense.

Garlic has been shown to be particularly effective in fighting **bacterial infections**, including **Staphylococcus aureus** and **Escherichia coli**. Studies have demonstrated that garlic extract, especially when consumed fresh, can reduce the growth of harmful bacteria in the gut and respiratory tract, making it an excellent remedy for **digestive disorders** and **respiratory infections**.

Furthermore, garlic has **anti-inflammatory** properties, which enhance immune system function and contribute to the body's ability to fight infections. By reducing inflammation, garlic also helps improve the body's overall ability to handle chronic conditions related to the immune system, such as **rheumatoid arthritis**.

Anti-cancer Properties in Colorectal and Gastric Cancers

Garlic has garnered significant attention for its potential **anticancer properties**, particularly in the prevention of **colorectal** and **gastric cancers**. Studies have shown that the sulfur compounds in garlic, including **allicin**, **diallyl sulfides**, and **diallyl trisulfides**, have the ability to reduce the risk of cancer by inhibiting **cancer cell proliferation**, inducing **apoptosis** (programmed cell death), and preventing the formation of **carcinogenic compounds**.

In a clinical trial published in *Cancer Prevention Research*, researchers found that individuals who consumed **raw garlic** regularly had a lower risk of developing **colorectal cancer**. The study concluded that the **organosulfur compounds** in garlic help inhibit the activity of **cyclooxygenase-2 (COX-2)**, an enzyme that plays a role in promoting inflammation and cancer cell growth. Additionally, **diallyl trisulfides** found in garlic have been shown to prevent the activation of **cancer-causing genes** and inhibit the spread of **tumor cells** in the colon and stomach.

Research published in *The American Journal of Clinical Nutrition* also investigated the role of garlic in **gastric cancer prevention**. The study found that a diet high in garlic was associated with a reduced risk of **gastric cancer**, especially when consumed regularly as part of a traditional Asian diet. The protective effects were linked to garlic's ability to detoxify **carcinogens**, reduce **inflammatory markers**, and modulate **gene expression** related to tumor development.

Liver Detoxification Support

Garlic has also been shown to support **liver detoxification**, promoting the removal of harmful toxins from the body. The **sulfur compounds** in garlic, particularly **diallyl sulfides**, play a crucial role in enhancing the body's ability to detoxify by supporting the **liver's phase I and phase II detoxification processes**. These compounds help to increase the production of **glutathione**, a potent antioxidant that is essential for neutralizing **free radicals** and eliminating **toxins** from the liver.

A study published in *The Journal of Nutritional Biochemistry* found that garlic supplementation could enhance the activity of liver enzymes involved in detoxification, such as **glutathione-S-transferase** and **catalase**. These enzymes help break down and eliminate toxins, such as **heavy metals** and **pollutants**, from the body. Garlic's detoxifying properties make it particularly beneficial for individuals exposed to environmental pollutants, heavy metals, or those with liver diseases like **fatty liver disease** or **hepatitis**.

Garlic's ability to support liver health and detoxification is also linked to its **anti-inflammatory** properties, which help reduce liver damage caused by inflammation and oxidative stress. By reducing inflammation, garlic helps protect the liver from long-term damage and supports its ability to regenerate and repair itself.

In conclusion, garlic offers a wide range of health benefits, from improving **cardiovascular health** and **immune function** to **preventing cancer** and supporting **liver detoxification**. Its **antimicrobial** and **anti-inflammatory** effects, along with its ability to regulate **blood pressure** and **cholesterol levels**, make it a potent natural remedy for various chronic health conditions. The bioactive sulfur compounds in garlic, particularly **allicin**, **diallyl sulfides**, and **diallyl trisulfides**, are responsible for many of these therapeutic effects, making garlic a valuable addition to any health regimen.

2.4.4 Clinical Research and Pharmacological Studies

Garlic and Cardiovascular Risk Reduction

Garlic has long been studied for its potential to reduce **cardiovascular risk** factors such as **high blood pressure**, **high cholesterol**, and **atherosclerosis**. Numerous clinical studies and pharmacological trials have investigated the effects of garlic on various aspects of cardiovascular health, and the results consistently demonstrate its beneficial impact.

One of the most prominent areas of research has focused on garlic's ability to **lower blood pressure**. A meta-analysis published in *The Journal of Clinical Hypertension* reviewed 16 randomized controlled trials (RCTs) involving over **900 participants**. The study found that garlic supplementation, particularly in the form of **garlic extract** or **aged garlic** (with dosages ranging from **600 mg to 1,500 mg per day**), resulted in a significant reduction in both **systolic** and **diastolic blood pressure**. On average, systolic blood pressure decreased by **5–8 mmHg**, and diastolic blood pressure decreased by **2–5 mmHg** in hypertensive individuals, which is clinically relevant in reducing the risk of heart disease and stroke.

Another well-known study published in *The American Journal of Clinical Nutrition* examined the effects of **garlic powder tablets** (containing **1,200 mg of garlic powder per day**) on **cholesterol levels**. The research showed that regular garlic supplementation led to a **7% reduction in total cholesterol** and a **10% reduction in LDL cholesterol** (the "bad" cholesterol). Garlic also increased **HDL cholesterol** (the "good" cholesterol) by **2–3%**. This lipid-modulating effect helps in reducing the formation of plaque in the arteries, thereby lowering the risk of **atherosclerosis**, a condition that can lead to heart attacks and strokes.

In addition to its effects on blood pressure and cholesterol, garlic has been shown to **improve endothelial function**, which is critical for maintaining healthy blood vessels. A study published in *Circulation* found that garlic supplementation improved the flexibility and health of arteries, which helps regulate blood flow and prevent **arterial stiffness**. The researchers concluded that regular garlic consumption could be an effective preventive measure against cardiovascular diseases.

Furthermore, garlic has been found to have **antiplatelet** properties, which help reduce the risk of **blood clot formation**. A study in *Thrombosis Research* showed that garlic extract inhibited platelet aggregation, which is essential in preventing conditions like **deep vein thrombosis** and **pulmonary embolism**.

Meta-analysis on Garlic's Impact on Immune Function

Garlic has been shown to have a significant impact on **immune function**, and several meta-analyses have evaluated its effects in this area. The immune-boosting properties of garlic are largely attributed to its **sulfur compounds**, such as **allicin**, which enhance the activity of immune cells, including **macrophages**, **natural killer cells**, and **T lymphocytes**. These cells play critical roles in the body's defense against infections, tumors, and other diseases.

One meta-analysis published in *The Journal of Nutrition* reviewed the effects of garlic supplementation on **immune system markers** in both healthy individuals and those with compromised immune function. The analysis included **19 studies** with a total of **over 2,000 participants**. The results showed that garlic supplementation significantly increased the levels of **interferon** and **interleukins**, proteins that help regulate immune responses and enhance the body's ability to fight off infections. The study also found that garlic consumption reduced the incidence of **upper respiratory tract infections** and helped reduce the severity and duration of cold symptoms.

A study in *The American Journal of Clinical Nutrition* investigated the impact of **aged garlic extract** on **immune function** in elderly individuals. The trial showed that **daily supplementation with 2.4 grams of aged garlic extract** for **12 weeks** resulted in a significant improvement in **immune cell function**, particularly in terms of **natural killer cell activity**. These findings suggest that garlic supplementation may help strengthen the immune system, particularly in older adults who are more vulnerable to infections.

Additionally, several studies have highlighted the **antimicrobial properties** of garlic, particularly its ability to fight bacterial, viral, and fungal infections. The antimicrobial effects of garlic have been well-documented in vitro, with research showing that **allicin** inhibits the growth of a wide range of pathogens, including **E. coli**, **Staphylococcus aureus**, and the **common cold virus**. A meta-analysis published in *Phytomedicine* showed that garlic supplementation was associated with a reduced risk of **flu** and **cold-related illnesses**, providing further evidence of its immune-enhancing effects.

Garlic's ability to enhance immune function and prevent infections is thought to be due to its **antioxidant** and **anti-inflammatory** properties. By reducing oxidative stress and inflammation, garlic helps to maintain immune system balance, which is essential for optimal immune responses.

In conclusion, the body of clinical research and meta-analyses strongly supports garlic's beneficial effects on cardiovascular health, particularly in reducing blood pressure, cholesterol, and atherosclerosis risk. Additionally, garlic's immune-boosting and antimicrobial properties make it an effective natural remedy for enhancing the body's defense mechanisms, improving overall immune function, and preventing infections. The active sulfur compounds, particularly **allicin**, are key to these health benefits, making garlic a valuable nutraceutical for supporting heart health and immune function.

2.5 Broccoli: Glucosinolates and Cancer Prevention

2.5.1 Introduction to Broccoli and Cruciferous Vegetables

Nutritional Importance of Cruciferous Vegetables

Cruciferous vegetables, belonging to the **Brassicaceae** family, are among the most nutritionally dense plant foods available. They include a variety of vegetables such as **broccoli, cauliflower, Brussels sprouts, cabbage**, and **kale.** These vegetables are rich in essential nutrients and bioactive compounds, making them beneficial for overall health and disease prevention.

Cruciferous vegetables are an excellent source of **vitamins, minerals, dietary fiber**, and **antioxidants**. They are particularly high in **vitamin C, folate**, and **vitamin K**, which play crucial roles in immune function, blood clotting, and tissue repair. The fiber content in these vegetables supports **digestive health** and helps in maintaining a healthy weight by providing satiety.

Moreover, cruciferous vegetables are rich in **bioactive compounds**, such as **glucosinolates**, which have been shown to have potent **detoxifying, anti-inflammatory**, and **anti-cancer properties**. These vegetables are also known to have a low glycemic index, making them suitable for individuals with **diabetes** or those looking to manage their blood sugar levels.

Broccoli vs. Other Cruciferous Vegetables

While all cruciferous vegetables offer significant health benefits, **broccoli** stands out due to its high levels of **sulforaphane** and **glucosinolates**. Broccoli has been the subject of numerous studies due to its potent **anti-cancer, anti-inflammatory**, and **detoxification** properties. Compared to other cruciferous vegetables, broccoli is particularly high in **sulforaphane**, a compound that plays a critical role in reducing the risk of cancer and supporting the body's **detoxification pathways.**

In terms of overall nutrition, **broccoli** is also one of the richest sources of **vitamin C** and **vitamin K** among cruciferous vegetables. It is an excellent source of **antioxidants**, such as **lutein** and **zeaxanthin**, which promote eye health and protect against oxidative stress. Additionally, broccoli provides **folate**, a vitamin crucial for DNA synthesis and repair, making it an essential food for cellular health.

Other cruciferous vegetables, such as **kale**, **Brussels sprouts**, and **cauliflower**, also provide similar nutrients but may have lower concentrations of certain beneficial compounds like **sulforaphane** compared to broccoli. Therefore, while all cruciferous vegetables should be included in a healthy diet, **broccoli** offers a particularly concentrated source of key bioactive compounds with a focus on **cancer prevention** and **overall health promotion**.

2.5.2 Key Bioactive Compounds in Broccoli

Glucosinolates and Isothiocyanates – Role in Detoxification

One of the most important groups of bioactive compounds found in broccoli are **glucosinolates**, sulfur-containing compounds that contribute to the plant's distinct taste and odor. When broccoli is consumed and metabolized by the body, these glucosinolates are broken down into **isothiocyanates**, which have been extensively studied for their **detoxifying** and **anti-cancer properties**.

The breakdown of glucosinolates into **sulforaphane** and other isothiocyanates plays a key role in the **body's detoxification processes**. Isothiocyanates activate **phase II detoxification enzymes** in the liver, which help neutralize and eliminate harmful compounds, including **carcinogens** and **toxins**. A study published in *The Journal of Nutritional Biochemistry* demonstrated that the consumption of broccoli, rich in **sulforaphane**, significantly increased the activity of **glutathione-S-transferase**, an enzyme involved in detoxifying harmful substances.

In addition to their detoxifying effects, **glucosinolates** and **isothiocyanates** have been shown to protect the body against **oxidative stress**, which can contribute to various chronic diseases, including **cancer** and **heart disease**. These compounds help neutralize **free radicals** and reduce the damage they cause to cells and tissues.

Sulforaphane – Anti-cancer and Anti-inflammatory Properties

Sulforaphane is one of the most extensively studied and powerful **isothiocyanates** derived from **glucoraphanin**, a type of glucosinolate found in broccoli. Sulforaphane has been shown to possess **anti-cancer, anti-**

inflammatory, and **antioxidant** properties, making it a key bioactive compound in broccoli's potential to reduce the risk of cancer and support overall health.

The **anti-cancer effects** of sulforaphane are primarily attributed to its ability to **induce apoptosis** (programmed cell death) in **cancerous cells** and inhibit the growth of **tumor cells**. Research published in *The Journal of Nutrition* demonstrated that sulforaphane significantly reduced the proliferation of **colon cancer cells** by promoting the expression of **tumor suppressor genes** and reducing the activation of **oncogenes**. Furthermore, sulforaphane has been shown to inhibit **angiogenesis**, the process by which tumors form new blood vessels, which is critical for tumor growth and metastasis.

In addition to its anti-cancer effects, sulforaphane has powerful **anti-inflammatory properties**. Chronic inflammation is a key factor in the development of several diseases, including **arthritis, cardiovascular disease**, and **cancer**. Sulforaphane helps reduce inflammation by modulating the production of **pro-inflammatory cytokines** and inhibiting the activation of inflammatory pathways such as the **NF-κB** signaling pathway. A study published in *The American Journal of Clinical Nutrition* found that sulforaphane supplementation significantly reduced **C-reactive protein** (CRP) levels, a marker of systemic inflammation, in individuals with **high levels of inflammation.**

Vitamins and Minerals (Vitamin C, K, Folate, Potassium)

Broccoli is a rich source of several essential vitamins and minerals that contribute to its overall health benefits. These include **vitamin C, vitamin K, folate**, and **potassium**, all of which play crucial roles in maintaining bodily functions and supporting overall well-being.

- **Vitamin C** is an important antioxidant that helps protect cells from oxidative damage. It is essential for the **synthesis of collagen**, a structural protein that supports skin, bones, and blood vessels. Vitamin C also enhances **immune function**, making it an important nutrient for fighting infections and improving overall health. Broccoli provides about **89 mg** of vitamin C per 100 grams, which is more than **100% of the daily recommended intake.**
- **Vitamin K** plays a vital role in **blood clotting** and maintaining bone health by regulating calcium metabolism. Broccoli is an excellent source of vitamin K, providing approximately **101.6 mcg** per 100 grams, which is

over **85% of the daily recommended intake.**

- **Folate** is essential for **DNA synthesis** and **cell division**, making it particularly important during pregnancy to support fetal development. It also helps in the production of red blood cells and the prevention of **anemia.** Broccoli provides approximately **63 mcg** of folate per 100 grams.
- **Potassium** is an important mineral that helps regulate **fluid balance, nerve function,** and **muscle contractions.** It also supports **blood pressure regulation.** Broccoli offers about **316 mg** of potassium per 100 grams, contributing to daily potassium intake and helping maintain heart health.

In conclusion, broccoli is a powerhouse of nutrition, with its rich content of **glucosinolates, sulforaphane, vitamins,** and **minerals** providing a wide range of health benefits. The **detoxifying, anti-cancer, anti-inflammatory,** and **immune-boosting properties** of broccoli make it an essential part of a healthy diet. By regularly consuming broccoli, individuals can support **cardiovascular health, immune function, bone health,** and **digestive health,** making it one of the most beneficial vegetables for promoting overall well-being and reducing the risk of chronic diseases.

2.6 Gingko Biloba: Active Constituents and Cognitive Health

2.6.1 Introduction to Gingko Biloba

Traditional Use in Cognitive Health

Gingko biloba, one of the oldest living tree species, has been used for over 2,000 years in traditional Chinese medicine. Historically, it has been valued for its **therapeutic benefits,** particularly in promoting **mental clarity,** enhancing **memory,** and improving **circulation.** Ancient practitioners of Chinese medicine used ginkgo leaves to treat a variety of ailments, including respiratory disorders, asthma, and poor circulation. It was particularly favored for its ability to **enhance cognitive function,** especially in the elderly population.

The primary traditional use of ginkgo was to treat **age-related cognitive decline** and improve **mental clarity.** It was often prescribed to improve **focus** and **concentration,** with its ability to enhance **blood flow to the brain,** which was believed to support brain function. In traditional Chinese medicine, ginkgo was thought to help balance the **Qi** (vital energy) and promote overall **brain health.**

Gingko biloba leaves contain several bioactive compounds, such as **flavonoids** and **terpenoids**, which contribute to its beneficial effects. These compounds were historically considered useful for improving **cognitive function**, combating **mental fatigue**, and supporting **overall brain health.**

Modern Applications in Dementia and Alzheimer's Disease

In modern times, ginkgo biloba has gained significant attention in the field of **neurology** and **pharmacology** for its potential use in the management of cognitive disorders such as **dementia** and **Alzheimer's disease.** Research has demonstrated that ginkgo may help improve **memory** and **cognitive function** in individuals with **mild cognitive impairment** and **early-stage Alzheimer's disease.**

Numerous clinical studies have been conducted to evaluate the efficacy of ginkgo in treating dementia-related symptoms. One of the largest and most influential studies was published in *The Journal of the American Medical Association* (JAMA), which showed that ginkgo biloba extract improved cognitive function and daily activities in individuals with **mild to moderate Alzheimer's disease.** The study involved over **300 participants** who took **120 mg** of ginkgo extract daily for **6 months**, with significant improvements in memory and cognitive performance.

Moreover, ginkgo's effects on **vascular dementia**, which results from impaired blood flow to the brain, have been widely studied. A clinical trial published in *The Lancet* found that ginkgo biloba extract was able to improve **cerebral circulation**, which, in turn, helped alleviate the symptoms of **vascular dementia.** The research concluded that **ginkgo biloba**, when taken regularly, can help **delay the progression of dementia** and potentially reduce the severity of symptoms.

Overall, ginkgo biloba is considered a potential natural remedy for improving **memory**, enhancing **cognitive function**, and supporting brain health, especially in the context of **age-related cognitive decline** and **neurodegenerative diseases** like **Alzheimer's** and **vascular dementia.**

2.6.2 Bioactive Components of Gingko Biloba

Flavonoids and Terpenoids – Antioxidant Properties

Gingko biloba contains a variety of **flavonoids** and **terpenoids**, which are responsible for its **antioxidant** and **anti-inflammatory** effects. These bioactive compounds have been shown to protect the brain and other tissues from **oxidative stress**, a condition caused by an imbalance between **free radicals** and **antioxidants** in the body. Oxidative stress plays a significant role in the aging process and the development of **neurodegenerative diseases** like Alzheimer's disease.

- **Flavonoids** in ginkgo biloba, including **quercetin, kaempferol**, and **myricetin**, possess strong **antioxidant** properties, which help neutralize **free radicals** and reduce oxidative damage. A study published in *Free Radical Biology and Medicine* showed that ginkgo flavonoids protect brain cells from oxidative damage by scavenging free radicals and upregulating the body's **natural antioxidant defenses**. By reducing oxidative stress, flavonoids contribute to improved **cognitive function** and may help **slow down neurodegenerative processes** in diseases like **Alzheimer's** and **Parkinson's**.
- **Terpenoids**, such as **ginkgolides** and **bilobalides**, are another key group of compounds found in ginkgo that contribute to its **antioxidant** effects. These terpenoids have been shown to **improve cerebral circulation** and promote the **flow of oxygen** and **nutrients** to brain tissues. A study published in *Pharmacology Biochemistry and Behavior* highlighted that ginkgolides possess **anti-inflammatory** properties, which can reduce **neuroinflammation** in the brain. Neuroinflammation is thought to be a major contributing factor in the development of neurodegenerative diseases.

The **antioxidant properties** of flavonoids and terpenoids in ginkgo biloba protect cells from oxidative damage, which not only benefits the brain but also supports overall **vascular health** by improving blood flow and reducing **inflammation**.

Ginkgolides and Bilobalides – Neuroprotective Activity

Ginkgolides and **bilobalides** are unique terpenoid compounds found in ginkgo biloba that have shown significant **neuroprotective activity**. These compounds have been shown to help **improve memory, cognitive performance**, and protect brain cells from damage caused by aging or disease.

- **Ginkgolides** are known for their ability to improve **cerebral blood flow** by promoting vasodilation (the widening of blood vessels). A study in *The Journal of Neuroscience* demonstrated that ginkgolides increased the **perfusion** of the brain, enhancing the delivery of oxygen and nutrients to brain cells. This effect is especially important in individuals with **cerebrovascular diseases** like **vascular dementia** or **stroke**, where blood flow to the brain is compromised.
- **Bilobalides** have been found to play a critical role in **neuroprotection**, especially in preventing **neuronal cell death** caused by oxidative stress and inflammation. Studies have shown that bilobalides protect brain cells by inhibiting the activity of **excitotoxic** amino acids, which can cause neuronal damage when present in excess. Additionally, bilobalides help regulate the activity of **neurotransmitters**, such as **dopamine** and **serotonin**, which are essential for mood regulation and cognitive function.

In clinical studies, the combination of ginkgolides and bilobalides has been shown to reduce the progression of **cognitive decline** in individuals with early-stage **Alzheimer's** and **vascular dementia**. Research has demonstrated that ginkgo extract containing these terpenoids may help improve **memory, concentration**, and **mental clarity**, while slowing the degeneration of brain tissue.

In conclusion, ginkgo biloba is a potent **nootropic** herb, with its **flavonoids, terpenoids, ginkgolides**, and **bilobalides** contributing to its impressive cognitive and neuroprotective effects. These compounds have shown potential in improving **memory**, reducing **neuroinflammation**, and enhancing **cerebral circulation**, making ginkgo biloba an effective natural remedy for improving cognitive function, especially in individuals with **age-related cognitive decline** and **neurodegenerative diseases** like **Alzheimer's** and **vascular dementia**.

2.6.3 Health Benefits of Ginkgo Biloba

Memory Enhancement and Cognitive Function Improvement

Ginkgo biloba is widely recognized for its potential to enhance **memory** and improve **cognitive function**, particularly in the elderly and those experiencing age-related cognitive decline. The key bioactive compounds in ginkgo, such as **flavonoids, terpenoids, ginkgolides**, and **bilobalides**, contribute to these cognitive benefits through various mechanisms.

One of the primary ways ginkgo biloba supports cognitive function is by improving **cerebral blood flow**. Ginkgo enhances the flow of oxygen and essential nutrients to the brain, which is crucial for maintaining optimal brain function. Research has shown that **ginkgo extract** helps increase **peripheral circulation**, ensuring better blood supply to the brain, especially in conditions where blood flow is compromised. A clinical study published in *The Journal of Neuroscience* revealed that ginkgo biloba improved blood flow to the **frontal lobe**, a part of the brain associated with higher cognitive functions, including memory and decision-making.

The effects of ginkgo on **memory** have been confirmed in several studies. A systematic review published in *The Cochrane Database of Systematic Reviews* found that **ginkgo biloba** extract significantly improved **memory retention** and **learning capacity** in individuals with **mild cognitive impairment** (MCI) and early stages of **Alzheimer's disease**. This study concluded that ginkgo supplementation improved short-term memory and **information processing** in participants with cognitive decline. Ginkgo is believed to work by **increasing acetylcholine** levels in the brain, a neurotransmitter essential for memory and learning.

Another randomized controlled trial conducted in elderly patients with **age-related cognitive decline** demonstrated that ginkgo biloba extract improved **working memory** and **mental clarity**, reducing symptoms of cognitive impairment. Participants who took **240 mg** of ginkgo extract daily for **6 months** showed significant improvements in **recall ability** and the **speed of cognitive processing** compared to those in the placebo group.

Vascular Health and Circulation Enhancement

Ginkgo biloba has well-documented **vascular health benefits**, particularly in improving **circulation** and ensuring optimal blood flow to various tissues in the body, including the brain. The compounds found in ginkgo, particularly **ginkgolides** and **bilobalides**, promote **vasodilation**, or the widening of blood vessels, which helps improve circulation and nutrient delivery.

The ability of ginkgo biloba to improve blood circulation extends beyond the brain, as it has also been shown to have **positive effects on peripheral circulation**. Studies have found that ginkgo supplementation increases **blood flow to the extremities**, making it useful in treating conditions such as **Raynaud's disease**, where blood flow to fingers and toes is restricted. A study published in *Phytomedicine* found that ginkgo extract significantly increased blood flow in patients with **chronic peripheral arterial disease**, improving symptoms such as leg pain and **muscle cramps**.

Furthermore, ginkgo's effect on circulation is also beneficial in managing **vascular dementia**. By enhancing **microcirculation** and improving **oxygen delivery** to brain tissues, ginkgo helps to alleviate the symptoms of dementia associated with poor cerebral blood flow. This vascular support helps prevent **cerebral ischemia**, a condition that can worsen cognitive decline.

Potential Role in Treating Neurodegenerative Diseases

Ginkgo biloba has shown promise in treating and managing various **neurodegenerative diseases**, including **Alzheimer's disease**, **Parkinson's disease**, and **vascular dementia**. Its neuroprotective properties are primarily attributed to its ability to improve **blood circulation**, its **antioxidant effects**, and its ability to regulate **neurotransmitter levels**.

In **Alzheimer's disease**, ginkgo has been shown to **improve cognitive function** and **delay disease progression**. Several clinical trials have investigated the effects of ginkgo in patients with **mild to moderate Alzheimer's**. A large-scale study published in *The Journal of the American Medical Association* (JAMA) demonstrated that ginkgo extract significantly improved cognitive function, social behavior, and daily living activities in Alzheimer's patients over a **24-week period**. This was attributed to ginkgo's ability to improve blood flow to the brain, reduce **oxidative stress**, and regulate **neurotransmitter levels**, such as **acetylcholine**.

Similarly, research in patients with **Parkinson's disease** has shown that ginkgo biloba extract can help manage **motor symptoms** and **cognitive decline**. A study published in *Pharmacology Biochemistry and Behavior* examined the impact of ginkgo on patients with **Parkinson's disease**, finding that it improved both **motor coordination** and **cognitive function** compared to the placebo. Ginkgo's **dopaminergic activity**—its ability to increase dopamine release in the brain—has been identified as a key factor in improving **movement** and reducing the tremors associated with Parkinson's.

In **vascular dementia**, ginkgo's role in improving **blood circulation** to the brain helps reduce the symptoms of cognitive decline associated with poor cerebral blood flow. A meta-analysis published in *The Cochrane Database of Systematic Reviews* concluded that ginkgo biloba may help slow the progression of **vascular dementia** and improve cognitive symptoms. By enhancing cerebral circulation and reducing oxidative damage, ginkgo provides **neuroprotection** in patients suffering from vascular-related cognitive impairments.

Overall, ginkgo biloba's neuroprotective, **anti-inflammatory**, and **antioxidant** properties make it a promising herbal remedy for managing and preventing the progression of **neurodegenerative diseases**. Its ability to improve **cognitive function**, enhance **blood circulation**, and support **brain health** makes it an important therapeutic agent for treating conditions like **Alzheimer's disease**, **Parkinson's disease**, and **vascular dementia**.

2.6.4 Clinical Evidence on Ginkgo Biloba

Studies on Ginkgo and Alzheimer's Disease Prevention

Ginkgo biloba has been extensively studied for its potential to prevent or delay the progression of **Alzheimer's disease** (AD), a degenerative condition that leads to cognitive decline and memory loss. The main focus of these studies is on ginkgo's ability to improve **cognitive function**, **enhance memory**, and **increase cerebral blood flow**, all of which are impaired in individuals with Alzheimer's.

One of the most notable studies is the **GEM (Ginkgo Evaluation of Memory) Study**, published in *The Journal of the American Medical Association* (JAMA). This large-scale, randomized, double-blind trial investigated the effects of **ginkgo biloba extract** in individuals aged 75 years or older who were at risk of **cognitive decline** or diagnosed with **mild cognitive impairment (MCI)**. The study found that ginkgo supplementation did not significantly reduce the incidence of Alzheimer's disease or improve cognitive function compared to a placebo over a period of **6 years**. However, there were modest improvements in some cognitive test scores in the group receiving ginkgo, suggesting potential benefits in individuals with early signs of cognitive impairment, though the study was not able to definitively prove its effectiveness in preventing Alzheimer's.

Another study, published in *Psychopharmacology*, assessed the effects of **ginkgo extract** in patients with **mild to moderate Alzheimer's disease**. The results showed that daily supplementation with **120 mg of ginkgo biloba extract** (split into two doses) for **24 weeks** resulted in significant improvements in cognitive performance, particularly in the areas of **memory**, **attention**, and **executive function**. The improvements were especially noticeable in patients who had early-stage Alzheimer's disease, suggesting that ginkgo might help delay the progression of cognitive decline in the earlier stages of the disease.

Moreover, a systematic review and meta-analysis of **ginkgo biloba** trials published in *The Cochrane Database of Systematic Reviews* examined multiple studies on ginkgo's effects in Alzheimer's patients. The review included both short-term and long-term trials, assessing outcomes related to cognitive function, activities of daily living, and neuropsychiatric symptoms. The review found that **ginkgo biloba** had a small but statistically significant effect on **cognitive function**, with better results seen in patients with **mild cognitive impairment** or early-stage Alzheimer's disease. However, the effects were not as pronounced in more severe stages of Alzheimer's, indicating that ginkgo might be more effective in early intervention rather than later stages of the disease.

Ginkgo's ability to enhance **cerebral blood flow** and its **antioxidant** properties are thought to contribute to its **neuroprotective effects** in Alzheimer's patients. Ginkgo has been shown to **increase blood circulation to the brain**, which may help improve the delivery of oxygen and essential nutrients, thus supporting brain function. In addition, its **antioxidant properties**, particularly through the inhibition of **free radicals** and **neuroinflammation**, may protect brain cells from oxidative damage, a key factor in the progression of Alzheimer's disease.

Further clinical trials have suggested that ginkgo's **memory-enhancing** properties might also extend to individuals with **vascular dementia**. A study published in *The Lancet* found that ginkgo extract was able to improve cognitive function and daily living activities in individuals with **vascular dementia**, which results from poor blood circulation in the brain. The study concluded that ginkgo may improve **vascular health**, which in turn helps maintain cognitive function in individuals with this form of dementia.

In summary, while the clinical evidence regarding ginkgo's ability to **prevent Alzheimer's disease** remains inconclusive, studies suggest that it may offer **modest benefits** in improving **cognitive function** and slowing the progression of **mild cognitive impairment** and **early-stage Alzheimer's.** Further research, especially larger and longer trials, is needed to better understand ginkgo's potential as a therapeutic agent in Alzheimer's disease prevention and treatment.

2.6.4 Clinical Evidence on Ginkgo Biloba

Studies on Ginkgo and Alzheimer's Disease Prevention

The potential of **ginkgo biloba** in preventing or delaying the progression of **Alzheimer's disease** (AD) has been the subject of extensive clinical research. Alzheimer's disease is a neurodegenerative condition characterized by progressive memory loss, cognitive decline, and behavioral changes. Ginkgo biloba has been suggested to have beneficial effects on cognitive function due to its ability to improve **cerebral circulation, neuroprotection,** and **neurotransmitter modulation,** all of which are impaired in Alzheimer's patients.

A large, multi-center **GEM (Ginkgo Evaluation of Memory)** study, published in *The Journal of the American Medical Association* (JAMA), aimed to evaluate the effectiveness of **ginkgo biloba** in the prevention of **Alzheimer's disease.** This study included **3,000 participants** aged 75 years and older who were either at risk for cognitive decline or had mild cognitive impairment (MCI), a condition that often precedes Alzheimer's disease. Participants were administered **120 mg of ginkgo extract** twice daily for **6 years.** However, the study found that ginkgo did not significantly reduce the incidence of Alzheimer's disease or improve cognitive function when compared to the placebo group. Despite these findings, some participants with early-stage cognitive decline showed minor improvements in memory and overall cognitive ability, suggesting that ginkgo might have a modest effect in preventing the onset of Alzheimer's in high-risk individuals.

In contrast, a study published in *Psychopharmacology* found more promising results. This **randomized controlled trial** (RCT) investigated the effect of **ginkgo biloba** on **mild to moderate Alzheimer's disease** patients. The study involved **118 participants**, who were given **120 mg of ginkgo**

extract twice daily for **24 weeks**. The results revealed that ginkgo significantly improved cognitive function in the patients, particularly in areas related to **memory** and **executive function.** The study concluded that **ginkgo biloba** could provide therapeutic benefits for patients in the early stages of Alzheimer's, suggesting it may help slow cognitive decline in these individuals.

Further research has supported the idea that ginkgo might be particularly beneficial in the **early stages** of Alzheimer's disease. A systematic review and meta-analysis published in *The Cochrane Database of Systematic Reviews* evaluated 9 clinical trials on ginkgo's effects in Alzheimer's patients. The analysis found that ginkgo supplementation led to small but statistically significant improvements in **cognitive function** in patients with **mild cognitive impairment** or **early-stage Alzheimer's.** However, the review found limited evidence of ginkgo's effectiveness in later stages of the disease, where cognitive decline is more severe.

The neuroprotective properties of ginkgo are believed to be attributed to its **bioactive compounds**, such as **ginkgolides** and **bilobalides**, which have been shown to **improve blood circulation** in the brain. These compounds also have strong **antioxidant** effects, reducing **oxidative stress** and **neuroinflammation**, both of which contribute to the progression of Alzheimer's disease. In addition, ginkgo's ability to **enhance acetylcholine activity** may help improve memory and cognitive function, as acetylcholine is a neurotransmitter that plays a key role in learning and memory.

In summary, while ginkgo biloba has shown **modest potential** in **preventing Alzheimer's disease** or slowing the progression of cognitive decline in some studies, its overall effectiveness remains inconclusive. The evidence suggests that ginkgo may be more effective in the **early stages** of cognitive impairment or Alzheimer's disease, particularly in improving **memory** and **cognitive function**. Further research with larger sample sizes and longer follow-up periods is needed to fully assess ginkgo's role in **Alzheimer's disease prevention** and treatment.

2.7.3 Health Benefits of Flaxseeds

Cardiovascular Benefits and Cholesterol Reduction

Flaxseeds are widely recognized for their **cardiovascular benefits**, particularly in reducing **cholesterol levels** and improving overall heart health. The health benefits of flaxseeds are largely attributed to their high content of **omega-3 fatty acids, lignans**, and **fiber**.

Flaxseeds are an excellent source of **alpha-linolenic acid (ALA)**, a type of **omega-3 fatty acid** that has been shown to reduce **LDL cholesterol** (the "bad" cholesterol) and **triglycerides** while increasing **HDL cholesterol** (the "good" cholesterol). Several clinical studies have demonstrated the effectiveness of flaxseed consumption in improving lipid profiles and supporting heart health. A meta-analysis published in *The American Journal of Clinical Nutrition* found that **flaxseed supplementation** led to a **10% reduction in total cholesterol** and **13% reduction in LDL cholesterol** in individuals with high cholesterol levels. These effects are particularly important for reducing the risk of **atherosclerosis, heart attack**, and **stroke**.

Moreover, flaxseeds have been shown to improve **blood pressure**. A study published in *Hypertension* found that **3 tablespoons of ground flaxseeds daily** significantly reduced **systolic** and **diastolic blood pressure** in individuals with high blood pressure. The study suggested that the **omega-3s** and **fiber** in flaxseeds, along with their **anti-inflammatory effects**, contribute to cardiovascular protection by improving **vascular function** and reducing **inflammation** in the arteries.

Hormonal Balance and Menopausal Health

Flaxseeds are also known for their potential to support **hormonal balance**, especially in women experiencing **menopausal symptoms**. The **lignans** found in flaxseeds are plant-based compounds that exhibit **phytoestrogenic** properties, meaning they can mimic or modulate the effects of estrogen in the body. This makes flaxseeds particularly beneficial for women during menopause, when estrogen levels naturally decline.

Research has shown that flaxseeds may help alleviate **menopausal symptoms** such as **hot flashes, night sweats**, and **mood swings**. A study published in *Menopause* found that **flaxseed supplementation** significantly reduced the frequency and severity of **hot flashes** in women experiencing menopause. The study involved **40 women** who consumed **40 grams of ground flaxseeds daily** for **6 weeks**. Participants reported a marked decrease in hot flashes, likely due to the **estrogenic activity** of lignans.

Flaxseeds may also help in **balancing hormonal levels** by regulating **estrogen metabolism**. This is beneficial not only for menopausal health but also for reducing the risk of **estrogen-related cancers**, such as **breast cancer**. Lignans in flaxseeds are thought to bind to estrogen receptors, thereby promoting healthy **estrogenic activity** and protecting against **hormone-dependent cancers**.

Gut Health Improvement Due to Fiber Content

Flaxseeds are an excellent source of both **soluble** and **insoluble fiber**, which play a crucial role in promoting **digestive health**. The fiber content in flaxseeds supports **regular bowel movements**, reduces **constipation**, and contributes to overall gut health.

Soluble fiber in flaxseeds forms a gel-like substance in the digestive tract, which helps to **slow down digestion** and **absorb excess cholesterol**. This can help improve **bowel function** and may contribute to cholesterol reduction. Insoluble fiber, on the other hand, adds bulk to the stool and promotes **regular bowel movements**, which helps prevent constipation and supports a healthy digestive system.

A study published in *The American Journal of Clinical Nutrition* found that individuals who consumed **ground flaxseeds** had an increased frequency of bowel movements and improved stool consistency compared to those who did not consume flaxseeds. Additionally, flaxseeds are thought to support a healthy **gut microbiome**, promoting the growth of beneficial bacteria and supporting overall **gut health**.

Anti-inflammatory and Antioxidant Properties

Flaxseeds have well-documented **anti-inflammatory** and **antioxidant** properties, which contribute to their health benefits, particularly in reducing the risk of chronic diseases such as **cardiovascular disease**, **diabetes**, and **cancer**.

The **omega-3 fatty acids** in flaxseeds, particularly **ALA**, are potent **anti-inflammatory agents** that help reduce the production of **pro-inflammatory cytokines** and **eicosanoids**. This makes flaxseeds particularly beneficial for conditions characterized by chronic inflammation, such as **rheumatoid arthritis** and **inflammatory bowel disease**. A study in *The Journal of Nutrition* found that flaxseed supplementation significantly reduced **C-**

reactive protein (CRP) levels, a marker of systemic inflammation, in individuals with inflammatory conditions.

In addition to their anti-inflammatory effects, flaxseeds are rich in **antioxidants**, particularly **lignans** and **polyphenols**, which help neutralize **free radicals** and reduce oxidative stress. Free radicals are unstable molecules that can cause cellular damage and contribute to the development of chronic diseases. By reducing oxidative stress, flaxseeds help protect against **cellular damage** and promote overall health.

2.7.4 Clinical Research on Flaxseeds

Studies on Flaxseed Consumption and Cardiovascular Health

Flaxseeds have been the subject of numerous clinical trials focusing on their effects on **cardiovascular health**. Several studies have demonstrated that flaxseed consumption can have a **positive impact** on **blood pressure, cholesterol levels**, and overall **heart health**.

In a clinical trial published in *The American Journal of Clinical Nutrition*, researchers studied the effects of **flaxseed consumption** on **blood pressure** and **lipid profiles** in individuals with **hypertension**. Participants were given **30 grams of ground flaxseeds** daily for **12 weeks**. The results showed a significant reduction in both **systolic** and **diastolic blood pressure**, as well as a decrease in **triglyceride** and **LDL cholesterol** levels. The study concluded that flaxseed supplementation could be an effective dietary intervention for individuals with high blood pressure and elevated cholesterol levels.

Another clinical trial, published in *The Journal of Nutrition*, evaluated the effects of **flaxseed oil** on **cholesterol metabolism** in hypercholesterolemic individuals. The trial found that **flaxseed oil** supplementation led to significant reductions in **total cholesterol** and **LDL cholesterol**, as well as a **10% increase in HDL cholesterol**. These effects were attributed to the high **omega-3 fatty acid content** of flaxseeds, which have well-documented benefits in improving lipid profiles and reducing the risk of cardiovascular diseases.

A meta-analysis published in *The Cochrane Database of Systematic Reviews* assessed multiple studies on the effects of **flaxseeds** on **cardiovascular**

health. The analysis found that flaxseed consumption was associated with improvements in **blood pressure, cholesterol levels,** and overall **heart health,** particularly in individuals with **hypertension** and **hyperlipidemia.** The review concluded that flaxseeds could be a beneficial dietary addition for those looking to improve their cardiovascular health.

In conclusion, clinical research consistently supports the cardiovascular benefits of flaxseeds, particularly in reducing **blood pressure,** improving **cholesterol profiles,** and promoting overall **heart health.** These benefits, combined with flaxseeds' high content of **omega-3 fatty acids** and **fiber,** make them an essential part of a heart-healthy diet.

Anti-diabetic Properties and Blood Sugar Regulation

Ginseng has been extensively studied for its **anti-diabetic** effects, particularly its ability to regulate **blood sugar levels** and improve **insulin sensitivity.** The ginsenosides in ginseng play a key role in modulating glucose metabolism by increasing the uptake of glucose into cells and improving the function of insulin. This makes ginseng a valuable supplement for individuals with **type 2 diabetes** or those at risk of developing the condition.

Research published in *Diabetes Care* demonstrated that ginseng supplementation led to a significant reduction in **fasting blood glucose levels** and improved **insulin sensitivity** in individuals with type 2 diabetes. In the study, participants who took **200 mg** of ginseng extract daily for **12 weeks** showed a marked improvement in blood glucose regulation and insulin resistance compared to the placebo group.

Ginseng has also been shown to increase the expression of key proteins involved in glucose metabolism, such as **GLUT4** (glucose transporter type 4), which helps transport glucose into muscle and fat cells. This enhances the body's ability to utilize glucose more effectively and reduces the accumulation of excess glucose in the bloodstream.

In addition to regulating blood sugar, ginseng has been found to reduce the oxidative stress and inflammation associated with diabetes. Chronic inflammation and oxidative damage are key contributors to the progression of diabetes and its complications, such as **retinopathy** and **neuropathy.** By reducing inflammation and oxidative stress, ginseng may help prevent or delay the complications of diabetes.

2.3.4 Clinical Trials and Research on Ginseng

Ginseng in Cognitive Function Improvement

Ginseng has been extensively researched for its potential benefits in improving cognitive function, particularly in the context of age-related cognitive decline and neurodegenerative diseases. Several clinical trials have demonstrated that ginseng, especially the ginsenosides found in *Panax ginseng*, can enhance memory, attention, and mental clarity.

A landmark study published in *The Journal of Psychopharmacology* examined the effects of ginseng on cognitive function in elderly individuals. In this double-blind, placebo-controlled trial, participants aged 55 to 75 received either **200 mg of ginseng extract** or a placebo daily for **12 weeks**. The results showed a significant improvement in cognitive performance, particularly in tasks related to memory and verbal fluency, for those taking ginseng. The study concluded that ginseng supplementation had a **neuroprotective effect** and could help mitigate age-related cognitive decline.

Another randomized controlled trial published in *The International Journal of Neuroscience* investigated the effects of ginseng on mental performance in young adults. The participants took **400 mg of ginseng extract** daily for **8 weeks**. The results revealed enhanced **working memory**, **attention**, and **reaction time** in the ginseng group compared to the placebo group. The researchers attributed these improvements to the ginsenosides, which help modulate neurotransmitter release and improve cerebral circulation.

Additionally, ginseng has been found to have potential in managing **Alzheimer's disease**. A study published in *Phytotherapy Research* evaluated the effects of ginseng in patients with mild cognitive impairment (MCI), a condition that often precedes Alzheimer's. The participants who received **ginseng extract** for **12 weeks** showed a significant improvement in cognitive function, compared to the control group. The study suggested that ginseng's neuroprotective properties might help slow the progression of Alzheimer's by reducing oxidative stress and inflammation in the brain.

Ginseng in Metabolic Syndrome Management

Metabolic syndrome is a cluster of conditions that increase the risk of heart disease, stroke, and diabetes. These conditions include abdominal obesity, high blood pressure, elevated blood sugar, and abnormal lipid levels. Ginseng has been studied for its potential role in managing metabolic syndrome, particularly in reducing risk factors like **insulin resistance**, **high blood pressure**, and **dyslipidemia**.

A clinical trial published in *The Journal of Clinical Endocrinology & Metabolism* investigated the effects of ginseng on individuals with metabolic syndrome. In this randomized, double-blind study, participants received **3 grams of ginseng root powder** daily for **8 weeks.** The results showed significant improvements in **fasting blood glucose levels, blood pressure,** and **lipid profiles.** Specifically, ginseng supplementation led to a reduction in **LDL cholesterol** and **triglyceride levels,** while **HDL cholesterol** levels increased. These improvements were attributed to ginseng's ability to regulate **glucose metabolism** and enhance **insulin sensitivity.**

Another study, published in *Diabetes & Metabolic Syndrome: Clinical Research & Reviews,* assessed the impact of ginseng on **obesity** and **insulin resistance** in individuals with metabolic syndrome. The participants consumed **100 mg of ginseng extract** daily for **12 weeks,** which resulted in a significant reduction in **waist circumference,** a key marker of abdominal obesity. Furthermore, ginseng supplementation led to improvements in **insulin resistance,** as evidenced by reduced levels of **HOMA-IR** (Homeostasis Model Assessment of Insulin Resistance).

A meta-analysis published in *The American Journal of Clinical Nutrition* reviewed 15 clinical trials on the effects of ginseng in metabolic syndrome management. The analysis concluded that ginseng supplementation was associated with a **moderate reduction in blood glucose** and **cholesterol levels,** as well as improvements in **blood pressure** and **inflammatory markers.** This analysis supported the potential of ginseng as a therapeutic agent for managing the risk factors of metabolic syndrome and preventing the progression to more serious conditions like type 2 diabetes and cardiovascular disease.

Ginseng's ability to regulate glucose metabolism, improve lipid profiles, and enhance insulin sensitivity makes it an effective herb for managing metabolic syndrome. The bioactive compounds in ginseng, particularly **ginsenosides,** work synergistically to improve several aspects of metabolic health, reducing the risk of developing chronic diseases.

THREE

PHYTOCHEMICALS AS NUTRACEUTICALS - CAROTENOIDS AND SULFIDES

3.1 Carotenoids - Types, Sources, and Benefits

3.1.1 Introduction to Carotenoids

Definition of Carotenoids

Carotenoids are a diverse group of fat-soluble pigments found naturally in many plants, algae, and photosynthetic bacteria. These pigments are responsible for the vibrant yellow, orange, and red colors observed in a variety of fruits and vegetables. Carotenoids play an essential role in photosynthesis by capturing light energy for the plant, and they also contribute to the protection of plant tissues from oxidative damage caused by sunlight.

In humans, carotenoids are important for their antioxidant properties and their ability to convert to vitamin A, which is essential for vision, immune function, and skin health. Carotenoids also contribute to the prevention of chronic diseases, such as heart disease and cancer, through their antioxidant and anti-inflammatory effects.

Classification of Carotenoids

Carotenoids are generally classified into two main groups based on their chemical structure: hydrocarbon carotenoids and oxygenated carotenoids.

- Hydrocarbon carotenoids (Carotenes): These carotenoids contain only carbon and hydrogen atoms, and they are the simplest form of carotenoids. Examples of hydrocarbon carotenoids include α-carotene, β-carotene, and lycopene. β-carotene is perhaps the most well-known carotenoid because it can be converted into vitamin A in the body. Lycopene, found in tomatoes and watermelon, is another important hydrocarbon carotenoid known for its powerful antioxidant properties.
- Oxygenated carotenoids (Xanthophylls): These carotenoids contain oxygen atoms in addition to carbon and hydrogen. Examples of xanthophylls include lutein, zeaxanthin, and astaxanthin. These carotenoids are often found in green leafy vegetables, corn, and egg yolk, where they play a critical role in protecting the eyes from oxidative damage caused by blue light and UV radiation.

Physiological Role of Carotenoids in Plants and Humans

In plants, carotenoids perform several important functions, including light absorption for photosynthesis, protection against photooxidation, and acting as antioxidants to neutralize free radicals. In humans, carotenoids serve a variety of physiological roles. They act as antioxidants, helping to protect cells and tissues from oxidative damage caused by free radicals. Some carotenoids, such as β-carotene, can be converted into vitamin A in the body, which is essential for maintaining good vision, immune function, and healthy skin.

Carotenoids like lutein and zeaxanthin are important for eye health, particularly in preventing age-related macular degeneration and cataracts, two major causes of vision impairment in the elderly. Carotenoids also support skin health by protecting the skin from UV-induced damage, and they play a role in immune system modulation by enhancing the activity of natural killer cells and macrophages.

Chemical Properties and Stability of Carotenoids

Carotenoids are lipophilic, meaning they are soluble in fats and oils but not in water. This property allows them to be stored in the body's fat tissues and transported via lipoproteins in the bloodstream. Carotenoids are also relatively unstable, and their structure can be easily broken down by light, heat, and oxygen, leading to a reduction in their bioactivity. The stability of carotenoids depends on their chemical structure, with hydrocarbon carotenoids like β-carotene being more susceptible to degradation than oxygenated carotenoids like lutein.

Carotenoids can be preserved and protected through proper storage methods, such as keeping them in dark, cool places and minimizing exposure to heat and oxygen. In food processing, carotenoids are often protected from degradation by using antioxidants and appropriate cooking methods that minimize oxidative damage.

3.1.2 Mechanism of Action of Carotenoids in Human Health

Antioxidant Mechanism

Carotenoids are well-known for their antioxidant properties, which play a crucial role in protecting the body against oxidative stress. Oxidative stress occurs when the body is overwhelmed by free radicals, unstable molecules that can cause damage to DNA, proteins, and lipids. This oxidative damage has been linked to various chronic diseases, including heart disease, cancer, and neurodegenerative conditions.

Carotenoids act as free radical scavengers, meaning they neutralize free radicals by donating an electron, thereby preventing the radical from causing cellular damage. β-carotene, lycopene, and lutein are examples of carotenoids with strong antioxidant properties. These carotenoids reduce oxidative stress by intercepting free radicals before they can interact with cell membranes and cellular components.

Provitamin A Activity

One of the most important roles of carotenoids, particularly β-carotene, is their ability to be converted into vitamin A (retinol) in the human body. Vitamin A is essential for vision, immune function, cell growth, and skin health. The conversion of carotenoids into vitamin A occurs in the small intestine and liver, where β-carotene is enzymatically converted to retinal and then to retinol, the active form of vitamin A.

- Vision: Vitamin A plays a critical role in maintaining good vision, particularly in low-light conditions. It is a key component of rhodopsin, a pigment found in the retina that is essential for vision in dim light. A deficiency in vitamin A can lead to night blindness and other vision problems.

- Immune Function: Vitamin A is vital for maintaining a healthy immune system by regulating the activity of immune cells, such as T lymphocytes and macrophages. It helps to strengthen the body's defenses against infections and diseases.
- Cell Growth: Vitamin A plays an important role in cellular differentiation, which is essential for the growth and development of epithelial tissues such as skin, respiratory, and intestinal cells.

Photoprotection

Carotenoids also play a significant role in photoprotection, particularly in preventing UV-induced DNA damage and protecting the skin from sunburn and skin aging. Carotenoids like lutein and zeaxanthin are found in high concentrations in the skin and eyes, where they protect tissues from damage caused by ultraviolet (UV) radiation.

- UV-Induced DNA Damage: Carotenoids act as photoprotectants, absorbing harmful UV rays and preventing DNA damage caused by UV-induced oxidative stress. Lutein and zeaxanthin, in particular, help filter blue light and protect the retina from light-induced damage.
- Skin Health: Carotenoids also protect the skin from sunburn and photoaging by neutralizing free radicals generated by UV exposure. Studies have shown that carotenoids, particularly lycopene, can reduce the formation of sunburn cells and enhance the skin's resistance to UV radiation.

Immune System Modulation

Carotenoids help modulate the immune system by enhancing the activity of natural killer (NK) cells, which are part of the body's innate immune response. NK cells play a crucial role in defending against viral infections and tumor formation.

- Enhancement of Natural Killer (NK) Cell Activity: Carotenoids, especially β-carotene and lycopene, have been shown to enhance the cytotoxic activity of NK cells, improving the body's ability to fight infections and cancers.
- Reduction of Inflammatory Mediators: Carotenoids also reduce the production of pro-inflammatory cytokines and inflammatory mediators, helping to modulate immune responses and reduce chronic

inflammation. This anti-inflammatory effect has been shown to be beneficial in preventing chronic diseases like cardiovascular disease, arthritis, and autoimmune disorders.

3.1.3 α-Carotene

3.1.3.1 Sources of α-Carotene

α-Carotene is a naturally occurring provitamin A carotenoid found in a wide variety of plant-based foods. It is primarily recognized for its antioxidant properties and its ability to be converted into vitamin A in the body, which is essential for vision, immune function, and skin health. α-Carotene is abundant in many orange and yellow vegetables, as well as certain dark leafy greens.

- Carrots: One of the richest sources of α-carotene is carrots, which are well known for their vibrant orange color. The orange pigment in carrots is primarily attributed to β-carotene, but it also contains significant amounts of α-carotene. A 100-gram serving of raw carrots provides approximately 1,500 micrograms of α-carotene. Carrots are widely consumed in various forms, such as raw, juiced, or cooked, and they play a crucial role in maintaining eye health due to their high carotenoid content.
- Pumpkins: Another excellent source of α-carotene is pumpkin. The bright orange color of pumpkins is due to the presence of carotenoids, including α-carotene. 100 grams of cooked pumpkin contains around 3,000 micrograms of α-carotene. Pumpkin is widely used in soups, pies, and stews, and its carotenoid content provides significant antioxidant protection and supports immune health.
- Sweet Potatoes: Sweet potatoes, particularly those with orange flesh, are rich in α-carotene. A 100-gram serving of cooked sweet potato can provide around 1,100 micrograms of α-carotene. These root vegetables are highly nutritious and are a popular food choice in many diets. In addition to α-carotene, sweet potatoes also contain vitamin C, fiber, and other important nutrients, making them beneficial for digestive health and immune support.

- Dark Leafy Greens: Although dark leafy greens like spinach, kale, and collard greens are often associated with lutein and zeaxanthin, they also contain significant amounts of α-carotene. These vegetables provide about 100–400 micrograms of α-carotene per 100 grams, and they offer a wealth of other nutrients such as vitamin K, vitamin A, and folate. The carotenoids in these leafy greens are important for eye health and skin protection.

3.1.3.2 Chemical Structure and Stability

Molecular Structure of α-Carotene

α-Carotene is a type of carotenoid with the chemical formula $C_{40}H_{56}$. It consists of a long chain of 40 carbon atoms with alternating single and double bonds, forming a structure known as a polyene chain. This structure is characteristic of carotenoids, allowing them to absorb light and act as antioxidants by neutralizing free radicals. The molecule is also composed of two β-ionone rings at either end of the polyene chain, which contribute to the molecule's chemical reactivity and biological activity.

The structure of α-carotene is very similar to β-carotene, but it has a subtle difference in its molecular configuration. While β-carotene has two β-ionone rings attached to its polyene chain, α-carotene has a slightly different arrangement, leading to a slightly different functional role in the human body. Specifically, α-carotene is not as potent as β-carotene in terms of provitamin A activity, meaning it is less efficient at being converted into vitamin A in the body. However, it still contributes to vitamin A synthesis and supports its antioxidant functions.

Sensitivity to Heat and Light Degradation

Carotenoids, including α-carotene, are highly sensitive to heat, light, and oxygen. This means that the stability of α-carotene can be compromised during food storage, processing, and cooking. The polyene chain in α-carotene makes it vulnerable to oxidative degradation, especially when exposed to high temperatures and prolonged light exposure.

- Heat Sensitivity: When exposed to heat, especially during cooking methods like boiling or frying, the structural integrity of α-carotene can be damaged, leading to decreased bioavailability. For example, studies have shown that cooking carrots can reduce the concentration of α-carotene by as much as 30-50%. However, some cooking methods, such as steaming, help retain more of the carotenoid content compared to boiling.

- Light Sensitivity: Light exposure can lead to photo-oxidation, a process where the carotenoid molecules are broken down due to the energy from light. This degradation reduces the antioxidant capacity and nutritional value of foods containing α-carotene. To prevent this, foods rich in α-carotene should be stored in dark containers or opaque packaging to limit exposure to light.
- Oxygen Sensitivity: Carotenoids like α-carotene are also prone to oxidation in the presence of oxygen. This is why it is important to store foods containing carotenoids in air-tight containers to reduce exposure to oxygen, which can lead to the loss of carotenoid content and overall nutritional value.

To maintain the maximum benefits of α-carotene, it is advisable to store food in cool, dark places and to use gentle cooking methods such as steaming or microwaving that minimize exposure to heat and light. Additionally, consuming raw or lightly cooked vegetables can help preserve the integrity of carotenoids like α-carotene.

3.1.3.3 Health Benefits of α-Carotene

Provitamin A Activity and Eye Health

One of the most significant health benefits of α-carotene is its provitamin A activity, meaning that it can be converted into vitamin A in the body. Vitamin A plays a crucial role in maintaining vision, particularly in low-light conditions. It is a vital component of rhodopsin, a pigment in the retina necessary for the conversion of light into neural signals for visual processing. α-Carotene, when ingested, is converted into retinol, the active form of vitamin A, which helps maintain healthy eyes and prevents night blindness, a condition caused by vitamin A deficiency.

In addition to supporting vision, α-carotene has been shown to contribute to overall eye health by protecting the eyes from oxidative damage caused by free radicals, particularly in the retina. This antioxidant action helps prevent conditions such as age-related macular degeneration (AMD) and cataracts, which are common age-related eye diseases. A study published in *The Archives of Ophthalmology* found that higher intake of carotenoids, including α-carotene, was associated with a lower risk of developing AMD in older adults.

Antioxidant Properties and Cancer Prevention

As a potent antioxidant, α-carotene plays a critical role in neutralizing free radicals and preventing oxidative damage to cells and tissues. Free radicals are unstable molecules that can cause damage to DNA, proteins, and lipids, leading to the development of chronic diseases, including cancer. α-Carotene, like other carotenoids, helps reduce oxidative stress by scavenging free radicals and thus protecting cells from damage.

There is considerable evidence suggesting that α-carotene, due to its antioxidant properties, may help in cancer prevention. Research indicates that regular consumption of α-carotene-rich foods is linked to a reduced risk of several cancers, particularly lung and prostate cancer. A large-scale study published in *The American Journal of Clinical Nutrition* found that individuals with higher blood levels of α-carotene had a significantly lower risk of developing lung cancer, especially in non-smokers. Similarly, another study showed that α-carotene intake was inversely related to the risk of prostate cancer, likely due to its ability to inhibit the growth of tumor cells and reduce inflammation in the prostate.

Cardiovascular Health and Cholesterol Modulation

α-Carotene also plays a role in cardiovascular health by influencing lipid metabolism and helping to lower cholesterol levels. Studies have shown that α-carotene can help modulate LDL cholesterol (low-density lipoprotein, often referred to as "bad cholesterol") by reducing its oxidation. Oxidized LDL is a key factor in the development of atherosclerosis, a condition where plaque builds up in the arteries, leading to heart disease and stroke. By acting as an antioxidant, α-carotene helps protect against the damage caused by oxidized LDL, thereby reducing the risk of cardiovascular diseases.

Additionally, α-carotene contributes to improving vascular health by enhancing blood flow and reducing inflammation in the blood vessels. Studies suggest that the consumption of α-carotene-rich foods can lead to improved endothelial function—the ability of blood vessels to expand and contract appropriately—thus reducing the risk of hypertension and improving overall heart health.

Anti-inflammatory Effects in Metabolic Disorders

Chronic inflammation is a hallmark of many metabolic disorders, including type 2 diabetes, obesity, and insulin resistance. α-Carotene's antioxidant properties extend to its ability to reduce inflammatory markers in the body. By neutralizing free radicals and reducing oxidative stress, α-carotene helps modulate the immune response, preventing the overproduction of inflammatory mediators such as C-reactive protein (CRP) and interleukins.

Research has shown that individuals with higher levels of α-carotene tend to have lower levels of systemic inflammation. A study published in *The Journal of Nutrition* demonstrated that α-carotene supplementation significantly reduced CRP levels in individuals with metabolic syndrome, suggesting that α-carotene could be beneficial in managing conditions associated with chronic low-grade inflammation. This effect may help in the prevention of type 2 diabetes and other metabolic disorders that are closely tied to inflammatory processes.

3.1.3.4 Clinical Studies on α-Carotene

α-Carotene Levels and Reduced Mortality Rates

Numerous epidemiological studies have linked higher α-carotene intake to reduced mortality rates, particularly from cardiovascular diseases and cancers. A large-scale study known as the Alpha-Tocopherol, Beta-Carotene Cancer Prevention Study (ATBC Study) followed more than 29,000 male smokers for 5-8 years and found that serum α-carotene levels were inversely associated with mortality rates from both cancer and cardiovascular diseases. The study showed that men with higher serum levels of α-carotene had a significantly lower risk of dying from coronary heart disease and lung cancer.

Moreover, a meta-analysis published in *The American Journal of Epidemiology* analyzed data from multiple studies and confirmed that higher dietary intake of carotenoids, including α-carotene, is associated with reduced all-cause mortality. The study concluded that individuals who consume a diet rich in fruits and vegetables—especially those high in carotenoids—have a lower risk of premature death, emphasizing the importance of including alpha-carotene-rich foods like carrots, pumpkins, and sweet potatoes in the diet.

Epidemiological Studies Linking α-Carotene to Cancer Prevention

Several epidemiological studies have highlighted the protective role of α-carotene against various cancers. A significant study published in *The International Journal of Cancer* found that individuals with higher dietary α-carotene intake had a lower incidence of lung cancer, particularly in non-smokers. The study found that α-carotene-rich diets may help reduce the risk of lung cancer through their antioxidant effects, which protect lung tissue from damage caused by air pollutants and free radicals.

Additionally, in a large cohort study published in *Cancer Epidemiology, Biomarkers & Prevention*, higher serum levels of α-carotene were associated with a reduced risk of colorectal cancer. The study followed more than 90,000 participants for 10 years and found that higher levels of α-carotene in the blood were correlated with a significant reduction in colon cancer risk, especially in men. These findings suggest that increased α-carotene consumption may help reduce the risk of cancer by acting as a protective antioxidant, reducing the oxidative damage that can lead to DNA mutations and tumor formation. 3.1.4.1 Sources of β-Carotene

3.1.4 β-Carotene

3.1.4.1 Sources of β-Carotene

β-Carotene is a type of provitamin A carotenoid that is widely found in various fruits and vegetables, particularly those that are orange, yellow, or dark green in color. As a precursor to vitamin A, β-carotene plays a significant role in maintaining vision, supporting immune health, and promoting skin health. The body can convert β-carotene into retinol, the active form of vitamin A, which is essential for healthy vision, immune function, and cellular health.

- Carrots: Carrots are one of the most well-known and rich sources of β-carotene. The orange pigment in carrots is primarily attributed to β-carotene, which gives them their characteristic color. A 100-gram serving of raw carrots provides approximately 8,000 micrograms of β-carotene. Carrots can be consumed in various forms, such as raw, juiced, or cooked, and are an excellent way to support eye health and overall well-being.
- Mangoes: Mangoes, particularly the ripe variety, are another excellent source of β-carotene. A single medium-sized mango can provide up to 2,000 micrograms of β-carotene. In addition to β-carotene, mangoes are rich in vitamin C, fiber, and antioxidants, making them a great addition to the diet for supporting immune function and skin health.

- Spinach: Although spinach is often associated with lutein and zeaxanthin, it also contains significant amounts of β-carotene. A 100-gram serving of spinach can provide around 6,000 micrograms of β-carotene. Spinach is highly nutritious and contains many other essential vitamins and minerals, including vitamin K, vitamin A, folate, and iron, making it an excellent vegetable for overall health.
- Red Bell Peppers: Red bell peppers are another great source of β-carotene, particularly when they are fully ripened. A 100-gram serving of red bell pepper provides approximately 1,200 micrograms of β-carotene. In addition to β-carotene, red bell peppers are rich in vitamin C, fiber, and flavonoids, making them a powerful food for immune support and skin protection.

3.1.4.2 Chemical Structure and Absorption

Comparison with α-Carotene

β-Carotene and α-carotene are both carotenoids that are provitamin A precursors, meaning that the body can convert them into vitamin A (retinol). While both carotenoids have a similar chemical structure, there are key differences that affect their conversion efficiency and biological activity.

- β-Carotene: The molecular structure of β-carotene consists of a polyene chain with 11 conjugated double bonds and two β-ionone rings at each end. This structure allows β-carotene to absorb light and exhibit antioxidant properties. When ingested, β-carotene is converted into vitamin A in the small intestine, where enzymes break down the carotenoid into retinal, which is further converted into retinol, the active form of vitamin A.
- α-Carotene: Although α-carotene has a similar structure to β-carotene, it differs in that it has one fewer β-ionone ring. As a result, α-carotene is less efficient at being converted into vitamin A than β-carotene. However, it still contributes to vitamin A intake and provides antioxidant benefits.

Factors Affecting Bioavailability

The bioavailability of β-carotene, or the body's ability to absorb and utilize it, is influenced by several factors, including dietary fat intake, food preparation methods, and the presence of other nutrients.

- Dietary Fat: Since β-carotene is fat-soluble, its absorption is enhanced when consumed with healthy fats, such as those found in olive oil, avocado, or nuts. A study published in *The Journal of Nutrition* found that consuming beta-carotene with 5 grams of fat increased its bioavailability by up to 6 times compared to when consumed without fat.
- Food Preparation: Cooking methods can also affect the bioavailability of β-carotene. Cooking vegetables, such as carrots and spinach, can break down cell walls, making the carotenoids more accessible for absorption. However, high heat can also cause some loss of carotenoid content, so steaming or light cooking is often preferred over boiling or frying.
- Presence of Other Nutrients: The absorption of β-carotene can also be influenced by the presence of other vitamins and minerals, such as vitamin E and vitamin C, which protect carotenoids from oxidative damage and enhance their absorption.

3.1.4.3 Health Benefits of β-Carotene

Role in Vision and Prevention of Night Blindness

β-Carotene is essential for maintaining good vision and preventing night blindness, a condition caused by vitamin A deficiency. Vitamin A is a critical component of rhodopsin, a protein in the retina responsible for the conversion of light into nerve signals for visual processing. A deficiency in vitamin A leads to impaired vision, particularly in low-light conditions. By converting β-carotene into vitamin A, the body ensures proper functioning of the retina and optimal vision.

Numerous studies have confirmed the role of β-carotene in preventing night blindness, particularly in children and pregnant women, who are at higher risk for vitamin A deficiency. A study in *The Lancet* found that β-carotene supplementation significantly improved vision and reduced the occurrence of night blindness in individuals with vitamin A deficiency.

Antioxidant Protection Against Free Radicals

As a potent antioxidant, β-carotene helps protect the body from oxidative stress, which is caused by an imbalance between free radicals and antioxidants. Free radicals are highly reactive molecules that can damage cells, proteins, and DNA, leading to the development of chronic diseases such as cardiovascular disease, cancer, and neurodegenerative diseases. β-Carotene scavenges free radicals and neutralizes their damaging effects, thereby protecting the body from oxidative damage.

Studies have shown that β-carotene supplementation can reduce oxidative stress and lower the risk of chronic diseases. For example, a study published in *The Journal of the American Medical Association* found that individuals with higher levels of β-carotene had significantly lower rates of heart disease and stroke compared to those with lower levels.

Cognitive Support and Brain Health

β-Carotene has also been linked to cognitive health and the prevention of cognitive decline. Due to its antioxidant properties, β-carotene helps protect the brain from oxidative damage and neuroinflammation, both of which are associated with cognitive decline and conditions like Alzheimer's disease.

Research suggests that a higher intake of β-carotene may reduce the risk of cognitive decline in the elderly. A study published in *The Journal of Nutrition, Health, and Aging* found that higher serum levels of β-carotene were associated with better cognitive performance in older adults. This suggests that β-carotene may play a role in maintaining cognitive function as people age.

Skin Protection from UV Radiation

β-Carotene is known for its ability to protect the skin from UV radiation and sunburn. It acts as a natural sunscreen by absorbing harmful UV rays and reducing the damage they cause to skin cells. Several studies have found that β-carotene can reduce the risk of sunburn, improve skin elasticity, and protect against skin aging.

A study published in *The American Journal of Clinical Nutrition* demonstrated that individuals who consumed β-carotene-rich foods for 12 weeks had increased resistance to sunburn and showed improved skin health compared to those who did not consume β-carotene.

3.1.4.4 Clinical Research on β-Carotene

β-Carotene Supplementation and Age-Related Macular Degeneration

Research on β-carotene has shown its potential role in preventing age-related macular degeneration (AMD), a leading cause of vision loss in older adults. A clinical trial published in *JAMA Ophthalmology* investigated the effect of β-carotene supplementation on AMD prevention in older adults. The study found that daily supplementation with 15 mg of β-carotene led to a significant reduction in the progression of AMD in high-risk individuals.

Additionally, a long-term study, the Age-Related Eye Disease Study (AREDS), found that a combination of β-carotene, vitamin C, vitamin E, and zinc helped slow the progression of AMD and preserve vision in individuals with advanced AMD. This study confirmed the potential of β-carotene in supporting eye health and preventing vision loss in older adults.

Studies on β-Carotene's Role in Immune System Enhancement

β-Carotene has also been studied for its immune-enhancing properties. Research has shown that β-carotene can modulate the immune response by increasing the activity of natural killer cells and promoting immune cell production. A study published in *The American Journal of Clinical Nutrition* found that β-carotene supplementation improved immune function in elderly individuals, enhancing their ability to fight infections. This suggests that β-carotene may play an important role in supporting the immune system, particularly in older adults and individuals with weakened immunity.

3.1.5 Lycopene

3.1.5.1 Sources of Lycopene

Lycopene is a carotenoid pigment responsible for the red, pink, and orange color in many fruits and vegetables. It is a potent antioxidant, and its consumption is associated with various health benefits, including heart health, cancer prevention, and skin protection. Lycopene is predominantly found in several commonly consumed fruits and vegetables.

- Tomatoes: Tomatoes are the most widely recognized and rich source of lycopene. A 100-gram serving of raw tomatoes contains approximately 4,000 to 5,000 micrograms of lycopene, which increases significantly when the tomatoes are cooked. Cooking tomatoes, such as in sauces, enhances the bioavailability of lycopene, making it more accessible to the body. Lycopene in tomatoes is a key factor in their heart-protective and cancer-preventing effects.
- Watermelon: Watermelon is another excellent source of lycopene. A 100-gram serving of watermelon can provide up to 4,500 micrograms of lycopene. This fruit is not only refreshing but also packed with lycopene, making it a great option for those seeking to improve their antioxidant

intake. Lycopene in watermelon is bioavailable even when consumed raw, and its antioxidant properties are beneficial for combating oxidative stress.

- Pink Grapefruit: Pink grapefruit, along with red grapefruit, contains significant amounts of lycopene, contributing to its distinctive color. 100 grams of pink grapefruit contains around 1,000 micrograms of lycopene. Studies have shown that grapefruit, particularly pink and red varieties, may have cardioprotective effects due to their lycopene content. Additionally, they offer other nutrients such as vitamin C and fiber.
- Papaya: Papaya is another tropical fruit that contains lycopene, though in slightly smaller amounts compared to tomatoes and watermelon. A 100-gram serving of papaya contains about 200 micrograms of lycopene. Despite being lower in lycopene than some other fruits, papaya offers a range of health benefits, including its high vitamin C content and its digestive support due to papain, an enzyme that aids in protein digestion.

3.1.5.2 Chemical Structure and Stability

Molecular Configuration of Lycopene

Lycopene is a polyunsaturated hydrocarbon and belongs to the carotenoid family. It has a chemical structure composed of 40 carbon atoms and 56 hydrogen atoms. Lycopene consists of 11 conjugated double bonds in a linear arrangement, making it highly reactive to light and oxygen, contributing to its antioxidant properties. This structure allows lycopene to absorb light in the orange-red spectrum, giving tomatoes, watermelon, and other lycopene-rich fruits their characteristic color.

The molecular configuration of lycopene is crucial for its ability to neutralize free radicals and act as an antioxidant. The conjugated double bonds in lycopene allow it to donate electrons and neutralize reactive oxygen species (ROS), which are unstable molecules that can cause damage to cells and tissues. By scavenging free radicals, lycopene helps protect the body from oxidative stress and the associated risk of chronic diseases such as cancer and cardiovascular disease.

Isomerization and Its Effect on Bioavailability

Lycopene exists in several isomeric forms, with the cis and trans isomers being the most common. The trans-lycopene form, which is linear, is the most abundant and stable form in food sources like tomatoes. However, when lycopene-rich foods are heated or processed, the lycopene molecules can undergo isomerization, changing from the trans-form to the cis-form.

The cis-isomers of lycopene are less stable than the trans-isomers, but they may have increased bioavailability. Studies have shown that cooking tomatoes, for example, increases the cis-lycopene content, which is more easily absorbed by the body. Cooking enhances the bioavailability of lycopene by breaking down the cell walls of the food, releasing more lycopene for absorption. This process makes lycopene in cooked tomatoes more accessible and usable by the body compared to raw tomatoes.

3.1.5.3 Health Benefits of Lycopene

Antioxidant and Anti-inflammatory Activity

Lycopene is a powerful antioxidant with the ability to neutralize free radicals, thereby reducing oxidative stress in the body. Oxidative stress is associated with the development of chronic diseases such as cancer, cardiovascular disease, and neurodegenerative diseases. Lycopene's strong antioxidant properties make it effective in preventing DNA damage, protecting cell membranes, and reducing the risk of inflammation.

Additionally, lycopene has demonstrated anti-inflammatory effects by lowering the levels of pro-inflammatory cytokines and other inflammatory markers in the body. Chronic inflammation is a contributing factor to several metabolic disorders, including obesity, diabetes, and heart disease. By reducing inflammation, lycopene helps support overall health and disease prevention.

Cancer Prevention, Particularly Prostate Cancer

Lycopene has garnered significant attention for its potential in cancer prevention, particularly in prostate cancer. Several epidemiological studies have linked higher intake of lycopene with a reduced risk of prostate cancer. Lycopene's ability to inhibit the growth of cancer cells, particularly in the prostate, is attributed to its antioxidant and anti-inflammatory properties. Lycopene may also reduce the proliferation of androgen-sensitive prostate cancer cells by inhibiting oxidative stress and interfering with tumor growth signaling pathways.

A study published in *The Journal of Nutrition* found that men with higher plasma levels of lycopene had a significantly lower risk of developing prostate cancer compared to men with lower levels of lycopene. Furthermore, lycopene has been shown to slow the progression of existing tumors by inhibiting angiogenesis (the formation of new blood vessels required for tumor growth) and inducing apoptosis (programmed cell death) in cancer cells.

Cardiovascular Benefits: Reduction of LDL Oxidation

Lycopene contributes to cardiovascular health by protecting LDL cholesterol from oxidation, which is a key process in the development of atherosclerosis (the buildup of plaque in the arteries). Oxidized LDL is a major risk factor for heart disease as it promotes plaque formation and inflammation in blood vessels. Lycopene has been shown to reduce LDL oxidation, thereby reducing the risk of atherosclerosis and improving overall heart health.

A clinical trial published in *The American Journal of Clinical Nutrition* found that lycopene supplementation significantly reduced LDL oxidation and improved arterial health in individuals with high cholesterol. This indicates that increasing lycopene intake through diet may help lower the risk of heart disease and stroke.

Skin Health and Photoprotection

Lycopene is also beneficial for skin health, particularly in providing photoprotection. Lycopene's antioxidant properties help protect the skin from UV-induced oxidative stress and sunburn. Studies have shown that lycopene-rich diets can reduce the erythema (redness) and inflammation associated with UV radiation exposure. Lycopene also contributes to maintaining skin elasticity, hydration, and overall appearance by reducing oxidative damage that accelerates skin aging.

A study published in *The Journal of Investigative Dermatology* found that lycopene supplementation protected the skin from UV-induced damage, reducing sunburn cell formation and improving skin health in subjects exposed to sunlight. This makes lycopene a valuable nutrient for skin care and anti-aging therapies.

3.1.5.4 Clinical Studies on Lycopene

Meta-analysis on Lycopene's Role in Cardiovascular Health

A meta-analysis published in *The American Journal of Clinical Nutrition* reviewed multiple studies to determine the impact of lycopene on cardiovascular health. The analysis found that higher consumption of lycopene-rich foods, particularly tomatoes and watermelon, was associated with a significant reduction in the risk of heart disease and stroke. The protective effects of lycopene were linked to its ability to reduce LDL oxidation, lower blood pressure, and improve vascular health.

The study concluded that dietary lycopene could be a valuable intervention for reducing cardiovascular disease risk, especially when combined with other antioxidant-rich foods.

Lycopene and Prostate Cancer Prevention Studies

Numerous studies have investigated the potential of lycopene in prostate cancer prevention. A well-known study published in *The Prostate* journal found that men who consumed high amounts of lycopene had a 40% lower risk of developing prostate cancer compared to those with low intake. The study highlighted that tomatoes, a primary source of lycopene, are particularly effective in reducing the risk of prostate cancer due to their high bioavailability of lycopene.

Additionally, a clinical trial published in *Cancer Epidemiology, Biomarkers & Prevention* found that lycopene supplementation resulted in reduced prostate cancer risk by decreasing oxidative stress and inflammatory markers in men at high risk for the disease.

These studies support the idea that increasing lycopene intake can significantly lower the risk of prostate cancer and promote overall prostate health.

3.1.5 Lycopene

3.1.5.1 Sources of Lycopene

Lycopene is a carotenoid pigment responsible for the red, pink, and orange color in many fruits and vegetables. It is a potent antioxidant, and its consumption is associated with various health benefits, including heart health, cancer prevention, and skin protection. Lycopene is predominantly found in several commonly consumed fruits and vegetables.

- Tomatoes: Tomatoes are the most widely recognized and rich source of lycopene. A 100-gram serving of raw tomatoes contains approximately 4,000 to 5,000 micrograms of lycopene, which increases significantly when the tomatoes are cooked. Cooking tomatoes, such as in sauces, enhances the bioavailability of lycopene, making it more accessible to the body. Lycopene in tomatoes is a key factor in their heart-protective and cancer-preventing effects.

- Watermelon: Watermelon is another excellent source of lycopene. A 100-gram serving of watermelon can provide up to 4,500 micrograms of lycopene. This fruit is not only refreshing but also packed with lycopene, making it a great option for those seeking to improve their antioxidant intake. Lycopene in watermelon is bioavailable even when consumed raw, and its antioxidant properties are beneficial for combating oxidative stress.
- Pink Grapefruit: Pink grapefruit, along with red grapefruit, contains significant amounts of lycopene, contributing to its distinctive color. 100 grams of pink grapefruit contains around 1,000 micrograms of lycopene. Studies have shown that grapefruit, particularly pink and red varieties, may have cardioprotective effects due to their lycopene content. Additionally, they offer other nutrients such as vitamin C and fiber.
- Papaya: Papaya is another tropical fruit that contains lycopene, though in slightly smaller amounts compared to tomatoes and watermelon. A 100-gram serving of papaya contains about 200 micrograms of lycopene. Despite being lower in lycopene than some other fruits, papaya offers a range of health benefits, including its high vitamin C content and its digestive support due to papain, an enzyme that aids in protein digestion.

3.1.5.2 Chemical Structure and Stability

Molecular Configuration of Lycopene

Lycopene is a polyunsaturated hydrocarbon and belongs to the carotenoid family. It has a chemical structure composed of 40 carbon atoms and 56 hydrogen atoms. Lycopene consists of 11 conjugated double bonds in a linear arrangement, making it highly reactive to light and oxygen, contributing to its antioxidant properties. This structure allows lycopene to absorb light in the orange-red spectrum, giving tomatoes, watermelon, and other lycopene-rich fruits their characteristic color.

The molecular configuration of lycopene is crucial for its ability to neutralize free radicals and act as an antioxidant. The conjugated double bonds in lycopene allow it to donate electrons and neutralize reactive oxygen species (ROS), which are unstable molecules that can cause damage to cells and tissues. By scavenging free radicals, lycopene helps protect the body from oxidative stress and the associated risk of chronic diseases such as cancer and cardiovascular disease.

Isomerization and Its Effect on Bioavailability

Lycopene exists in several isomeric forms, with the cis and trans isomers being the most common. The trans-lycopene form, which is linear, is the most abundant and stable form in food sources like tomatoes. However, when lycopene-rich foods are heated or processed, the lycopene molecules can undergo isomerization, changing from the trans-form to the cis-form.

The cis-isomers of lycopene are less stable than the trans-isomers, but they may have increased bioavailability. Studies have shown that cooking tomatoes, for example, increases the cis-lycopene content, which is more easily absorbed by the body. Cooking enhances the bioavailability of lycopene by breaking down the cell walls of the food, releasing more lycopene for absorption. This process makes lycopene in cooked tomatoes more accessible and usable by the body compared to raw tomatoes.

3.1.5.3 Health Benefits of Lycopene

Antioxidant and Anti-inflammatory Activity

Lycopene is a powerful antioxidant with the ability to neutralize free radicals, thereby reducing oxidative stress in the body. Oxidative stress is associated with the development of chronic diseases such as cancer, cardiovascular disease, and neurodegenerative diseases. Lycopene's strong antioxidant properties make it effective in preventing DNA damage, protecting cell membranes, and reducing the risk of inflammation.

Additionally, lycopene has demonstrated anti-inflammatory effects by lowering the levels of pro-inflammatory cytokines and other inflammatory markers in the body. Chronic inflammation is a contributing factor to several metabolic disorders, including obesity, diabetes, and heart disease. By reducing inflammation, lycopene helps support overall health and disease prevention.

Cancer Prevention, Particularly Prostate Cancer

Lycopene has garnered significant attention for its potential in cancer prevention, particularly in prostate cancer. Several epidemiological studies have linked higher intake of lycopene with a reduced risk of prostate cancer. Lycopene's ability to inhibit the growth of cancer cells, particularly in the prostate, is attributed to its antioxidant and anti-inflammatory properties. Lycopene may also reduce the proliferation of androgen-sensitive prostate cancer cells by inhibiting oxidative stress and interfering with tumor growth signaling pathways.

A study published in *The Journal of Nutrition* found that men with higher plasma levels of lycopene had a significantly lower risk of developing prostate cancer compared to men with lower levels of lycopene. Furthermore, lycopene has been shown to slow the progression of existing tumors by inhibiting angiogenesis (the formation of new blood vessels required for tumor growth) and inducing apoptosis (programmed cell death) in cancer cells.

Cardiovascular Benefits: Reduction of LDL Oxidation

Lycopene contributes to cardiovascular health by protecting LDL cholesterol from oxidation, which is a key process in the development of atherosclerosis (the buildup of plaque in the arteries). Oxidized LDL is a major risk factor for heart disease as it promotes plaque formation and inflammation in blood vessels. Lycopene has been shown to reduce LDL oxidation, thereby reducing the risk of atherosclerosis and improving overall heart health.

A clinical trial published in *The American Journal of Clinical Nutrition* found that lycopene supplementation significantly reduced LDL oxidation and improved arterial health in individuals with high cholesterol. This indicates that increasing lycopene intake through diet may help lower the risk of heart disease and stroke.

Skin Health and Photoprotection

Lycopene is also beneficial for skin health, particularly in providing photoprotection. Lycopene's antioxidant properties help protect the skin from UV-induced oxidative stress and sunburn. Studies have shown that lycopene-rich diets can reduce the erythema (redness) and inflammation associated with UV radiation exposure. Lycopene also contributes to maintaining skin elasticity, hydration, and overall appearance by reducing oxidative damage that accelerates skin aging.

A study published in *The Journal of Investigative Dermatology* found that lycopene supplementation protected the skin from UV-induced damage, reducing sunburn cell formation and improving skin health in subjects exposed to sunlight. This makes lycopene a valuable nutrient for skin care and anti-aging therapies.

3.1.5.4 Clinical Studies on Lycopene

Meta-analysis on Lycopene's Role in Cardiovascular Health

A meta-analysis published in *The American Journal of Clinical Nutrition* reviewed multiple studies to determine the impact of lycopene on cardiovascular health. The analysis found that higher consumption of lycopene-rich foods, particularly tomatoes and watermelon, was associated with a significant reduction in the risk of heart disease and stroke. The protective effects of lycopene were linked to its ability to reduce LDL oxidation, lower blood pressure, and improve vascular health.

The study concluded that dietary lycopene could be a valuable intervention for reducing cardiovascular disease risk, especially when combined with other antioxidant-rich foods.

Lycopene and Prostate Cancer Prevention Studies

Numerous studies have investigated the potential of lycopene in prostate cancer prevention. A well-known study published in *The Prostate* journal found that men who consumed high amounts of lycopene had a 40% lower risk of developing prostate cancer compared to those with low intake. The study highlighted that tomatoes, a primary source of lycopene, are particularly effective in reducing the risk of prostate cancer due to their high bioavailability of lycopene.

Additionally, a clinical trial published in *Cancer Epidemiology, Biomarkers & Prevention* found that lycopene supplementation resulted in reduced prostate cancer risk by decreasing oxidative stress and inflammatory markers in men at high risk for the disease.

These studies support the idea that increasing lycopene intake can significantly lower the risk of prostate cancer and promote overall prostate health.

3.1.5 Lycopene

3.1.5.1 Sources of Lycopene

Lycopene is a carotenoid pigment responsible for the red, pink, and orange color in many fruits and vegetables. It is a potent antioxidant, and its consumption is associated with various health benefits, including heart health, cancer prevention, and skin protection. Lycopene is predominantly found in several commonly consumed fruits and vegetables.

- Tomatoes: Tomatoes are the most widely recognized and rich source of lycopene. A 100-gram serving of raw tomatoes contains approximately 4,000 to 5,000 micrograms of lycopene, which increases significantly when the tomatoes are cooked. Cooking tomatoes, such as in sauces, enhances the bioavailability of lycopene, making it more accessible to the body. Lycopene in tomatoes is a key factor in their heart-protective and cancer-preventing effects.
- Watermelon: Watermelon is another excellent source of lycopene. A 100-gram serving of watermelon can provide up to 4,500 micrograms of lycopene. This fruit is not only refreshing but also packed with lycopene, making it a great option for those seeking to improve their antioxidant intake. Lycopene in watermelon is bioavailable even when consumed raw, and its antioxidant properties are beneficial for combating oxidative stress.
- Pink Grapefruit: Pink grapefruit, along with red grapefruit, contains significant amounts of lycopene, contributing to its distinctive color. 100 grams of pink grapefruit contains around 1,000 micrograms of lycopene. Studies have shown that grapefruit, particularly pink and red varieties, may have cardioprotective effects due to their lycopene content. Additionally, they offer other nutrients such as vitamin C and fiber.
- Papaya: Papaya is another tropical fruit that contains lycopene, though in slightly smaller amounts compared to tomatoes and watermelon. A 100-gram serving of papaya contains about 200 micrograms of lycopene. Despite being lower in lycopene than some other fruits, papaya offers a range of health benefits, including its high vitamin C content and its digestive support due to papain, an enzyme that aids in protein digestion.

3.1.5.2 Chemical Structure and Stability

Molecular Configuration of Lycopene

Lycopene is a polyunsaturated hydrocarbon and belongs to the carotenoid family. It has a chemical structure composed of 40 carbon atoms and 56 hydrogen atoms. Lycopene consists of 11 conjugated double bonds in a linear arrangement, making it highly reactive to light and oxygen, contributing to its antioxidant properties. This structure allows lycopene to absorb light in the orange-red spectrum, giving tomatoes, watermelon, and other lycopene-rich fruits their characteristic color.

The molecular configuration of lycopene is crucial for its ability to neutralize free radicals and act as an antioxidant. The conjugated double bonds in lycopene allow it to donate electrons and neutralize reactive oxygen species (ROS), which are unstable molecules that can cause damage to cells and tissues. By scavenging free radicals, lycopene helps protect the body from oxidative stress and the associated risk of chronic diseases such as cancer and cardiovascular disease.

Isomerization and Its Effect on Bioavailability

Lycopene exists in several isomeric forms, with the cis and trans isomers being the most common. The trans-lycopene form, which is linear, is the most abundant and stable form in food sources like tomatoes. However, when lycopene-rich foods are heated or processed, the lycopene molecules can undergo isomerization, changing from the trans-form to the cis-form.

The cis-isomers of lycopene are less stable than the trans-isomers, but they may have increased bioavailability. Studies have shown that cooking tomatoes, for example, increases the cis-lycopene content, which is more easily absorbed by the body. Cooking enhances the bioavailability of lycopene by breaking down the cell walls of the food, releasing more lycopene for absorption. This process makes lycopene in cooked tomatoes more accessible and usable by the body compared to raw tomatoes.

3.1.5.3 Health Benefits of Lycopene

Antioxidant and Anti-inflammatory Activity

Lycopene is a powerful antioxidant with the ability to neutralize free radicals, thereby reducing oxidative stress in the body. Oxidative stress is associated with the development of chronic diseases such as cancer, cardiovascular disease, and neurodegenerative diseases. Lycopene's strong antioxidant properties make it effective in preventing DNA damage, protecting cell membranes, and reducing the risk of inflammation.

Additionally, lycopene has demonstrated anti-inflammatory effects by lowering the levels of pro-inflammatory cytokines and other inflammatory markers in the body. Chronic inflammation is a contributing factor to several metabolic disorders, including obesity, diabetes, and heart disease. By reducing inflammation, lycopene helps support overall health and disease prevention.

Cancer Prevention, Particularly Prostate Cancer

Lycopene has garnered significant attention for its potential in cancer prevention, particularly in prostate cancer. Several epidemiological studies have linked higher intake of lycopene with a reduced risk of prostate cancer. Lycopene's ability to inhibit the growth of cancer cells, particularly in the prostate, is attributed to its antioxidant and anti-inflammatory properties. Lycopene may also reduce the proliferation of androgen-sensitive prostate cancer cells by inhibiting oxidative stress and interfering with tumor growth signaling pathways.

A study published in *The Journal of Nutrition* found that men with higher plasma levels of lycopene had a significantly lower risk of developing prostate cancer compared to men with lower levels of lycopene. Furthermore, lycopene has been shown to slow the progression of existing tumors by inhibiting angiogenesis (the formation of new blood vessels required for tumor growth) and inducing apoptosis (programmed cell death) in cancer cells.

Cardiovascular Benefits: Reduction of LDL Oxidation

Lycopene contributes to cardiovascular health by protecting LDL cholesterol from oxidation, which is a key process in the development of atherosclerosis (the buildup of plaque in the arteries). Oxidized LDL is a major risk factor for heart disease as it promotes plaque formation and inflammation in blood vessels. Lycopene has been shown to reduce LDL oxidation, thereby reducing the risk of atherosclerosis and improving overall heart health.

A clinical trial published in *The American Journal of Clinical Nutrition* found that lycopene supplementation significantly reduced LDL oxidation and improved arterial health in individuals with high cholesterol. This indicates that increasing lycopene intake through diet may help lower the risk of heart disease and stroke.

Skin Health and Photoprotection

Lycopene is also beneficial for skin health, particularly in providing photoprotection. Lycopene's antioxidant properties help protect the skin from UV-induced oxidative stress and sunburn. Studies have shown that lycopene-rich diets can reduce the erythema (redness) and inflammation associated with UV radiation exposure. Lycopene also contributes to maintaining skin elasticity, hydration, and overall appearance by reducing oxidative damage that accelerates skin aging.

A study published in *The Journal of Investigative Dermatology* found that lycopene supplementation protected the skin from UV-induced damage, reducing sunburn cell formation and improving skin health in subjects exposed to sunlight. This makes lycopene a valuable nutrient for skin care and anti-aging therapies.

3.1.5.4 Clinical Studies on Lycopene

Meta-analysis on Lycopene's Role in Cardiovascular Health

A meta-analysis published in *The American Journal of Clinical Nutrition* reviewed multiple studies to determine the impact of lycopene on cardiovascular health. The analysis found that higher consumption of lycopene-rich foods, particularly tomatoes and watermelon, was associated with a significant reduction in the risk of heart disease and stroke. The protective effects of lycopene were linked to its ability to reduce LDL oxidation, lower blood pressure, and improve vascular health.

The study concluded that dietary lycopene could be a valuable intervention for reducing cardiovascular disease risk, especially when combined with other antioxidant-rich foods.

Lycopene and Prostate Cancer Prevention Studies

Numerous studies have investigated the potential of lycopene in prostate cancer prevention. A well-known study published in *The Prostate* journal found that men who consumed high amounts of lycopene had a 40% lower risk of developing prostate cancer compared to those with low intake. The study highlighted that tomatoes, a primary source of lycopene, are particularly effective in reducing the risk of prostate cancer due to their high bioavailability of lycopene.

Additionally, a clinical trial published in *Cancer Epidemiology, Biomarkers & Prevention* found that lycopene supplementation resulted in reduced prostate cancer risk by decreasing oxidative stress and inflammatory markers in men at high risk for the disease.

These studies support the idea that increasing lycopene intake can significantly lower the risk of prostate cancer and promote overall prostate health.

3.1.5 Lycopene

3.1.5.1 Sources of Lycopene

Lycopene is a carotenoid pigment responsible for the red, pink, and orange color in many fruits and vegetables. It is a potent antioxidant, and its consumption is associated with various health benefits, including heart health, cancer prevention, and skin protection. Lycopene is predominantly found in several commonly consumed fruits and vegetables.

- Tomatoes: Tomatoes are the most widely recognized and rich source of lycopene. A 100-gram serving of raw tomatoes contains approximately 4,000 to 5,000 micrograms of lycopene, which increases significantly when the tomatoes are cooked. Cooking tomatoes, such as in sauces, enhances the bioavailability of lycopene, making it more accessible to the body. Lycopene in tomatoes is a key factor in their heart-protective and cancer-preventing effects.
- Watermelon: Watermelon is another excellent source of lycopene. A 100-gram serving of watermelon can provide up to 4,500 micrograms of lycopene. This fruit is not only refreshing but also packed with lycopene, making it a great option for those seeking to improve their antioxidant intake. Lycopene in watermelon is bioavailable even when consumed raw, and its antioxidant properties are beneficial for combating oxidative stress.
- Pink Grapefruit: Pink grapefruit, along with red grapefruit, contains significant amounts of lycopene, contributing to its distinctive color. 100 grams of pink grapefruit contains around 1,000 micrograms of lycopene. Studies have shown that grapefruit, particularly pink and red varieties, may have cardioprotective effects due to their lycopene content. Additionally, they offer other nutrients such as vitamin C and fiber.
- Papaya: Papaya is another tropical fruit that contains lycopene, though in slightly smaller amounts compared to tomatoes and watermelon. A 100-gram serving of papaya contains about 200 micrograms of lycopene. Despite being lower in lycopene than some other fruits, papaya offers a range of health benefits, including its high vitamin C content and its digestive support due to papain, an enzyme that aids in protein digestion.

3.1.5.2 Chemical Structure and Stability

Molecular Configuration of Lycopene

Lycopene is a polyunsaturated hydrocarbon and belongs to the carotenoid family. It has a chemical structure composed of 40 carbon atoms and 56 hydrogen atoms. Lycopene consists of 11 conjugated double bonds in a linear arrangement, making it highly reactive to light and oxygen, contributing to its antioxidant properties. This structure allows lycopene to absorb light in the orange-red spectrum, giving tomatoes, watermelon, and other lycopene-rich fruits their characteristic color.

The molecular configuration of lycopene is crucial for its ability to neutralize free radicals and act as an antioxidant. The conjugated double bonds in lycopene allow it to donate electrons and neutralize reactive oxygen species (ROS), which are unstable molecules that can cause damage to cells and tissues. By scavenging free radicals, lycopene helps protect the body from oxidative stress and the associated risk of chronic diseases such as cancer and cardiovascular disease.

Isomerization and Its Effect on Bioavailability

Lycopene exists in several isomeric forms, with the cis and trans isomers being the most common. The trans-lycopene form, which is linear, is the most abundant and stable form in food sources like tomatoes. However, when lycopene-rich foods are heated or processed, the lycopene molecules can undergo isomerization, changing from the trans-form to the cis-form.

The cis-isomers of lycopene are less stable than the trans-isomers, but they may have increased bioavailability. Studies have shown that cooking tomatoes, for example, increases the cis-lycopene content, which is more easily absorbed by the body. Cooking enhances the bioavailability of lycopene by breaking down the cell walls of the food, releasing more lycopene for absorption. This process makes lycopene in cooked tomatoes more accessible and usable by the body compared to raw tomatoes.

3.1.5.3 Health Benefits of Lycopene

Antioxidant and Anti-inflammatory Activity

Lycopene is a powerful antioxidant with the ability to neutralize free radicals, thereby reducing oxidative stress in the body. Oxidative stress is associated with the development of chronic diseases such as cancer, cardiovascular disease, and neurodegenerative diseases. Lycopene's strong antioxidant properties make it effective in preventing DNA damage, protecting cell membranes, and reducing the risk of inflammation.

Additionally, lycopene has demonstrated anti-inflammatory effects by lowering the levels of pro-inflammatory cytokines and other inflammatory markers in the body. Chronic inflammation is a contributing factor to several metabolic disorders, including obesity, diabetes, and heart disease. By reducing inflammation, lycopene helps support overall health and disease prevention.

Cancer Prevention, Particularly Prostate Cancer

Lycopene has garnered significant attention for its potential in cancer prevention, particularly in prostate cancer. Several epidemiological studies have linked higher intake of lycopene with a reduced risk of prostate cancer. Lycopene's ability to inhibit the growth of cancer cells, particularly in the prostate, is attributed to its antioxidant and anti-inflammatory properties. Lycopene may also reduce the proliferation of androgen-sensitive prostate cancer cells by inhibiting oxidative stress and interfering with tumor growth signaling pathways.

A study published in *The Journal of Nutrition* found that men with higher plasma levels of lycopene had a significantly lower risk of developing prostate cancer compared to men with lower levels of lycopene. Furthermore, lycopene has been shown to slow the progression of existing tumors by inhibiting angiogenesis (the formation of new blood vessels required for tumor growth) and inducing apoptosis (programmed cell death) in cancer cells.

Cardiovascular Benefits: Reduction of LDL Oxidation

Lycopene contributes to cardiovascular health by protecting LDL cholesterol from oxidation, which is a key process in the development of atherosclerosis (the buildup of plaque in the arteries). Oxidized LDL is a major risk factor for heart disease as it promotes plaque formation and inflammation in blood vessels. Lycopene has been shown to reduce LDL oxidation, thereby reducing the risk of atherosclerosis and improving overall heart health.

A clinical trial published in *The American Journal of Clinical Nutrition* found that lycopene supplementation significantly reduced LDL oxidation and improved arterial health in individuals with high cholesterol. This indicates that increasing lycopene intake through diet may help lower the risk of heart disease and stroke.

Skin Health and Photoprotection

Lycopene is also beneficial for skin health, particularly in providing photoprotection. Lycopene's antioxidant properties help protect the skin from UV-induced oxidative stress and sunburn. Studies have shown that lycopene-rich diets can reduce the erythema (redness) and inflammation associated with UV radiation exposure. Lycopene also contributes to maintaining skin elasticity, hydration, and overall appearance by reducing oxidative damage that accelerates skin aging.

A study published in *The Journal of Investigative Dermatology* found that lycopene supplementation protected the skin from UV-induced damage, reducing sunburn cell formation and improving skin health in subjects exposed to sunlight. This makes lycopene a valuable nutrient for skin care and anti-aging therapies.

3.1.5.4 Clinical Studies on Lycopene

Meta-analysis on Lycopene's Role in Cardiovascular Health

A meta-analysis published in *The American Journal of Clinical Nutrition* reviewed multiple studies to determine the impact of lycopene on cardiovascular health. The analysis found that higher consumption of lycopene-rich foods, particularly tomatoes and watermelon, was associated with a significant reduction in the risk of heart disease and stroke. The protective effects of lycopene were linked to its ability to reduce LDL oxidation, lower blood pressure, and improve vascular health.

The study concluded that dietary lycopene could be a valuable intervention for reducing cardiovascular disease risk, especially when combined with other antioxidant-rich foods.

Lycopene and Prostate Cancer Prevention Studies

Numerous studies have investigated the potential of lycopene in prostate cancer prevention. A well-known study published in *The Prostate* journal found that men who consumed high amounts of lycopene had a 40% lower risk of developing prostate cancer compared to those with low intake. The study highlighted that tomatoes, a primary source of lycopene, are particularly effective in reducing the risk of prostate cancer due to their high bioavailability of lycopene.

Additionally, a clinical trial published in *Cancer Epidemiology, Biomarkers & Prevention* found that lycopene supplementation resulted in reduced prostate cancer risk by decreasing oxidative stress and inflammatory markers in men at high risk for the disease.

These studies support the idea that increasing lycopene intake can significantly lower the risk of prostate cancer and promote overall prostate health.

3.1.5 Lycopene

3.1.5.1 Sources of Lycopene

Lycopene is a carotenoid pigment responsible for the red, pink, and orange color in many fruits and vegetables. It is a potent antioxidant, and its consumption is associated with various health benefits, including heart health, cancer prevention, and skin protection. Lycopene is predominantly found in several commonly consumed fruits and vegetables.

- Tomatoes: Tomatoes are the most widely recognized and rich source of lycopene. A 100-gram serving of raw tomatoes contains approximately 4,000 to 5,000 micrograms of lycopene, which increases significantly when the tomatoes are cooked. Cooking tomatoes, such as in sauces, enhances the bioavailability of lycopene, making it more accessible to the body. Lycopene in tomatoes is a key factor in their heart-protective and cancer-preventing effects.
- Watermelon: Watermelon is another excellent source of lycopene. A 100-gram serving of watermelon can provide up to 4,500 micrograms of lycopene. This fruit is not only refreshing but also packed with lycopene, making it a great option for those seeking to improve their antioxidant intake. Lycopene in watermelon is bioavailable even when consumed raw, and its antioxidant properties are beneficial for combating oxidative stress.
- Pink Grapefruit: Pink grapefruit, along with red grapefruit, contains significant amounts of lycopene, contributing to its distinctive color. 100 grams of pink grapefruit contains around 1,000 micrograms of lycopene. Studies have shown that grapefruit, particularly pink and red varieties, may have cardioprotective effects due to their lycopene content. Additionally, they offer other nutrients such as vitamin C and fiber.
- Papaya: Papaya is another tropical fruit that contains lycopene, though in slightly smaller amounts compared to tomatoes and watermelon. A 100-gram serving of papaya contains about 200 micrograms of lycopene. Despite being lower in lycopene than some other fruits, papaya offers a range of health benefits, including its high vitamin C content and its

digestive support due to papain, an enzyme that aids in protein digestion.

3.1.5.2 Chemical Structure and Stability

Molecular Configuration of Lycopene

Lycopene is a polyunsaturated hydrocarbon and belongs to the carotenoid family. It has a chemical structure composed of 40 carbon atoms and 56 hydrogen atoms. Lycopene consists of 11 conjugated double bonds in a linear arrangement, making it highly reactive to light and oxygen, contributing to its antioxidant properties. This structure allows lycopene to absorb light in the orange-red spectrum, giving tomatoes, watermelon, and other lycopene-rich fruits their characteristic color.

The molecular configuration of lycopene is crucial for its ability to neutralize free radicals and act as an antioxidant. The conjugated double bonds in lycopene allow it to donate electrons and neutralize reactive oxygen species (ROS), which are unstable molecules that can cause damage to cells and tissues. By scavenging free radicals, lycopene helps protect the body from oxidative stress and the associated risk of chronic diseases such as cancer and cardiovascular disease.

Isomerization and Its Effect on Bioavailability

Lycopene exists in several isomeric forms, with the cis and trans isomers being the most common. The trans-lycopene form, which is linear, is the most abundant and stable form in food sources like tomatoes. However, when lycopene-rich foods are heated or processed, the lycopene molecules can undergo isomerization, changing from the trans-form to the cis-form.

The cis-isomers of lycopene are less stable than the trans-isomers, but they may have increased bioavailability. Studies have shown that cooking tomatoes, for example, increases the cis-lycopene content, which is more easily absorbed by the body. Cooking enhances the bioavailability of lycopene by breaking down the cell walls of the food, releasing more lycopene for absorption. This process makes lycopene in cooked tomatoes more accessible and usable by the body compared to raw tomatoes.

3.1.5.3 Health Benefits of Lycopene

Antioxidant and Anti-inflammatory Activity

Lycopene is a powerful antioxidant with the ability to neutralize free radicals, thereby reducing oxidative stress in the body. Oxidative stress is associated with the development of chronic diseases such as cancer, cardiovascular disease, and neurodegenerative diseases. Lycopene's strong antioxidant properties make it effective in preventing DNA damage, protecting cell membranes, and reducing the risk of inflammation.

Additionally, lycopene has demonstrated anti-inflammatory effects by lowering the levels of pro-inflammatory cytokines and other inflammatory markers in the body. Chronic inflammation is a contributing factor to several metabolic disorders, including obesity, diabetes, and heart disease. By reducing inflammation, lycopene helps support overall health and disease prevention.

Cancer Prevention, Particularly Prostate Cancer

Lycopene has garnered significant attention for its potential in cancer prevention, particularly in prostate cancer. Several epidemiological studies have linked higher intake of lycopene with a reduced risk of prostate cancer. Lycopene's ability to inhibit the growth of cancer cells, particularly in the prostate, is attributed to its antioxidant and anti-inflammatory properties. Lycopene may also reduce the proliferation of androgen-sensitive prostate cancer cells by inhibiting oxidative stress and interfering with tumor growth signaling pathways.

A study published in *The Journal of Nutrition* found that men with higher plasma levels of lycopene had a significantly lower risk of developing prostate cancer compared to men with lower levels of lycopene. Furthermore, lycopene has been shown to slow the progression of existing tumors by inhibiting angiogenesis (the formation of new blood vessels required for tumor growth) and inducing apoptosis (programmed cell death) in cancer cells.

Cardiovascular Benefits: Reduction of LDL Oxidation

Lycopene contributes to cardiovascular health by protecting LDL cholesterol from oxidation, which is a key process in the development of atherosclerosis (the buildup of plaque in the arteries). Oxidized LDL is a major risk factor for heart disease as it promotes plaque formation and inflammation in blood vessels. Lycopene has been shown to reduce LDL oxidation, thereby reducing the risk of atherosclerosis and improving overall heart health.

A clinical trial published in *The American Journal of Clinical Nutrition* found that lycopene supplementation significantly reduced LDL oxidation and improved arterial health in individuals with high cholesterol. This indicates that increasing lycopene intake through diet may help lower the risk of heart disease and stroke.

Skin Health and Photoprotection

Lycopene is also beneficial for skin health, particularly in providing photoprotection. Lycopene's antioxidant properties help protect the skin from UV-induced oxidative stress and sunburn. Studies have shown that lycopene-rich diets can reduce the erythema (redness) and inflammation associated with UV radiation exposure. Lycopene also contributes to maintaining skin elasticity, hydration, and overall appearance by reducing oxidative damage that accelerates skin aging.

A study published in *The Journal of Investigative Dermatology* found that lycopene supplementation protected the skin from UV-induced damage, reducing sunburn cell formation and improving skin health in subjects exposed to sunlight. This makes lycopene a valuable nutrient for skin care and anti-aging therapies.

3.1.5.4 Clinical Studies on Lycopene

Meta-analysis on Lycopene's Role in Cardiovascular Health

A meta-analysis published in *The American Journal of Clinical Nutrition* reviewed multiple studies to determine the impact of lycopene on cardiovascular health. The analysis found that higher consumption of lycopene-rich foods, particularly tomatoes and watermelon, was associated with a significant reduction in the risk of heart disease and stroke. The protective effects of lycopene were linked to its ability to reduce LDL oxidation, lower blood pressure, and improve vascular health.

The study concluded that dietary lycopene could be a valuable intervention for reducing cardiovascular disease risk, especially when combined with other antioxidant-rich foods.

Lycopene and Prostate Cancer Prevention Studies

Numerous studies have investigated the potential of lycopene in prostate cancer prevention. A well-known study published in *The Prostate* journal found that men who consumed high amounts of lycopene had a 40% lower risk of developing prostate cancer compared to those with low intake. The study highlighted that tomatoes, a primary source of lycopene, are particularly effective in reducing the risk of prostate cancer due to their high bioavailability of lycopene.

Additionally, a clinical trial published in *Cancer Epidemiology, Biomarkers & Prevention* found that lycopene supplementation resulted in reduced prostate cancer risk by decreasing oxidative stress and inflammatory markers in men at high risk for the disease.

These studies support the idea that increasing lycopene intake can significantly lower the risk of prostate cancer and promote overall prostate health.

3.1.6 Xanthophylls

3.1.6.1 Definition and Types of Xanthophylls

Xanthophylls are a class of oxygen-containing carotenoids that are naturally occurring pigments in plants. Unlike carotenes (which are pure hydrocarbons), xanthophylls contain oxygen atoms, which impart a yellow or golden color to the compounds. These pigments are primarily involved in the plant's photosynthetic process, helping in light absorption and protection from oxidative damage.

Types of Xanthophylls include:

- Lutein: Found in high concentrations in the retina and responsible for protecting the eyes from oxidative damage.
- Zeaxanthin: Often found in combination with lutein in the retina, playing a role in protecting against UV light-induced damage.
- Astaxanthin: Found in certain marine organisms, this xanthophyll is known for its potent antioxidant properties.
- Canthaxanthin: Commonly found in certain algae and fruits, canthaxanthin is also used as a food coloring agent in the industry.

These xanthophylls are crucial in biological systems due to their ability to quench free radicals and protect cells from damage. Their presence in the human diet has been linked to various health benefits, particularly in eye health and cognitive function.

3.1.6.2 Dietary Sources of Xanthophylls

Xanthophylls are found abundantly in a variety of dietary sources, particularly in foods that are rich in yellow and green pigments. These foods provide a substantial intake of both lutein and zeaxanthin, which are key for eye health.

- Egg yolks: One of the richest sources of lutein and zeaxanthin, egg yolks are highly bioavailable and contribute significantly to dietary intake.
- Corn: Yellow corn is a good source of lutein, making it a common dietary component in various cultures. Corn and its derivatives are also consumed as part of a staple diet.
- Leafy greens: Vegetables such as spinach, kale, collard greens, and broccoli are packed with lutein and zeaxanthin. These dark green vegetables are considered one of the best natural sources of xanthophylls.
- Other sources: Other foods that contain xanthophylls include yellow peppers, squash, and kiwi fruit.

Incorporating these foods into the diet can significantly increase the intake of xanthophylls, promoting better health and providing protective benefits to the eyes and brain.

3.1.6.3 Health Benefits of Xanthophylls

Xanthophylls, especially lutein and zeaxanthin, have been associated with several health benefits, primarily in the areas of eye health, cognitive function, and cardiovascular protection.

1. Neuroprotection and Cognitive Function:

   - Xanthophylls have been shown to have neuroprotective effects, helping to preserve brain health, particularly in aging individuals. Lutein, for example, has been associated with improved cognitive performance and memory retention, especially in older adults. It helps protect neurons from oxidative damage and inflammation, which are key contributors to age-related cognitive decline.
   - The antioxidant properties of xanthophylls support the reduction of oxidative stress in the brain, improving overall brain function and potentially slowing cognitive aging.

2. Eye Health and Prevention of Age-Related Macular Degeneration (AMD):

- Lutein and zeaxanthin are particularly abundant in the macula of the eye, where they act as filters to protect the retina from harmful blue light and oxidative damage. Their antioxidant activity protects the retina from UV radiation and reduces the risk of developing age-related macular degeneration (AMD), a leading cause of vision loss in older adults.
- Xanthophylls also play a role in maintaining visual acuity and preventing the decline of visual function due to aging.

3. Cardiovascular Health and Anti-Inflammatory Effects:

- Xanthophylls possess anti-inflammatory properties that help reduce the risk of cardiovascular diseases by reducing inflammation in the arteries and veins. They help prevent the buildup of plaque in the arteries, which can lead to atherosclerosis and heart disease.
- By improving blood flow and reducing oxidative damage in the vascular system, xanthophylls contribute to overall heart health. Their anti-inflammatory effects further support the management of blood pressure and cholesterol levels.

3.1.6.4 Clinical Studies on Xanthophylls

Numerous clinical studies have investigated the health benefits of xanthophylls, particularly their roles in cognitive aging and eye health.

1. Xanthophyll Intake and Cognitive Aging:

- A number of studies have shown that higher lutein and zeaxanthin intake is associated with better cognitive performance in older adults. Research has demonstrated that individuals with higher levels of these xanthophylls in their diets tend to perform better on tests of memory, attention, and information processing speed.
- One significant study published in the Journal of Alzheimer's Disease found that lutein supplementation in older adults improved cognitive function, particularly in individuals who showed early signs of

cognitive decline.

2. Studies on AMD Prevention:

- Clinical research has strongly supported the role of lutein and zeaxanthin in preventing and managing age-related macular degeneration (AMD). A study conducted by the Age-Related Eye Disease Study (AREDS) showed that higher dietary intake of lutein and zeaxanthin significantly reduced the progression of AMD in participants.
- Additional research has found that xanthophyll-rich diets protect the macula from oxidative stress and UV-induced damage, thereby maintaining visual health and retinal function.

3.1.7 Lutein

3.1.7.1 Sources of Lutein

Lutein is a carotenoid known for its antioxidant properties, particularly in protecting the eyes and improving overall eye health. Lutein is primarily found in green leafy vegetables, but it can also be sourced from other fruits and vegetables.

- Kale: Kale is one of the richest sources of lutein, offering an abundance of this carotenoid to help maintain eye health. A 100-gram serving of cooked kale provides around 20-30 mg of lutein. Kale's deep green color, due to high concentrations of chlorophyll, is a direct indicator of its lutein content. Regular consumption of kale can help prevent macular degeneration and support overall vision health.
- Spinach: Spinach is another excellent source of lutein, particularly when it is cooked. A 100-gram serving of cooked spinach provides 12-15 mg of lutein, making it one of the top dietary sources of this carotenoid. Spinach also contains zeaxanthin, another carotenoid that works synergistically with lutein to protect the eyes from oxidative damage caused by UV light.

- Peas: Peas, especially green peas, are a good source of lutein, providing around 2-4 mg per 100 grams. While they may not have as high a concentration as leafy greens, peas are still an excellent source of lutein, and they offer a convenient and versatile option for adding lutein to the diet. Apart from lutein, peas are rich in vitamins, minerals, and fiber, supporting general health and immune function.

3.1.7.2 Mechanism of Lutein in Health

Retinal Protection and Blue Light Filtration

One of the primary mechanisms through which lutein contributes to eye health is its ability to filter blue light and protect the retina from oxidative damage. The retina is particularly vulnerable to damage from high-energy visible (HEV) blue light, which comes from both natural sunlight and artificial sources like screens. Lutein, along with zeaxanthin, accumulates in the macula of the eye, a small region in the retina responsible for central vision.

Lutein acts as a natural filter, absorbing blue light and protecting the sensitive cells of the retina from damage. This protection helps reduce the risk of age-related macular degeneration (AMD), a leading cause of vision loss in older adults. Studies have shown that individuals with higher lutein levels in the retina have better protection against blue light-induced damage and a reduced risk of AMD.

Antioxidant Effects in Neural Tissues

Lutein also serves as a potent antioxidant in neural tissues, including the brain and eyes. It scavenges free radicals and reduces oxidative stress, which can lead to neurodegeneration and age-related diseases like Alzheimer's disease. Lutein's antioxidant properties help protect brain cells from oxidative damage and inflammation, which are key contributors to the aging process and the development of neurodegenerative disorders.

Research has shown that lutein not only protects the eyes but also plays a significant role in maintaining brain function. A study published in *Frontiers in Aging Neuroscience* found that higher levels of lutein in the blood were associated with improved cognitive function and memory performance in older adults. This suggests that lutein's antioxidant action extends beyond the eyes, contributing to overall brain health.

3.1.7.3 Health Benefits of Lutein

Macular Degeneration Prevention

Lutein is best known for its role in preventing age-related macular degeneration (AMD), a condition that leads to loss of vision in the central part of the visual field. AMD is associated with oxidative damage and inflammation in the retina, especially in the macula, where the highest concentration of light-sensitive cells resides. Lutein helps by accumulating in the macula and providing photoprotection. Studies have shown that individuals with higher dietary intake or higher serum levels of lutein have a significantly lower risk of developing AMD.

A study published in *The Archives of Ophthalmology* found that individuals with higher intake of lutein had a 45% lower risk of AMD compared to those with lower levels. The study also highlighted the beneficial effects of lutein in preventing cataract formation, which often co-occurs with macular degeneration.

Cognitive Support and Memory Enhancement

Lutein also contributes to cognitive health and memory enhancement. Research has shown that lutein, due to its antioxidant properties, helps reduce oxidative stress and inflammation in the brain, which are known factors in cognitive decline. Lutein is found in high concentrations in the brain, particularly in the occipital cortex and prefrontal cortex, which are associated with vision and cognitive function.

A study published in *The Journal of Nutrition* found that older adults with higher levels of lutein had better cognitive performance, particularly in areas related to memory and processing speed. The study suggests that lutein may help protect against age-related cognitive decline and may be beneficial in conditions such as Alzheimer's disease.

Reduction of Oxidative Stress in Chronic Diseases

Oxidative stress is a common underlying factor in several chronic diseases, including heart disease, diabetes, and neurodegenerative diseases. Lutein's ability to scavenge free radicals and reduce oxidative damage helps mitigate the effects of oxidative stress in these conditions. By protecting cells from damage, lutein contributes to reducing inflammation and protecting against disease progression.

A study published in *Free Radical Biology and Medicine* found that lutein supplementation significantly reduced oxidative stress markers in individuals with type 2 diabetes, a condition associated with chronic inflammation and oxidative damage. Lutein's antioxidant properties make it a valuable nutrient for individuals at risk of chronic diseases linked to oxidative stress.

3.1.7.4 Clinical Research on Lutein

Lutein Supplementation in Macular Degeneration

Numerous clinical studies have examined the effect of lutein supplementation on macular degeneration and other eye diseases. A clinical trial published in *Ophthalmology* found that lutein supplementation significantly improved macular pigment density in individuals with early-stage AMD, suggesting that lutein may help slow the progression of the disease. The study involved 10 mg of lutein daily for 6 months, resulting in improved visual function and reduced risk of further damage to the retina.

Furthermore, the Age-Related Eye Disease Study (AREDS2), a large-scale, multi-center clinical trial, found that lutein and zeaxanthin supplementation helped reduce the risk of advanced AMD by 25% in individuals with intermediate AMD. This study confirmed the effectiveness of lutein in maintaining retinal health and reducing the risk of vision loss due to macular degeneration.

Role of Lutein in Alzheimer's Disease Prevention

Lutein has also been studied for its potential role in the prevention of Alzheimer's disease and other forms of cognitive decline. Research has suggested that lutein's antioxidant and anti-inflammatory properties help protect brain cells from oxidative damage and reduce the inflammation associated with neurodegenerative diseases.

In a clinical study published in *The Journal of the American Geriatrics Society*, older adults with higher levels of lutein in their blood had better cognitive function and a reduced risk of developing Alzheimer's disease. The study found that lutein helped preserve brain structure and enhance memory performance in participants, suggesting that lutein may play a key role in cognitive health and Alzheimer's prevention.

Lutein's effects on neuroprotection and memory enhancement indicate its potential as a valuable nutrient for maintaining cognitive function in aging adults and preventing diseases like Alzheimer's.

3.2 Sulfides - Organosulfur Compounds and Their Health Benefits

3.2.1 Introduction to Organosulfur Compounds

Definition and Classification

Organosulfur compounds are organic molecules that contain sulfur atoms in their structure. These compounds are widespread in nature and are particularly abundant in various plants, vegetables, and fruits. Sulfur is an essential element in the human diet and plays a key role in various biological processes. Organosulfur compounds can be classified into several types, based on their chemical structure and function. Some of the most important classes include:

- Thioethers: Compounds where sulfur is bonded to two carbon atoms, such as methylsulfonylmethane (MSM) and dimethyl sulfoxide (DMSO).
- Thiol compounds: These compounds contain a sulfur atom bonded to a hydrogen atom (–SH), such as cysteine and glutathione.
- Disulfides: These compounds contain two sulfur atoms linked together, often in the form of dimethyl disulfide (DMDS), which occurs naturally in garlic.
- Sulfones and sulfoxides: Compounds that contain sulfur doubly bonded to oxygen atoms, such as sulforaphane, a powerful antioxidant found in cruciferous vegetables like broccoli.

These sulfur-containing compounds are found in a wide range of foods, especially in garlic, onions, cruciferous vegetables, and alliums, where they are responsible for much of their characteristic odor and taste.

Sulfur Metabolism in Plants and Its Impact on Human Health

In plants, sulfur plays an essential role in metabolism, particularly in the synthesis of amino acids such as cysteine and methionine, which are critical for protein synthesis and enzyme function. Plants also produce sulfur-containing compounds such as glucosinolates (in cruciferous vegetables) and allyl sulfides (in garlic and onions), which are believed to have important health benefits for humans.

When consumed, these sulfur compounds are metabolized in the body, contributing to various detoxification processes in the liver and providing protection against free radical damage. For instance, sulforaphane, a compound found in broccoli, helps activate phase II detoxification enzymes, which aid in the neutralization and elimination of toxic substances from the body.

Sulfur-containing compounds also support immune function, cardiovascular health, and cancer prevention by reducing oxidative stress and inflammation. The presence of sulfur in the diet is vital for the synthesis of important antioxidants such as glutathione, which is a key player in the body's defense against oxidative damage.

Importance of Sulfur-Containing Phytochemicals

Sulfur-containing phytochemicals are critical for human health, particularly because they have the ability to regulate various biological processes, including immune function, detoxification, and cardiovascular protection. These compounds often work synergistically with other nutrients and enzymes in the body to enhance overall health and prevent chronic diseases such as cancer, heart disease, and diabetes.

Organosulfur compounds have been linked to anti-inflammatory, antimicrobial, antioxidant, and anticancer properties, making them highly valuable in both preventive health and therapeutic health. For example, sulforaphane (from broccoli) and allyl sulfides (from garlic) are both considered to have antioxidant properties that help protect the body from chronic oxidative stress and inflammation, two factors that contribute to the onset of many diseases.

3.2.2 Mechanism of Action of Organosulfur Compounds

Detoxification and Liver Function Enhancement

One of the most important mechanisms of action of organosulfur compounds is their ability to support detoxification processes in the body. Many sulfur-containing compounds, such as sulforaphane and glutathione, play crucial roles in activating phase II detoxification enzymes, including glutathione S-transferase and NAD(P)H quinone oxidoreductase. These enzymes help in the neutralization of toxins, heavy metals, and carcinogens by binding to them and facilitating their elimination through the liver and kidneys.

- Glutathione, a sulfur-containing tripeptide (composed of glutamine, cysteine, and glycine), is particularly important for detoxification. It helps in neutralizing free radicals, reactive oxygen species (ROS), and free radicals produced during normal metabolic processes. By doing so, glutathione reduces oxidative damage to liver cells and plays a critical role in protecting against liver diseases such as fatty liver and hepatitis.

In addition, sulfur compounds such as diallyl sulfide, found in garlic, can stimulate the production of glutathione in the liver, thus enhancing the body's ability to detoxify harmful substances and maintain liver health.

Antimicrobial and Antifungal Properties

Organosulfur compounds, especially those found in garlic and onions, have well-documented antimicrobial and antifungal properties. Allicin, the main active compound in garlic, has been shown to exhibit strong antibacterial, antiviral, and antifungal activity. Allicin works by interfering with the cellular metabolism of microbes, disrupting their cell membranes, and preventing their growth and reproduction.

Similarly, allyl sulfides and diallyl disulfide have been found to exhibit potent antifungal activity, particularly against Candida albicans, a yeast that can cause infections in humans. This antimicrobial action is not limited to bacteria and fungi; organosulfur compounds have also demonstrated antiviral effects, particularly against respiratory infections caused by viruses like influenza.

Cardiovascular Protection via Nitric Oxide Regulation

Another mechanism by which organosulfur compounds promote health is through the regulation of nitric oxide (NO), a key molecule involved in vascular health. Garlic, in particular, has been studied for its ability to enhance the production of nitric oxide in the endothelium (the lining of blood vessels). Nitric oxide helps dilate blood vessels, improving blood flow and reducing blood pressure.

In studies, garlic supplementation has been shown to lower LDL cholesterol levels, reduce blood pressure, and improve vascular function, all of which contribute to cardiovascular protection. Organosulfur compounds can also help reduce inflammation and oxidative stress in blood vessels, further supporting cardiovascular health.

Cancer Prevention Through Apoptosis Induction

One of the most promising roles of organosulfur compounds is in the prevention of cancer. Sulfur compounds, particularly those in cruciferous vegetables like broccoli, have been shown to induce apoptosis (programmed cell death) in cancer cells. The key compound involved is sulforaphane, which activates transcription factors like Nrf2 and p53. These factors regulate the expression of genes responsible for detoxification, antioxidant production, and cell cycle regulation.

Sulforaphane has been shown to inhibit the proliferation of cancer cells and promote the self-destruction of tumor cells without affecting healthy cells. Furthermore, sulforaphane can enhance the immune system's ability to target and destroy cancer cells. Studies have demonstrated that organosulfur compounds are particularly effective in preventing lung cancer, breast cancer, and colon cancer by reducing oxidative DNA damage and inflammation in cells.

In addition to sulforaphane, diallyl sulfide from garlic has been found to suppress the growth of colon cancer cells by modulating cell cycle proteins and promoting apoptosis.

Organosulfur compounds are a class of phytochemicals with profound health benefits. They support detoxification, enhance liver function, exhibit antimicrobial properties, protect the cardiovascular system, and provide cancer protection. Through their mechanisms of action, these compounds play vital roles in maintaining overall health and preventing chronic diseases.

3.2.3 Diallyl Sulfides

3.2.3.1 Chemical Structure and Metabolism

Structure of Diallyl Sulfides

Diallyl sulfides are a group of organosulfur compounds consisting of a sulfur atom bound to two allyl groups (C_3H_5), each of which is a propene molecule ($CH_2=CH-CH_2$). The basic structure of diallyl sulfides is represented by the formula $C_6H_{10}S$, and it typically consists of a sulfur atom (S) positioned between two allyl groups ($CH_2=CH-CH_2$). The structure is relatively simple, with the sulfur atom acting as a central link between the two propene side chains.

There are different variations of diallyl sulfides, depending on the number of allyl groups and the position of the sulfur atoms. The simplest diallyl sulfide is diallyl disulfide, which consists of two sulfur atoms, each bonded to one of the allyl groups. More complex forms include compounds with multiple sulfur atoms in the chain, such as diallyl trisulfide.

The structure of diallyl sulfides allows them to be highly reactive, particularly in biochemical reactions that involve the metabolism of sulfur or the interaction with enzymes.

Metabolism and Bioavailability

The metabolism of diallyl sulfides primarily occurs in the liver, where they are broken down by a variety of enzymes. After ingestion, diallyl sulfides are absorbed into the bloodstream through the gastrointestinal tract. The bioavailability of diallyl sulfides is influenced by factors such as cooking and food matrix, which can impact the absorption rates.

Once absorbed, diallyl sulfides undergo metabolic conversion in the liver, where they are processed into water-soluble metabolites that can be easily excreted through urine. Some of the key enzymes involved in the metabolism of diallyl sulfides include cytochrome P450 enzymes, which play a crucial role in detoxification processes. These enzymes help break down the sulfur compounds into sulfate conjugates or methylated derivatives, which are less toxic and more easily excreted.

The bioavailability of diallyl sulfides is enhanced by their fat-solubility, meaning that when they are consumed with a fatty meal, absorption tends to be greater. Furthermore, cooking methods, such as crushing or chopping garlic, enhance the bioavailability of diallyl sulfides by activating enzymes that release sulfur compounds. However, cooking at high temperatures can cause the volatilization of some of these sulfur compounds, thus reducing their availability.

3.2.3.2 Dietary Sources of Diallyl Sulfides

Garlic

Garlic is the richest and most well-known source of diallyl sulfides. The major diallyl sulfide in garlic is diallyl disulfide (DADS), which is responsible for the characteristic smell and health benefits associated with garlic. A 100-gram serving of fresh garlic contains up to 3.5 grams of diallyl sulfides, though the actual bioavailability can vary based on preparation and cooking methods. When raw garlic is crushed or chopped, the enzyme alliinase converts alliin into allicin, which is then further converted into diallyl sulfides, including diallyl disulfide.

Garlic has long been recognized for its cardioprotective effects, antimicrobial properties, and anti-cancer benefits, all of which are attributed to its high diallyl sulfide content. Regular consumption of garlic has been shown to lower blood pressure, reduce cholesterol levels, and enhance immune function.

Onions

Onions, particularly red onions, are another rich source of diallyl sulfides, although the concentration is lower compared to garlic. The main organosulfur compound in onions is dipropyl disulfide, which shares similar health-promoting effects. A 100-gram serving of raw onions contains about 1-2 grams of sulfur compounds.

Onions, like garlic, have anti-inflammatory, antioxidant, and antimicrobial properties. They are commonly used in culinary preparations around the world and contribute significantly to cardiovascular health by reducing blood pressure and cholesterol levels.

Shallots

Shallots are another allium vegetable that contain significant amounts of diallyl sulfides, especially diallyl trisulfide, which is more concentrated in shallots than in other alliums. A 100-gram serving of raw shallots contains roughly 0.5-1 gram of sulfur compounds. Shallots have similar health benefits to garlic and onions, contributing to heart health, anti-cancer properties, and immune enhancement. They are widely used in cooking for their mild, sweet flavor.

3.2.3.3 Health Benefits of Diallyl Sulfides

Cardiovascular Benefits and Cholesterol Regulation

One of the key health benefits of diallyl sulfides is their ability to support cardiovascular health. Studies have shown that diallyl sulfides can reduce LDL cholesterol oxidation, which is a key factor in the development of atherosclerosis (plaque buildup in arteries). By reducing the oxidation of LDL cholesterol, diallyl sulfides help prevent plaque formation and maintain healthy blood vessels.

Research has shown that diallyl sulfides, particularly those from garlic, can lower blood pressure and improve vascular function. A clinical trial published in *The Journal of Nutrition* found that garlic supplementation significantly reduced systolic blood pressure in individuals with hypertension. Diallyl sulfides may also promote endothelial function, improving the ability of blood vessels to dilate and contract properly.

Immune System Modulation

Diallyl sulfides also play a role in immune system modulation. These compounds stimulate the production of immune cells, including natural killer (NK) cells and macrophages, which are crucial for fighting infections

and preventing tumor development. In animal studies, diallyl sulfides have
been shown to enhance immune cell activity, increasing the body's defense
against pathogens.

In addition to stimulating the immune system, diallyl sulfides have anti-
inflammatory properties that help reduce chronic inflammation, which is
linked to various diseases, including cardiovascular disease, diabetes, and
arthritis.

Anti-Cancer Effects Through Inhibition of Carcinogen Activation

One of the most notable health benefits of diallyl sulfides is their anti-
cancer potential. Diallyl sulfides, particularly diallyl disulfide (DADS) and
diallyl trisulfide (DATS), have been shown to inhibit the activation of
carcinogens by modulating detoxification pathways. These compounds
activate phase II detoxification enzymes, which neutralize harmful
substances before they can cause DNA damage and promote tumor
formation.

In vitro and animal studies have demonstrated that diallyl sulfides can
suppress the growth of cancer cells by inducing apoptosis (programmed cell
death) in tumor cells. This action has been particularly observed in breast,
colon, and liver cancer cells.

Antimicrobial Activity Against Bacterial Infections

Diallyl sulfides, especially from garlic, exhibit strong antimicrobial
activity against a wide range of pathogens, including bacteria, viruses, and
fungi. Studies have shown that diallyl sulfides can inhibit the growth of
common pathogens such as Escherichia coli (E. coli), Staphylococcus aureus,
and Salmonella species. The antimicrobial action is attributed to the ability
of diallyl sulfides to disrupt cell membranes, inhibit bacterial enzyme
activity, and prevent bacterial replication.

This makes diallyl sulfides a valuable addition to the diet for supporting
immune function and preventing infections, particularly gastrointestinal
infections and respiratory infections.

3.2.3.4 Clinical Research on Diallyl Sulfides

Studies on Diallyl Sulfides and Cancer Risk Reduction

Clinical studies have shown that garlic-derived diallyl sulfides can
significantly reduce the risk of developing certain cancers, particularly
gastrointestinal and lung cancer. A study published in *Cancer Prevention
Research* found that individuals who consumed higher amounts of garlic

and its active compounds, including diallyl sulfides, had a significantly lower risk of developing colon cancer compared to those with lower intake.

Another study published in *The American Journal of Clinical Nutrition* found that diallyl sulfides from garlic inhibited the growth of lung cancer cells by inducing apoptosis and blocking cancer cell migration.

Research on Cardiovascular Effects of Garlic-Derived Sulfides

Several clinical trials have investigated the effects of garlic-derived diallyl sulfides on cardiovascular health. One large-scale study published in *The Journal of Nutrition* found that garlic supplementation resulted in a significant reduction in both LDL cholesterol and blood pressure. Additionally, garlic consumption improved vascular elasticity, helping to protect the arteries from damage and reduce the risk of cardiovascular events such as heart attack and stroke

3.2.4 Allyl Trisulfide

3.2.4.1 Chemical Structure and Properties

Allyl trisulfide is a sulfur-containing compound primarily found in garlic and other allium vegetables, and is one of the key organosulfur compounds that contribute to the characteristic odor and health benefits of garlic. Its structure consists of a sulfur atom (S) bonded to three allyl groups (C_3H_5), forming the compound with the chemical formula $C_6H_{12}S_3$.

In human metabolism, allyl trisulfide is primarily broken down in the liver through enzymatic reactions. The enzymatic breakdown involves the cytochrome P450 enzyme system, which helps in detoxifying and metabolizing allyl trisulfide into water-soluble metabolites, such as allyl methyl sulfide (AMS). This breakdown process enhances the bioavailability and ensures that the compound can be safely eliminated through the urine. The bioavailability of allyl trisulfide varies depending on how it is consumed. It is most readily available when garlic is crushed or chopped, as this process activates the enzymes that release sulfur compounds like allyl trisulfide. The presence of fatty acids can enhance its absorption, as with other fat-soluble compounds.

3.2.4.2 Dietary Sources of Allyl Trisulfide

Fermented Garlic

Fermented garlic is a rich source of allyl trisulfide. The fermentation process enhances the formation of sulfur compounds, including allyl trisulfide, by breaking down alliin into allicin, which then undergoes further conversion into more stable sulfur-containing compounds. Fermented garlic also has higher bioavailability, as the fermentation process increases the release and absorption of these beneficial compounds. A 100-gram serving of fermented garlic can provide significant amounts of allyl trisulfide, contributing to detoxification and cardiovascular protection.

Onions

Onions, particularly red onions, are another source of allyl trisulfide, though in lower concentrations than garlic. Onions contain sulfide compounds, which are chemically similar to those found in garlic. While allyl trisulfide is not the most abundant sulfur compound in onions, the health benefits of consuming onions regularly—such as immune enhancement and anti-inflammatory properties—can still be partly attributed to their sulfur content. A 100-gram serving of raw onion contains small but significant amounts of sulfur compounds, including allyl trisulfide, contributing to its antimicrobial and cardiovascular benefits.

Cruciferous Vegetables

Cruciferous vegetables like broccoli, cauliflower, cabbage, and brussels sprouts contain glucosinolates, which are sulfur-containing compounds. While allyl trisulfide is not the predominant sulfur compound in these vegetables, they are still excellent sources of other sulfur-rich phytochemicals that have similar health benefits, including detoxification, cancer prevention, and anti-inflammatory effects. These vegetables also support liver function by enhancing the body's natural detoxification processes through phase II enzymes.

3.2.4.3 Health Benefits of Allyl Trisulfide

Detoxification of Harmful Compounds in the Liver

One of the most significant health benefits of allyl trisulfide is its role in liver detoxification. Allyl trisulfide stimulates the production of phase II detoxification enzymes, including glutathione S-transferase and NAD(P)H quinone oxidoreductase, which help to neutralize and eliminate toxins and carcinogens from the body. The ability of allyl trisulfide to activate these enzymes makes it an important compound for protecting the liver against damage from toxic substances and environmental pollutants.

Studies have shown that allyl trisulfide enhances liver detoxification by increasing the production of glutathione, one of the body's most important antioxidants. This boosts the liver's ability to neutralize reactive oxygen species (ROS) and free radicals, protecting the liver from oxidative damage and maintaining its optimal functioning.

Antioxidant Properties in Neurodegenerative Diseases

Allyl trisulfide also demonstrates antioxidant properties, which are beneficial for neurodegenerative diseases like Parkinson's disease and Alzheimer's disease. Oxidative stress and free radical damage are key contributors to the progression of these conditions, and allyl trisulfide's ability to scavenge free radicals and reduce oxidative damage in the brain may help slow down neurodegeneration.

A study published in *Neurochemical Research* demonstrated that allyl trisulfide could reduce inflammation and oxidative stress in neural tissues, showing promise as a neuroprotective agent. This makes allyl trisulfide a potential candidate for the prevention or management of neurodegenerative disorders, such as Parkinson's disease, where oxidative stress plays a significant role in neuronal loss and cognitive decline.

Potential Anti-Cancer Properties Through Apoptosis Regulation

Allyl trisulfide has shown anti-cancer potential by regulating apoptosis (programmed cell death) and preventing the activation of carcinogens in the body. The compound has been shown to inhibit the growth of cancer cells and induce apoptosis in tumor cells, particularly in cancers such as breast cancer and colon cancer.

Research has demonstrated that allyl trisulfide activates the Nrf2 pathway, which is involved in the expression of detoxifying enzymes and antioxidants. By activating this pathway, allyl trisulfide helps protect healthy cells from carcinogens and reduces the risk of tumor formation. Additionally, allyl trisulfide has been found to inhibit cell proliferation and metastasis in cancerous cells, thus contributing to its anti-cancer effects.

Antimicrobial Activity Against Bacterial Infections

Allyl trisulfide, like other sulfur-containing compounds, also exhibits strong antimicrobial activity. It has been shown to be effective against a range of bacterial infections, including those caused by Escherichia coli (E. coli), Staphylococcus aureus, and Salmonella. Allyl trisulfide works by disrupting the membranes of bacterial cells, thereby preventing their replication and growth.

The antibacterial properties of allyl trisulfide make it a valuable compound in preventing infections and promoting overall immune health. It also has antifungal properties, particularly against fungi like Candida albicans, which can cause infections in humans.

3.2.4.4 Clinical Studies on Allyl Trisulfide

Research on Allyl Trisulfide in Liver Detoxification

Several studies have focused on the role of allyl trisulfide in liver detoxification. A study published in *Toxicology* demonstrated that allyl trisulfide significantly enhanced liver detoxification by stimulating phase II detoxification enzymes and glutathione production. The study showed that oral administration of allyl trisulfide in animal models increased the liver's ability to neutralize toxic substances and protect against liver damage.

In addition, a clinical trial published in *The Journal of Nutritional Biochemistry* showed that garlic supplementation containing allyl trisulfide improved liver function in patients with non-alcoholic fatty liver disease (NAFLD). The study found that allyl trisulfide helped reduce liver inflammation and oxidative stress, leading to improved liver health.

Studies on Sulfur Compounds in Neurodegeneration Prevention

A series of clinical studies has also investigated the role of sulfur compounds, including allyl trisulfide, in neurodegeneration prevention. A study in *Free Radical Biology & Medicine* found that garlic-derived sulfur compounds helped protect brain cells from oxidative damage and reduced the risk of neurodegenerative diseases like Alzheimer's and Parkinson's disease. The study concluded that allyl trisulfide's antioxidant and anti-inflammatory properties could potentially slow the progression of these diseases.

These findings underscore the importance of allyl trisulfide in protecting the brain from oxidative stress and inflammation, which are central to the pathogenesis of neurodegenerative diseases.

FOUR

PHYTOCHEMICALS AS NUTRACEUTICALS – POLYPHENOLS AND FLAVONOIDS

4.1.1 Introduction to Polyphenols

Definition and Classification

Polyphenols are a group of naturally occurring micronutrients found in plant-based foods. They are characterized by the presence of multiple phenolic rings in their structure, which provide antioxidant properties. These compounds are widely distributed in the plant kingdom and play a vital role in the plant's ability to resist diseases, UV radiation, and other environmental stressors. In humans, polyphenols are recognized for their antioxidant, anti-inflammatory, and cardioprotective effects, making them an important part of a healthy diet.

Polyphenols are classified based on their chemical structure and the number of phenolic units they contain. They can be broadly divided into several categories:

- Flavonoids: This is the largest group of polyphenols and includes subgroups such as flavones, flavonols, flavonones, and anthocyanins. Flavonoids are found in a variety of fruits, vegetables, and beverages such as tea and wine.
- Phenolic Acids: These include hydroxybenzoic acid and hydroxycinnamic acid and are mainly found in fruits, vegetables, whole grains, and seeds.
- Stilbenes: This category includes resveratrol, found in grapes and red wine, which has been extensively studied for its anti-aging and cardiovascular benefits.
- Lignans: These polyphenols are found in seeds, particularly flaxseeds, and have been associated with antioxidant and anti-cancer properties.
- Other Polyphenols: This category includes ellagic acid, tannins, and lignans, each of which has unique health benefits related to disease prevention and health maintenance.

Polyphenols can also be categorized based on their molecular structure. Some polyphenols contain a single phenolic unit, while others are composed of several phenolic units connected by various bonds.

Sources of Polyphenols in Diet

Polyphenols are widely distributed in plant-based foods, and they are most commonly consumed through fruits, vegetables, nuts, seeds, whole grains, legumes, and beverages such as tea, coffee, and red wine. Here are some of the primary sources of polyphenols in the human diet:

- Fruits: Many fruits are rich in polyphenols, particularly berries such as blueberries, strawberries, blackberries, and raspberries. These fruits contain high levels of anthocyanins and other polyphenolic compounds. Other fruits like apples, grapes, pomegranates, and cherries also provide significant amounts of polyphenols, with grapes being particularly rich in flavonoids like resveratrol.
- Vegetables: Spinach, broccoli, artichokes, and red onions are examples of vegetables rich in polyphenols. Spinach and broccoli are particularly high in flavonoids and phenolic acids, offering strong antioxidant protection.

- Nuts and Seeds: Nuts such as almonds, walnuts, and hazelnuts contain polyphenols, including flavonoids and phenolic acids. Flaxseeds are an excellent source of lignans, a class of polyphenols that have been linked to reduced cancer risk and improved hormonal balance.
- Whole Grains: Whole grains, particularly oats, barley, and brown rice, provide polyphenols, mostly in the form of phenolic acids. These grains contribute to overall health by improving digestive health and reducing the risk of heart disease.
- Beverages: Tea (particularly green tea) and coffee are rich sources of polyphenols, especially flavonoids. Both drinks have been extensively studied for their antioxidant properties, which contribute to heart health and anti-aging effects. Red wine is also a well-known source of polyphenols, particularly resveratrol, a powerful antioxidant.
- Legumes: Beans, lentils, and chickpeas contain polyphenols such as flavonoids and phenolic acids, which support metabolic health and reduce oxidative stress.

Role in Plant Defense Mechanisms

In plants, polyphenols play an essential role in defense mechanisms against environmental stresses, such as herbivores, pathogens, UV radiation, and oxidative damage. Polyphenols are involved in several protective functions within plants:

- Protection Against UV Radiation: Polyphenols, particularly flavonoids and phenolic acids, help protect plants from UV-induced damage. They act as natural sunscreens, absorbing harmful UV light and preventing oxidative damage to plant cells. This function is especially critical for plants exposed to intense sunlight.
- Defense Against Herbivores: Many polyphenols, such as tannins and flavonoids, serve as antifeedants by making plant tissues unpalatable or toxic to herbivores. These compounds can also interfere with the digestion of herbivores by binding to proteins and other nutrients, reducing the plant's susceptibility to grazing.
- Antimicrobial Activity: Polyphenols also act as natural antibiotics in plants, helping to inhibit the growth of harmful bacteria, fungi, and viruses. Allicin, found in garlic, is a prime example of a polyphenol with

strong antimicrobial properties.

- Oxidative Stress Response: Polyphenols help plants counteract oxidative stress caused by environmental factors like pollution and drought. They act as antioxidants, neutralizing free radicals and reducing damage to plant cells, thereby enhancing the plant's ability to survive in challenging conditions.

In summary, polyphenols are not only vital for plant health but also offer significant health benefits to humans. By acting as antioxidants, anti-inflammatory agents, and cardioprotective agents, they help in the prevention and management of chronic diseases, contributing to overall well-being.

4.1.2 Types of Polyphenols

Polyphenols are a diverse group of plant-derived compounds that can be broadly categorized based on their chemical structure. Each type of polyphenol offers distinct health benefits, such as antioxidant protection, anti-inflammatory effects, and contributions to cardiovascular health and cancer prevention. The major types of polyphenols are phenolic acids, flavonoids, stilbenes, and lignans, each of which can be further subdivided into specific compounds with unique properties.

Phenolic Acids

Phenolic acids are one of the most abundant groups of polyphenols found in the human diet. They are typically classified into two categories based on their chemical structure:

- Hydroxybenzoic acids (e.g., gallic acid, p-coumaric acid)
- Hydroxycinnamic acids (e.g., caffeic acid, ferulic acid)

Caffeic Acid

Caffeic acid is a hydroxycinnamic acid that is widely distributed in fruits, vegetables, and coffee. It is a potent antioxidant that helps neutralize free radicals, reducing the risk of oxidative stress-related diseases like cardiovascular disease and cancer. In addition to its antioxidant properties, caffeic acid has anti-inflammatory effects, contributing to immune function and joint health. Studies have shown that caffeic acid may also help regulate blood sugar levels, making it beneficial for managing type 2 diabetes.

Ferulic Acid

Ferulic acid is another hydroxycinnamic acid found primarily in whole grains, fruits, and vegetables. It has a strong antioxidant effect, similar to caffeic acid, and can scavenge free radicals, thus protecting cells from oxidative damage. Research suggests that ferulic acid plays a significant role in improving cardiovascular health by reducing inflammation and lipid oxidation, which are key contributors to the development of atherosclerosis. Additionally, it has anti-cancer properties and is believed to inhibit the growth of tumor cells in cancers such as breast cancer and colon cancer.

Flavonoids

Flavonoids are a large group of polyphenols that are widely distributed in nature and are responsible for the color and flavor of many fruits and vegetables. These compounds are classified into several subgroups, each with unique health benefits.

Flavones

Flavones, such as apigenin and luteolin, are common in parsley, celery, and peppers. They have potent anti-inflammatory and antioxidant properties, helping to reduce chronic inflammation and lower the risk of heart disease and stroke. Flavones also have neuroprotective effects, making them useful for improving cognitive function and potentially reducing the risk of neurodegenerative diseases such as Alzheimer's.

Flavonols

Flavonols, such as quercetin, kaempferol, and myricetin, are primarily found in onions, apples, grapes, and tea. These flavonoids are widely recognized for their antioxidant and anti-inflammatory effects, which help protect the body from oxidative stress and reduce the risk of cardiovascular diseases, diabetes, and cancer. Quercetin, in particular, has been studied for its potential to reduce allergy symptoms, lower blood pressure, and improve immune function.

Isoflavones

Isoflavones, such as genistein, daidzein, and glycitein, are primarily found in soybeans and other legumes. These flavonoids have phytoestrogenic properties, meaning they can mimic estrogen in the body. As a result, isoflavones are particularly beneficial for hormonal balance and menopausal symptom relief. They have also been shown to reduce the risk of breast cancer, prostate cancer, and osteoporosis. Isoflavones are believed to modulate estrogen receptors in a way that supports cardiovascular health and bone density, especially in postmenopausal women.

Stilbenes

Stilbenes are a class of polyphenols characterized by a stilbene backbone, which consists of two phenolic rings connected by a double bond. The most well-known stilbene is resveratrol, which has gained significant attention for its potential health benefits.

Resveratrol

Resveratrol is a polyphenolic compound found in grapes, red wine, berries, and peanuts. It has been widely studied for its anti-aging and cardioprotective effects. Resveratrol works by activating sirtuins, a group of enzymes that regulate cell survival, metabolism, and aging processes. It has been shown to protect blood vessels, reduce LDL cholesterol oxidation, and improve vascular function. Resveratrol also exhibits anti-inflammatory properties and may help reduce the risk of heart disease and stroke. Furthermore, it has anticancer effects by inhibiting the growth of cancer cells and promoting apoptosis in tumors.

Lignans

Lignans are another type of polyphenol found in seeds, whole grains, and legumes. These compounds are precursors to enterolignans, which are metabolized in the gut by intestinal bacteria.

Sesamin

Sesamin is a lignan found in sesame seeds. It has been shown to possess antioxidant and anti-inflammatory properties, making it beneficial for cardiovascular health. Sesamin has been linked to cholesterol reduction, blood pressure regulation, and liver protection. It also has the potential to improve insulin sensitivity and prevent type 2 diabetes.

Secoisolariciresinol

Secoisolariciresinol is another lignan found in flaxseeds, sesame seeds, and whole grains. It has been shown to have anti-cancer properties, particularly in preventing breast cancer and prostate cancer. It also contributes to hormonal balance and bone health, offering protection against osteoporosis.

Summary

Polyphenols are diverse compounds found in a wide variety of foods, including fruits, vegetables, whole grains, legumes, nuts, and seeds. Their health benefits are primarily attributed to their antioxidant, anti-inflammatory, cardioprotective, and anti-cancer effects. The key types of polyphenols—phenolic acids, flavonoids, stilbenes, and lignans—each offer unique benefits, contributing to chronic disease prevention, cognitive health, and immune function. Consuming a variety of polyphenol-rich foods can help promote overall health and protect against age-related diseases.

4.1.3 Mechanism of Action of Polyphenols

Polyphenols exert a wide range of health benefits through their interactions with various biological systems. Their mechanisms of action are multifaceted and involve antioxidant activity, anti-inflammatory effects, and the modulation of cell signaling pathways. These activities collectively contribute to the prevention and management of chronic diseases such as cardiovascular diseases, cancer, diabetes, and neurodegenerative diseases.

Antioxidant Activity and Free Radical Scavenging

The primary mechanism through which polyphenols exert their health benefits is by acting as antioxidants. Polyphenols are effective free radical scavengers, neutralizing highly reactive free radicals and reactive oxygen species (ROS) that can cause oxidative stress in the body. Oxidative stress occurs when there is an imbalance between free radicals and the body's ability to neutralize them with antioxidants, leading to damage of cells, proteins, lipids, and DNA. This oxidative damage is a key factor in the development of chronic diseases and aging.

Polyphenols possess a phenolic hydroxyl group (-OH) that is capable of donating electrons to free radicals, rendering them less reactive and thus inactivating them. The ability of polyphenols to scavenge free radicals is particularly important in reducing oxidative damage to tissues and organs, including the heart, brain, liver, and lungs. For example, polyphenols such as flavonoids and phenolic acids have been shown to reduce lipid peroxidation, thereby protecting cell membranes from damage. Additionally, polyphenols enhance the body's natural antioxidant defenses by activating antioxidant enzymes, such as superoxide dismutase (SOD) and catalase, which further protect cells from oxidative damage.

In summary, the antioxidant properties of polyphenols play a key role in preventing cell damage and maintaining overall health, particularly in relation to age-related diseases and conditions associated with oxidative stress, including cardiovascular diseases, diabetes, and neurodegeneration.

Anti-inflammatory Effects via NF-κB Inhibition

Polyphenols also exert anti-inflammatory effects, which contribute to the prevention of various inflammatory diseases such as arthritis, heart disease, and cancer. Chronic inflammation is a key factor in the pathogenesis of many diseases and is often driven by the activation of pro-inflammatory pathways within the body. One of the most important of these pathways involves the nuclear factor-kappa B (NF-κB) signaling pathway.

NF-κB is a transcription factor that regulates the expression of pro-inflammatory cytokines, such as TNF-α, IL-6, and IL-1β, which play a significant role in the inflammatory response. Under normal conditions, NF-κB is kept inactive in the cytoplasm. However, in response to inflammatory stimuli, NF-κB translocates to the nucleus, where it binds to DNA and induces the transcription of genes that promote inflammation.

Polyphenols have been shown to inhibit the activation of NF-κB, thereby reducing the production of pro-inflammatory cytokines and mitigating chronic inflammation. For example, flavonoids like quercetin and curcumin (found in turmeric) have demonstrated significant inhibitory effects on NF-κB activation, making them valuable compounds for managing inflammatory diseases. By blocking the NF-κB pathway, polyphenols help to reduce inflammatory responses and prevent the escalation of diseases such as rheumatoid arthritis, asthma, heart disease, and even cancer.

Furthermore, polyphenols such as resveratrol (found in grapes and red wine) also reduce the activity of COX-2, an enzyme involved in the production of prostaglandins, which promote inflammation. By inhibiting both NF-κB and COX-2, polyphenols have broad anti-inflammatory effects that help mitigate the symptoms of chronic inflammation and prevent tissue damage.

Modulation of Cell Signaling Pathways

In addition to their antioxidant and anti-inflammatory effects, polyphenols also influence cell signaling pathways that regulate cell growth, survival, apoptosis, and differentiation. Through these pathways, polyphenols can help prevent cancer, promote healthy cell function, and protect against cell death caused by oxidative stress.

Regulation of the MAPK Pathway

The mitogen-activated protein kinase (MAPK) pathway is involved in various cellular processes, including growth, differentiation, and survival. Polyphenols have been shown to modulate this pathway by activating or inhibiting different MAPK proteins. For example, epigallocatechin gallate (EGCG), a polyphenol found in green tea, activates the p38 MAPK pathway, which plays a crucial role in cell stress responses and apoptosis (programmed cell death). By activating apoptosis in damaged or cancerous cells, EGCG helps to prevent tumorigenesis and supports overall cell health.

Activation of the Nrf2 Pathway

The Nrf2 pathway is another important mechanism through which polyphenols exert their protective effects. Nrf2 is a transcription factor that regulates the expression of antioxidant genes and detoxifying enzymes. Polyphenols, such as sulforaphane (from broccoli), curcumin, and resveratrol, can activate Nrf2, thereby increasing the body's ability to detoxify harmful substances and neutralize oxidative stress. This action is particularly important in protecting against chronic diseases like cancer and cardiovascular diseases, which are closely linked to oxidative damage and inflammation.

Inhibition of the Akt Pathway

The Akt pathway, also known as the protein kinase B (PKB) pathway, is involved in regulating cell survival, metabolism, and growth. In cancer cells, the Akt pathway is often overactivated, promoting uncontrolled cell proliferation and tumor growth. Polyphenols such as epicatechin (found in green tea and dark chocolate) can inhibit the Akt pathway, leading to cell cycle arrest and apoptosis in cancer cells. By modulating the Akt pathway, polyphenols help prevent cancer cell proliferation and promote the normal functioning of healthy cells.

4.1.4 Resveratrol

4.1.4.1 Sources of Resveratrol

Red Grapes

Red grapes are one of the most well-known sources of resveratrol, particularly the skin of the grapes. Resveratrol is a phytoalexin, a compound produced by the grapevine in response to stress or injury. It is found in higher concentrations in red and purple grapes, as opposed to green grapes, due to the pigments in the skins. A 100-gram serving of red grapes can contain about 0.2-2.5 mg of resveratrol, with the concentration varying based on the grape variety and ripeness.

Red Wine

Red wine, particularly dry red wine, is one of the richest dietary sources of resveratrol. The process of fermentation contributes to the extraction of resveratrol from the skins of the grapes into the wine. The resveratrol content in red wine typically ranges from 0.2 to 5 mg per liter, depending on factors such as the grape variety, fermentation method, and aging process. While red wine contains resveratrol, it should be consumed in moderation due to the alcohol content.

Peanuts

Peanuts are another important source of resveratrol, albeit in smaller amounts than red grapes or red wine. They contain trans-resveratrol, which has similar health benefits to the resveratrol found in grapes. A 100-gram serving of peanuts provides approximately 0.01–0.04 mg of resveratrol, making them a good snack option for adding a small amount of resveratrol to the diet.

Blueberries

Blueberries, especially wild blueberries, are also a source of resveratrol, although the concentration is lower compared to grapes. Blueberries contain other flavonoids, such as anthocyanins, which also contribute to their antioxidant properties. A 100-gram serving of blueberries may contain approximately 0.01-0.02 mg of resveratrol. Despite this lower content, the combination of resveratrol with other polyphenols in blueberries provides powerful health benefits, particularly for heart health and cognitive function.

4.1.4.2 Chemical Structure and Bioavailability

Molecular Structure of Resveratrol

Resveratrol (3,5,4'-trihydroxy-trans-stilbene) is a stilbene compound that features two phenolic rings connected by an ethene (C=C) bridge. It exists in two isomeric forms: cis and trans, with the trans form being more stable and the one most commonly found in food sources. The hydroxyl groups (-OH) attached to the phenolic rings are responsible for the compound's antioxidant and anti-inflammatory properties, allowing it to scavenge free radicals and neutralize reactive oxygen species (ROS).

The chemical structure of resveratrol enables it to interact with various biological targets, including enzymes, receptors, and cellular signaling pathways, which underpins its health-promoting properties. In its trans form, resveratrol is more easily absorbed into the bloodstream and exhibits higher bioactivity.

Factors Affecting Absorption and Metabolism

The bioavailability of resveratrol is relatively low due to poor absorption and rapid metabolism in the body. After consumption, resveratrol is absorbed in the gastrointestinal tract but undergoes extensive first-pass metabolism in the liver, where it is converted into glucuronide and sulfate conjugates. These metabolites are less bioactive than the parent compound, but they are more easily excreted through the urine.

Several factors influence the absorption and metabolism of resveratrol, including:

- Food matrix: Resveratrol is often consumed in foods like grapes, peanuts, and wine, which contain other compounds that may influence its absorption. For instance, the alcohol in wine may enhance the absorption of resveratrol, while fiber in whole foods may slow down its absorption.
- Dosage and form: Resveratrol supplements are often taken in higher doses than those typically found in food, and their bioavailability can be enhanced by formulating the compound in a more bioavailable form, such as liposomal resveratrol or resveratrol nanoparticles.
- Gut microbiota: The composition of an individual's gut microbiota can also affect the metabolism of resveratrol, with certain bacteria being capable of converting resveratrol into more bioactive metabolites.

4.1.4.3 Health Benefits of Resveratrol

Cardiovascular Protection

One of the most extensively studied health benefits of resveratrol is its ability to protect the cardiovascular system. Resveratrol has been shown to:

- Prevent atherosclerosis: Resveratrol inhibits the oxidation of LDL cholesterol, one of the key processes that contributes to the development of plaque in the arteries. It also reduces the formation of platelet aggregates, thereby improving blood flow and reducing the risk of heart attacks and stroke.
- Regulate blood pressure: Resveratrol has been found to lower blood pressure by relaxing blood vessels and improving endothelial function. It does so by enhancing the production of nitric oxide, a molecule that dilates blood vessels, leading to better blood circulation and reduced hypertension.
- Enhance nitric oxide production: By stimulating endothelial nitric oxide synthase (eNOS), resveratrol helps produce nitric oxide, which is crucial for maintaining vascular health and preventing arterial stiffness.

Anti-Cancer Properties

Resveratrol exhibits significant anti-cancer effects by:

- Inhibiting tumor growth: Resveratrol has been shown to suppress the growth of various types of cancer cells, including those in breast, colon, and lung cancer. It works by inducing cell cycle arrest, preventing cancer cells from proliferating.
- Modulation of apoptosis: Resveratrol promotes apoptosis (programmed cell death) in cancer cells by activating certain enzymes that regulate cell death. It also modulates tumor suppressor genes like p53 and Bax, which are involved in initiating apoptosis in cancer cells.

Neuroprotection and Cognitive Benefits

Resveratrol has shown promising potential in protecting the brain and improving cognitive function. Its benefits include:

- Prevention of Alzheimer's disease: Resveratrol has been shown to reduce the formation of amyloid plaques, which are a hallmark of Alzheimer's disease. It does so by reducing oxidative stress and promoting the clearance of toxic proteins from the brain.

- Neuroprotective effects: Resveratrol also enhances brain-derived neurotrophic factor (BDNF), a protein essential for the survival and growth of neurons, thereby supporting cognitive function and memory.

4.1.4.4 Clinical Studies on Resveratrol

Research on Resveratrol and Heart Disease Prevention

Numerous clinical studies have explored the effects of resveratrol on cardiovascular health. One prominent study published in the *Journal of the American College of Cardiology* demonstrated that resveratrol supplementation improved blood vessel function and reduced the risk of heart disease by promoting vascular health and reducing inflammation. A meta-analysis found that resveratrol supplementation led to significant reductions in systolic and diastolic blood pressure in individuals with hypertension.

Clinical Trials on Resveratrol and Longevity

Resveratrol has also garnered attention for its potential to extend lifespan. Research in model organisms, such as yeast, worms, and mice, has shown that resveratrol can activate sirtuins, a group of enzymes involved in cellular repair and longevity. A clinical trial published in *Cell Metabolism* explored the effects of resveratrol on human health and found that it may improve insulin sensitivity and reduce inflammation, which are both linked to aging and age-related diseases. However, while these results are promising, more studies are needed to confirm its effects on human lifespan.

In conclusion, resveratrol is a powerful polyphenol with diverse health benefits. From cardiovascular protection to anti-cancer and neuroprotective effects, resveratrol is a promising compound for improving overall health and preventing age-related diseases. However, its bioavailability remains a challenge, and further research is needed to determine optimal dosages and forms for therapeutic use.

4.2 Flavonoids - Types and Health Benefits

4.2.1 Introduction to Flavonoids

Definition and Chemical Classification

Flavonoids are a diverse group of naturally occurring polyphenolic compounds found primarily in plants. They are responsible for the color, flavor, and health benefits of many fruits, vegetables, and beverages like tea and wine. Chemically, flavonoids are characterized by their basic structure, which consists of a 15-carbon skeleton containing two phenolic rings linked by a three-carbon bridge. This structure allows flavonoids to exhibit various biological activities.

Flavonoids can be classified into several subtypes, based on the structure of their skeleton and the type of functional groups attached to the phenolic rings. These subtypes include:

- Flavones: Found in parsley, thyme, and celery, with compounds like apigenin and luteolin.
- Flavonols: Found in onions, apples, and tea, with key compounds such as quercetin and kaempferol.
- Isoflavones: Found primarily in soybeans and other legumes, with genistein and daidzein as prominent examples.
- Anthocyanins: Found in red, purple, and blue fruits, such as berries and grapes, with compounds like cyanidin and delphinidin.
- Flavanones: Found in citrus fruits, with key compounds like hesperidin and naringin.
- Flavonones: Present in citrus fruits, contributing to their distinctive flavor and antioxidant properties.

This diversity in structure leads to the wide variety of biological effects flavonoids have on human health.

Comparison of Flavonoids with Other Polyphenols

Flavonoids belong to the broader group of polyphenols, but they are distinguished by their specific chemical structure. While both flavonoids and other polyphenols (such as phenolic acids or stilbenes) possess antioxidant properties, flavonoids have unique characteristics that set them apart:

- Phenolic Acids vs. Flavonoids: Phenolic acids, like caffeic acid and ferulic acid, are often simpler in structure and are primarily found in grains and fruits. They function mainly as antioxidants, whereas flavonoids possess additional anti-inflammatory and immune-modulating properties, which are often linked to their more complex structure.

- Stilbenes vs. Flavonoids: Stilbenes, such as resveratrol, are more commonly found in grapes and red wine. Resveratrol, while also a potent antioxidant, is particularly noted for its anti-aging effects, whereas flavonoids, with their broader classification, exert a wider range of biological effects, such as immunomodulation, cardiovascular protection, and cancer prevention.

In essence, flavonoids provide a more diverse array of health benefits compared to other polyphenolic compounds due to their ability to interact with multiple biological pathways.

Importance of Flavonoids in Human Health

Flavonoids are integral to maintaining human health. As antioxidants, anti-inflammatory agents, and immunomodulators, they play a central role in reducing the risk of chronic diseases such as cardiovascular diseases, cancer, diabetes, and neurodegenerative diseases. Their consumption through fruits, vegetables, and beverages is associated with:

- Reduced risk of heart disease by improving vascular health, reducing LDL cholesterol, and preventing arterial plaque formation.
- Cancer prevention through inhibition of cancer cell proliferation and induction of apoptosis (programmed cell death).
- Brain health by promoting cognitive function, reducing oxidative stress, and protecting against neurodegenerative diseases like Alzheimer's.
- Improved immune function and protection against infections and inflammatory diseases.

As part of a balanced diet, flavonoids contribute significantly to disease prevention and overall well-being.

4.2.2 Mechanism of Action of Flavonoids

Antioxidant and Free Radical Scavenging Activity

Flavonoids are best known for their antioxidant properties, which are crucial for combating oxidative stress in the body. Oxidative stress occurs when free radicals or reactive oxygen species (ROS) accumulate and cause damage to cells, proteins, lipids, and DNA, which can contribute to various diseases, including cardiovascular diseases, cancer, and diabetes.

Flavonoids possess phenolic hydroxyl groups (-OH) in their structure, which are capable of donating electrons to free radicals, neutralizing them and preventing oxidative damage. In doing so, flavonoids protect cell membranes, DNA, and mitochondria from damage caused by free radicals. Flavonoids such as quercetin and epicatechin are particularly effective at scavenging free radicals and reducing the oxidative burden on cells.

Furthermore, flavonoids enhance the body's natural antioxidant defenses by stimulating the production of endogenous antioxidants, including superoxide dismutase (SOD), catalase, and glutathione peroxidase, which further protect cells from damage. This broad antioxidant activity helps reduce the risk of age-related diseases and promotes cell longevity.

Anti-inflammatory Properties

Flavonoids also exert anti-inflammatory effects through the inhibition of key molecules and pathways involved in the inflammatory response. One of the primary mechanisms of action involves the inhibition of NF-κB (nuclear factor kappa B), a transcription factor that regulates the production of pro-inflammatory cytokines like IL-6, TNF-α, and IL-1β. These cytokines play a significant role in the inflammatory response and are associated with conditions like arthritis, cardiovascular diseases, and inflammatory bowel diseases.

Flavonoids such as quercetin, apigenin, and curcumin (found in turmeric) suppress NF-κB activation, thereby reducing the production of these inflammatory cytokines. Additionally, flavonoids can inhibit COX-2 (cyclooxygenase-2) and LOX (lipoxygenase) enzymes, which are responsible for the production of prostaglandins and leukotrienes, molecules that promote inflammation. By modulating these enzymes, flavonoids help reduce chronic inflammation, improving conditions such as rheumatoid arthritis and asthma.

Immune-modulating Effects

Flavonoids also play a key role in modulating immune responses. They have been shown to stimulate the activity of immune cells such as macrophages, natural killer (NK) cells, and T lymphocytes, enhancing the body's ability to defend against infections and tumors. Moreover, flavonoids can regulate the production of cytokines and chemokines, proteins involved in immune signaling, thus promoting a balanced immune response.

Some flavonoids, such as quercetin, have been shown to increase NK cell activity, which is important for viral defense and tumor suppression. Others, like epigallocatechin gallate (EGCG) from green tea, can enhance the production of interferons, which help to inhibit the replication of viruses. Additionally, flavonoids may help to downregulate excessive immune responses, thus preventing autoimmune conditions and promoting immune tolerance.

Regulation of Enzyme Activity (CYP450, Cyclooxygenase, Lipoxygenase)

Flavonoids can regulate enzyme activity involved in the metabolism of toxins, hormones, and drugs, influencing drug bioavailability and detoxification processes. For example, flavonoids interact with cytochrome P450 enzymes (CYP450), which are involved in the metabolism of various compounds in the liver. Some flavonoids act as inhibitors of specific CYP450 enzymes, slowing down the metabolism of certain drugs, while others enhance the activity of these enzymes, facilitating the elimination of toxins.

Flavonoids also modulate cyclooxygenase (COX) and lipoxygenase (LOX), enzymes that are involved in the synthesis of prostaglandins and leukotrienes, respectively. By inhibiting COX-2 and LOX, flavonoids help reduce inflammation and pain, making them beneficial for conditions such as arthritis and inflammatory bowel disease.

4.2.3 Rutin

4.2.3.1 Sources of Rutin

Buckwheat

Buckwheat is one of the most significant dietary sources of rutin, a flavonoid glycoside. Rutin is found in high concentrations in buckwheat seeds, especially in unprocessed or whole forms. Buckwheat is considered a superfood due to its high nutritional content, including rutin, which is beneficial for vascular health. A 100-gram serving of cooked buckwheat can provide up to 0.8 to 1.2 mg of rutin.

Citrus Fruits

Citrus fruits such as oranges, lemons, and grapefruits are rich in flavonoids, including rutin. These fruits, particularly the peel, contain significant amounts of rutin, which contributes to their antioxidant and anti-inflammatory properties. Rutin content in citrus fruits varies depending on the type, but oranges can contain approximately 0.5–1.5 mg of rutin per 100 grams.

Apples

Apples, especially with their peel, are another excellent source of rutin. The content of rutin in apples varies based on the variety and ripeness. On average, 100 grams of apple contains about 0.1–1 mg of rutin, making them a great source for daily flavonoid intake. Consuming apples with the skin maximizes the intake of this beneficial compound.

Green Tea

Green tea, a popular beverage, contains a range of polyphenols, including rutin. Green tea is often consumed for its antioxidant and metabolic benefits. While it contains lower amounts of rutin compared to buckwheat, it still offers an important source of flavonoid intake. The amount of rutin in a cup of green tea (approximately 240 ml) can vary but typically ranges between 0.5–1 mg. Consuming green tea regularly can contribute to cardiovascular protection and anti-inflammatory benefits.

4.2.3.2 Chemical Structure and Metabolism

Quercetin-Rutinose Glycoside Structure

Rutin is a glycoside composed of quercetin, a flavonoid, bound to a rutinose sugar molecule. Its molecular structure consists of a quercetin backbone (a polyphenolic compound) attached to a disaccharide unit called rutinose. The glycosidic bond between quercetin and rutinose is key to its bioactivity. The structure allows rutin to exhibit antioxidant properties by donating hydrogen atoms to free radicals, thereby neutralizing them.

The unique structure of rutin provides it with water-solubility and makes it more bioavailable in the body compared to quercetin alone. When consumed, rutin is often hydrolyzed by intestinal enzymes, releasing the active quercetin, which is then absorbed and utilized by the body.

Enzymatic Hydrolysis and Bioavailability

After ingestion, rutin undergoes enzymatic hydrolysis in the digestive system. The hydrolysis process involves the breaking of the glycosidic bond between quercetin and rutinose by the enzyme β-glucosidase. This process releases free quercetin, which is then absorbed in the small intestine and enters the bloodstream.

However, the bioavailability of rutin is influenced by several factors, including the presence of other dietary compounds, the food matrix, and the intestinal microbiota. Bioavailability can be enhanced when rutin is consumed in combination with other nutrients, such as vitamin C, which can facilitate absorption. On the other hand, factors like fiber content in food or the use of heat processing can reduce the absorption rate of rutin.

4.2.3.3 Health Benefits of Rutin

Cardiovascular Protection and Capillary Strengthening

Rutin is most widely known for its cardiovascular benefits, particularly its ability to strengthen blood vessels and capillaries. It has been shown to reduce capillary permeability, helping to maintain the integrity of blood vessel walls. This action is particularly beneficial in preventing conditions like hemorrhoids and varicose veins. Rutin also improves blood circulation by reducing blood clot formation and lowering blood pressure. By promoting vascular health, rutin reduces the risk of atherosclerosis and other cardiovascular diseases.

Rutin works by enhancing the activity of endothelial cells that line the blood vessels, leading to the increased production of nitric oxide (NO). Nitric oxide helps dilate the blood vessels, improving blood flow and reducing the strain on the heart. The antioxidant properties of rutin also prevent the oxidation of LDL cholesterol, a key step in the development of plaque in arteries.

Anti-inflammatory and Anti-thrombotic Effects

Rutin's anti-inflammatory properties help reduce the inflammatory responses associated with chronic conditions such as arthritis and cardiovascular diseases. It inhibits the production of pro-inflammatory cytokines and reduces the activation of NF-κB, a key regulator of inflammation in the body.

In addition, rutin has anti-thrombotic effects, meaning it can prevent the formation of blood clots (thrombosis). It inhibits the aggregation of platelets and the activation of fibrinogen, reducing the risk of heart attacks and stroke. This makes rutin particularly useful in managing hypertension and high cholesterol levels.

Role in Neuroprotection and Cognitive Function

Rutin is also beneficial for brain health due to its neuroprotective effects. It has been shown to reduce oxidative stress in brain cells and protect against neurodegenerative diseases like Alzheimer's and Parkinson's. By scavenging free radicals, rutin helps to reduce neuronal damage and promote better brain function.

Rutin may also support cognitive health by enhancing blood flow to the brain, improving memory, and reducing the risk of cognitive decline. Its ability to modulate neuroinflammation plays a key role in protecting neurons from damage associated with diseases like Alzheimer's and vascular dementia.

4.2.3.4 Clinical Studies on Rutin

Studies on Rutin and Vascular Health

Numerous clinical studies have examined the effects of rutin on vascular health. A study published in the *Journal of Nutritional Biochemistry* found that rutin supplementation significantly improved endothelial function in individuals with hypertension. The study showed that rutin helped reduce blood pressure, enhance blood vessel elasticity, and reduce vascular inflammation. Additionally, rutin supplementation has been found to reduce capillary fragility and increase blood circulation, making it beneficial for conditions like varicose veins and hemorrhoids.

Rutin in Diabetes Management

Rutin has also shown promising results in the management of diabetes. A study in the *European Journal of Pharmacology* found that rutin supplementation in diabetic rats improved blood glucose levels and insulin sensitivity. The compound works by modulating glucose metabolism and reducing the accumulation of advanced glycation end-products (AGEs), which are implicated in diabetic complications.

Clinical trials have also shown that rutin can help reduce oxidative stress and inflammation in individuals with type 2 diabetes, further supporting its role in diabetes management. By improving the vascular health of individuals with diabetes, rutin may help prevent complications like diabetic retinopathy and diabetic neuropathy.

In conclusion, rutin is a versatile flavonoid with significant health benefits. From cardiovascular protection to neuroprotection and anti-inflammatory effects, rutin plays an important role in maintaining overall health and preventing chronic diseases. Through its vascular protective effects, cognitive support, and anti-cancer properties, rutin offers a wide range of potential therapeutic applications.

4.2.4 Naringin

4.2.4.1 Sources of Naringin

Grapefruit

Grapefruit, particularly pink and red varieties, is the most significant natural source of naringin, a flavonoid glycoside. The bitter taste of grapefruit comes primarily from naringin, which is found in the peel and flesh of the fruit. Naringin is most concentrated in the peel, but it is also present in smaller amounts in the pulp and juice. A 100-gram serving of grapefruit can contain approximately 0.3-1.2 mg of naringin, with the concentration varying based on the type and ripeness of the fruit.

Oranges

Oranges, particularly bitter oranges, also contain naringin. The concentration of naringin in oranges is lower compared to grapefruit, but it still provides a good source of this bioactive flavonoid. Naringin is found predominantly in the peel and the white pith of the fruit. The juice and flesh of oranges contain trace amounts of naringin, but it is less concentrated compared to other citrus fruits like grapefruit. Oranges can contain 0.01-0.05 mg of naringin per 100 grams of fruit.

Lemons

Lemons, while not as rich in naringin as grapefruit, do contain this flavonoid, especially in the peel. Lemon zest contains a higher concentration of naringin, while the juice has a lesser amount. Lemons also contain limonene, a compound that adds to their health benefits. A 100-gram serving of lemon peel can contain approximately 0.2-0.3 mg of naringin, although the fruit's overall naringin content is still lower than that found in grapefruit.

4.2.4.2 Chemical Structure and Bioavailability

Flavanone Glycoside Nature

Naringin is classified as a flavonoid glycoside, meaning it consists of a flavonoid molecule (in this case, naringenin) attached to a sugar molecule (specifically rhamnose). Its chemical structure includes two phenolic rings connected by a three-carbon bridge, a hallmark of flavonoid compounds. The glycosidic bond between naringenin and rhamnose is what gives naringin its characteristic bitter taste and biological activity.

Flavonoid glycosides, such as naringin, are often inactive until they are metabolized in the human body. The conversion of naringin into its aglycone form, naringenin, is a key step in its bioavailability and action.

Conversion to Naringenin in Metabolism

After ingestion, naringin undergoes enzymatic hydrolysis in the small intestine by the enzyme β-glucosidase, which cleaves the glycosidic bond, releasing the active compound naringenin. Naringenin is more bioavailable than naringin due to its higher absorption in the intestines. Once absorbed, naringenin enters the bloodstream, where it exerts various biological effects, including antioxidant, anti-inflammatory, and lipid-modulating actions.

Naringenin, after being absorbed, is further metabolized in the liver by phase II metabolic enzymes such as UDP-glucuronosyltransferase and sulfotransferase, forming glucuronide and sulfate conjugates. These metabolites are then excreted via urine. The bioavailability of naringin can be influenced by food matrix, intestinal microbiota, and individual metabolism.

4.2.4.3 Health Benefits of Naringin

Antioxidant and Liver Protective Effects

Naringin has significant antioxidant properties that contribute to its liver-protective effects. Naringin helps to scavenge free radicals, particularly reactive oxygen species (ROS), which are implicated in the oxidative stress that damages liver cells. By neutralizing free radicals, naringin protects liver cells from oxidative damage and supports liver detoxification processes. In animal studies, naringin has shown the ability to reduce liver enzyme levels and prevent liver fibrosis, suggesting its protective role in liver diseases such as non-alcoholic fatty liver disease (NAFLD).

Anti-inflammatory and Immune-enhancing Properties

Naringin exhibits anti-inflammatory effects by inhibiting the production of pro-inflammatory cytokines like TNF-α, IL-1β, and IL-6. It does so by modulating the NF-κB pathway, a key signaling pathway involved in the inflammatory response. Naringin also enhances immune function by increasing the activity of natural killer (NK) cells and promoting the production of interferons, which are important for antiviral defense. Its immune-modulating properties make naringin a useful compound in reducing chronic inflammation and improving immune function.

Role in Obesity Management and Metabolic Health

Naringin has demonstrated anti-obesity effects through its ability to regulate lipid metabolism. It helps reduce fat accumulation by inhibiting lipogenesis (fat formation) and promoting lipolysis (fat breakdown). Naringin can enhance thermogenesis, leading to increased energy expenditure and reduced fat stores. It also improves insulin sensitivity, which is crucial for managing metabolic disorders such as type 2 diabetes.

In addition, naringin can reduce plasma cholesterol levels by modulating lipid metabolism, thus contributing to better cardiovascular health. Naringin also helps lower triglyceride levels, a key risk factor for obesity and heart disease.

4.2.4.4 Clinical Research on Naringin

Naringin Supplementation and Weight Loss Studies

Several studies have explored the effects of naringin supplementation on weight loss and obesity management. In animal models, naringin has been shown to reduce adiposity by increasing fat oxidation and promoting energy expenditure. A human clinical trial published in the *Journal of Nutritional Biochemistry* found that naringin supplementation in overweight individuals led to significant reductions in body fat percentage, particularly in those with high blood sugar levels. Naringin also improved insulin sensitivity, which is key in the management of obesity-related diseases such as type 2 diabetes.

Effect of Naringin on Lipid Metabolism

Clinical research has also demonstrated the role of naringin in improving lipid metabolism. A study published in the *International Journal of Obesity* found that naringin supplementation significantly reduced total cholesterol and LDL cholesterol levels in individuals with hyperlipidemia. Naringin has been shown to modulate the expression of lipid-metabolizing enzymes, such as HMG-CoA reductase, which is involved in cholesterol synthesis. By lowering LDL cholesterol and raising HDL cholesterol levels, naringin helps improve cardiovascular health and reduce the risk of atherosclerosis and heart disease.

In conclusion, naringin is a bioactive flavonoid with antioxidant, anti-inflammatory, and lipid-modulating properties. Its beneficial effects on cardiovascular health, obesity management, and immune function make it a valuable dietary component. Further clinical research is necessary to fully elucidate its potential therapeutic applications, particularly in managing metabolic disorders like diabetes and obesity.

4.2.5 Quercetin

4.2.5.1 Sources of Quercetin

Onions

Onions, particularly red and yellow onions, are one of the richest dietary sources of quercetin, a potent flavonoid. Quercetin is found primarily in the outer layers and peels of the onion. A 100-gram serving of raw onion provides approximately 20–40 mg of quercetin, although the amount can vary depending on the variety and how the onion is prepared. Consuming raw onions or minimally processed onions can maximize the intake of quercetin, as cooking can reduce the flavonoid content.

Apples

Apples, especially those with red skin, are another excellent source of quercetin. The skin of apples contains the highest concentration of this flavonoid, and varieties like Red Delicious have higher quercetin content than other apple types. A medium-sized apple (approximately 150 grams) can provide 2–5 mg of quercetin. Eating apples with the skin intact ensures maximum quercetin intake. Apples are also rich in other beneficial polyphenols that work synergistically with quercetin to support heart health and immune function.

Berries

Berries, such as blueberries, blackberries, and cranberries, also contain significant amounts of quercetin. While the concentration of quercetin in berries is lower compared to onions or apples, they still contribute to overall flavonoid intake. A 100-gram serving of blueberries or blackberries may provide approximately 1–3 mg of quercetin. Berries, in general, are also rich in other antioxidants like anthocyanins, which further enhance their health benefits.

4.2.5.2 Chemical Properties and Metabolism

Flavonol Backbone Structure

Quercetin is a member of the flavonol subclass of flavonoids and has a structure characterized by a 15-carbon skeleton, consisting of two phenolic rings (A and B) connected by a three-carbon chain (C-ring). This structure includes multiple hydroxyl groups (-OH) attached to the rings, which give quercetin its antioxidant and anti-inflammatory properties. Quercetin is often found as a glycoside, bound to a sugar molecule, which enhances its solubility in water and influences its bioavailability.

The molecular structure of quercetin enables it to scavenge free radicals and inhibit the formation of reactive oxygen species (ROS), contributing to its antioxidant effects. The hydroxyl groups also make quercetin highly reactive with various biological targets, including enzymes, cell receptors, and proteins.

Absorption and Enzyme Interactions

Quercetin, in its free or glycosylated form, is absorbed primarily in the small intestine, but its bioavailability is limited due to its rapid metabolism and extensive first-pass effect in the liver. Once absorbed, quercetin is metabolized into its glucuronide and sulfate conjugates by enzymes such as UDP-glucuronosyltransferase and sulfotransferase. These metabolites are less bioactive than quercetin itself but are easier to excrete via urine.

The bioavailability of quercetin can be influenced by several factors, including the food matrix in which it is consumed. For example, quercetin absorption may be enhanced when consumed with fats, which can improve its intestinal permeability. Additionally, the gut microbiota plays a significant role in converting quercetin into more bioactive metabolites, such as dihydroquercetin and 3'-methoxyquercetin, which can have distinct biological activities compared to the parent compound.

4.2.5.3 Health Benefits of Quercetin

Anti-inflammatory and Pain-relieving Effects

Quercetin is widely recognized for its anti-inflammatory properties, which are beneficial in managing various chronic inflammatory diseases such as rheumatoid arthritis, asthma, and inflammatory bowel disease. It works by inhibiting the activation of pro-inflammatory cytokines such as TNF-α, IL-1β, and IL-6, which are key players in the inflammatory response. Quercetin has been shown to downregulate the NF-κB pathway, a major regulator of inflammation, thereby reducing inflammation in tissues.

Quercetin also possesses analgesic (pain-relieving) properties, which contribute to its role in alleviating symptoms of painful conditions such as osteoarthritis and fibromyalgia. By inhibiting COX-2 (cyclooxygenase-2), an enzyme involved in pain and inflammation pathways, quercetin provides a natural alternative to non-steroidal anti-inflammatory drugs (NSAIDs).

Immune System Regulation

Quercetin has significant immune-modulating effects, enhancing the body's ability to respond to infections while preventing excessive immune responses that lead to autoimmune diseases. It has been shown to stimulate natural killer (NK) cell activity, a key component of the innate immune system, which plays a crucial role in viral defense and tumor suppression. Furthermore, quercetin can enhance the production of interferons, which help combat infections and inhibit viral replication.

Quercetin's ability to modulate T-cell and B-cell activity helps balance the immune response, reducing chronic inflammation and promoting immune tolerance. This makes quercetin beneficial for managing conditions like allergies and autoimmune disorders.

Cardiovascular Benefits and Blood Pressure Modulation

Quercetin contributes to cardiovascular health by improving endothelial function, reducing oxidative stress, and enhancing blood circulation. Studies have shown that quercetin helps lower blood pressure, especially in individuals with hypertension. It acts by increasing nitric oxide production, which dilates blood vessels and improves blood flow, thereby reducing blood pressure.

Additionally, quercetin has been shown to lower LDL cholesterol and reduce oxidation of LDL, which is a key step in the development of atherosclerosis. It also helps prevent platelet aggregation, further reducing the risk of heart attacks and stroke.

4.2.5.4 Clinical Studies on Quercetin

Studies on Quercetin's Impact on Allergies

Quercetin has demonstrated effectiveness in managing allergic conditions such as hay fever and asthma. A study published in the *Journal of Immunology* found that quercetin inhibits histamine release from mast cells, which are responsible for triggering allergic responses. By stabilizing mast cells and reducing inflammatory cytokine release, quercetin helps alleviate the symptoms of allergic rhinitis and bronchial asthma.

Other clinical trials have confirmed that quercetin reduces allergic symptoms in individuals by inhibiting the release of pro-inflammatory mediators, which helps mitigate the effects of common allergens like pollen and dust mites.

Quercetin in Cardiovascular Disease Prevention

Numerous studies have explored the role of quercetin in preventing cardiovascular diseases. A clinical trial published in *The American Journal of Clinical Nutrition* showed that quercetin supplementation reduced blood pressure and improved vascular function in individuals with hypertension. Other research has shown that quercetin helps lower LDL cholesterol and triglyceride levels, both of which are major risk factors for heart disease.

A meta-analysis published in *Frontiers in Nutrition* confirmed that quercetin supplementation led to significant reductions in systolic and diastolic blood pressure in individuals with pre-hypertension and hypertension, further supporting its role as a cardiovascular protective agent.

In conclusion, quercetin is a potent flavonoid with diverse health benefits. From its anti-inflammatory and immune-modulating effects to its role in cardiovascular protection and allergy management, quercetin is an important dietary compound for improving overall health and preventing chronic diseases. Further clinical research will continue to uncover its full therapeutic potential.

4.2.6 Anthocyanidins

4.2.6.1 Sources of Anthocyanidins

Berries (Blueberries, Raspberries)

Berries, particularly blueberries, blackberries, and raspberries, are the richest sources of anthocyanidins, the aglycone form of anthocyanins. These pigments are responsible for the characteristic blue, purple, and red colors of these fruits. Among these, blueberries are particularly high in anthocyanidins, providing a significant amount of antioxidants that are beneficial for health. A 100-gram serving of blueberries can contain approximately 50-80 mg of anthocyanidins, depending on the variety. Consuming berries regularly is an excellent way to increase intake of these powerful antioxidants.

Red Cabbage

Red cabbage is another significant source of anthocyanidins. It contains anthocyanins that give it its deep purple-red color. Anthocyanidins are present in both raw and cooked red cabbage, though cooking can reduce the total content due to heat degradation. A 100-gram serving of raw red cabbage may contain approximately 30-50 mg of anthocyanidins. Red cabbage is a healthy addition to the diet, as it provides both fiber and vitamins along with these beneficial antioxidants.

Eggplant

Eggplant, particularly the skin of the fruit, contains anthocyanidins in the form of nasunin, a type of anthocyanin that contributes to the fruit's deep purple color. Eggplant is not as rich in anthocyanidins as berries or cabbage, but it still provides a notable amount, particularly when consumed with the skin. A 100-gram serving of eggplant contains about 5-10 mg of anthocyanidins. Nasunin in eggplant has been shown to have potent antioxidant and anti-inflammatory effects, contributing to the health benefits of this vegetable.

4.2.6.2 Chemical Structure and Stability

Anthocyanin Glycosides and pH-Dependent Color Change

Anthocyanidins are the aglycone forms of anthocyanins, which are flavonoid glycosides consisting of an anthocyanidin molecule bound to a sugar molecule. These glycosides are responsible for the colors seen in red, purple, and blue fruits and vegetables. The basic chemical structure of anthocyanidins consists of flavonoid skeletons attached to hydroxyl groups (-OH) at different positions, which are essential for their color properties.

The color of anthocyanidins is highly pH-dependent. At acidic pH, they appear red to purple, while at a more alkaline pH, they shift to a blue hue. This color change is due to the chemical structure of anthocyanidins, where the molecular arrangement of their phenolic rings can vary depending on the acidity or alkalinity of the environment. This property makes anthocyanidins particularly useful for natural food coloring in various industries.

Factors Affecting Stability in Food Processing

The stability of anthocyanidins is affected by several factors during food processing. High temperatures, light, oxygen, and acidic conditions can degrade anthocyanins, converting them into colorless forms or altering their chemical structure, thus diminishing their antioxidant properties. Food processing techniques such as boiling, blanching, and freeze-drying can result in significant loss of anthocyanin content, particularly in fruits like blueberries and raspberries.

To preserve the anthocyanin content during food processing, careful techniques such as low-temperature storage, vacuum packaging, and adding acid (to maintain an acidic pH) can help retain the beneficial properties of these antioxidants. The stability of anthocyanidins can be enhanced by protecting them from light exposure and reducing oxygen exposure during processing.

4.2.6.3 Health Benefits of Anthocyanidins

Antioxidant Properties and Vascular Health

Anthocyanidins, as potent antioxidants, play a critical role in scavenging free radicals and protecting the body from oxidative stress, which contributes to aging and the development of various diseases. In particular, they help protect vascular health by reducing the oxidation of LDL cholesterol, thus lowering the risk of atherosclerosis and cardiovascular disease. Anthocyanidins have been shown to enhance endothelial function, which is critical for maintaining healthy blood vessels and blood pressure. They help increase the production of nitric oxide (NO), which relaxes blood vessels and improves circulation.

Studies have demonstrated that anthocyanidin-rich diets are associated with improved blood vessel function and a reduced risk of stroke and heart disease. Anthocyanidins also reduce inflammation in the blood vessels and have been shown to lower the levels of C-reactive protein (CRP), a marker of inflammation linked to heart disease.

Neuroprotection and Cognitive Function Improvement

Anthocyanidins play a significant role in neuroprotection, particularly in the prevention of age-related cognitive decline and neurodegenerative diseases. They help protect neurons from oxidative damage and improve memory and cognitive function. Anthocyanidins, by reducing oxidative stress and inflammation in the brain, may help prevent or delay the onset of diseases such as Alzheimer's disease and Parkinson's disease.

Research has shown that anthocyanidin-rich foods like blueberries and blackberries can improve short-term memory, learning abilities, and overall brain health, particularly in aging populations. By reducing inflammation and enhancing brain plasticity, anthocyanidins have therapeutic potential in improving cognitive function and brain health.

Cancer Prevention and DNA Protection

Anthocyanidins have shown promising anti-cancer properties, particularly in preventing the growth and spread of tumor cells. They help protect DNA from oxidative damage and mutations that may lead to cancer development. By inducing apoptosis (programmed cell death) in damaged or cancerous cells, anthocyanidins help prevent the proliferation of cancer cells. Additionally, they inhibit tumor metastasis by blocking the enzymes that promote cancer cell invasion.

The anti-cancer effects of anthocyanidins have been studied in various cancers, including breast, colon, lung, and prostate cancer. Anthocyanidin-rich foods have been found to inhibit angiogenesis (the formation of new blood vessels that supply tumors) and reduce the growth of tumors, thereby lowering the risk of cancer.

4.2.6.4 Clinical Research on Anthocyanidins

Anthocyanidin-rich Diets and Cognitive Health Studies

Clinical research has shown that diets rich in anthocyanidins can help improve cognitive function and reduce the risk of neurodegenerative diseases. A study published in the *Journal of Nutritional Biochemistry* demonstrated that blueberry supplementation significantly improved memory and learning in aging adults, with participants experiencing enhanced brain performance after consuming anthocyanidin-rich diets. Other studies have shown that anthocyanidins can help improve short-term memory, focus, and cognitive abilities in older adults at risk for dementia.

Studies on Anthocyanidins and Eye Health

Research has also explored the role of anthocyanidins in eye health, particularly in the prevention of age-related macular degeneration (AMD) and retinal damage. A study published in *Current Eye Research* found that anthocyanidin-rich foods, particularly blueberries, can protect the retina from oxidative damage and reduce the risk of vision loss. Anthocyanidins help regenerate visual purple in the retina, which is crucial for night vision and overall eye function. These compounds have also been shown to improve visual acuity and protect against the deleterious effects of UV light exposure.

In conclusion, anthocyanidins are powerful antioxidants with diverse health benefits, particularly in cardiovascular health, brain function, and cancer prevention. Their ability to protect against oxidative stress, inflammation, and DNA damage makes them an essential component of a healthy diet. Further clinical studies are needed to fully establish their therapeutic potential in various chronic diseases and age-related conditions.

4.2.7 Catechins

4.2.7.1 Sources of Catechins

Green Tea

Green tea is one of the richest natural sources of catechins, particularly epigallocatechin gallate (EGCG) and epicatechin (EC). Catechins, which belong to the flavonoid family, are the primary active compounds in green tea and contribute to its health-promoting properties. A typical cup of green tea (about 240 ml) contains around 50–100 mg of catechins, with EGCG accounting for the majority. The concentration of catechins is highest in fresh, unprocessed leaves, and various brewing methods (such as water temperature and steeping time) can affect catechin content.

Cocoa

Cocoa, especially in its dark chocolate form, is another rich source of catechins, particularly epicatechin and catechin. Dark chocolate with a 70% or higher cocoa content contains substantial amounts of catechins, which contribute to its antioxidant and cardioprotective effects. A 40-gram piece of dark chocolate can provide up to 40 mg of catechins, depending on its cocoa content. Cocoa also contains other beneficial compounds, such as theobromine and flavonoids, that enhance the health benefits of catechins.

Apples

Apples, particularly red-skinned varieties, also contain catechins, although in lower concentrations compared to green tea and cocoa. The peel of apples is especially rich in these antioxidants, and consuming apples with their skin can maximize intake. On average, a 100-gram serving of apple may contain about 1–3 mg of catechins, with the levels varying based on the apple variety and ripeness. Besides catechins, apples also provide fiber, vitamins, and other antioxidants, contributing to their overall health benefits.

4.2.7.2 Chemical Properties and Absorption

Epicatechin and Epigallocatechin Gallate (EGCG) Structure

Catechins are a subclass of flavonoids, with epicatechin (EC) and epigallocatechin gallate (EGCG) being two of the most studied compounds in this category. Both epicatechin and EGCG have a flavonoid backbone, consisting of a 15-carbon skeleton with two phenolic rings and a three-carbon bridge. EGCG, in particular, has an additional gallate group (a type of ester) attached to its structure, which enhances its antioxidant activity and contributes to its biological effects.

Both catechins share the ability to scavenge free radicals and inhibit oxidative stress, which are key to their health benefits. EGCG is considered the most potent catechin in terms of its antioxidant capacity and has been linked to various health-promoting effects, including anti-inflammatory and cardiovascular benefits.

Factors Influencing Bioavailability

The bioavailability of catechins, particularly EGCG and epicatechin, is relatively low, meaning that only a small fraction of these compounds is absorbed into the bloodstream after ingestion. Several factors influence the absorption and bioavailability of catechins:

- Food Matrix: Consuming catechins with fatty foods or proteins can improve their absorption, as catechins are better absorbed when taken with a meal containing fat.
- Gastrointestinal Conditions: The pH of the stomach and the enzymatic environment in the digestive tract can affect the breakdown and absorption of catechins.
- Microbial Metabolism: Gut bacteria play an important role in metabolizing catechins into more bioavailable forms. The gut microbiome can convert EGCG into more bioactive metabolites, improving its absorption and efficacy.
- Formulation and Processing: The processing method (e.g., fermentation of tea or cocoa) can affect catechin content and their bioavailability. Additionally, extraction methods and supplement forms can influence the absorption rates of catechins.

4.2.7.3 Health Benefits of Catechins

Cardiovascular Health and Cholesterol Reduction

Catechins, especially EGCG, have been widely studied for their cardioprotective effects. They help reduce the risk of cardiovascular diseases by improving vascular health, reducing LDL cholesterol oxidation, and regulating blood pressure. Catechins have been shown to enhance endothelial function, which improves blood flow and reduces arterial stiffness, thus lowering the risk of atherosclerosis and hypertension.

Catechins also help reduce total cholesterol levels, particularly LDL cholesterol (often referred to as "bad cholesterol"), which is a major contributor to heart disease. Studies have shown that regular consumption of catechin-rich foods like green tea and dark chocolate can significantly reduce LDL levels while increasing HDL cholesterol (good cholesterol).

Anti-inflammatory and Weight Management Properties

Catechins exhibit potent anti-inflammatory properties, which play a key role in managing obesity and metabolic syndrome. They help reduce systemic inflammation, which is commonly associated with insulin resistance, obesity, and chronic diseases like type 2 diabetes and heart disease. Catechins also enhance fat metabolism and fat oxidation, helping in weight management.

One of the primary mechanisms by which catechins support weight loss is through the increase in thermogenesis and energy expenditure, particularly EGCG. By stimulating brown adipose tissue (BAT) activity, catechins increase fat burning and reduce fat accumulation in the body.

Role in Neurodegeneration Prevention

Catechins are known for their neuroprotective effects. They help reduce oxidative stress and inflammation in the brain, which are key factors in the progression of neurodegenerative diseases such as Alzheimer's disease and Parkinson's disease. By scavenging free radicals and reducing oxidative damage, catechins protect neurons and promote brain health.

Catechins also support cognitive function by improving blood circulation to the brain and stimulating the production of brain-derived neurotrophic factor (BDNF), a protein that promotes neurogenesis and supports learning and memory processes. The neuroprotective effects of catechins have been linked to the reduction of beta-amyloid plaques and the prevention of tau protein aggregation, both of which are hallmark features of Alzheimer's disease.

4.2.7.4 Clinical Studies on Catechins

Catechin-rich Diets and Cardiovascular Outcomes
Clinical studies have shown that catechin-rich diets, particularly those that include green tea, can have significant positive effects on cardiovascular health. A study published in the *American Journal of Clinical Nutrition* found that green tea catechins improved blood pressure, arterial stiffness, and cholesterol levels in people with hypertension. Another meta-analysis concluded that green tea consumption significantly reduces the risk of heart disease, specifically through the reduction of LDL cholesterol and increased HDL cholesterol levels.

EGCG Supplementation and Weight Loss Trials
Several clinical trials have examined the role of EGCG in weight loss and metabolic health. A randomized controlled trial published in *Obesity* found that EGCG supplementation significantly increased fat oxidation and energy expenditure, leading to fat loss in overweight individuals. Other studies have shown that EGCG enhances thermogenesis and fat burning, especially when combined with exercise, contributing to weight management and obesity prevention.

In conclusion, catechins, especially EGCG, provide a wide array of health benefits, from cardiovascular protection to anti-inflammatory and neuroprotective effects. Their ability to regulate lipid metabolism, reduce inflammation, and prevent neurodegeneration makes them an essential part of a health-promoting diet. Further research and clinical studies are needed to fully establish their therapeutic potential in the prevention and management of chronic diseases.

4.2.8 Flavones

4.2.8.1 Sources of Flavones

Parsley
Parsley is a rich source of flavones, particularly apigenin, which contributes to its anti-inflammatory and antioxidant properties. The leafy part of parsley, particularly when used fresh or dried, contains a significant amount of flavones. Parsley is commonly consumed in small amounts as

a garnish, but it is a potent source of flavones, with 1 cup of fresh parsley providing approximately 4–5 mg of flavones. It is also an excellent source of vitamins like vitamin K, C, and A, which support overall health.

Celery

Celery, often used in salads and juices, contains apigenin and luteolin, which are major flavonoid compounds. These flavones contribute to its anti-inflammatory and cardioprotective effects. A 100-gram serving of celery provides around 1–2 mg of flavones, with higher amounts present in the seeds. Celery is a common ingredient in various dishes, and it also offers other health benefits due to its high water content and rich mineral profile.

Chamomile

Chamomile, particularly German chamomile (Matricaria chamomilla), is an herb known for its high flavonoid content, specifically apigenin. Chamomile tea is one of the most popular ways to consume this herb, offering a mild sedative effect that promotes relaxation and sleep. A cup of chamomile tea (approximately 200 ml) contains 1–2 mg of flavones, mostly in the form of apigenin. Chamomile also possesses anti-inflammatory, digestive, and immune-boosting properties, making it an important source of flavonoids for overall health.

4.2.8.2 Chemical Structure and Metabolism

Core Flavone Structure and Functional Groups

Flavones are a subclass of flavonoids and have a basic C6-C3-C6 structure, consisting of two aromatic rings (A and B) connected by a three-carbon bridge (C-ring). The core flavone structure includes a carbonyl group (C=O) in the C-ring, which differentiates flavones from other flavonoids like flavonols. The A-ring usually has hydroxyl (-OH) groups attached, and the B-ring contains various functional groups such as methoxy (-OCH3) or hydroxy groups, contributing to the flavones' antioxidant and anti-inflammatory effects.

The flavones found in herbs like parsley, celery, and chamomile are primarily apigenin and luteolin, both of which have similar structures but differ slightly in the placement of their hydroxyl or methoxy groups. These structural differences give each flavone distinct biological properties, such as their ability to act on various molecular pathways involved in inflammation, immune modulation, and neuroprotection.

Flavone Metabolism in the Human Body

Upon ingestion, flavones undergo intestinal absorption and are metabolized primarily in the liver. The absorption of flavones, including apigenin and luteolin, is generally moderate and depends on their form (e.g., free flavone or glycoside form). After absorption, flavones are conjugated with glucuronic acid or sulfate in the liver, enhancing their solubility for easier excretion in urine. The bioavailability of flavones is generally low due to their rapid metabolism, but certain compounds like apigenin and luteolin have been shown to produce significant health effects despite their limited bioavailability.

The gut microbiota also plays a crucial role in the metabolism of flavones. Some gut bacteria can further modify flavones into bioactive metabolites, which may have enhanced effects on inflammatory pathways and oxidative stress.

4.2.8.3 Health Benefits of Flavones

Anti-inflammatory and Neuroprotective Properties

Flavones, particularly apigenin and luteolin, exhibit potent anti-inflammatory effects by inhibiting the NF-κB pathway, a major regulator of inflammation. These flavones reduce the production of pro-inflammatory cytokines such as TNF-α and IL-6, which are linked to chronic inflammatory conditions like rheumatoid arthritis and asthma. They also protect against neuroinflammation by modulating pathways involved in brain cell signaling, thus contributing to neuroprotection in conditions like Alzheimer's disease and Parkinson's disease.

Flavones like luteolin have shown promise in reducing oxidative stress in neural tissues, helping to prevent damage to brain cells. By protecting neurons from oxidative damage, flavones contribute to cognitive health and memory retention, making them valuable in preventing neurodegenerative diseases.

Cardiovascular and Blood Pressure Regulation

Flavones play a crucial role in cardiovascular health by improving blood vessel function and reducing blood pressure. Studies have shown that apigenin and luteolin can dilate blood vessels, enhancing blood flow and reducing vascular stiffness. They also reduce LDL cholesterol oxidation, which is a key factor in the development of atherosclerosis. By enhancing endothelial function, flavones help prevent the formation of plaques in the arteries, reducing the risk of heart attack and stroke.

In addition to improving blood circulation, flavones are involved in regulating blood pressure by increasing the production of nitric oxide (NO), which relaxes blood vessels. Regular consumption of flavone-rich foods has been linked to lower systolic and diastolic blood pressure in individuals with hypertension.

Role in Estrogenic Activity and Hormonal Balance

Certain flavones, particularly apigenin and luteolin, have mild estrogenic effects, meaning they can bind to estrogen receptors and mimic some of the actions of estrogen. This property makes flavones particularly useful in supporting hormonal balance in women, particularly during menopause when estrogen levels decline. Flavones can help alleviate menopausal symptoms, such as hot flashes, by modulating estrogen receptors in the brain and reproductive organs.

Furthermore, flavones may offer protection against hormone-dependent cancers like breast cancer by blocking the effects of excess estrogen. Their ability to modulate estrogen activity may also reduce the risk of endometrial cancer and ovarian cancer.

4.2.8.4 Clinical Studies on Flavones

Research on Flavones and Estrogenic Effects

Clinical research has highlighted the estrogenic properties of flavones, particularly apigenin and luteolin, which help to modulate hormonal balance. Studies have demonstrated that apigenin from parsley and chamomile may reduce the severity of menopausal symptoms by mimicking estrogen's effects on hot flashes and vaginal dryness. These flavones have also shown potential in reducing the risk of hormone-related cancers, such as breast cancer, by binding to estrogen receptors and competing with endogenous estrogens.

Flavone Supplementation and Heart Disease Prevention

Flavone supplementation has been shown to have beneficial effects on cardiovascular health. A clinical trial published in the *Journal of Nutritional Biochemistry* found that luteolin supplementation significantly reduced blood pressure and cholesterol levels in people with hypertension. The study concluded that flavones improve vascular function, reduce oxidative stress, and enhance blood flow, all of which contribute to the prevention of heart disease.

Another study showed that apigenin, a flavone found in parsley and chamomile, could reduce LDL cholesterol levels and inhibit inflammatory pathways associated with atherosclerosis, making it a promising supplement for individuals at high risk of cardiovascular disease.

In conclusion, flavones such as apigenin and luteolin offer significant health benefits, particularly in cardiovascular health, neuroprotection, and hormonal balance. Their anti-inflammatory and anti-oxidant properties make them valuable compounds for preventing chronic diseases like heart disease, cancer, and neurodegenerative conditions. Further clinical studies are needed to fully explore the therapeutic potential of flavones in various health conditions.

FIVE

PREBIOTICS, PROBIOTICS, AND OTHER PHYTOCHEMICALS

5.1 Prebiotics and Probiotics: Types, Functions, and Benefits

5.1.1 Introduction to Gut Microbiota and Digestive Health

Definition of Gut Microbiota

The gut microbiota refers to the diverse community of microorganisms, including bacteria, fungi, viruses, and protozoa, that inhabit the human gastrointestinal tract. These microorganisms play a crucial role in digestion, immune function, and metabolic processes. The gut microbiome is composed of trillions of microbial cells, outnumbering human cells by a significant factor. The diversity of this microbial community is essential for maintaining digestive health, and disruptions in the balance of these microbes can lead to various gastrointestinal disorders and other systemic health problems.

The gut microbiota is involved in the breakdown of complex carbohydrates (such as fiber) that the human body cannot digest on its own, producing short-chain fatty acids (SCFAs) such as butyrate, propionate, and acetate, which are beneficial for gut health. The diversity and composition of the gut microbiome can vary greatly depending on diet, lifestyle, age, and environmental factors.

Importance of a Balanced Gut Microbiome

A balanced gut microbiome is essential for overall health. When the balance of beneficial and harmful bacteria is disturbed, a condition called dysbiosis can occur. Dysbiosis has been linked to several digestive issues, such as irritable bowel syndrome (IBS), inflammatory bowel disease (IBD), and gastroesophageal reflux disease (GERD). Furthermore, an imbalanced microbiome is associated with obesity, diabetes, and even mental health conditions such as anxiety and depression, often referred to as the gut-brain axis.

A balanced microbiome helps with the synthesis of essential vitamins (like B vitamins and vitamin K), enhances nutrient absorption, and regulates intestinal motility. The gut microbiota also plays a critical role in the immune system by modulating immune responses, preventing the overgrowth of pathogens, and promoting gut barrier function. By maintaining microbial diversity and a healthy balance between different strains, the gut microbiome contributes significantly to digestive health and immune function.

Interaction Between Gut Microbiota and Host Health

The interaction between the gut microbiota and host health is complex and bidirectional. The host provides a suitable environment for the microbiota to thrive, including nutrients and a favorable pH in the intestines. In return, the gut microbiota influences digestion, nutrient absorption, and immune function. Beneficial bacteria, for example, produce SCFAs, which not only provide energy to the cells lining the intestines but also help to regulate intestinal inflammation and maintain the integrity of the gut barrier.

The gut microbiota also plays an essential role in the metabolism of xenobiotics (foreign substances such as drugs and toxins), influencing how the body reacts to medications and other chemicals. Studies have shown that the gut microbiota affects the bioavailability of certain medications and can alter the efficacy and side effects of drugs, especially in treatments for cancer and autoimmune diseases.

Furthermore, the gut microbiota interacts with the central nervous system through the gut-brain axis. The microbial community can influence mood, stress response, and cognitive function through the production of neurotransmitters like serotonin, which is predominantly synthesized in the gut. Disruption of this interaction has been linked to mental health disorders such as depression and anxiety.

5.1.2 Definition and Mechanism of Prebiotics

Definition of Prebiotics

Prebiotics are non-digestible food components, typically fiber or complex carbohydrates, that stimulate the growth and activity of beneficial gut microbiota. They are distinct from probiotics, which are live beneficial microorganisms. Prebiotics act as a food source for beneficial bacteria, promoting their growth and activity. Unlike probiotics, prebiotics do not have to be living organisms. The most common prebiotics are oligosaccharides, such as inulin, fructooligosaccharides (FOS), and galactooligosaccharides (GOS), as well as resistant starch and pectin.

Prebiotics selectively stimulate the growth of beneficial bacteria such as Bifidobacteria and Lactobacilli while inhibiting the growth of pathogenic microbes. They help enhance the microbial diversity in the gut, fostering a healthier gut environment that supports digestive health, immune function, and overall well-being.

How Prebiotics Stimulate Beneficial Gut Bacteria

Prebiotics stimulate beneficial bacteria in the gut by serving as a food source for these microbes. Beneficial bacteria such as Bifidobacteria and Lactobacillus have specific enzymes that allow them to ferment prebiotics, producing short-chain fatty acids (SCFAs) like acetate, propionate, and butyrate. These SCFAs provide energy for the cells lining the colon, promote the growth of beneficial microbes, and help maintain gut health by reducing intestinal inflammation.

SCFAs also lower the pH of the gut environment, making it less conducive for the growth of harmful bacteria while promoting the growth of beneficial bacteria. This process is critical for maintaining gut homeostasis and preventing the overgrowth of pathogenic microorganisms that can lead to diseases such as IBD, C. difficile infections, and gastrointestinal disorders.

Mechanism of Prebiotic Action in Gut Microbiota Modulation

Prebiotics work by promoting the selective growth and activity of beneficial bacteria. Upon consumption, prebiotics reach the colon undigested, where they are fermented by the gut microbiota. This fermentation process generates SCFAs, which have several health benefits, including reducing gut inflammation, improving intestinal barrier function, and enhancing the production of mucus that protects the gut lining. SCFAs also play a key role in regulating gene expression in the colon cells, further supporting gut health.

The consumption of prebiotics can also enhance the absorption of minerals such as calcium and magnesium by altering gut pH and increasing mineral solubility. Additionally, prebiotics have been shown to modulate the immune system by promoting the growth of beneficial bacteria that produce anti-inflammatory compounds and immune-enhancing substances, which help in the prevention of infections and autoimmune diseases.

In conclusion, prebiotics are essential dietary components that promote the health of the gut microbiota by stimulating the growth of beneficial bacteria. They contribute significantly to digestive health, immune function, and disease prevention, making them an important part of a healthy diet.

5.1.3 Common Types of Prebiotics

Fructooligosaccharides (FOS)

Chemical Structure and Properties

Fructooligosaccharides (FOS) are a type of oligosaccharide made up of short chains of fructose molecules, typically linked to a glucose molecule at the end. FOS are classified as non-digestible carbohydrates because the human digestive enzymes cannot break them down. These compounds consist of 2–10 monosaccharide units and have a sweet taste, but they do not contribute significantly to caloric intake. Their non-digestibility allows them to pass through the small intestine and reach the colon, where they are fermented by gut bacteria.

FOS act as prebiotics by stimulating the growth of beneficial bacteria such as Bifidobacteria and Lactobacilli, which are essential for maintaining gut health.

Natural Sources

FOS can be naturally found in several plant-based foods, including:

- Onions: One of the richest natural sources of FOS.

- Garlic: Contains a high amount of prebiotics that promote the growth of beneficial bacteria.
- Bananas: Especially unripe bananas, which are high in FOS and act as a source of dietary fiber.
- Asparagus: Contains a notable amount of FOS that contribute to gut health.

A 100-gram serving of onions contains about 0.5–1 gram of FOS, while garlic, depending on preparation, can provide 2–6 grams per 100 grams. These natural sources of FOS are often consumed in various culinary forms, offering both nutritional value and gut health benefits.

Role in Gut Fermentation and Production of Short-chain Fatty Acids (SCFAs)

Once consumed, FOS are fermented by beneficial gut bacteria, leading to the production of short-chain fatty acids (SCFAs) such as acetate, propionate, and butyrate. These SCFAs are beneficial for gut health, as they provide energy to the cells lining the colon, help maintain the gut barrier, and reduce gut inflammation. Additionally, they lower the pH of the gut, creating an environment that is unfavorable to harmful bacteria and promoting the growth of healthy microbiota.

FOS fermentation contributes significantly to the regulation of intestinal motility and digestive function, which is crucial for overall digestive health.

Health Benefits

FOS offer several health benefits due to their prebiotic effects:

- Improved Digestion: FOS help in the fermentation process that enhances nutrient absorption, particularly minerals like calcium and magnesium.
- Reduced Gut Inflammation: SCFAs produced from FOS fermentation have anti-inflammatory effects, which help reduce the symptoms of IBD and irritable bowel syndrome (IBS).
- Enhanced Immune Function: By promoting the growth of beneficial bacteria, FOS can help strengthen the gut's immune system, preventing the overgrowth of harmful pathogens.

FOS have also been linked to improved bowel regularity, increased stool frequency, and reduced symptoms of constipation.

Clinical Studies on FOS and Digestive Health

Numerous studies have examined the role of FOS in gut health and digestive disorders. A clinical trial published in the *Journal of Nutritional*

Science and Vitaminology showed that FOS supplementation significantly increased Bifidobacteria counts and improved gut microbiome diversity in individuals with constipation. Another study found that FOS intake was associated with reduced gut inflammation and improved intestinal permeability, making them a promising intervention for IBD.

Galactooligosaccharides (GOS)

Composition and Prebiotic Activity

Galactooligosaccharides (GOS) are prebiotics composed of short chains of galactose molecules, usually derived from lactose (milk sugar). These prebiotics are non-digestible by humans, which allows them to reach the colon, where they stimulate the growth of beneficial Bifidobacteria and Lactobacilli. GOS are particularly effective in increasing the levels of beneficial bacteria in the gut, which play an essential role in immune regulation and gut health.

Role in Modulating Gut Flora

GOS selectively stimulates the growth of Bifidobacteria, which are key players in maintaining gut homeostasis and immune function. These beneficial bacteria help inhibit the growth of harmful pathogens in the intestines, reduce intestinal inflammation, and contribute to overall digestive health. GOS supplementation can also help reduce bloating and gas production, which are common symptoms associated with gut dysbiosis.

Health Effects on Infants and Elderly Populations

GOS is particularly beneficial for infants and elderly populations:

- In infants, GOS supplementation is often used in infant formula to mimic the effects of human milk oligosaccharides (HMOs), which support the development of a healthy gut microbiome in infants. Studies have shown that GOS-enriched formula improves gut flora composition, strengthens immune responses, and supports intestinal health.
- In elderly individuals, GOS has been shown to improve intestinal health, prevent constipation, and support cognitive function. A study in *The Journal of Nutrition* found that GOS supplementation improved gut microbiota composition and reduced the incidence of gastrointestinal disorders in older adults.

Inulin

Dietary Sources and Structure

Inulin is a type of soluble fiber found in a variety of plants. It is composed of a chain of fructose molecules with a glucose molecule at the end, making it a type of fructooligosaccharide. Inulin is found naturally in foods such as chicory root, Jerusalem artichokes, onions, garlic, and asparagus. Chicory root is one of the most concentrated sources of inulin, providing up to 75% inulin by dry weight.

Fermentation Process in the Gut

Inulin is not digestible by human enzymes and passes through the small intestine to be fermented by the gut microbiota in the colon. It is fermented by beneficial gut bacteria such as Bifidobacteria and Lactobacilli, producing SCFAs that provide energy for colon cells and help reduce intestinal inflammation. The fermentation of inulin also promotes the production of gas (such as hydrogen), but this is typically well-tolerated by individuals without gut sensitivities.

Effect on Calcium Absorption and Bone Health

Inulin has been shown to enhance the absorption of calcium in the colon, which contributes to bone health. By lowering the pH of the colon and increasing the solubility of minerals, inulin improves calcium absorption and helps reduce the risk of osteoporosis and other bone-related diseases, particularly in elderly individuals and those with calcium deficiencies.

In addition to supporting calcium absorption, inulin promotes gut health by enhancing mineral absorption, improving intestinal motility, and supporting the growth of beneficial gut microbiota. Regular consumption of inulin-rich foods can help improve digestive function and bone mineral density.

In conclusion, prebiotics such as FOS, GOS, and inulin play vital roles in gut health by promoting the growth of beneficial gut bacteria, enhancing nutrient absorption, and supporting immune function. Their diverse health benefits, particularly in digestive health, bone health, and weight management, make them important components of a healthy diet.

5.1.4 Definition and Mechanism of Probiotics

Definition of Probiotics

Probiotics are live microorganisms that, when administered in adequate amounts, confer health benefits to the host, particularly by improving or restoring the gut microbiota. The term "probiotic" is derived from the Greek word "pro bios", meaning "for life." These beneficial microbes can include bacteria, yeasts, and other microorganisms that naturally reside in the gastrointestinal tract and are essential for maintaining digestive health and overall wellness.

Probiotics work by restoring balance to the gut microbiota, which may be disrupted due to factors like dietary changes, stress, antibiotic use, and infections. They help promote the growth of beneficial bacteria while inhibiting the growth of harmful microbes, supporting immune function, intestinal integrity, and digestive health.

How Probiotics Colonize and Maintain Gut Health

Probiotics colonize the gut primarily through adhesion to the intestinal lining, where they interact with the gut's mucosal surface and establish a healthy balance of microorganisms. After ingestion, probiotics pass through the acidic environment of the stomach and arrive in the small intestine and colon, where they adhere to intestinal cells using specialized receptors. This process enhances their survival and allows them to multiply and maintain their presence in the gut.

Probiotics also produce metabolites like lactic acid, which lowers the pH of the gut, making it less favorable for harmful bacteria. They can also compete for nutrients and attachment sites on the intestinal wall, outcompeting harmful pathogens. By doing so, they balance the gut microbiota and maintain intestinal homeostasis.

Relationship Between Probiotics and Immune Modulation

Probiotics play a crucial role in immune modulation by interacting with the immune cells in the gut-associated lymphoid tissue (GALT). They help enhance the activity of macrophages, dendritic cells, and T cells, which are essential for the body's immune defense. Probiotics also contribute to the production of antibodies and the activation of immune responses that protect the body against infections.

Additionally, probiotics produce short-chain fatty acids (SCFAs), such as butyrate, that help regulate immune function and maintain intestinal barrier integrity. These SCFAs play a key role in reducing intestinal inflammation and promoting the health of intestinal epithelial cells. By modulating immune responses, probiotics help prevent the development of chronic diseases such as autoimmune disorders and inflammatory bowel diseases (IBD).

5.1.5 Common Probiotic Species and Their Health Benefits

Lactobacillus Species

Role in Lactose Digestion and Gut pH Balance

Lactobacillus is one of the most well-known probiotic genera. These bacteria are primarily involved in the fermentation of lactose, the sugar found in milk, into lactic acid. Lactobacillus species, such as Lactobacillus acidophilus, are particularly beneficial for individuals who have lactose intolerance, as they help in the digestion of lactose by breaking it down into simpler sugars that can be absorbed by the body. This process reduces the discomfort associated with lactose intolerance, such as bloating and gas.

In addition to lactose digestion, Lactobacillus helps in maintaining the gut pH by producing lactic acid. This acidic environment inhibits the growth of harmful bacteria and supports the growth of beneficial gut microbiota, promoting overall gut health.

Prevention of Diarrhea and Gastrointestinal Infections

Lactobacillus has shown strong protective effects in preventing and managing various types of gastrointestinal infections and diarrhea. For example, Lactobacillus rhamnosus GG has been shown to prevent antibiotic-associated diarrhea (AAD) by maintaining the gut flora balance during antibiotic treatment. Lactobacillus species also help reduce the duration and severity of infectious diarrhea, particularly in children, by enhancing the gut immune response and inhibiting the adhesion of pathogenic bacteria to the gut wall.

Enhancement of Immune Function

Lactobacillus species are important in immune modulation. They stimulate the production of immunoglobulin A (IgA), a key antibody in mucosal immunity that protects the gastrointestinal lining from harmful pathogens. Lactobacillus also promotes the activity of macrophages and T lymphocytes, enhancing the body's ability to fight infections. Studies have shown that regular intake of Lactobacillus probiotics can improve immune responses and reduce the incidence of upper respiratory infections.

Clinical Studies on Lactobacillus Probiotics in Gut Disorders

Numerous clinical studies have demonstrated the effectiveness of Lactobacillus probiotics in managing gastrointestinal disorders such as irritable bowel syndrome (IBS), inflammatory bowel disease (IBD), and diarrhea. A clinical trial published in *The Lancet* found that Lactobacillus rhamnosus GG significantly improved symptoms in patients with IBS, reducing bloating, abdominal pain, and diarrhea. Other studies have shown that Lactobacillus probiotics help manage the symptoms of ulcerative colitis and Crohn's disease, contributing to gut healing and reducing intestinal inflammation.

Bifidobacterium Species

Role in Gut Health and Digestion

Bifidobacterium species are among the first microorganisms to colonize the human gut at birth and play a crucial role in digestion and gut health. They are involved in the fermentation of fiber and other complex carbohydrates, producing short-chain fatty acids (SCFAs) that help nourish gut epithelial cells and maintain the intestinal barrier. Bifidobacterium also plays a role in synthesizing vitamins like B vitamins and vitamin K, which are essential for overall health.

Prevention of Irritable Bowel Syndrome (IBS)

Bifidobacterium species, particularly Bifidobacterium infantis and Bifidobacterium longum, have been shown to help alleviate the symptoms of irritable bowel syndrome (IBS), including abdominal pain, bloating, and diarrhea. A study in *Alimentary Pharmacology and Therapeutics* found that Bifidobacterium infantis supplementation significantly reduced IBS symptoms and improved gut function. By enhancing intestinal motility and reducing gut inflammation, Bifidobacterium species offer relief to individuals suffering from this common gastrointestinal disorder.

Effect on Lipid Metabolism and Cardiovascular Health

Bifidobacterium species may also have a positive impact on lipid metabolism and cardiovascular health. Several studies have suggested that Bifidobacterium can lower serum cholesterol levels by reducing LDL cholesterol and increasing HDL cholesterol. In addition, Bifidobacterium has been shown to reduce blood pressure and improve vascular health, which can help in the prevention of cardiovascular diseases.

Saccharomyces Boulardii

Yeast-based Probiotic and Its Role in Gut Health

Saccharomyces boulardii is a non-pathogenic yeast that has been widely studied for its probiotic properties. Unlike bacterial probiotics, S. boulardii is a yeast-based microorganism that supports gut health by balancing gut flora and protecting against intestinal pathogens. It works by enhancing the production of SCFAs, promoting intestinal barrier integrity, and modulating immune responses in the gastrointestinal tract.

S. boulardii has been particularly effective in preventing and managing antibiotic-associated diarrhea (AAD), Clostridium difficile infections, and traveler's diarrhea.

Prevention of Antibiotic-Associated Diarrhea

Saccharomyces boulardii has been shown to effectively prevent antibiotic-associated diarrhea (AAD), which often occurs as a side effect of antibiotic treatment. Studies have demonstrated that S. boulardii supplementation significantly reduces the incidence and duration of AAD by restoring gut microbial balance and inhibiting the growth of harmful pathogens like Clostridium difficile. A study published in *The American Journal of Gastroenterology* concluded that S. boulardii was effective in reducing the risk of diarrhea caused by antibiotic use and improved intestinal health in both adults and children.

5.1.6 Synergistic Effects of Prebiotics and Probiotics (Synbiotics)

Definition and Importance of Synbiotics

Synbiotics refer to a combination of prebiotics and probiotics that work together to enhance the health benefits of the gut microbiota. A synbiotic formulation contains both live beneficial microorganisms (probiotics) and their food sources (prebiotics) that promote the growth and activity of these microorganisms in the gut. The primary aim of synbiotics is to provide a synergistic effect, where the prebiotics enhance the survival and colonization of the probiotics, and the probiotics, in turn, ferment the prebiotics into short-chain fatty acids (SCFAs) and other beneficial metabolites.

The use of synbiotics can be more effective than using prebiotics or probiotics alone because the prebiotics selectively stimulate the growth of the probiotics, ensuring that these beneficial bacteria thrive and exert their health-promoting effects. Synbiotics have been associated with improved gut health, immune function, and digestion, as well as the prevention and management of various gastrointestinal disorders such as IBS, constipation, and inflammatory bowel diseases (IBD).

Mechanism of Combined Prebiotic-Probiotic Therapy

The combined use of prebiotics and probiotics in synbiotics offers several mechanisms of action that enhance gut health:

- Prebiotics serve as food sources for probiotics, stimulating the growth and activity of beneficial gut bacteria such as Bifidobacteria and Lactobacilli.
- The probiotics, after being administered, colonize the gut, producing lactic acid and SCFAs that reduce gut pH, creating an environment that inhibits the growth of harmful bacteria.
- Probiotics produce antimicrobial compounds, including bacteriocins and hydrogen peroxide, which help control pathogenic bacteria and promote a balanced microbiome.
- Immune modulation is another important aspect, as synbiotics help stimulate the production of immunoglobulin A (IgA) and enhance the activity of immune cells, such as macrophages and T cells, thereby improving gut immunity and overall immune function.

This combination provides a holistic approach to managing gut dysbiosis and improving digestive health.

Clinical Benefits of Synbiotic Supplementation

Synbiotic supplementation has been studied extensively for its clinical benefits in various health conditions:

- Gut Health: Clinical trials have shown that synbiotics help improve intestinal microbiota composition, enhancing the growth of beneficial bacteria and reducing the overgrowth of harmful microorganisms. They are particularly beneficial in conditions like IBS, inflammatory bowel diseases (IBD), and antibiotic-associated diarrhea.
- Immune System Enhancement: Synbiotics improve immune response by modulating the gut-associated lymphoid tissue (GALT) and increasing the production of IgA and other immune cells that protect the gut from pathogens.
- Metabolic Health: Studies have indicated that synbiotics may aid in managing metabolic syndrome, obesity, and diabetes by regulating insulin sensitivity, lipid metabolism, and blood glucose levels.
- Allergy Prevention: Clinical research has also demonstrated that synbiotics can help in the prevention and management of allergic diseases like atopic dermatitis and asthma by modulating the immune system and reducing inflammation.

5.2 Phytoestrogens and Isoflavones

5.2.1 Introduction to Phytoestrogens and Their Mechanism of Action

Definition of Phytoestrogens

Phytoestrogens are naturally occurring plant compounds that have a chemical structure similar to that of estrogen, the primary female sex hormone. Because of this structural similarity, phytoestrogens can bind to estrogen receptors and mimic or modulate the effects of estrogen in the body. Unlike synthetic estrogens, phytoestrogens are generally considered to have weaker estrogenic effects, but they can still influence estrogenic activity, especially in tissues where estrogen plays a vital role, such as the breast, bone, and cardiovascular system.

Phytoestrogens are primarily found in soybeans, legumes, whole grains, fruits, and vegetables, and they are often consumed as part of a plant-based diet.

Structure and Similarity to Human Estrogen

The chemical structure of phytoestrogens resembles that of estradiol, a form of estrogen, and consists of a phenolic ring structure that can interact with estrogen receptors (ERs). The two main classes of phytoestrogens are flavonoids (including isoflavones) and lignans, which have distinct structural features but share the ability to bind to estrogen receptors and modulate estrogenic activity in the body.

Mechanism of Action in Estrogen Receptors

Phytoestrogens can exert estrogenic effects by binding to estrogen receptors (ER-α and ER-β) in various tissues. Depending on the concentration and the tissue type, they may either mimic the effects of estrogen or block estrogen receptors from binding with the body's natural estrogens. This dual action is referred to as selective estrogen receptor modulation (SERM). Phytoestrogens also interact with other signaling pathways, such as those involved in bone metabolism, cardiovascular health, and breast cancer risk.

5.2.2 Classification of Phytoestrogens

Isoflavones (Daidzein, Genistein)

Isoflavones are the most widely studied class of phytoestrogens and are found predominantly in soybeans and soy products. The two primary isoflavones are daidzein and genistein, both of which can be metabolized into other bioactive compounds in the gut. These compounds mimic estrogen in the body, particularly in tissues like the breast and bones, providing protective effects against diseases such as osteoporosis and breast cancer.

Lignans

Lignans are another type of phytoestrogen found in flaxseeds, sesame seeds, whole grains, and berries. Lignans are converted by gut bacteria into enterolignans such as enterodiol and enterolactone, which exhibit estrogen-like effects. They are known for their antioxidant and anti-inflammatory properties and their potential role in reducing the risk of breast cancer and cardiovascular diseases.

Coumestans

Coumestans are found in legumes, sprouts, and alfalfa. The most well-known coumestan is coumestrol, which has strong estrogenic activity and may play a role in modulating menopausal symptoms and breast cancer risk.

5.2.3 Isoflavones and Their Health Benefits

5.2.3.1 Daidzein

Sources of Daidzein

Daidzein is found predominantly in soybeans and soy products such as tofu, tempeh, and soy milk. It is also present in smaller quantities in chickpeas and lentils.

Chemical Structure and Estrogenic Activity

Daidzein is an isoflavone with a chemical structure similar to estradiol, enabling it to bind to estrogen receptors and exhibit weak estrogenic activity. In the body, daidzein is metabolized by gut bacteria into equol, a metabolite that has more potent estrogen-like effects. This conversion is critical in determining the overall estrogenic effects of daidzein in the body.

Health Benefits of Daidzein

- Bone Health and Osteoporosis Prevention: Daidzein has been shown to help maintain bone density and prevent osteoporosis, especially in postmenopausal women, by mimicking the effects of estrogen on bone cells.
- Cardiovascular Protection and Lipid Regulation: Daidzein helps lower LDL cholesterol and regulate lipid metabolism, reducing the risk of cardiovascular diseases.
- Anti-cancer Effects in Breast and Prostate Cancer: Studies suggest that daidzein may reduce the risk of breast cancer and prostate cancer by inhibiting tumor growth and promoting apoptosis in cancer cells.

Clinical Studies on Daidzein

Clinical research on daidzein, especially in postmenopausal women, has shown promising results in improving bone health, reducing hot flashes, and offering cardiovascular benefits. A study in *The Journal of Clinical Endocrinology & Metabolism* demonstrated that daidzein supplementation increased bone mineral density in postmenopausal women and improved lipid profiles.

In conclusion, phytoestrogens, particularly isoflavones like daidzein, offer a range of health benefits, including cardiovascular protection, bone health, and anti-cancer effects. Their ability to modulate estrogenic activity makes them a valuable tool for preventing and managing menopausal symptoms and hormone-related diseases.

5.2.3.2 Genistein

Sources of Genistein

Genistein is a naturally occurring isoflavone found primarily in soy-based foods and fermented soy products. It is most abundant in foods such as:

- Soybeans: The primary source of genistein, both in its natural and processed forms.
- Tofu: Made from soybeans, it contains high concentrations of genistein.
- Tempeh: Another fermented soy product, also rich in isoflavones.
- Soy Milk: A popular dairy substitute derived from soybeans.
- Miso and Natto: Fermented soy products that contribute to the intake of genistein.

These foods are a significant part of many Asian diets, especially in Japan and China, where soy consumption has been linked to lower rates of hormone-related cancers and cardiovascular diseases.

Mechanism of Genistein in Hormonal Balance

Genistein is known for its estrogenic activity, meaning it can interact with estrogen receptors in the body. Genistein has a chemical structure similar to estradiol, the body's primary estrogen, allowing it to bind to estrogen receptors (specifically ER-α and ER-β). This interaction can mimic or modify the effects of estrogen in various tissues, which is particularly important for maintaining hormonal balance.

- Estrogen Receptor Interaction: Genistein binds primarily to ER-β, a receptor involved in regulating bone health, cardiovascular health, and immune responses. Its action at these receptors is beneficial in modulating the effects of estrogen, particularly during periods of low estrogen levels, such as menopause.
- Selective Estrogen Receptor Modulation: Genistein acts as a selective estrogen receptor modulator (SERM), meaning it can mimic estrogen activity in some tissues (such as the bones and vascular system) while

blocking estrogen in other tissues (such as the breast), potentially reducing the risk of breast cancer.

Health Benefits of Genistein

Menopausal Symptom Relief

One of the key benefits of genistein is its ability to alleviate menopausal symptoms. During menopause, estrogen levels decline, which can lead to symptoms such as hot flashes, night sweats, and mood swings. Genistein's estrogen-like effects help to modulate estrogen receptors in tissues sensitive to estrogen, providing symptom relief for women undergoing menopause. Several studies have shown that genistein supplementation can significantly reduce the severity and frequency of hot flashes and improve quality of life during menopause.

Cancer Prevention and Cell Cycle Modulation

Genistein has shown potential in cancer prevention, particularly in breast and prostate cancer. It works by regulating the cell cycle and inducing apoptosis (programmed cell death) in cancerous cells. Genistein inhibits the activity of cancer-promoting proteins, such as protein tyrosine kinases, and modulates estrogen receptor activity, which can prevent the uncontrolled cell division that characterizes cancer.

- Breast Cancer: Genistein has been linked to a reduced risk of breast cancer in women, especially in those who consume it from an early age. Its ability to bind to estrogen receptors and prevent estrogen-driven cell proliferation makes it a protective agent against hormone-related cancers.
- Prostate Cancer: Genistein also exerts anti-cancer effects in prostate cancer by inhibiting angiogenesis (the formation of new blood vessels that supply tumors) and modulating testosterone-driven tumor growth.

Cardiovascular Health and Blood Vessel Relaxation

Genistein contributes to cardiovascular health by promoting blood vessel relaxation, which can help reduce blood pressure and improve blood flow. It works by enhancing nitric oxide production, which helps dilate blood vessels and reduce vascular resistance. Genistein also regulates lipid metabolism by decreasing LDL cholesterol and increasing HDL cholesterol, which is beneficial for preventing atherosclerosis and other cardiovascular conditions.

The cardioprotective effects of genistein are attributed to its antioxidant properties, which help prevent oxidative stress and inflammation in the cardiovascular system.

Clinical Research on Genistein

Genistein's Effect on Breast Cancer Risk Reduction

Research on genistein's role in breast cancer prevention has yielded promising results. Several studies suggest that genistein-rich diets may lower the risk of breast cancer by regulating estrogen activity. A clinical trial published in *The Journal of Clinical Oncology* showed that genistein supplementation reduced tumor growth and increased apoptosis in breast cancer cells. Additionally, epidemiological studies have shown that women who consume higher amounts of soy-based foods, which are rich in genistein, have a lower incidence of breast cancer compared to those with low consumption.

Moreover, genistein has been shown to be effective in reducing the recurrence of breast cancer in women who have undergone treatment, making it a potential adjunct therapy for breast cancer survivors.

In conclusion, genistein, as a phytoestrogen, offers a wide range of health benefits, particularly for women's health. Its ability to balance hormonal activity, reduce menopausal symptoms, prevent cancer, and promote cardiovascular health underscores its importance in both preventive and therapeutic applications. Ongoing clinical research continues to investigate its potential in cancer prevention, cardioprotection, and the treatment of hormone-related diseases.

5.2.4 Lignans and Their Health Effects

5.2.4.1 Sources of Lignans

Lignans are a group of phytoestrogens primarily found in plant-based foods, particularly in seeds, whole grains, and certain vegetables and fruits. The richest sources of lignans include:

- Flaxseeds: Flaxseeds are by far the most concentrated source of lignans. A typical serving of flaxseeds (around 1 ounce) can provide approximately 85-100 mg of lignans.
- Sesame Seeds: These seeds contain lignans, especially sesamin and sesamolin, with sesame seeds providing about 20-30 mg of lignans per serving.
- Whole Grains: Whole grains such as wheat, rye, barley, and oats also contribute to lignan intake. Whole wheat bread or cooked barley can provide around 2–3 mg of lignans per serving.
- Berries and Vegetables: Certain fruits and vegetables, like berries (strawberries, raspberries) and cruciferous vegetables (broccoli, cabbage), also contain small amounts of lignans.

Incorporating these foods into the diet can provide a significant source of lignans, which contribute to overall health by providing antioxidant and hormonal regulation benefits.

5.2.4.2 Chemical Structure and Metabolism

Lignans are a type of polyphenol characterized by their chemical structure, which consists of two phenylpropanoid units linked by a carbon-carbon bond. The structure of lignans allows them to exhibit estrogen-like activity, which is why they are classified as phytoestrogens. In their natural form, lignans are bound to sugars, but once consumed, they are metabolized in the gut into enterolignans, such as enterodiol and enterolactone.

The gut microbiota plays a critical role in this conversion, as specific bacteria in the colon break down the lignans into enterolignans. These metabolites exhibit weak estrogenic effects, which may help modulate hormonal activity in the body, particularly in balancing estrogen levels in women. Enterolignans also have antioxidant properties, which contribute to their beneficial health effects.

5.2.4.3 Health Benefits of Lignans

Antioxidant Effects in Reducing Oxidative Stress
Lignans are powerful antioxidants that help combat oxidative stress in the body. They neutralize free radicals, which are unstable molecules that can damage cells and tissues. By scavenging free radicals, lignans reduce

oxidative stress, which is a key factor in the development of several chronic diseases, including cardiovascular diseases, diabetes, and cancer. Studies have shown that lignans' antioxidant activity helps protect DNA from damage and supports cellular health by reducing inflammation and preventing the accumulation of oxidized lipids.

Estrogenic Activity and Hormonal Balance

Lignans are considered phytoestrogens, meaning they can bind to estrogen receptors in the body and either mimic or modulate the effects of estrogen. This property makes them especially beneficial for hormonal balance, particularly in postmenopausal women, who experience a natural decrease in estrogen levels. By interacting with estrogen receptors, lignans help alleviate symptoms of menopause, such as hot flashes, night sweats, and vaginal dryness. Furthermore, lignans may reduce the risk of hormone-related cancers, including breast cancer, by modulating estrogen metabolism and promoting balanced estrogen levels in the body.

Cardiovascular Benefits and Cholesterol-Lowering Properties

Lignans have been shown to contribute to cardiovascular health by improving lipid profiles. They help reduce LDL cholesterol (the "bad" cholesterol) and increase HDL cholesterol (the "good" cholesterol), which contributes to heart health. The antioxidant properties of lignans also help reduce oxidized LDL, a form of LDL that contributes to the formation of arterial plaques and the development of atherosclerosis. Additionally, lignans' anti-inflammatory effects can help reduce vascular inflammation, further supporting cardiovascular health.

Anti-cancer Effects Through Modulation of Estrogen Metabolism

Lignans, particularly enterolactone, have been shown to exhibit anti-cancer properties by influencing estrogen metabolism. Lignans can regulate the conversion of estrone (a type of estrogen) to less potent forms of estrogen, potentially reducing the risk of breast cancer. They also support apoptosis (programmed cell death) in cancer cells and inhibit tumor cell proliferation. Lignans' ability to reduce estrogen-dependent cancer cell growth makes them a promising component in the prevention of breast cancer and possibly endometrial cancer.

5.2.4.4 Clinical Research on Lignans

Studies on Lignan-rich Diets and Hormone-related Cancers

Several studies have examined the relationship between lignan-rich diets and cancer prevention. Epidemiological studies have found that populations with high lignan intake, particularly those consuming flaxseeds and whole grains, have a lower risk of breast cancer and other hormone-related cancers. One study published in *The American Journal of Clinical Nutrition* demonstrated that enterolignans, the metabolites of lignans, were associated with a reduced risk of breast cancer recurrence in women with early-stage breast cancer.

Furthermore, research in *Cancer Epidemiology, Biomarkers & Prevention* suggested that a diet rich in lignans was linked to a lower incidence of prostate cancer, with the estrogen-modulating effects of lignans potentially playing a protective role against this cancer.

Lignan Supplementation in Cardiovascular Disease Prevention

Lignan supplementation has been shown to improve cardiovascular health, particularly by modulating cholesterol levels and reducing vascular inflammation. In a clinical study published in *The Journal of Nutrition*, flaxseed lignans were associated with lower cholesterol levels and improved arterial health in individuals with hyperlipidemia. Additionally, a study published in *Hypertension* showed that lignans could help reduce blood pressure and improve vascular function in hypertensive individuals..

5.3 Tocopherols and Their Role in Antioxidant Defense

5.3.1 Introduction to Tocopherols and Tocotrienols

Definition and Classification of Vitamin E Compounds

Vitamin E refers to a group of fat-soluble compounds that function as antioxidants, helping to neutralize harmful free radicals in the body. These compounds are tocopherols and tocotrienols, both of which belong to the vitamin E family. Vitamin E is essential for maintaining cellular integrity and preventing oxidative damage to lipid membranes and other cell components.

- Tocopherols and tocotrienols both contain a chromanol ring and a long isoprenoid side chain. The primary distinction between these two forms of vitamin E is in the unsaturation of the side chain. Tocopherols have a saturated side chain, whereas tocotrienols have an unsaturated side chain. This difference gives tocotrienols unique properties in terms of bioactivity and antioxidant effectiveness.

- Vitamin E compounds are classified into four types: alpha (α)-tocopherol, beta (β)-tocopherol, gamma (γ)-tocopherol, and delta (δ)-tocopherol. Each of these forms varies in antioxidant potency, with alpha-tocopherol being the most well-known and biologically active form in humans.

Difference Between Tocopherols and Tocotrienols

Tocopherols and tocotrienols both have significant antioxidant properties, but they differ in structure, bioactivity, and tissue distribution. While tocopherols are the dominant form in the human body, tocotrienols, with their unsaturated side chain, offer additional antioxidant benefits and have been shown to have unique anti-inflammatory and cardioprotective properties.

- Tocopherols: These compounds are primarily antioxidants and are critical in protecting cell membranes from oxidative damage. They are typically found in vegetable oils, nuts, and seeds. Tocopherols can help prevent lipid peroxidation and maintain cellular integrity.
- Tocotrienols: While also potent antioxidants, tocotrienols offer additional health benefits, such as reducing cholesterol levels, protecting against neurodegeneration, and enhancing cardiovascular health. Tocotrienols are found in palm oil, rice bran oil, barley, and oats.

Role in Lipid-soluble Antioxidant Defense

Tocopherols play a crucial role in the body's lipid-soluble antioxidant defense system. They protect lipid membranes from oxidative stress caused by free radicals and reactive oxygen species (ROS), which can lead to cell membrane damage, inflammation, and chronic diseases such as atherosclerosis and neurodegenerative diseases.

As fat-soluble compounds, tocopherols are well-suited to integrate into lipid-rich areas of the body, such as cell membranes, where they neutralize free radicals. This role is especially important in mitochondria, where oxidative stress is commonly high due to the production of ROS during cellular respiration.

5.3.2 Types of Tocopherols

Alpha-tocopherol (Most Bioactive Form)

Alpha-tocopherol is the most biologically active form of vitamin E in humans. It is the form of vitamin E that is most commonly present in the blood and tissues and is recognized for its superior ability to act as an antioxidant. Alpha-tocopherol neutralizes free radicals, protecting lipids and cell membranes from oxidative damage. It is commonly found in vegetable oils, nuts, seeds, and green leafy vegetables.

As an essential antioxidant, alpha-tocopherol helps prevent oxidative damage associated with aging, cardiovascular disease, and some cancers. It also plays a role in immune function, skin health, and eye health by preventing oxidative stress in the tissues.

Beta-tocopherol

Beta-tocopherol is less biologically active than alpha-tocopherol but still has antioxidant properties. It is found in a variety of vegetable oils, including sunflower oil and safflower oil. While beta-tocopherol has antioxidant activity, its role is less prominent in human metabolism compared to alpha-tocopherol.

Despite its lesser activity, beta-tocopherol still contributes to overall antioxidant defense and may offer benefits in reducing oxidative stress and supporting immune function.

Gamma-tocopherol

Gamma-tocopherol is the predominant form of tocopherol in the American diet. It is most commonly found in corn oil, soybean oil, and nuts. Gamma-tocopherol has unique properties that set it apart from other forms of vitamin E. It is especially effective at neutralizing reactive nitrogen species (RNS), which are involved in inflammation and disease processes.

Gamma-tocopherol has been linked to cardiovascular protection, as it can reduce inflammation and inhibit the oxidation of LDL cholesterol, a critical step in the development of atherosclerosis. It also plays a role in preventing cancer by reducing DNA damage caused by oxidative stress.

Delta-tocopherol

Delta-tocopherol is the least common form of tocopherol in the diet and is found in some plant oils, such as corn oil and soybean oil. It has been shown to possess potent antioxidant properties, although its presence in the body is much less significant than alpha-tocopherol and gamma-tocopherol.

While delta-tocopherol has antioxidant capabilities, its role in human health remains less studied compared to the other forms of tocopherols. However, it is likely to contribute to the overall antioxidant defense system and may have a role in reducing inflammation and oxidative stress in tissues.

In conclusion, the different types of tocopherols—alpha-tocopherol, beta-tocopherol, gamma-tocopherol, and delta-tocopherol—each play unique roles in protecting cells from oxidative damage, supporting immune function, and promoting cardiovascular health. The most biologically active form, alpha-tocopherol, is essential for maintaining lipid-soluble antioxidant defense, while other forms like gamma-tocopherol provide additional benefits, especially in the context of inflammation and vascular health.

5.3.3 Sources of Tocopherols in Diet

Plant-based Sources

Tocopherols, especially alpha-tocopherol, are abundant in various plant-based foods, making them a key component of a healthy, plant-based diet. The primary sources include:

- Nuts: Almonds, hazelnuts, and walnuts are excellent sources of tocopherols, particularly alpha-tocopherol, which is the most biologically active form in humans. A handful of almonds (about 28 grams) can provide approximately 7.3 mg of vitamin E.
- Seeds: Sunflower seeds are one of the richest sources of tocopherols. Just 1 ounce (28 grams) of sunflower seeds contains around 7.4 mg of vitamin E, primarily in the form of alpha-tocopherol.
- Vegetable Oils: Vegetable oils are among the most concentrated sources of tocopherols. Oils like sunflower oil, safflower oil, and olive oil contain high amounts of vitamin E. Sunflower oil, for example, provides about 5.6 mg of vitamin E per tablespoon (14 grams).

These sources not only provide tocopherols but also offer other healthy fats, such as omega-3 and omega-6 fatty acids, which contribute to overall cardiovascular health.

Animal-based Sources

While plant-based foods are the primary sources of tocopherols, they can also be found in animal-based products, though in smaller amounts:

- Dairy Products: Milk, cheese, and yogurt provide moderate amounts of tocopherols. One cup of whole milk contains approximately 0.3 mg of vitamin E.
- Eggs: Egg yolks are another source of tocopherols. A single large egg yolk contains about 0.4 mg of vitamin E, primarily in the form of alpha-tocopherol. However, egg yolks contain fat-soluble vitamins, making them a good source of fat along with tocopherols.

Although animal products contribute to vitamin E intake, they provide lower levels compared to plant-based sources. Therefore, plant-based oils, seeds, and nuts are the preferred sources of tocopherols for optimal health.

5.3.4 Mechanism of Antioxidant Action of Tocopherols

Free Radical Scavenging and Lipid Peroxidation Inhibition

Tocopherols, particularly alpha-tocopherol, function as potent antioxidants. They neutralize free radicals, which are highly reactive molecules that can damage cellular structures, including lipids, proteins, and DNA. By scavenging these free radicals, tocopherols help protect the integrity of cell membranes.

One of the key mechanisms by which tocopherols protect cells is by preventing lipid peroxidation, a process where free radicals attack unsaturated lipids in the cell membrane, leading to membrane damage. Alpha-tocopherol directly inhibits lipid peroxidation by donating a hydrogen atom to free radicals, stabilizing them and preventing further damage to cellular membranes. This antioxidant action is essential in preventing oxidative stress, which is a key factor in the development of chronic diseases like atherosclerosis and neurodegenerative disorders.

Role in Maintaining Cellular Membrane Integrity

Tocopherols are crucial in maintaining the structural integrity of cell membranes. The lipid bilayer of the cell membrane is composed of unsaturated fatty acids, which are susceptible to oxidative damage by free radicals. Alpha-tocopherol acts as a protective shield by integrating into the membrane, where it stabilizes the lipid structure, preventing oxidation. This helps ensure the fluidity and permeability of the cell membrane, facilitating cellular communication and maintaining cell function.

Moreover, tocopherols are involved in protecting mitochondria, which are the energy-producing organelles in cells. As mitochondria generate energy, they also produce free radicals, making them particularly vulnerable to oxidative damage. Tocopherols help preserve mitochondrial function, which is essential for overall cellular health.

Protection Against Oxidative Stress in Mitochondria

Mitochondria are not only involved in energy production but are also major sites of oxidative stress, due to their involvement in electron transport chain processes that produce reactive oxygen species (ROS). Tocopherols protect mitochondria by neutralizing these free radicals and reducing the oxidative damage that could impair mitochondrial function. This role is particularly important in the context of aging and age-related diseases, where mitochondrial dysfunction is a key factor in the development of neurodegenerative disorders like Alzheimer's and Parkinson's diseases.

5.3.5 Health Benefits of Tocopherols

Cardiovascular Health

Prevention of Atherosclerosis

Tocopherols, particularly alpha-tocopherol, play a vital role in cardiovascular health by reducing oxidative damage in blood vessels. One of the key mechanisms through which tocopherols exert their protective effects is by inhibiting the oxidation of LDL cholesterol, a major factor in the formation of atherosclerotic plaques. By preventing LDL oxidation, tocopherols reduce the risk of atherosclerosis, a condition characterized by the buildup of plaque in the arteries, which can lead to heart attacks and stroke.

Reduction of LDL Oxidation

Tocopherols also contribute to the reduction of oxidized LDL (oxLDL), which is more harmful than native LDL. OxLDL can trigger inflammation in the arteries, contributing to plaque formation and the development of cardiovascular diseases. By reducing LDL oxidation, tocopherols help protect against vascular inflammation and arterial thickening, both of which are precursors to atherosclerosis.

Neuroprotection

Role in Alzheimer's Disease Prevention

Tocopherols have shown potential in neuroprotection, particularly in the prevention of Alzheimer's disease. The antioxidant properties of tocopherols help reduce oxidative damage in brain cells. Oxidative stress is a significant factor in the development of Alzheimer's disease, where the accumulation of beta-amyloid plaques and tau tangles leads to neuronal dysfunction. Alpha-tocopherol has been shown to slow down cognitive decline in Alzheimer's patients by reducing oxidative stress and promoting cell survival in the brain.

Maintenance of Cognitive Function in Aging

Tocopherols are also beneficial in maintaining cognitive function as individuals age. Vitamin E supplementation has been linked to improved memory and mental clarity in older adults, particularly in those at risk for cognitive decline. Studies have suggested that tocopherols protect brain cells from damage caused by oxidative stress, which is a major contributor to age-related cognitive decline.

Skin Health and Anti-aging Effects

Protection from UV Radiation and Oxidative Damage

Tocopherols play an essential role in skin health, offering protection from UV radiation and oxidative damage caused by exposure to sunlight. Alpha-tocopherol, in particular, is widely used in cosmetic formulations for its ability to protect the skin from sunburns and photoaging. It helps to neutralize free radicals generated by UV exposure, which can lead to premature aging of the skin, wrinkles, and skin cancer.

Cancer Prevention

Tocopherol's Role in Modulating Tumor Suppressor Genes

Tocopherols have been shown to play a role in cancer prevention, particularly through their ability to modulate tumor suppressor genes. Tocopherols, by reducing oxidative stress, help regulate gene expression and cell cycle in ways that prevent the initiation and progression of tumors. They have been particularly studied for their pro-apoptotic (cell death-inducing) effects on cancer cells, and their ability to reduce angiogenesis, the formation of new blood vessels that tumors need to grow.

5.3.6 Clinical Research on Tocopherols

Meta-analysis of Tocopherols in Heart Disease Prevention

Several meta-analyses have investigated the role of tocopherols, particularly alpha-tocopherol, in preventing heart disease. One large meta-analysis found that vitamin E supplementation significantly reduced the risk of heart disease and stroke, especially in individuals with high cardiovascular risk. Another study, published in *Circulation*, showed that tocopherol supplementation led to improved endothelial function, which is essential for maintaining healthy blood vessels.

Studies on Tocopherol Supplementation and Cognitive Function

Tocopherol supplementation has been extensively studied for its impact on cognitive function. Research published in *The Archives of Neurology* showed that alpha-tocopherol supplementation slowed down the progression of Alzheimer's disease and improved memory performance in older adults. Further studies have suggested that vitamin E could play a role in delaying cognitive decline and improving brain health in aging populations.

SIX

FREE RADICALS AND THEIR IMPACT ON HEALTH

6.1 Introduction to Free Radicals and Reactive Oxygen Species (ROS)

6.1.1 Definition and Basic Chemistry of Free Radicals

What are Free Radicals?

Free radicals are highly reactive molecules or atoms that contain one or more unpaired electrons in their outermost orbital. This unpaired electron makes free radicals unstable and highly reactive, as they seek to pair their unpaired electron by gaining or losing electrons from other molecules. This reactivity allows free radicals to participate in chain reactions, leading to the formation of more free radicals and causing damage to cellular components such as DNA, proteins, and lipids.

Chemical Structure and Instability of Free Radicals

The chemical structure of free radicals is characterized by the presence of an unpaired electron, which makes them highly unstable and reactive. For example, the hydroxyl radical ($\cdot OH$) has an unpaired electron on the oxygen atom, making it one of the most reactive and damaging free radicals. The instability of free radicals arises from their tendency to achieve a stable electron configuration by reacting with other molecules, often leading to oxidative stress and cellular damage.

Differences Between Free Radicals and Stable Molecules

Stable molecules have paired electrons in their outermost orbitals, making them chemically inert and less reactive. In contrast, free radicals have unpaired electrons, making them highly reactive and capable of initiating chain reactions. For example, molecular oxygen (O_2) is relatively stable because it has paired electrons, whereas the superoxide anion (O_2^-) is a free radical with an unpaired electron, making it highly reactive.

6.1.2 Types of Free Radicals

Free radicals can be classified into two main categories: Reactive Oxygen Species (ROS) and Reactive Nitrogen Species (RNS). These molecules play a dual role in the body, acting as both signaling molecules and agents of oxidative damage.

Reactive Oxygen Species (ROS)

ROS are oxygen-containing molecules that are highly reactive due to the presence of unpaired electrons. They are generated as byproducts of cellular metabolism, particularly in the mitochondria during oxidative phosphorylation. Common ROS include:

1. **Superoxide Anion (O_2^-)**

   - Chemical Formula: O_2^-
   - Formation: Produced during the reduction of molecular oxygen (O_2) in the electron transport chain.
   - Role: Acts as a precursor to other ROS, such as hydrogen peroxide and hydroxyl radicals. It can damage cellular components and contribute to oxidative stress.

2. **Hydrogen Peroxide (H_2O_2)**

   - Chemical Formula: H_2O_2
   - Formation: Produced by the dismutation of superoxide anions catalyzed by superoxide dismutase (SOD).
   - Role: Less reactive than other ROS but can diffuse across cell membranes and generate highly reactive hydroxyl radicals in the presence of transition metals (e.g., iron or copper) through the Fenton reaction.

3. **Hydroxyl Radical (·OH)**

   - Chemical Formula: ·OH
   - Formation: Generated from hydrogen peroxide in the presence of transition metals (Fenton reaction) or from the reaction of superoxide anions with nitric oxide.
   - Role: The most reactive and damaging ROS, capable of attacking and damaging DNA, proteins, and lipids.

4. **Singlet Oxygen ($^1O_2$)**

   - Chemical Formula: $^1O_2$
   - Formation: Produced during photosensitization reactions, such as those involving chlorophyll or porphyrins.
   - Role: Highly reactive and can cause oxidative damage to cellular components, particularly in the presence of light.

Reactive Nitrogen Species (RNS)

RNS are nitrogen-containing molecules that are highly reactive and play a role in cellular signaling and oxidative damage. Common RNS include:

1. **Nitric Oxide (NO·)**

   - Chemical Formula: NO·
   - Formation: Produced by nitric oxide synthase (NOS) enzymes from the amino acid L-arginine.
   - Role: Acts as a signaling molecule in vasodilation, neurotransmission, and immune response. However, excessive NO· can react with superoxide anions to form peroxynitrite, a highly reactive RNS.

2. **Peroxynitrite ($ONOO^-$)**

   - Chemical Formula: $ONOO^-$
   - Formation: Produced by the reaction of nitric oxide (NO·) with superoxide anions (O_2^-).
   - Role: Highly reactive and can cause nitrosative stress, leading to damage to proteins, lipids, and DNA.

6.1.3 Free Radical Formation and Stability

How Free Radicals Form in Biological Systems
Free radicals are generated in biological systems through both endogenous and exogenous mechanisms. Endogenous sources include normal cellular metabolic processes, while exogenous sources involve external factors such as radiation, pollution, and toxins.

1. **Endogenous Sources**:

   - **Mitochondrial Electron Transport Chain (ETC)**: During oxidative phosphorylation, electrons can leak from the ETC and react with oxygen, forming superoxide anions (O_2^-).
   - **Enzymatic Reactions**: Enzymes such as NADPH oxidase, xanthine oxidase, and cytochrome P450 can produce free radicals as byproducts of their catalytic activity.
   - **Inflammatory Response**: Immune cells, such as macrophages and neutrophils, produce free radicals (e.g., superoxide and nitric oxide) to destroy pathogens.

2. **Exogenous Sources**:

   - **Radiation**: Ultraviolet (UV) light and ionizing radiation can generate free radicals by breaking chemical bonds in molecules.
   - **Environmental Pollutants**: Exposure to pollutants, such as cigarette smoke and industrial chemicals, can introduce free radicals into the body.
   - **Toxins**: Certain drugs and chemicals can undergo redox cycling, generating free radicals during their metabolism.

Stability and Reactivity of Different Radical Species
The stability and reactivity of free radicals depend on their chemical structure and the presence of unpaired electrons. Some radicals are highly reactive and short-lived, while others are more stable and can persist longer in biological systems.

1. **Highly Reactive Radicals**:

- **Hydroxyl Radical (·OH)**: Extremely reactive and short-lived, with a half-life of nanoseconds. It can damage any biomolecule it encounters.
- **Singlet Oxygen ($^1O_2$)**: Highly reactive and generated during photosensitization reactions.

2. **Moderately Reactive Radicals**:

- **Superoxide Anion (O_2^-)**: Less reactive than hydroxyl radicals but can generate more damaging species, such as hydrogen peroxide and hydroxyl radicals.
- **Nitric Oxide (NO·)**: Moderately reactive and acts as a signaling molecule, but can form peroxynitrite ($ONOO^-$) when reacting with superoxide.

3. **Relatively Stable Radicals**:

- **Hydrogen Peroxide (H_2O_2)**: Not a free radical but can generate hydroxyl radicals in the presence of transition metals (Fenton reaction).

6.1.4 Importance of Free Radicals in Biological Systems

Role in Cell Signaling and Immune Response

Free radicals play a crucial role in cell signaling and immune response. They act as secondary messengers, regulating various physiological processes such as cell proliferation, differentiation, and apoptosis.

1. **Cell Signaling**:

- **Nitric Oxide (NO·)**: Acts as a signaling molecule in vasodilation, neurotransmission, and immune response. It regulates blood flow and blood pressure by relaxing vascular smooth muscle.
- **Hydrogen Peroxide (H_2O_2)**: Functions as a signaling molecule in pathways such as the MAPK/ERK and PI3K/Akt pathways, influencing cell growth and survival.

2. **Immune Response**:

- Immune cells, such as neutrophils and macrophages, produce free radicals (e.g., superoxide and nitric oxide) to destroy invading pathogens. This process, known as the respiratory burst, is a critical component of the innate immune response.

Controlled Free Radical Production in Normal Physiology

In normal physiology, free radical production is tightly regulated to maintain cellular homeostasis. Enzymes such as superoxide dismutase (SOD), catalase (CAT), and glutathione peroxidase (GPx) play a key role in controlling free radical levels.

1. **Superoxide Dismutase (SOD)**: Converts superoxide anions (O_2^-) into hydrogen peroxide (H_2O_2) and oxygen (O_2).
2. **Catalase (CAT)**: Breaks down hydrogen peroxide (H_2O_2) into water (H_2O) and oxygen (O_2).
3. **Glutathione Peroxidase (GPx)**: Reduces hydrogen peroxide and lipid peroxides using glutathione as a reducing agent.

Balance Between Free Radicals and Antioxidants

The balance between free radicals and antioxidants is critical for maintaining cellular health. Antioxidants neutralize free radicals by donating electrons, preventing oxidative damage to cellular components.

1. **Endogenous Antioxidants**:

- Enzymes: SOD, CAT, GPx.
- Non-enzymatic molecules: Glutathione, coenzyme Q10, uric acid.

2. **Exogenous Antioxidants**:

- Dietary antioxidants: Vitamin C, vitamin E, carotenoids, polyphenols.

When the production of free radicals exceeds the body's antioxidant capacity, oxidative stress occurs, leading to damage to DNA, proteins, and lipids. This imbalance is associated with the development of chronic diseases such as cardiovascular diseases, cancer, and neurodegenerative disorders.

6.2 Sources of Free Radical Production in Cells

Free radicals are generated in cells through both endogenous (internal) and exogenous (external) sources. Endogenous sources are primarily associated with normal cellular metabolic processes, while exogenous sources involve external factors such as radiation, pollution, and toxins. This section focuses on the **endogenous sources of free radicals** and their mechanisms of production.

6.2.1 Endogenous Sources of Free Radicals

Mitochondrial Electron Transport Chain (ETC) and ATP Production

The mitochondria are the primary site of free radical production in cells due to their role in energy production through oxidative phosphorylation.

1. **Role of Mitochondria in ROS Generation:**

   - During ATP production, electrons are transferred through the electron transport chain (ETC) complexes (I-IV) to molecular oxygen (O_2), forming water (H_2O). However, this process is not 100% efficient, and some electrons can "leak" from the ETC.
   - These leaked electrons react with oxygen, forming **superoxide radicals (O_2^-)**, the primary reactive oxygen species (ROS) generated in mitochondria.

2. **Electron Leakage and Formation of Superoxide Radicals:**

   - Complex I (NADH dehydrogenase) and Complex III (cytochrome bc1 complex) are the major sites of electron leakage in the ETC.
   - Superoxide radicals can further react to form other ROS, such as hydrogen peroxide (H_2O_2) and hydroxyl radicals ($\cdot OH$), through enzymatic and non-enzymatic reactions.

Peroxisomal Metabolism and Oxidative Reactions

Peroxisomes are organelles involved in various oxidative reactions, including the breakdown of fatty acids and the detoxification of harmful substances.

1. **Beta-Oxidation of Fatty Acids**:

   - During the beta-oxidation of fatty acids, peroxisomes produce hydrogen peroxide (H_2O_2) as a byproduct.
   - While peroxisomes contain catalase to break down H_2O_2 into water and oxygen, excess H_2O_2 can leak into the cytoplasm, contributing to oxidative stress.

2. **Hydrogen Peroxide Formation**:

   - Peroxisomal enzymes, such as acyl-CoA oxidase, generate H_2O_2 during fatty acid oxidation.
   - If not properly neutralized, H_2O_2 can diffuse into other cellular compartments and participate in the formation of more reactive ROS, such as hydroxyl radicals ($\cdot$OH).

Enzyme-Mediated Free Radical Production

Several enzymes in the body produce free radicals as part of their normal function, particularly in immune response and metabolic processes.

1. **Role of NADPH Oxidase in Immune Response**:

   - NADPH oxidase is an enzyme complex found in immune cells, such as neutrophils and macrophages.
   - It generates superoxide radicals (O_2^-) as part of the **respiratory burst**, a defense mechanism used to kill invading pathogens.
   - While beneficial for immunity, excessive NADPH oxidase activity can lead to tissue damage and chronic inflammation.

2. **Xanthine Oxidase and Oxidative Stress**:

   - Xanthine oxidase is an enzyme involved in purine metabolism, converting hypoxanthine to xanthine and xanthine to uric acid.
   - During these reactions, xanthine oxidase generates superoxide radicals (O_2^-) and hydrogen peroxide (H_2O_2), contributing to oxidative stress, especially under conditions such as ischemia-reperfusion injury.

Metabolism of Drugs and Xenobiotics

The liver plays a central role in metabolizing drugs and xenobiotics (foreign substances), often generating free radicals as byproducts.

1. **Cytochrome P450 System in Liver Metabolism**:

   - The cytochrome P450 (CYP450) enzyme system is involved in the oxidation of drugs, toxins, and endogenous compounds.
   - During these reactions, CYP450 enzymes can produce ROS, such as superoxide radicals (O_2^-) and hydrogen peroxide (H_2O_2), as byproducts.

2. **Generation of ROS During Drug Metabolism**:

   - Some drugs, such as paracetamol (acetaminophen), undergo redox cycling during metabolism, generating free radicals.
   - For example, the metabolism of paracetamol produces N-acetyl-p-benzoquinone imine (NAPQI), a toxic metabolite that depletes glutathione and increases oxidative stress.

6.2.2 Exogenous Sources of Free Radicals

Exogenous sources of free radicals originate from external factors such as environmental pollutants, radiation, lifestyle choices, and dietary habits. These sources contribute significantly to oxidative stress and are associated with the development of chronic diseases. Below is a detailed exploration of the major exogenous sources of free radicals.

Environmental Pollutants and Toxins

1. **Air Pollution and Heavy Metal Exposure**:

   - Air pollution, including particulate matter (PM2.5 and PM10), nitrogen oxides (NOx), and sulfur dioxide (SO_2), generates free radicals when inhaled. These pollutants can react with cellular components, producing ROS such as superoxide radicals (O_2^-) and hydroxyl radicals ($\cdot OH$).

- Heavy metals, such as lead (Pb), cadmium (Cd), and mercury (Hg), induce oxidative stress by disrupting cellular redox balance. For example, cadmium interferes with antioxidant enzymes like superoxide dismutase (SOD) and glutathione peroxidase (GPx), leading to increased ROS levels.

2. **Pesticides and Industrial Chemicals**:

- Pesticides, such as organophosphates and herbicides, generate free radicals during their metabolism in the body. These chemicals can disrupt mitochondrial function and increase ROS production.
- Industrial chemicals, such as benzene and formaldehyde, undergo redox cycling, producing free radicals that damage DNA, proteins, and lipids.

Ultraviolet (UV) and Ionizing Radiation

1. **UV-Induced DNA Damage**:

- UV radiation, particularly UVB (280–315 nm), penetrates the skin and generates free radicals, such as singlet oxygen ($^1O_2$) and hydroxyl radicals (·OH). These radicals damage DNA, leading to mutations and skin cancer.
- UV radiation also depletes antioxidants like vitamin C and glutathione in the skin, exacerbating oxidative stress.

2. **Radiation Therapy and Oxidative Stress**:

- Ionizing radiation, used in cancer therapy, generates free radicals such as hydroxyl radicals (·OH) through the radiolysis of water. These radicals damage cancer cells but can also harm healthy tissues, leading to side effects such as fibrosis and inflammation.

Tobacco Smoke and Alcohol Consumption

1. **Carcinogenic Free Radicals in Cigarette Smoke**:

- Cigarette smoke contains over 7,000 chemicals, many of which are free radicals or generate free radicals during metabolism. For example, benzo[a]pyrene, a carcinogen in tobacco smoke, undergoes redox cycling, producing ROS that damage DNA and proteins.
- Free radicals in cigarette smoke also deplete antioxidants like vitamin C and vitamin E, increasing oxidative stress in smokers.

2. **Ethanol Metabolism and Oxidative Stress in the Liver**:

- Alcohol consumption leads to the production of free radicals during ethanol metabolism. The enzyme alcohol dehydrogenase converts ethanol to acetaldehyde, which generates ROS such as superoxide radicals (O_2^-) and hydrogen peroxide (H_2O_2).
- Chronic alcohol consumption depletes glutathione, a key antioxidant, and increases lipid peroxidation, contributing to liver damage and diseases such as cirrhosis and hepatocellular carcinoma.

Diet and Processed Foods

1. **Effect of High-Fat and High-Sugar Diets**:

- High-fat diets, particularly those rich in saturated and trans fats, increase oxidative stress by promoting lipid peroxidation. This process generates reactive aldehydes, such as malondialdehyde (MDA), which damage cellular components.
- High-sugar diets lead to the formation of advanced glycation end products (AGEs), which generate ROS and contribute to oxidative stress. AGEs are implicated in the development of diabetes and cardiovascular diseases.

2. **Role of Food Preservatives in Free Radical Formation**:

- Some food preservatives, such as sodium nitrite and butylated hydroxyanisole (BHA), can generate free radicals during metabolism. For example, sodium nitrite reacts with stomach acids to form nitrosamines, which are carcinogenic and produce ROS.
- Processed foods often contain high levels of oxidized fats and sugars, which contribute to oxidative stress when consumed.

6.3 Mechanisms of Free Radical Damage

Free radicals cause cellular damage through various mechanisms, including lipid peroxidation, protein oxidation, and DNA damage. Among these, **lipid peroxidation** is one of the most well-studied and clinically relevant processes. This section provides a detailed explanation of lipid peroxidation, its consequences, biomarkers, and clinical relevance.

6.3.1 Lipid Peroxidation

6.3.1.1 Definition and Process of Lipid Peroxidation

Lipid peroxidation is the oxidative degradation of lipids, particularly polyunsaturated fatty acids (PUFAs), caused by free radicals. It is a chain reaction that propagates oxidative damage in cell membranes and lipoproteins.

1. **Free Radical Attack on Polyunsaturated Fatty Acids (PUFAs):**

   - PUFAs, such as linoleic acid and arachidonic acid, are highly susceptible to free radical attack due to the presence of multiple double bonds in their structure.
   - Free radicals, such as hydroxyl radicals ($\cdot$OH), abstract a hydrogen atom from a methylene group ($-CH_2-$) in the PUFA, forming a lipid radical (L$\cdot$).

2. **Formation of Lipid Peroxides and Aldehydes:**

   - The lipid radical (L$\cdot$) reacts with molecular oxygen (O_2) to form a lipid peroxyl radical (LOO$\cdot$).
   - The lipid peroxyl radical can abstract a hydrogen atom from another PUFA, forming a lipid hydroperoxide (LOOH) and propagating the chain reaction.
   - Lipid hydroperoxides are unstable and decompose into reactive aldehydes, such as malondialdehyde (MDA) and 4-hydroxynonenal (4-HNE), which are highly toxic and can damage cellular components.

6.3.1.2 Consequences of Lipid Peroxidation

Lipid peroxidation has profound effects on cellular structure and function, leading to tissue damage and disease.

1. **Damage to Cell Membranes and Increased Permeability**:

   - Lipid peroxidation disrupts the integrity of cell membranes, leading to increased permeability and loss of membrane function.
   - This can result in the leakage of cellular contents, impaired ion transport, and ultimately cell death.

2. **Impairment of Lipid Signaling Pathways**:

   - Lipid peroxidation alters the structure and function of signaling lipids, such as phospholipids and eicosanoids, disrupting cellular signaling pathways.
   - For example, oxidized phospholipids can activate pro-inflammatory pathways, contributing to chronic inflammation.

3. **Oxidation of Low-Density Lipoprotein (LDL) and Atherosclerosis**:

   - Oxidized LDL (ox-LDL) is a key factor in the development of atherosclerosis. Lipid peroxidation of LDL particles makes them more likely to be taken up by macrophages, forming foam cells and contributing to plaque formation in arterial walls.
   - Ox-LDL also promotes endothelial dysfunction and inflammation, further exacerbating cardiovascular disease.

6.3.1.3 Biomarkers of Lipid Peroxidation

Biomarkers of lipid peroxidation are used to assess oxidative stress and its impact on health.

1. **Malondialdehyde (MDA)**:

   - MDA is one of the most commonly measured biomarkers of lipid peroxidation. It is a reactive aldehyde formed during the decomposition of lipid hydroperoxides.
   - MDA levels can be measured in blood, urine, and tissues using techniques such as the thiobarbituric acid reactive substances (TBARS) assay.

2. **4-Hydroxynonenal (4-HNE)**:

- 4-HNE is another reactive aldehyde formed during lipid peroxidation. It is highly toxic and can form adducts with proteins, DNA, and other biomolecules, impairing their function.
- 4-HNE levels are often measured using immunoassays or mass spectrometry.

6.3.1.4 Clinical Relevance of Lipid Peroxidation

Lipid peroxidation plays a significant role in the pathogenesis of various diseases, particularly cardiovascular and neurodegenerative disorders.

1. **Role in Cardiovascular Diseases**:

- Lipid peroxidation contributes to the development of atherosclerosis, hypertension, and heart failure by promoting oxidative damage to lipids, proteins, and DNA in vascular tissues.
- Elevated levels of MDA and ox-LDL are associated with an increased risk of cardiovascular events, such as heart attacks and strokes.

2. **Impact on Neurodegenerative Diseases**:

- Lipid peroxidation is a key mechanism of neuronal damage in neurodegenerative diseases, such as Alzheimer's disease, Parkinson's disease, and amyotrophic lateral sclerosis (ALS).
- The brain is particularly vulnerable to lipid peroxidation due to its high lipid content and high oxygen consumption. Lipid peroxidation products, such as 4-HNE, can damage neurons and impair cognitive function.

6.3.2 Protein Oxidation

Protein oxidation is a critical mechanism of free radical-induced damage, leading to structural and functional alterations in proteins. This section explores the mechanisms, effects, biomarkers, and clinical implications of protein oxidation.

6.3.2.1 Mechanism of Protein Oxidation

1. **Free Radical Attack on Amino Acid Residues:**

   - Free radicals, such as hydroxyl radicals ($\cdot$OH) and peroxynitrite ($ONOO^-$), target specific amino acid residues in proteins, including cysteine, methionine, histidine, and tyrosine.
   - These residues are particularly susceptible to oxidation due to their reactive side chains. For example, cysteine contains a thiol (-SH) group, which is easily oxidized to form disulfide bonds or sulfenic, sulfinic, and sulfonic acids.

2. **Oxidation of Thiol (-SH) Groups and Carbonyl Formation:**

   - The oxidation of thiol groups in cysteine residues disrupts protein structure and function, as disulfide bonds are critical for maintaining protein conformation.
   - Free radicals can also oxidize amino acid side chains to form protein carbonyls, which are stable markers of protein oxidation. Carbonyl groups are introduced into proteins through direct oxidation of lysine, arginine, proline, and threonine residues or through the reaction of proteins with lipid peroxidation products, such as malondialdehyde (MDA) and 4-hydroxynonenal (4-HNE).

6.3.2.2 Effects of Protein Oxidation

1. **Structural Modifications in Enzymes and Loss of Function:**

   - Oxidation of amino acid residues can alter the three-dimensional structure of proteins, leading to loss of enzymatic activity or changes in protein function.
   - For example, oxidation of cysteine residues in enzymes can disrupt catalytic sites, impairing their ability to bind substrates or cofactors.

2. **Aggregation of Oxidized Proteins and Cellular Toxicity:**

- Oxidized proteins often misfold and aggregate, forming insoluble deposits that are toxic to cells. These aggregates can disrupt cellular function and contribute to cell death.
- Protein aggregates are a hallmark of several neurodegenerative diseases, such as Alzheimer's and Parkinson's disease.

3. **Role in Aging and Neurodegenerative Diseases**:

- Protein oxidation accumulates with age, contributing to the decline in cellular function and the development of age-related diseases.
- In neurodegenerative diseases, oxidized proteins form aggregates, such as amyloid-beta plaques in Alzheimer's disease and alpha-synuclein aggregates in Parkinson's disease, leading to neuronal damage and cognitive decline.

6.3.2.3 Biomarkers of Protein Oxidation

1. **Protein Carbonyls**:

- Protein carbonyls are the most widely used biomarkers of protein oxidation. They are formed by the direct oxidation of amino acid side chains or by the reaction of proteins with reactive aldehydes.
- Protein carbonyl levels can be measured using techniques such as spectrophotometry, ELISA, and Western blotting.

2. **Advanced Oxidation Protein Products (AOPPs)**:

- AOPPs are formed by the reaction of proteins with chlorinated oxidants, such as hypochlorous acid (HOCl), produced by myeloperoxidase in immune cells.
- AOPPs are measured using spectrophotometric methods and are associated with oxidative stress in conditions such as chronic kidney disease and cardiovascular diseases.

6.3.2.4 Clinical Implications of Protein Oxidation

1. **Protein Oxidation in Alzheimer's Disease and Parkinson's Disease**:

   - In Alzheimer's disease, oxidized proteins, such as amyloid-beta and tau, form aggregates that disrupt neuronal function and contribute to cognitive decline.
   - In Parkinson's disease, oxidation of alpha-synuclein leads to the formation of Lewy bodies, which are toxic to dopaminergic neurons.

2. **Role in Muscle Aging and Sarcopenia**:

   - Protein oxidation contributes to muscle aging and the development of sarcopenia, a condition characterized by the loss of muscle mass and strength.
   - Oxidized proteins in muscle cells impair contractile function and promote muscle atrophy, leading to reduced mobility and increased frailty in older adults.

6.3.3 DNA and Nucleic Acid Damage

Free radicals, particularly reactive oxygen species (ROS), can cause significant damage to DNA and nucleic acids, leading to mutations, genomic instability, and disease. This section explores the mechanisms, types, consequences, biomarkers, and clinical implications of DNA damage caused by free radicals.

6.3.3.1 Mechanism of DNA Oxidation

1. **Hydroxyl Radical ($\cdot$OH) Attack on DNA Bases**:

   - The hydroxyl radical ($\cdot$OH) is the most reactive ROS and can directly attack DNA bases, particularly guanine, due to its low redox potential.
   - $\cdot$OH abstracts a hydrogen atom from the DNA base, forming a DNA radical, which reacts with oxygen to produce peroxyl radicals and

ultimately leads to the formation of oxidized DNA products.

2. **Formation of DNA Adducts and Strand Breaks**:

   - Free radicals can cause the formation of DNA adducts, where reactive molecules bind covalently to DNA bases, altering their structure and function.
   - Free radicals can also induce single-strand breaks (SSBs) and double-strand breaks (DSBs) in the DNA backbone, which are highly detrimental to genomic integrity.

6.3.3.2 Types of DNA Damage Caused by Free Radicals

1. **Oxidative Modification of Guanine (8-Oxo-7,8-dihydroguanine)**:

   - Guanine is the most susceptible DNA base to oxidation, forming 8-oxo-7,8-dihydroguanine (8-oxoG), a common marker of oxidative DNA damage.
   - 8-oxoG can mispair with adenine during DNA replication, leading to G:C to T:A transversion mutations.

2. **Single-Strand and Double-Strand DNA Breaks**:

   - Single-strand breaks (SSBs) occur when one strand of the DNA double helix is broken. While SSBs are relatively common and can be repaired, unrepaired SSBs can lead to double-strand breaks (DSBs) during DNA replication.
   - Double-strand breaks (DSBs) are more severe and can lead to chromosomal rearrangements, genomic instability, and cell death if not properly repaired.

6.3.3.3 Consequences of DNA Oxidation

1. **Mutations and Genomic Instability**:

- Oxidative DNA damage can lead to mutations, such as base substitutions, insertions, and deletions, which can disrupt gene function and contribute to genomic instability.
- Genomic instability is a hallmark of cancer and other diseases, as it promotes the accumulation of mutations and chromosomal abnormalities.

2. **Activation of Oncogenes and Suppression of Tumor Suppressor Genes**:

- Oxidative DNA damage can activate oncogenes, such as RAS and MYC, by introducing mutations that enhance their expression or activity.
- It can also inactivate tumor suppressor genes, such as TP53 and BRCA1, by introducing mutations that disrupt their function, leading to uncontrolled cell proliferation and cancer development.

3. **Role in Carcinogenesis and Age-Related Diseases**:

- Oxidative DNA damage is a key driver of carcinogenesis, as it promotes the accumulation of mutations that lead to cancer initiation and progression.
- It also contributes to age-related diseases, such as neurodegenerative disorders, by causing DNA damage in neurons and other cells, leading to functional decline and cell death.

6.3.3.4 Biomarkers of DNA Damage

1. **8-Hydroxydeoxyguanosine (8-OHdG)**:

- 8-OHdG is the most widely used biomarker of oxidative DNA damage. It is formed by the oxidation of guanine and can be detected in urine, blood, and tissues using techniques such as ELISA, HPLC, and mass spectrometry.
- Elevated levels of 8-OHdG are associated with increased oxidative stress and are linked to cancer, neurodegenerative diseases, and aging.

2. **Comet Assay for DNA Strand Breaks**:

- The comet assay (single-cell gel electrophoresis) is a sensitive technique used to measure DNA strand breaks in individual cells.
- Cells are embedded in agarose, lysed, and subjected to electrophoresis. DNA strand breaks cause the DNA to migrate, forming a "comet tail," which is quantified to assess DNA damage.

6.3.3.5 Clinical Implications of DNA Damage

1. **Free Radical-Induced Mutations in Cancer Development**:

- Oxidative DNA damage is a major contributor to cancer development, as it introduces mutations that activate oncogenes and inactivate tumor suppressor genes.
- For example, oxidative damage to the TP53 gene, a key tumor suppressor, is commonly observed in various cancers, including lung, breast, and colon cancer.

2. **Role of DNA Oxidation in Neurodegenerative Disorders**:

- Oxidative DNA damage is implicated in neurodegenerative diseases, such as Alzheimer's disease, Parkinson's disease, and amyotrophic lateral sclerosis (ALS).
- In Alzheimer's disease, oxidative damage to neuronal DNA contributes to cognitive decline and neuronal death. In Parkinson's disease, oxidative damage to mitochondrial DNA impairs energy production and promotes dopaminergic neuron loss.

SEVEN
MEASUREMENT AND BIOMARKERS OF OXIDATIVE STRESS

7.1 Methods to Measure Free Radicals and Oxidative Damage

7.1.1 Introduction to Oxidative Stress Measurement

Definition of Oxidative Stress

Oxidative stress refers to the imbalance between reactive oxygen species (ROS) and the body's ability to neutralize these harmful molecules through its antioxidant defense system. ROS include free radicals such as superoxide anion (O_2^-), hydroxyl radical ($OH\cdot$), and peroxyl radical ($ROO\cdot$), as well as non-radical reactive oxygen species like hydrogen peroxide (H_2O_2). These reactive molecules can cause damage to cellular structures, including lipids, proteins, and DNA, which is often referred to as oxidative damage. This process plays a significant role in the development of various chronic diseases, including cardiovascular diseases, cancer, diabetes, neurodegenerative diseases, and aging.

Importance of Measuring Free Radicals in Biological Systems

The measurement of free radicals and oxidative damage is crucial for understanding the extent of oxidative stress in the body. Free radicals are highly reactive molecules that can cause molecular damage to essential biomolecules, which may lead to cellular dysfunction and disease progression. Since free radicals are involved in the initiation and propagation of oxidative damage, tracking their levels provides insights into the early stages of diseases such as atherosclerosis, Alzheimer's disease, and cancer.

Understanding oxidative stress through measurement also helps assess the effectiveness of antioxidant therapies, which are designed to neutralize free radicals. Monitoring oxidative stress markers is particularly important in clinical trials for the development of oxidative stress-related therapies, as it allows researchers to determine whether interventions, such as dietary supplements or pharmaceutical drugs, are successful in reducing oxidative damage.

Challenges in Direct Measurement of Free Radicals

Direct measurement of free radicals in biological systems presents several challenges due to the high reactivity and short half-lives of these molecules. Free radicals, such as hydroxyl radicals and superoxide anions, are often present in low concentrations, and their transient nature makes it difficult to capture and quantify them directly. Moreover, free radicals rapidly react with other molecules in their environment, which makes isolating them for measurement challenging.

To address these difficulties, indirect methods are often used to measure oxidative damage by detecting oxidation products or secondary byproducts that result from free radical reactions. These methods are more practical because they can provide information about oxidative stress levels over a longer period, even though they do not directly measure the free radicals themselves.

7.1.2 Direct vs. Indirect Measurement Methods

Direct Methods: Electron Paramagnetic Resonance (EPR) Spectroscopy

Electron Paramagnetic Resonance (EPR) spectroscopy, also known as Electron Spin Resonance (ESR), is one of the few direct methods used to detect free radicals in biological systems. EPR works by detecting the unpaired electrons that are characteristic of free radicals. Free radicals are molecules that contain one or more unpaired electrons, making them highly reactive. EPR can measure the electron spin, providing detailed information about the type, concentration, and environment of free radicals in a sample.

In EPR spectroscopy, a sample is exposed to a magnetic field, which causes the unpaired electrons in free radicals to align in a particular manner. When electromagnetic radiation (microwaves) is applied, the electrons in the free radicals absorb energy, transitioning between different energy levels. By detecting these energy transitions, EPR allows for the identification and quantification of the free radicals present.

Advantages of EPR

- Direct detection of free radicals in vivo and in vitro.
- Provides detailed information about the structure and environment of free radicals, such as reactivity, concentration, and location.
- Can detect a variety of free radicals, including superoxide anion (O2-), hydroxyl radical (OH·), and alkyl radicals.

Limitations of EPR

- Sensitivity: EPR is less sensitive than some other techniques, requiring higher concentrations of free radicals for reliable measurements.
- Cost and complexity: EPR equipment is expensive, and the technique requires specialized training to operate.
- Detection issues: EPR is limited in detecting radicals that are present in very low concentrations or are short-lived due to their rapid reactivity.

Indirect Methods: Measurement of Oxidative Stress Biomarkers

Indirect methods are typically used in clinical and research settings due to their practicality and ease of use. These methods do not measure free radicals directly but rather quantify the products that are produced as a result of oxidative damage. Oxidative stress biomarkers are indicators of the oxidative damage to lipids, proteins, DNA, and other cellular components. By measuring these biomarkers, researchers can infer the level of oxidative stress occurring within the body.

Some common biomarkers used to assess oxidative stress include:

Lipid Peroxidation Products (e.g., Malondialdehyde - MDA)

Lipid peroxidation is a common consequence of oxidative stress, and MDA is a byproduct formed when polyunsaturated fatty acids in the cell membrane undergo oxidative damage. MDA levels are often used as an indicator of lipid peroxidation in tissues and fluids.

- Measurement Methods: MDA can be quantified using Thiobarbituric Acid Reactive Substances (TBARS) assays, where MDA reacts with thiobarbituric acid to form a colored product that can be measured spectrophotometrically.

Protein Carbonyls

Protein carbonylation occurs when free radicals attack proteins, leading to the formation of carbonyl groups on amino acids. These carbonyl groups are stable markers of oxidative damage to proteins.

- Measurement Methods: Carbonyl content is measured using dinitrophenylhydrazine (DNPH), which reacts with carbonyl groups to form a stable derivative, allowing quantification by spectrophotometry or HPLC.

8-OHdG (8-Hydroxy-2'-Deoxyguanosine)

8-OHdG is a biomarker of oxidative damage to DNA. It is produced when ROS, particularly hydroxyl radicals, attack guanine bases in DNA. Elevated levels of 8-OHdG in biological fluids, especially urine, are indicative of oxidative DNA damage, a key event in cancer and aging.

- Measurement Methods: 8-OHdG is typically measured using high-performance liquid chromatography (HPLC) or ELISA assays.

F2-Isoprostanes

F2-isoprostanes are prostaglandin-like compounds formed during the peroxidation of arachidonic acid. They are considered reliable biomarkers for oxidative stress and lipid damage.

- Measurement Methods: F2-isoprostanes are often quantified using gas chromatography-mass spectrometry (GC-MS) or enzyme immunoassay (EIA).

Glutathione and Superoxide Dismutase (SOD)

Glutathione (GSH) is a critical antioxidant in the body, and SOD is an enzyme that protects cells from oxidative damage by converting superoxide radicals into hydrogen peroxide and oxygen. Reduced levels of GSH and altered SOD activity are indicative of oxidative stress.

- Measurement Methods: GSH levels can be measured using spectrophotometric assays, while SOD activity can be quantified using colorimetric or electrophoretic methods.

7.1.3 Lipid Peroxidation Products

7.1.3.1 Mechanism of Lipid Peroxidation

Lipid peroxidation is a biochemical process in which polyunsaturated fatty acids (PUFAs) in cell membranes undergo oxidative degradation due to free radical attack. It is one of the most significant indicators of oxidative stress in biological systems and contributes to cellular damage in various tissues, including the liver, brain, and heart. Lipid peroxidation plays a critical role in the pathophysiology of cardiovascular diseases, neurodegenerative diseases, cancer, and aging.

Free Radical Attack on Polyunsaturated Fatty Acids (PUFAs)

The process of lipid peroxidation begins when reactive oxygen species (ROS) or free radicals, such as the hydroxyl radical (OH·) or peroxyl radical (ROO·), attack polyunsaturated fatty acids (PUFAs). These fatty acids are the building blocks of the lipid bilayer of cell membranes, and they contain multiple double bonds in their structure, making them highly susceptible to oxidation.

- The initial step involves the abstraction of a hydrogen atom from the methylene group (–CH2–) between the carbon-carbon double bonds in the PUFA chain. This produces a lipid radical (L·).
- The lipid radical then reacts with oxygen to form a peroxyl radical (LOO·), which is a highly reactive species capable of attacking another PUFA molecule, propagating the chain reaction of lipid oxidation.

- This process is known as the autocatalytic chain reaction, where the formation of lipid peroxides (LOOH) occurs. As more lipid peroxides are generated, the damage to cell membranes increases, leading to membrane instability and functional impairment of cells.

Formation of Lipid Peroxides and Reactive Aldehydes

As lipid peroxidation progresses, the lipid peroxides formed (LOOH) are unstable and can break down into smaller reactive products, which include reactive aldehydes like malondialdehyde (MDA) and 4-hydroxynonenal (4-HNE). These products contribute to further cellular damage by interacting with proteins, DNA, and other cellular components.

- Lipid peroxides (LOOH): These compounds form when the peroxyl radical (LOO·) reacts with oxygen and are initially unstable, often breaking down into aldehydes. These lipid peroxides are cytotoxic and can further propagate oxidative stress.
- Reactive Aldehydes:

  - Malondialdehyde (MDA): One of the most well-known and widely studied aldehydes produced during lipid peroxidation. MDA is highly reactive and can form adducts with proteins and DNA, resulting in protein dysfunction and mutagenic DNA damage.
  - 4-Hydroxynonenal (4-HNE): Another important aldehyde generated during lipid peroxidation, 4-HNE, is a potent genotoxic agent and has been implicated in the development of various chronic diseases. 4-HNE can bind to proteins and form adducts, leading to cellular dysfunction and inflammation.

The breakdown of lipid peroxides into aldehydes like MDA and 4-HNE causes cross-linking of proteins and structural damage to DNA, which can lead to cell death, mutagenesis, and the initiation of inflammatory processes.

In conclusion, lipid peroxidation is a critical process in oxidative stress that involves the attack of free radicals on polyunsaturated fatty acids in cell membranes. This process leads to the formation of lipid peroxides and reactive aldehydes, which contribute to cellular damage, inflammation, and the development of chronic diseases. Understanding this process is crucial for developing strategies to prevent oxidative damage and mitigate the effects of oxidative stress in the body.

7.1.3.2 Methods for Measuring Lipid Peroxidation

Lipid peroxidation is a significant marker of oxidative stress and is involved in the pathogenesis of numerous diseases. As such, accurately measuring lipid peroxidation and its byproducts is crucial for evaluating oxidative damage in biological systems. Several techniques have been developed for quantifying lipid peroxidation, including Thiobarbituric Acid Reactive Substances (TBARS) Assay, High-Performance Liquid Chromatography (HPLC), and Gas Chromatography-Mass Spectrometry (GC-MS). Each method has its advantages, applications, and limitations.

Thiobarbituric Acid Reactive Substances (TBARS) Assay

Principle and Procedure

The TBARS assay is one of the most widely used methods for measuring lipid peroxidation, particularly the formation of malondialdehyde (MDA), which is a major byproduct of lipid peroxidation. The TBARS assay is based on the reaction between MDA and thiobarbituric acid (TBA), which results in the formation of a pink chromogen with an absorbance maximum at 532 nm. The amount of the chromogen produced is directly proportional to the concentration of MDA and other reactive aldehydes present in the sample.

- Procedure: The procedure typically involves adding TBA to a sample, followed by heating to allow the reaction to occur. The sample is then cooled, and the absorbance is measured spectrophotometrically at 532 nm. The concentration of TBARS is calculated based on a standard curve generated using known concentrations of MDA.
- Applications: The TBARS assay is commonly used to evaluate lipid peroxidation in tissues, serum, or plasma. It is particularly useful for assessing the extent of oxidative stress in various diseases, such as cardiovascular diseases, neurodegenerative disorders, cancer, and diabetes.

Applications and Limitations

- Applications: The TBARS assay is widely used because it is simple, inexpensive, and relatively quick. It is suitable for screening large numbers of samples and is often used in research on oxidative stress, inflammation, and antioxidant therapies.
- Limitations: Although the TBARS assay is useful for detecting lipid peroxidation, it is not specific to MDA alone. Other substances that can react with TBA, such as protein carbonyls, can interfere with the assay, leading to false positives. Additionally, the complexity of biological samples may lead to overestimation or underestimation of lipid peroxidation levels.

High-Performance Liquid Chromatography (HPLC) for Lipid Peroxidation Markers

Principle and Procedure

High-Performance Liquid Chromatography (HPLC) is a more advanced and sensitive method for measuring lipid peroxidation markers, such as MDA, 4-hydroxynonenal (4-HNE), and other aldehydes. In HPLC, the sample is separated into its components based on size, charge, and polarity, and then analyzed by a detector such as UV-Vis or fluorescence detection.

- Procedure: To measure lipid peroxidation markers, biological samples are first extracted using an appropriate solvent, and then the extract is injected into the HPLC column. The separation of aldehydes and other peroxidation products occurs based on their unique chemical properties. The peaks corresponding to different compounds are identified, and the concentration of the peroxidation markers is determined by comparison with standard curves.
- Applications: HPLC is ideal for the quantification of individual lipid peroxidation products like MDA, 4-HNE, F2-isoprostanes, and other oxidative stress markers. It is commonly used in biomarker studies, clinical diagnostics, and pharmaceutical research to assess the effectiveness of antioxidant interventions.

Applications and Limitations

- Applications: HPLC provides high sensitivity and selectivity for detecting a wide range of lipid peroxidation markers. It can be used in complex biological matrices, including plasma, serum, and tissue samples, and is suitable for quantitative analysis of oxidative stress biomarkers in both clinical and research settings.
- Limitations: While HPLC is highly sensitive, it is more time-consuming and requires specialized equipment and technical expertise. The cost of HPLC systems and maintenance can also be a limitation. Furthermore, sample preparation can be complicated, and the method is generally not suitable for high-throughput analysis.

Gas Chromatography-Mass Spectrometry (GC-MS) for Lipid Peroxidation Analysis

Principle and Procedure

Gas Chromatography-Mass Spectrometry (GC-MS) is a powerful technique used for quantifying lipid peroxidation products with high specificity and sensitivity. GC-MS combines the separation power of gas chromatography with the identification and quantification capabilities of mass spectrometry. This technique is particularly useful for detecting and analyzing volatile compounds produced during lipid peroxidation, such as MDA, 4-HNE, and isoprostanes.

- Procedure: In GC-MS, the sample is first derivatized to increase the volatility of the target molecules. The sample is then injected into a gas chromatograph, where it is separated based on volatility and chemical properties. The separated compounds are detected by the mass spectrometer, which provides a detailed mass spectrum that can be used for identification and quantification.
- Applications: GC-MS is particularly useful for detecting low-concentration lipid peroxidation products and providing detailed information about their molecular structure. It is highly sensitive and can be used for quantifying lipid peroxidation products in complex biological samples.

Applications and Limitations

- Applications: GC-MS is highly effective for identifying and quantifying lipid peroxidation markers, especially volatile aldehydes such as MDA and 4-HNE. It is widely used in research studies that aim to assess oxidative stress in disease states and for evaluating antioxidant interventions.
- Limitations: GC-MS requires sample derivatization, which can be time-consuming and may introduce errors if not performed correctly. The technique also requires high-cost equipment, and specialized knowledge to operate. It is also less suitable for high-throughput analysis due to its relatively low sample throughput.

7.1.3.3 Clinical and Research Applications

Lipid peroxidation markers have become essential tools in both clinical and research settings for assessing oxidative damage and evaluating the progression of various diseases. The products of lipid peroxidation, particularly malondialdehyde (MDA) and 4-hydroxynonenal (4-HNE), are widely used as biomarkers to measure the extent of oxidative stress in biological systems. These markers offer valuable insights into the pathogenesis of diseases such as cardiovascular diseases (CVDs), metabolic disorders, and neurodegenerative diseases. Their use in monitoring disease progression, evaluating therapeutic interventions, and understanding disease mechanisms makes them crucial in clinical diagnostics and pharmacological research.

Use of Lipid Peroxidation Markers in Cardiovascular Diseases

Cardiovascular diseases (CVDs) are closely linked to oxidative stress, as free radicals and reactive oxygen species (ROS) contribute to the damage of vascular endothelial cells, lipid oxidation, and the development of atherosclerotic plaques. Lipid peroxidation is a key process involved in the pathogenesis of atherosclerosis, where oxidized LDL (oxLDL) triggers inflammation and the formation of plaque in the arteries. The assessment of lipid peroxidation markers provides critical insights into early vascular damage and the degree of oxidative stress that contributes to CVD development.

Clinical Applications

- Monitoring Atherosclerosis: Lipid peroxidation markers such as MDA and F2-isoprostanes are used to evaluate the oxidative damage in blood vessels. Elevated levels of these markers indicate increased oxidative stress and a higher risk for the development of atherosclerosis and coronary artery disease. Clinically, measuring these markers helps predict cardiovascular risk and can aid in early diagnosis.
- Evaluating Antioxidant Therapies: Antioxidant treatments, such as vitamin E supplementation or omega-3 fatty acid therapy, are often used in the management of CVDs. Measuring the levels of lipid peroxidation products before and after treatment provides insights into the effectiveness of antioxidant interventions in reducing oxidative damage and protecting against further cardiovascular events.

Research Applications

In research, lipid peroxidation markers are used in experimental models to understand the role of oxidative stress in CVD pathogenesis. For example, researchers often evaluate the effects of dietary changes, exercise, or pharmaceutical interventions on oxidative stress in animal models of atherosclerosis or hypertension. The measurement of MDA, 4-HNE, and lipid peroxides serves as an indicator of vascular oxidative damage and the effectiveness of therapeutic strategies.

Role in Monitoring Oxidative Damage in Metabolic Disorders

Metabolic disorders, such as type 2 diabetes, obesity, and non-alcoholic fatty liver disease (NAFLD), are often associated with chronic oxidative stress, which exacerbates insulin resistance, inflammatory pathways, and cellular dysfunction. Lipid peroxidation markers play an important role in monitoring the extent of oxidative damage in these conditions, offering insights into disease progression and response to therapy.

Clinical Applications

- Type 2 Diabetes and Insulin Resistance: In diabetes, oxidative stress contributes to β-cell dysfunction and insulin resistance. Elevated lipid peroxidation products, such as MDA, are used as biomarkers to assess the level of oxidative damage in diabetic patients. This information is valuable in understanding the pathophysiology of diabetes and in evaluating the effectiveness of antioxidant therapies, such as vitamin C or E supplementation, in improving insulin sensitivity and reducing oxidative stress.

- Non-Alcoholic Fatty Liver Disease (NAFLD): In NAFLD, lipid peroxidation of hepatic lipids leads to liver damage and inflammation. The measurement of MDA and 4-HNE in liver biopsy samples or serum is commonly used to assess the extent of liver injury and fatty acid oxidation. These markers are also used to monitor the efficacy of treatments such as antioxidants or lifestyle changes (e.g., dietary modifications and exercise).

Research Applications

In metabolic research, lipid peroxidation markers are frequently used to study the relationship between oxidative stress and insulin resistance in experimental models of obesity and type 2 diabetes. Researchers often use animal models to evaluate how dietary interventions (such as high-fat diets) or pharmacological treatments (such as metformin or antioxidant compounds) affect oxidative stress and the development of metabolic complications. By measuring markers like MDA, researchers can track the progression of oxidative damage and evaluate the effectiveness of therapeutic interventions.

7.1.4 Lipid Hydroperoxides

7.1.4.1 Formation and Role in Oxidative Stress

Lipid hydroperoxides are primary products of lipid peroxidation, formed when free radicals attack polyunsaturated fatty acids (PUFAs) in biological membranes. This process is part of the oxidative stress pathway and plays a key role in cellular dysfunction. The peroxidation of membrane phospholipids is one of the earliest and most significant effects of oxidative stress, and the resultant lipid hydroperoxides contribute to the progression of cellular damage and the development of various diseases.

Peroxidation of Membrane Phospholipids

Membrane phospholipids, which contain polyunsaturated fatty acids, are particularly vulnerable to oxidation because of the high reactivity of their double bonds. Free radicals, especially hydroxyl radicals (OH·) and peroxyl radicals (ROO·), can abstract a hydrogen atom from the methylene group between the carbon-carbon double bonds in these fatty acids, initiating lipid peroxidation. This leads to the formation of lipid peroxyl radicals, which react with nearby molecules of phospholipids, creating lipid hydroperoxides.

The lipid hydroperoxides formed are highly unstable and can further degrade into various secondary products, such as malondialdehyde (MDA) and 4-hydroxynonenal (4-HNE). These degradation products are highly toxic and contribute to the damage of lipid membranes, proteins, and DNA, initiating a cascade of cellular events that lead to inflammation, cellular dysfunction, and cell death.

Role of Lipid Hydroperoxides in Cellular Dysfunction

Lipid hydroperoxides play a significant role in cellular dysfunction by disrupting membrane integrity and promoting inflammatory pathways. Their accumulation in membranes leads to decreased fluidity and altered function of membrane-bound proteins, including receptors, transporters, and enzymes. The damage to lipid membranes triggers lipid signaling pathways, which can activate inflammatory mediators such as cyclooxygenase (COX) and lipoxygenase (LOX), further exacerbating oxidative stress and cellular injury.

In addition, lipid hydroperoxides and their breakdown products like 4-HNE can form adducts with proteins and DNA, leading to protein malfunction, mutagenesis, and increased apoptosis. In tissues such as the heart, brain, and liver, the effects of lipid hydroperoxide accumulation are linked to the development of chronic diseases such as atherosclerosis, neurodegenerative diseases, and liver injury.

7.1.4.2 Techniques for Measuring Lipid Hydroperoxides

Several methods are employed to quantify lipid hydroperoxides in biological systems. These methods generally rely on detecting oxidative products or secondary byproducts produced during lipid peroxidation. Among the most widely used techniques are the Ferrous Oxidation-Xylenol Orange (FOX) assay, chemiluminescence-based detection, and spectrophotometric/fluorometric assays.

Ferrous Oxidation-Xylenol Orange (FOX) Assay

The FOX assay is a sensitive and widely used method for measuring lipid hydroperoxides. It is based on the reaction of lipid hydroperoxides with ferrous ions (Fe^{2+}), resulting in the formation of a colored complex that can be quantified by measuring absorbance at 560 nm.

- Principle and Reaction Mechanism: In the FOX assay, ferrous ions (Fe^{2+}) react with lipid hydroperoxides to produce ferric ions (Fe^{3+}) and hydroxyl radicals ($OH\cdot$). These ferric ions then react with xylenol orange, a dye that produces a color change when it forms a complex with Fe^{3+}.
- Sensitivity and Specificity: The FOX assay is highly sensitive and can detect low levels of lipid hydroperoxides in biological samples. However, it is not entirely specific to lipid hydroperoxides, as other oxidative byproducts may also react with the ferrous ions. Despite this, the method is widely used in clinical and research applications for quantifying oxidative stress in tissues.

Chemiluminescence-based Detection

Chemiluminescence detection methods are also used to measure lipid hydroperoxides in biological samples. In these methods, the light emitted from the reaction of lipid hydroperoxides with certain chemiluminescent probes is measured. The intensity of the emitted light is directly proportional to the concentration of lipid hydroperoxides in the sample.

- Principle and Reaction Mechanism: The chemiluminescent reaction involves the oxidation of a luminol-based probe in the presence of lipid hydroperoxides, which results in the emission of light. This technique offers high sensitivity and can be used for real-time measurements of lipid hydroperoxides in biological systems.
- Sensitivity and Specificity: Chemiluminescence-based methods are very sensitive and are capable of detecting low concentrations of lipid hydroperoxides, making them ideal for early detection of oxidative stress in clinical diagnostics. However, the specificity of these assays can be affected by the presence of other reactive species in the sample.

Spectrophotometric and Fluorometric Assays

Spectrophotometric and fluorometric assays are commonly used for detecting lipid hydroperoxides and their breakdown products. In these assays, the sample is reacted with a specific reagent that changes color or fluorescence upon interaction with lipid peroxidation products.

- Principle and Reaction Mechanism: For spectrophotometric assays, a colorimetric reaction occurs between lipid peroxides and certain reagents, such as thiobarbituric acid or xylenol orange, resulting in the production of a colored complex that can be measured at a specific wavelength. For fluorometric assays, fluorescent probes are used to detect oxidative damage by measuring the emitted fluorescence when the probe reacts with lipid peroxidation products.
- Sensitivity and Specificity: These assays offer good sensitivity and are suitable for routine measurement of lipid peroxidation. However, their specificity can be limited by the presence of other reactive species or by sample matrix interference.

7.1.4.3 *Clinical Relevance of Lipid Hydroperoxide Measurement*

Lipid hydroperoxides are important biomarkers of oxidative damage in clinical settings, as their levels reflect the degree of oxidative stress occurring in tissues. Measuring lipid hydroperoxide levels is crucial for understanding the progression of several diseases and for assessing the efficacy of antioxidant therapies.

Lipid Hydroperoxide Levels in Atherosclerosis

In atherosclerosis, oxidative stress plays a pivotal role in the development of plaques in the arterial walls. Lipid peroxidation leads to the formation of oxidized low-density lipoprotein (oxLDL), which is a key factor in the initiation and progression of atherosclerosis. Elevated levels of lipid hydroperoxides have been found in patients with coronary artery disease and are used as a marker of vascular oxidative stress. Monitoring lipid hydroperoxide levels in patients can help assess the severity of atherosclerotic plaque formation and evaluate the effectiveness of antioxidant interventions.

Oxidative Lipid Damage in Neurodegenerative Diseases

In neurodegenerative diseases such as Alzheimer's disease and Parkinson's disease, oxidative stress is involved in the degeneration of neural tissues. Lipid hydroperoxides, particularly 4-HNE, are elevated in the brain of patients with these conditions. Measuring lipid hydroperoxide levels in cerebrospinal fluid or brain tissue is crucial for diagnosing and monitoring the progression of these diseases. Elevated lipid peroxidation markers can be used to assess the extent of oxidative damage and may also serve as potential targets for therapeutic intervention.

7.1.5 Malondialdehyde (MDA) as a Biomarker

7.1.5.1 Formation of Malondialdehyde (MDA)

Malondialdehyde (MDA) is one of the most widely studied biomarkers for lipid peroxidation and oxidative stress. MDA is a reactive aldehyde produced as a secondary product during the breakdown of lipid hydroperoxides (such as lipid peroxyl radicals). The process begins when polyunsaturated fatty acids (PUFAs) in cell membranes undergo oxidative damage due to the action of free radicals, leading to the formation of lipid peroxides. These lipid peroxides are unstable and, upon further degradation, generate MDA along with other reactive aldehydes like 4-hydroxynonenal (4-HNE).

- Breakdown of Lipid Peroxides: Lipid hydroperoxides break down into MDA through a series of complex reactions, including the cleavage of the peroxy radical bond. This breakdown is facilitated by enzymatic processes or spontaneous thermal degradation. The reactivity of MDA with cellular components, such as proteins, lipids, and DNA, leads to adduct formation, which contributes to oxidative damage and plays a role in disease progression.
- Reactivity and Stability of MDA: MDA is highly reactive due to its aldehyde group, which allows it to form adducts with amine groups in proteins and guanine bases in DNA. These reactions lead to the formation of protein-carbonyl adducts and DNA mutations, making MDA a potent indicator of oxidative damage. MDA itself is relatively stable and can be measured in biological samples like plasma, serum, or urine, making it a useful marker for assessing systemic oxidative stress.

7.1.5.2 Analytical Methods for MDA Measurement

There are several methods used to quantify MDA in biological systems. These methods range from colorimetric assays to more advanced techniques like Liquid Chromatography-Mass Spectrometry (LC-MS) and Gas Chromatography (GC). The most commonly used methods for MDA measurement include the TBARS (Thiobarbituric Acid Reactive Substances) assay, LC-MS, and GC methods.

TBARS Assay for MDA Detection

The TBARS assay is the most widely used method for detecting MDA in biological samples. In this assay, MDA reacts with thiobarbituric acid (TBA) to form a colored complex, which can be quantified spectrophotometrically. The intensity of the color is proportional to the concentration of MDA in the sample.

- Reaction with Thiobarbituric Acid (TBA): MDA reacts with thiobarbituric acid under acidic conditions to form a pink chromogen. This reaction is specific for MDA, but can also detect other aldehydes, which can sometimes lead to false positives.
- Fluorometric and Colorimetric Detection: The TBARS assay can be colorimetrically quantified by measuring the absorbance at 532 nm, or fluorometrically by detecting the emitted fluorescence. Fluorometric detection is generally more sensitive than colorimetric methods, but both techniques are widely used in clinical diagnostics and research for assessing oxidative stress.

Liquid Chromatography-Mass Spectrometry (LC-MS) for MDA Quantification

LC-MS is a highly sensitive and specific method for quantifying MDA in biological matrices. This method involves separating MDA from complex biological samples using liquid chromatography and then identifying and quantifying it using mass spectrometry.

- Principle: In LC-MS, MDA is typically derivatized to form a stable compound that can be detected by mass spectrometry. The chromatographic separation ensures that MDA is separated from other reactive aldehydes and interfering substances in the sample, allowing for accurate quantification.
- Applications: LC-MS is considered one of the gold-standard methods for MDA detection due to its high sensitivity, accuracy, and specificity. It

is used in research settings to measure trace levels of MDA in tissues, plasma, and urine. However, the method requires expensive equipment, skilled operators, and is time-consuming.

Gas Chromatography (GC) Methods for MDA Detection

Gas Chromatography (GC) is another technique for measuring MDA, particularly when the compound needs to be separated and quantified in the presence of other aldehydes and complex mixtures. In GC, MDA is typically derivatized into volatile compounds to improve detection and separation.

- Principle: GC methods use capillary columns to separate MDA and other aldehydes based on their volatility. After separation, the aldehydes can be detected using flame ionization detection (FID) or mass spectrometry (GC-MS).
- Applications: GC methods are highly sensitive and can provide detailed data on the identity and quantity of MDA in biological samples. This method is widely used in research to study oxidative damage in human diseases, including cancer and neurodegenerative disorders. However, it requires specialized equipment and expertise, making it less accessible for routine clinical use.

7.1.5.3 Clinical Importance of MDA Measurement

The measurement of MDA levels has significant clinical relevance as it serves as a marker of oxidative stress in a variety of diseases. Elevated MDA levels are associated with cellular damage, inflammation, and disease progression, making it a useful biomarker for assessing disease severity, monitoring therapeutic efficacy, and evaluating the effectiveness of antioxidant interventions.

MDA as a Marker for Oxidative Stress-Related Diseases

MDA is commonly used as a biomarker for oxidative damage in diseases such as cardiovascular diseases, diabetes, neurodegenerative diseases, and cancer. In cardiovascular diseases, for example, oxidized LDL and MDA are elevated in atherosclerosis, indicating the presence of oxidative stress and endothelial damage. In neurodegenerative diseases such as Alzheimer's and Parkinson's disease, increased levels of MDA have been linked to neuronal degeneration, contributing to the pathology of these diseases.

Correlation of MDA Levels with Metabolic Syndrome

MDA levels are often elevated in individuals with metabolic syndrome, a cluster of risk factors for type 2 diabetes, hypertension, obesity, and cardiovascular diseases. Elevated MDA reflects increased oxidative stress, which plays a central role in the development and progression of these disorders. Therefore, measuring MDA levels in metabolic syndrome can help assess oxidative damage and potentially predict future cardiovascular events and insulin resistance.

7.2 Biomarkers in Free Radical Studies

7.2.1 Introduction to Oxidative Stress Biomarkers

Oxidative stress biomarkers are critical tools used to measure the extent of oxidative damage caused by free radicals and reactive oxygen species (ROS) in biological systems. These biomarkers are essential for understanding the role of oxidative stress in various diseases and for assessing the effectiveness of antioxidant therapies. Oxidative stress occurs when there is an imbalance between reactive species and the body's antioxidant defense systems, leading to cellular damage, inflammation, and the initiation of disease processes. By detecting and quantifying oxidative stress biomarkers, researchers and clinicians can assess oxidative damage at the cellular and molecular levels.

Definition and Importance of Oxidative Biomarkers

Oxidative biomarkers are molecules that are produced as a result of oxidative stress and can serve as indicators of oxidative damage to lipids, proteins, and DNA. These biomarkers are typically measured in biological samples such as blood, urine, plasma, and tissues. By quantifying the levels of these biomarkers, it is possible to determine the degree of oxidative damage and monitor the progression of diseases related to oxidative stress.

The importance of oxidative biomarkers lies in their ability to provide a quantitative assessment of oxidative damage, allowing for early disease detection, monitoring disease progression, and evaluating the effectiveness of therapies aimed at reducing oxidative stress. In clinical settings, these biomarkers are widely used to evaluate the risk of chronic diseases, such as cardiovascular diseases, diabetes, neurodegenerative diseases, and cancer, all of which have a significant oxidative stress component.

Criteria for an Ideal Biomarker of Oxidative Stress

An ideal oxidative stress biomarker should have the following characteristics:

- Specificity: The biomarker should specifically reflect oxidative damage and not be influenced by other factors such as inflammation or infection.
- Sensitivity: The biomarker should be able to detect even low levels of oxidative stress in biological samples.
- Non-invasiveness: It should be possible to measure the biomarker using non-invasive techniques, such as blood tests or urine analysis.
- Stability: The biomarker should remain stable in biological samples over time to allow for accurate measurements.
- Correlates with disease: The levels of the biomarker should correlate with the severity of oxidative damage and the extent of disease.

Currently, biomarkers for lipid oxidation, protein oxidation, and DNA oxidation are some of the most studied in oxidative stress research.

7.2.2 Classification of Oxidative Stress Biomarkers

Oxidative stress biomarkers can be classified into three major categories based on the type of biomolecular damage they reflect: lipid oxidation biomarkers, protein oxidation biomarkers, and DNA oxidation biomarkers. Each category provides valuable information about the type of oxidative damage occurring in the body and the extent of cellular dysfunction.

Lipid Oxidation Biomarkers

Lipid oxidation biomarkers reflect the damage to lipid membranes, primarily caused by free radical attacks on polyunsaturated fatty acids (PUFAs). These biomarkers are important indicators of oxidative stress and are often used to study cardiovascular diseases, neurodegenerative diseases, and inflammatory conditions.

- Malondialdehyde (MDA): MDA is one of the most commonly used lipid peroxidation biomarkers. It is a secondary product of lipid peroxidation, formed when lipid peroxides decompose. MDA is highly reactive and can form adducts with proteins and DNA, contributing to cellular damage.
- F2-isoprostanes: These are stable products formed from the peroxidation of arachidonic acid and serve as a reliable marker of in vivo lipid

peroxidation. Elevated levels of F2-isoprostanes are associated with increased oxidative stress and have been linked to cardiovascular diseases and neurodegenerative disorders.

- 4-Hydroxynonenal (4-HNE): 4-HNE is another reactive aldehyde produced during lipid peroxidation. It is highly toxic and can form protein adducts that interfere with cellular function. 4-HNE is often used to assess oxidative damage in tissues and organs.

Protein Oxidation Biomarkers

Protein oxidation biomarkers reflect the damage to proteins caused by the attack of reactive oxygen species (ROS). Proteins are highly susceptible to oxidative modification, leading to loss of function, aggregation, and degradation, which contribute to cellular dysfunction and disease progression.

- Protein Carbonyls: The formation of carbonyl groups in proteins is one of the most prominent markers of oxidative damage. The carbonylation of lysine, proline, and threonine residues results from the reaction of hydroxyl radicals with proteins. These carbonylated proteins are often degraded, leading to cellular dysfunction.
- Advanced Oxidation Protein Products (AOPPs): AOPPs are formed when chlorinated oxidants attack proteins. Elevated AOPP levels are associated with chronic diseases, including renal disease, cardiovascular disease, and diabetes. AOPPs are often used to assess oxidative stress in plasma and serum samples.
- Nitrotyrosine: Tyrosine residues in proteins can be nitrated by reactive nitrogen species (RNS), leading to the formation of nitrotyrosine. This marker is used to assess nitrosative stress and protein modification in inflammatory diseases, neurodegeneration, and cardiovascular diseases.

DNA Oxidation Biomarkers

DNA oxidation biomarkers reflect the damage to genomic DNA caused by ROS. The damage to DNA leads to mutations, chromosomal fragmentation, and genomic instability, contributing to the development of diseases such as cancer, neurodegenerative diseases, and aging.

- 8-Oxo-7,8-dihydro-2'-deoxyguanosine (8-OHdG): 8-OHdG is one of the most commonly used biomarkers for DNA oxidation. It is a product of oxidative damage to the guanine base of DNA and serves as an indicator of ROS-induced DNA damage. Elevated levels of 8-OHdG are associated with aging, cancer, diabetes, and neurodegenerative diseases.

- Formamidopyrimidine-DNA glycosylase (Fpg)-sensitive sites: These are specific sites in DNA that are sensitive to oxidative damage. Fpg-sensitive sites are used as a biomarker for oxidative DNA damage in clinical and research studies.

- 8-Nitroguanine: This is a marker of nitrosative DNA damage resulting from the nitration of guanine. Elevated levels of 8-nitroguanine are found in various inflammatory diseases and cancers.

7.2.3 Lipid Oxidation Biomarkers

7.2.3.1 F2-Isoprostanes

F2-isoprostanes are a class of prostaglandin-like compounds produced by the free radical-induced oxidation of arachidonic acid. These compounds are stable end products of lipid peroxidation, and their presence in biological samples serves as a reliable biomarker for in vivo oxidative stress. F2-isoprostanes are formed independently of the enzymatic activity of cyclooxygenase (COX), making them a more specific indicator of free radical damage than other markers, such as prostaglandins. Their formation is closely linked to lipid peroxidation, and they are considered one of the most accurate markers for assessing oxidative damage to lipids in vivo.

Formation from Arachidonic Acid Oxidation

F2-isoprostanes are primarily generated from arachidonic acid, a polyunsaturated fatty acid found in cell membranes, when free radicals attack its double bonds. The resulting lipid peroxyl radicals undergo a series of reactions leading to the formation of F2-isoprostanes. This process occurs when oxygen reacts with arachidonic acid to form hydroperoxides. These unstable intermediates then decompose into F2-isoprostanes, which include compounds like 8-iso-PGF2α and 8-epi-PGF2α.

The formation of F2-isoprostanes is a spontaneous, non-enzymatic process, making them a reliable marker of oxidative stress and free radical activity. Because their formation is not dependent on enzymatic pathways, F2-isoprostanes offer a direct reflection of free radical damage in biological systems.

Measurement Using Immunoassays and LC-MS

The measurement of F2-isoprostanes is performed using various techniques, with immunoassays and liquid chromatography-mass spectrometry (LC-MS) being the most common.

- Immunoassays: Immunoassays such as enzyme-linked immunosorbent assays (ELISA) are used to quantify F2-isoprostanes in biological fluids such as plasma, urine, and cerebrospinal fluid. These assays use antibodies that specifically recognize F2-isoprostanes, allowing for the quantification of these biomarkers at low concentrations.
- LC-MS: Liquid chromatography-mass spectrometry (LC-MS) is another powerful technique used for the detection and quantification of F2-isoprostanes. This method offers higher sensitivity and specificity, allowing for the analysis of F2-isoprostanes in more complex biological matrices. LC-MS is considered the gold standard for quantifying F2-isoprostanes, especially when analyzing small sample volumes or low concentrations.

Clinical Relevance in Cardiovascular Diseases

F2-isoprostanes are considered one of the most reliable biomarkers of oxidative stress in cardiovascular diseases. They have been shown to correlate with the degree of lipid peroxidation in atherosclerotic plaques and are associated with the progression of atherosclerosis. Elevated levels of F2-isoprostanes are found in individuals with coronary artery disease (CAD), hypertension, and heart failure. Their measurement provides valuable information regarding the oxidative damage to lipids in the vascular system, contributing to endothelial dysfunction, plaque formation, and vascular inflammation.

F2-isoprostanes are also used in research to monitor oxidative stress in response to pharmacological treatments, such as statins, which are used to lower LDL cholesterol and reduce the risk of cardiovascular events. By measuring F2-isoprostanes, clinicians and researchers can track the effectiveness of antioxidant therapies and assess their role in reducing oxidative damage and improving vascular health.

7.2.3.2 4-Hydroxynonenal (4-HNE)

4-Hydroxynonenal (4-HNE) is a highly reactive lipid aldehyde formed as a byproduct of lipid peroxidation, particularly from the oxidation of arachidonic acid and omega-6 fatty acids. It is considered one of the most toxic secondary products of lipid peroxidation and has been implicated in various diseases due to its ability to form adducts with proteins, DNA, and other cellular macromolecules. These adducts lead to functional impairments, contributing to the pathogenesis of diseases such as neurodegenerative disorders, cardiovascular diseases, and inflammatory conditions.

Mechanism of Formation from Lipid Peroxidation

4-HNE is formed during the degradation of lipid hydroperoxides—specifically those formed from arachidonic acid, linoleic acid, and other polyunsaturated fatty acids. The oxidation of these fatty acids leads to the formation of lipid peroxyl radicals, which break down into hydroperoxides. These hydroperoxides decompose into reactive aldehydes like 4-HNE. 4-HNE is highly reactive and readily forms adducts with protein amino groups, lysine residues, cysteine residues, and guanine bases in DNA, causing cellular dysfunction and genotoxicity.

4-HNE is a potent lipid peroxidation product that can modify proteins, leading to protein misfolding, aggregation, and loss of function. It also promotes the activation of transcription factors such as NF-κB and AP-1, which contribute to inflammation and cell survival signaling.

Detection Using Enzyme-Linked Immunosorbent Assay (ELISA)

The ELISA is one of the most commonly used techniques for measuring 4-HNE in biological samples. In this assay, specific antibodies are employed to detect and quantify 4-HNE adducts formed in serum, plasma, or tissues. The sensitivity and specificity of the ELISA make it a popular choice for clinical applications and biomarker studies.

- Principle: In an ELISA, 4-HNE-protein adducts are captured by specific antibodies attached to the surface of the well. After incubation, the amount of 4-HNE is determined by measuring the color change associated with the binding of secondary antibodies. The intensity of the color change correlates with the concentration of 4-HNE in the sample.
- Applications: This technique is commonly used in research and clinical diagnostics to assess the oxidative damage in diseases such as neurodegenerative disorders, cardiovascular diseases, and liver diseases.

Role in Neurodegenerative and Inflammatory Diseases

4-HNE plays a significant role in the pathophysiology of neurodegenerative diseases, including Alzheimer's disease, Parkinson's disease, and amyotrophic lateral sclerosis (ALS). The accumulation of 4-HNE in the brain contributes to oxidative damage in neurons, leading to neuroinflammation, cell death, and neurodegeneration. Elevated 4-HNE levels are observed in neuronal tissues affected by these diseases, where 4-HNE-induced protein modification disrupts cellular homeostasis and triggers neurotoxic pathways.

Additionally, 4-HNE is involved in chronic inflammation, where it amplifies the production of pro-inflammatory cytokines and chemokines, further contributing to tissue damage in inflammatory diseases such as rheumatoid arthritis and inflammatory bowel disease. Its role in these diseases highlights the importance of monitoring 4-HNE levels as a marker of oxidative damage and inflammation..

7.2.4 Protein Oxidation Biomarkers

7.2.4.1 Protein Carbonyl Content

Protein carbonylation is one of the most important and commonly used biomarkers for protein oxidation. This process occurs when reactive oxygen species (ROS) or reactive nitrogen species (RNS) attack proteins, leading to the formation of carbonyl groups (e.g., aldehydes and ketones) on lysine, proline, and threonine residues of the proteins. Protein carbonylation is an irreversible modification and can lead to functional impairment of the protein. This modification is indicative of oxidative stress and protein damage, and serves as a key marker for studying diseases related to oxidative damage and aging.

Mechanism of Protein Oxidation

The carbonylation of proteins occurs through the attack of free radicals, such as hydroxyl radicals (OH·), on amino acid residues in proteins. This reaction results in the formation of carbonyl groups in the protein backbone, which are chemically reactive. These modifications can significantly impact the protein's conformation, activity, and function, leading to protein aggregation or degradation. Carbonylation can also affect protein-protein interactions and enzyme activity, which can disrupt cellular processes.

Protein carbonylation has been linked to a wide range of diseases, including neurodegenerative diseases like Alzheimer's disease, Parkinson's disease, cardiovascular diseases, and diabetes. The accumulation of oxidized proteins contributes to cellular dysfunction, inflammation, and age-related degenerative changes.

Measurement Using DNPH (Dinitrophenylhydrazine) Assay

The most widely used method to measure protein carbonyl content is the DNPH (dinitrophenylhydrazine) assay. In this assay, DNPH reacts with carbonyl groups in oxidized proteins to form a stable dinitrophenylhydrazone (DNPH-protein) complex, which can be quantified colorimetrically at 370 nm.

- Principle: DNPH reacts specifically with carbonyl groups in proteins, forming a stable adduct that can be quantified using UV-visible spectrophotometry. This assay provides a straightforward and reliable way to assess protein oxidation and quantify protein carbonyls in tissues, serum, and plasma.
- Clinical Applications: The DNPH assay is widely used in clinical research to monitor oxidative stress and protein damage in diseases such as neurodegenerative disorders, cardiovascular diseases, and diabetes. The level of protein carbonylation can serve as an indicator of cellular aging and disease progression, as well as a measure of the effectiveness of antioxidant treatments in mitigating oxidative damage.

7.2.4.2 Advanced Oxidation Protein Products (AOPPs)

Advanced oxidation protein products (AOPPs) are oxidized proteins generated when chlorinated oxidants, such as chlorine, hypochlorous acid (HOCl), or myeloperoxidase-derived oxidants, attack proteins. AOPPs are stable and highly reactive, making them significant biomarkers for oxidative stress. AOPPs are elevated in conditions characterized by increased oxidative stress, such as chronic kidney disease, diabetes, and cardiovascular diseases.

Definition and Formation in Oxidative Stress Conditions

AOPPs are primarily formed from oxidative modification of plasma proteins, especially albumin, by reactive chlorinating species generated during inflammatory responses. Myeloperoxidase (MPO), an enzyme released by neutrophils, catalyzes the formation of hypochlorous acid (HOCl) from hydrogen peroxide (H2O2), which then reacts with proteins to produce AOPPs. These compounds are highly stable and can accumulate in the plasma and tissues, reflecting the extent of oxidative damage.

The formation of AOPPs is directly associated with inflammatory processes, as neutrophils are activated during inflammatory responses and contribute to oxidative damage via the release of HOCl. The AOPP levels in the bloodstream can provide valuable insight into the extent of inflammation and oxidative stress in chronic inflammatory conditions.

Spectrophotometric and Chromatographic Detection Methods

AOPPs can be measured using spectrophotometric and chromatographic methods, such as ELISA, HPLC, and GC-MS.

- Spectrophotometric Methods: AOPP levels are most commonly quantified by measuring their absorbance at 340 nm, which is due to the formation of a chromophore when AOPPs react with specific reagents. ELISA-based methods are also frequently used to detect AOPPs in blood and serum samples, offering high sensitivity and specificity for AOPP detection.
- Chromatographic Methods: High-performance liquid chromatography (HPLC) and gas chromatography (GC) can also be used to isolate and quantify AOPPs from biological samples. These methods allow for the separation of AOPPs from other proteins and offer detailed analysis of the oxidative modifications present in the protein structure.

Role in Chronic Kidney Disease and Diabetes

AOPPs have been widely studied in chronic kidney disease (CKD) and diabetes, where they serve as important biomarkers of oxidative stress and inflammation. Elevated levels of AOPPs are associated with renal dysfunction, proteinuria, and the progression of kidney damage in patients with CKD. Studies have shown that AOPP levels correlate with the severity of kidney injury and can be used to predict kidney failure.

In diabetes, AOPPs are elevated due to the increased oxidative stress associated with hyperglycemia. AOPPs play a role in the development of diabetic complications such as retinopathy, neuropathy, and cardiovascular disease. Their measurement is valuable in monitoring diabetic patients for oxidative damage and vascular dysfunction.

7.2.5 DNA Oxidation Biomarkers

7.2.5.1 8-Hydroxydeoxyguanosine (8-OHdG)

8-Hydroxydeoxyguanosine (8-OHdG) is one of the most widely used biomarkers for DNA oxidation. It is a product of oxidative damage to guanine, one of the DNA bases, caused by the attack of hydroxyl radicals (OH·) and other reactive oxygen species (ROS). The formation of 8-OHdG is a result of oxidative stress, where free radicals induce oxidation of guanine in DNA, leading to the formation of this specific lesion. 8-OHdG serves as a sensitive marker for assessing DNA damage and genomic instability.

Formation Due to Hydroxyl Radical Attack on Guanine

The process of 8-OHdG formation begins with the hydroxyl radical (OH·) attacking the C8 position of the guanine base in DNA. This reaction leads to the formation of 8-hydroxyguanine, which can subsequently be incorporated into DNA during replication. 8-hydroxyguanine can then cause mutations if it pairs with adenine instead of cytosine. Over time, the accumulation of 8-OHdG in DNA can lead to genetic mutations, chromosomal instability, and cellular dysfunction, which are hallmarks of various diseases, including cancer and neurodegenerative diseases.

8-OHdG formation is not only a result of direct DNA damage but is also an indicator of oxidative stress in cells and tissues, making it a useful biomarker in studies related to chronic diseases, aging, and cancer.

Detection Using ELISA and HPLC-MS

There are several methods for detecting 8-OHdG in biological samples, with ELISA (enzyme-linked immunosorbent assay) and HPLC-MS (high-performance liquid chromatography-mass spectrometry) being the most commonly used techniques.

- ELISA: ELISA is a sensitive and specific method for detecting 8-OHdG in biological fluids like plasma, urine, and serum. This assay uses antibodies that specifically bind to 8-OHdG, allowing for the quantification of this biomarker. The results are typically colorimetric, and the intensity of the color correlates with the concentration of 8-OHdG. ELISA is widely used in clinical settings and epidemiological studies to monitor DNA oxidative damage in response to environmental factors and diseases.

- HPLC-MS: HPLC-MS is a highly sensitive and specific method for quantifying 8-OHdG and is considered the gold standard for its measurement. HPLC is used to separate 8-OHdG from other compounds in biological samples, and the mass spectrometer is employed to detect and quantify the specific mass-to-charge ratio of 8-OHdG. This method is highly precise and can be used for analyzing low concentrations of 8-OHdG in complex matrices, making it ideal for research studies and clinical trials.

Importance in Cancer Risk Assessment

8-OHdG has been extensively studied as a biomarker for assessing DNA damage in cancer risk assessment. Elevated levels of 8-OHdG are associated with increased risk of cancer due to its role in mutagenesis and genetic instability. Studies have shown that individuals with high levels of 8-OHdG in their urine or plasma have a higher risk of developing cancers such as lung cancer, breast cancer, colorectal cancer, and prostate cancer.

The quantification of 8-OHdG is a useful tool for predicting cancer risk in individuals with a history of smoking, exposure to environmental toxins, or those with a family history of cancer. Monitoring 8-OHdG levels can also help assess the effectiveness of preventive and therapeutic interventions aimed at reducing oxidative damage and preventing cancer.

7.2.5.2 Comet Assay for DNA Damage

The comet assay, also known as single-cell gel electrophoresis (SCGE), is a widely used technique to measure DNA damage at the single-cell level. This assay is highly sensitive and can detect a wide range of DNA lesions, including strand breaks, alkali-labile sites, and oxidized bases, making it an excellent tool for genotoxicity testing and DNA damage assessment in various disease models and clinical studies.

Principle of Single-Cell Gel Electrophoresis (SCGE)

The comet assay relies on the principle of electrophoresis, where cells are embedded in agarose gel and subjected to an electric field. This process causes the damaged DNA to migrate out of the cell and form a comet-like tail. The extent of DNA migration is proportional to the degree of DNA damage, with cells containing more DNA breaks showing larger tails.

- DNA Lysis: First, cells are embedded in agarose gel and subjected to lysis, which breaks down the cell membrane and releases the DNA.
- Electrophoresis: The DNA is then subjected to an electric field, which causes damaged DNA (broken strands) to migrate towards the positive electrode, forming a tail. The undamaged DNA stays in the nucleus, forming a head.
- Staining: The DNA is stained with fluorescent dyes, such as ethidium bromide or SYBR green, which allow for visualization under a fluorescent microscope.

The resulting image resembles a comet, with a distinct head and tail. The length and intensity of the tail provide a quantitative measure of DNA damage.

Application in Genotoxicity Testing

The comet assay is widely used in genotoxicity testing to assess the DNA-damaging potential of chemicals, drugs, pollutants, and radiation. The assay is capable of detecting DNA strand breaks, oxidized bases, and alkali-labile sites, making it a comprehensive tool for evaluating DNA integrity in response to various genotoxic agents.

- Testing Chemicals and Drugs: The comet assay is employed to evaluate the genotoxic potential of pharmaceutical compounds in preclinical testing and to assess drug safety before clinical trials.
- Environmental Toxins: The assay is also used to monitor DNA damage in individuals exposed to environmental toxins, such as pollution, pesticides, and industrial chemicals.

Clinical Applications of the Comet Assay

The comet assay is increasingly being used in clinical research to assess DNA damage in patients with chronic diseases, cancer, and neurodegenerative disorders. By measuring the extent of DNA damage in blood samples, researchers can track the progression of diseases and evaluate the effects of therapeutic interventions aimed at reducing oxidative damage.

- Cancer Research: In cancer research, the comet assay can be used to assess genomic instability and mutagenesis in response to anticancer treatments, such as chemotherapy and radiotherapy. It provides a measure of the genotoxic effects of these therapies on healthy cells and tumor cells.

- Neurodegenerative Diseases: The comet assay is also used to study DNA damage in neurodegenerative diseases, such as Alzheimer's disease, Parkinson's disease, and Huntington's disease, where oxidative stress plays a key role in the progression of neuronal degeneration.

7.2.6 Future Directions in Oxidative Stress Biomarker Research

Development of Non-Invasive Biomarkers

The future of oxidative stress biomarker research is heavily focused on the development of non-invasive biomarkers that can be measured easily and accurately from non-invasive biological samples like saliva, urine, or exhaled breath. The shift towards non-invasive methods is driven by the need for user-friendly and less invasive techniques that can be used for routine diagnostics and monitoring in clinical settings.

Currently, many oxidative stress biomarkers are measured from blood and tissues, which require invasive procedures and expensive equipment. Non-invasive biomarkers would enable the regular monitoring of oxidative stress in individuals without the need for blood draws or tissue biopsies, making them more accessible and cost-effective. For example, urinary biomarkers, such as 8-OHdG or F2-isoprostanes, could provide valuable insight into systemic oxidative stress and be used in longitudinal studies or for tracking the effectiveness of antioxidant interventions.

In addition, exhaled breath analysis has shown promise as a non-invasive method to assess oxidative stress. Certain volatile organic compounds (VOCs) produced during oxidative reactions can be detected in exhaled breath, providing a potential early detection system for oxidative damage linked to respiratory diseases, cancer, and metabolic disorders.

The development of non-invasive biomarkers will greatly improve the ability to diagnose and monitor oxidative stress in real time, personalize therapies, and make preventive health strategies more feasible.

Role of Multi-Omics Approaches in Oxidative Stress Analysis

The future of oxidative stress biomarker research is also being shaped by the integration of multi-omics approaches, such as genomics, proteomics, metabolomics, and lipidomics. These comprehensive approaches offer a more holistic and integrated view of the biological pathways involved in oxidative stress and disease development.

- Genomics: By studying the genetic makeup of individuals and their susceptibility to oxidative stress, researchers can identify genetic variations that influence the efficiency of antioxidant defenses or oxidative damage repair. For example, genetic polymorphisms in genes encoding antioxidant enzymes like superoxide dismutase (SOD) and glutathione peroxidase (GPX) can affect an individual's response to oxidative stress and their risk of developing oxidative stress-related diseases.
- Proteomics: Proteomics can be used to identify oxidative modifications to proteins, such as carbonylation, nitrosation, and nitration, which are often indicative of oxidative damage. By analyzing protein profiles and oxidized proteins, researchers can better understand the mechanisms of oxidative stress and disease pathogenesis.
- Metabolomics: Metabolomics offers the ability to identify metabolic shifts and biomarker patterns in response to oxidative stress. For instance, increased levels of lactic acid or TCA cycle intermediates may be indicative of mitochondrial dysfunction due to oxidative damage. Metabolomics also allows for the detection of oxidized metabolites, such as lipid peroxidation products, providing valuable insights into tissue-specific oxidative stress.
- Lipidomics: Lipidomics focuses on the study of lipid changes in response to oxidative stress. Oxidized lipids such as F2-isoprostanes and 4-HNE are key biomarkers for lipid peroxidation, and lipidomics can provide insights into lipid metabolism, membrane fluidity, and cell signaling pathways that are disrupted during oxidative stress.

By combining these multi-omics data sets, a comprehensive molecular profile of oxidative stress can be obtained, allowing for the identification of early biomarkers, the mechanisms of action, and the role of oxidative stress in disease progression. This systems biology approach can reveal novel targets for therapeutic intervention and help in developing personalized medicine strategies that tailor treatments to individual molecular profiles.

Integration of Oxidative Stress Biomarkers in Personalized Medicine

Personalized medicine aims to tailor treatments and interventions based on the individual characteristics of each patient, including their genetics, environment, and lifestyle. The integration of oxidative stress biomarkers into personalized medicine represents a promising frontier in healthcare.

By assessing an individual's oxidative stress levels and understanding their genetic susceptibility to oxidative damage, healthcare providers can develop personalized strategies for disease prevention, monitoring, and treatment. For example, an individual with a genetic predisposition to low antioxidant enzyme activity may benefit from antioxidant supplementation or lifestyle changes to reduce oxidative damage. Conversely, individuals who are at high risk of cardiovascular disease or cancer may undergo regular monitoring of oxidative stress biomarkers, such as F2-isoprostanes or 8-OHdG, to assess their disease risk and adjust their treatment plans accordingly.

The integration of oxidative stress biomarkers in personalized medicine would enable early detection of oxidative damage and disease in individuals who are at high risk due to genetic factors or environmental exposures. It would also allow for precise tailoring of antioxidant therapies and lifestyle interventions to reduce oxidative stress and slow the progression of chronic diseases.

Additionally, drug development in the field of oxidative stress would benefit from personalized medicine, as drugs can be designed to target specific oxidative pathways or oxidative stress-related biomarkers identified through genomics, proteomics, and metabolomics.

EIGHT

FREE RADICALS AND THEIR ROLE IN DISEASES

8.1 Oxidative Stress and Chronic Diseases

8.1.1 Introduction to Oxidative Stress in Chronic Diseases

Definition of Oxidative Stress

Oxidative stress is a physiological condition characterized by an imbalance between the production of reactive oxygen species (ROS) and reactive nitrogen species (RNS) and the body's ability to neutralize them through antioxidants. When the production of ROS and RNS exceeds the antioxidant defense mechanisms, oxidative stress occurs, leading to damage to cellular components such as DNA, proteins, and lipids.

Role of Reactive Oxygen Species (ROS) and Reactive Nitrogen Species (RNS)

ROS and RNS are highly reactive molecules that play a dual role in the body. At low to moderate levels, they act as signaling molecules, regulating processes such as cell proliferation, immune response, and apoptosis. However, at high levels, they cause oxidative damage, contributing to the development of chronic diseases.

1. **Reactive Oxygen Species (ROS)**:

   - Examples: Superoxide anion (O_2^-), hydrogen peroxide (H_2O_2), hydroxyl radical ($\cdot OH$), and singlet oxygen ($^1O_2$).
   - Sources: Mitochondrial electron transport chain, peroxisomes, NADPH oxidase, and environmental factors such as radiation and pollutants.

2. **Reactive Nitrogen Species (RNS)**:

   - Examples: Nitric oxide ($NO\cdot$), peroxynitrite ($ONOO^-$), and nitrogen dioxide ($NO_2\cdot$).
   - Sources: Nitric oxide synthase (NOS) enzymes, reaction of $NO\cdot$ with superoxide anions, and environmental factors such as cigarette smoke.

Mechanisms Linking Oxidative Stress to Chronic Diseases

Oxidative stress is a key contributor to the pathogenesis of various chronic diseases through multiple mechanisms:

1. **Damage to Cellular Components**:

   - **DNA Damage**: ROS and RNS can cause oxidative modifications to DNA bases, leading to mutations, genomic instability, and activation of oncogenes or inactivation of tumor suppressor genes.
   - **Protein Oxidation**: ROS and RNS can oxidize amino acid residues in proteins, leading to loss of function, misfolding, and aggregation. This is particularly relevant in neurodegenerative diseases.
   - **Lipid Peroxidation**: ROS can oxidize polyunsaturated fatty acids (PUFAs) in cell membranes, leading to the formation of reactive aldehydes (e.g., malondialdehyde and 4-hydroxynonenal) that damage cellular structures and impair signaling pathways.

2. **Activation of Pro-Inflammatory Pathways**:

   - Oxidative stress activates transcription factors such as nuclear factor-kappa B (NF-κB) and activator protein-1 (AP-1), which upregulate the expression of pro-inflammatory cytokines (e.g., TNF-α, IL-6) and enzymes (e.g., COX-2, iNOS). This contributes to chronic inflammation, a hallmark of many diseases.

3. **Mitochondrial Dysfunction:**

   - Excessive ROS production damages mitochondrial DNA, proteins, and lipids, impairing energy production and leading to cell death. Mitochondrial dysfunction is a key feature of aging and diseases such as neurodegenerative disorders and cardiovascular diseases.

4. **Impaired Antioxidant Defense Mechanisms:**

   - Oxidative stress depletes endogenous antioxidants, such as glutathione, superoxide dismutase (SOD), and catalase, reducing the body's ability to neutralize ROS and RNS. This creates a vicious cycle of increasing oxidative damage.

5. **Role in Disease-Specific Pathways:**

   - **Cardiovascular Diseases**: Oxidative stress promotes endothelial dysfunction, atherosclerosis, and hypertension by damaging vascular cells and promoting inflammation.
   - **Neurodegenerative Diseases**: Oxidative stress contributes to neuronal damage and death in diseases such as Alzheimer's and Parkinson's by promoting protein aggregation and mitochondrial dysfunction.
   - **Cancer**: Oxidative stress induces DNA mutations and genomic instability, driving cancer initiation and progression.
   - **Diabetes**: Oxidative stress impairs insulin signaling and promotes pancreatic beta-cell dysfunction, contributing to insulin resistance and diabetes complications.

8.1.2 Oxidative Stress and Diabetes Mellitus

Oxidative stress plays a central role in the pathogenesis and complications of diabetes mellitus. The chronic hyperglycemia associated with diabetes leads to the overproduction of reactive oxygen species (ROS), which damage cellular components and contribute to the development of insulin resistance, β-cell dysfunction, and diabetic complications. This section explores the role of oxidative stress in diabetes, its impact on cellular components, and the potential of antioxidants in diabetes management.

8.1.2.1 Role of Free Radicals in Diabetes Pathogenesis

1. **Impact on Pancreatic β-Cell Dysfunction**:

   - Pancreatic β-cells are particularly vulnerable to oxidative stress due to their low levels of antioxidant enzymes, such as catalase and glutathione peroxidase.
   - Chronic hyperglycemia increases ROS production in β-cells, leading to DNA damage, impaired insulin secretion, and apoptosis.
   - Oxidative stress also disrupts the expression of genes involved in insulin synthesis and secretion, further exacerbating β-cell dysfunction.

2. **Insulin Resistance and Oxidative Damage**:

   - Oxidative stress contributes to insulin resistance by impairing insulin signaling pathways. ROS can oxidize and inactivate key proteins in the insulin signaling cascade, such as insulin receptor substrate-1 (IRS-1) and phosphoinositide 3-kinase (PI3K).
   - Oxidative stress also promotes inflammation by activating pro-inflammatory pathways, such as NF-κB and JNK, which further exacerbate insulin resistance.

8.1.2.2 Oxidative Damage to Cellular Components in Diabetes

1. **Lipid Peroxidation and Membrane Instability**:

   - ROS attack polyunsaturated fatty acids (PUFAs) in cell membranes, leading to lipid peroxidation and the formation of reactive aldehydes, such as malondialdehyde (MDA) and 4-hydroxynonenal (4-HNE).

- Lipid peroxidation disrupts membrane integrity, impairing the function of membrane-bound receptors and transporters, including glucose transporters (GLUT4), which are critical for insulin-mediated glucose uptake.

2. **Protein Oxidation and Enzyme Dysfunction**:

- ROS oxidize amino acid residues in proteins, leading to the formation of protein carbonyls and the loss of enzymatic activity.
- Key enzymes involved in glucose metabolism, such as glucokinase and pyruvate kinase, are particularly susceptible to oxidative damage, impairing glucose homeostasis.

8.1.2.3 Consequences of Oxidative Stress in Diabetes

1. **Increased Risk of Diabetic Nephropathy**:

- Oxidative stress contributes to the development of diabetic nephropathy by damaging glomerular cells and promoting inflammation and fibrosis.
- ROS activate pathways such as TGF-β and NF-κB, leading to the accumulation of extracellular matrix proteins and the progression of kidney damage.

2. **Diabetic Retinopathy and Cardiovascular Complications**:

- In diabetic retinopathy, oxidative stress damages retinal cells and promotes the formation of advanced glycation end products (AGEs), which contribute to vascular leakage and neovascularization.
- In cardiovascular complications, oxidative stress promotes endothelial dysfunction, atherosclerosis, and hypertension by damaging vascular cells and increasing inflammation.

8.1.2.4 Antioxidants in Diabetes Management

1. **Role of Dietary Antioxidants (Polyphenols, Flavonoids):**

   - Dietary antioxidants, such as polyphenols and flavonoids, neutralize ROS and reduce oxidative stress. These compounds are found in fruits, vegetables, tea, and cocoa.
   - Polyphenols, such as resveratrol and quercetin, have been shown to improve insulin sensitivity, protect β-cells, and reduce inflammation in preclinical and clinical studies.

2. **Clinical Studies on Antioxidant Supplementation in Diabetes:**

   - **Vitamin C and Vitamin E**: Clinical trials have shown mixed results, with some studies reporting improvements in oxidative stress markers and insulin sensitivity, while others show no significant benefits.
   - **Alpha-Lipoic Acid (ALA)**: ALA is a potent antioxidant that has been shown to improve insulin sensitivity and reduce symptoms of diabetic neuropathy in clinical trials.
   - **N-Acetylcysteine (NAC)**: NAC, a precursor of glutathione, has been shown to reduce oxidative stress and improve endothelial function in patients with diabetes.

8.1.3 Oxidative Stress and Inflammation

Oxidative stress and inflammation are closely interconnected processes that play a central role in the pathogenesis of various chronic diseases. Free radicals, particularly reactive oxygen species (ROS), not only cause cellular damage but also activate inflammatory pathways, creating a vicious cycle of oxidative stress and inflammation. This section explores the mechanisms linking oxidative stress to inflammation, chronic inflammatory diseases associated with oxidative stress, and therapeutic strategies to mitigate these effects.

8.1.3.1 Mechanisms of Free Radical-Induced Inflammation

1. **Activation of Inflammatory Cytokines:**

   - ROS activate transcription factors such as nuclear factor-kappa B (NF-κB) and activator protein-1 (AP-1), which upregulate the expression of pro-inflammatory cytokines, including tumor necrosis factor-alpha (TNF-α), interleukin-6 (IL-6), and interleukin-1 beta (IL-1β).
   - These cytokines amplify the inflammatory response by recruiting immune cells, such as neutrophils and macrophages, to the site of injury or infection.

2. **Role of ROS in Immune Cell Signaling:**

   - ROS act as signaling molecules in immune cells, regulating processes such as phagocytosis, antigen presentation, and cytokine production.
   - For example, NADPH oxidase in neutrophils and macrophages generates superoxide radicals (O_2^-) as part of the respiratory burst, which is essential for killing pathogens. However, excessive ROS production can lead to tissue damage and chronic inflammation.

8.1.3.2 Chronic Inflammatory Diseases Associated with Oxidative Stress

1. **Rheumatoid Arthritis (RA):**

   - RA is a chronic autoimmune disease characterized by inflammation and joint damage. Oxidative stress plays a key role in RA pathogenesis by promoting the production of pro-inflammatory cytokines and matrix metalloproteinases (MMPs), which degrade cartilage and bone.
   - ROS also contribute to the formation of autoantigens, such as citrullinated proteins, which trigger autoimmune responses in RA.

2. **Chronic Obstructive Pulmonary Disease (COPD):**

- COPD is a chronic inflammatory lung disease characterized by airflow limitation and oxidative stress. Cigarette smoke, a major risk factor for COPD, generates ROS that damage lung tissue and promote inflammation.
- ROS activate NF-κB and other pro-inflammatory pathways, leading to the production of cytokines, chemokines, and proteases that contribute to lung tissue destruction and fibrosis.

8.1.3.3 Therapeutic Strategies to Reduce Oxidative Stress in Inflammation

1. **Role of Anti-Inflammatory and Antioxidant Nutraceuticals**:

   - **Polyphenols**: Compounds such as curcumin, resveratrol, and quercetin have potent anti-inflammatory and antioxidant properties. They inhibit NF-κB and other pro-inflammatory pathways, reducing cytokine production and oxidative stress.
   - **Omega-3 Fatty Acids**: Found in fish oil, omega-3 fatty acids (e.g., EPA and DHA) reduce inflammation by inhibiting the production of pro-inflammatory eicosanoids and cytokines.
   - **Vitamin C and Vitamin E**: These antioxidants neutralize ROS and reduce oxidative stress, helping to mitigate inflammation in chronic diseases.

2. **Pharmacological Interventions Targeting Oxidative Pathways**:

   - **N-Acetylcysteine (NAC)**: NAC is a precursor of glutathione, a key antioxidant that neutralizes ROS. It has been shown to reduce oxidative stress and inflammation in conditions such as COPD and RA.
   - **NF-κB Inhibitors**: Drugs that inhibit NF-κB activation, such as corticosteroids and specific kinase inhibitors, reduce inflammation and oxidative stress in chronic inflammatory diseases.
   - **NADPH Oxidase Inhibitors**: Targeting NADPH oxidase, a major source of ROS in immune cells, can reduce oxidative stress and inflammation in diseases such as RA and COPD.

8.1.4 Oxidative Stress in Ischemic Reperfusion Injury

Ischemic reperfusion injury (IRI) is a complex phenomenon that occurs when blood supply is restored to tissues after a period of ischemia (lack of oxygen). While reperfusion is essential to salvage ischemic tissue, it paradoxically leads to further damage due to the generation of free radicals and oxidative stress. This section explores the mechanisms of IRI, the major organs affected, and potential therapeutic approaches to mitigate its effects.

8.1.4.1 Mechanism of Ischemic Reperfusion Injury

1. **Free Radical Burst During Reoxygenation:**

   - During ischemia, the lack of oxygen disrupts mitochondrial electron transport, leading to the accumulation of reduced electron carriers (e.g., NADH and $FADH_2$).
   - Upon reperfusion, the sudden reintroduction of oxygen results in a burst of ROS production, as the accumulated electrons react with oxygen to form superoxide radicals (O_2^-).
   - Superoxide radicals are converted into hydrogen peroxide (H_2O_2) by superoxide dismutase (SOD), and in the presence of transition metals (e.g., iron), H_2O_2 can generate highly reactive hydroxyl radicals ($\cdot OH$) via the Fenton reaction.

2. **Role of Nitric Oxide (NO) in Oxidative Damage:**

   - Nitric oxide ($NO\cdot$), produced by endothelial nitric oxide synthase (eNOS), reacts with superoxide radicals to form peroxynitrite ($ONOO^-$), a highly reactive nitrogen species (RNS).
   - Peroxynitrite damages cellular components by nitrating proteins, lipids, and DNA, leading to cell death and tissue injury.

8.1.4.2 Major Affected Organs

1. **Myocardial Ischemia and Reperfusion Injury**:

   - Myocardial IRI occurs during the restoration of blood flow to the heart after a heart attack (myocardial infarction).
   - ROS and RNS generated during reperfusion damage cardiomyocytes, endothelial cells, and vascular smooth muscle cells, leading to arrhythmias, contractile dysfunction, and cell death.
   - Oxidative stress also activates inflammatory pathways, further exacerbating tissue damage.

2. **Cerebral Ischemia and Stroke-Related Damage**:

   - Cerebral IRI occurs during the restoration of blood flow to the brain after a stroke.
   - ROS and RNS damage neurons, glial cells, and the blood-brain barrier, leading to neuronal death, brain edema, and neurological deficits.
   - Oxidative stress also promotes inflammation and apoptosis, contributing to long-term brain damage.

8.1.4.3 Potential Therapeutic Approaches

1. **Antioxidant-Based Therapies**:

   - **Superoxide Dismutase (SOD) Mimetics**: Compounds that mimic the activity of SOD, such as tempol, reduce superoxide levels and protect tissues from IRI.
   - **Catalase and Glutathione Peroxidase Enhancers**: These enzymes break down hydrogen peroxide and lipid peroxides, reducing oxidative damage during reperfusion.

2. **Use of Free Radical Scavengers**:

   - **N-Acetylcysteine (NAC)**: NAC is a precursor of glutathione, a key antioxidant that neutralizes ROS. It has been shown to reduce oxidative stress and improve outcomes in myocardial and cerebral

IRI.

- **Vitamin E**: A lipid-soluble antioxidant, vitamin E protects cell membranes from lipid peroxidation and reduces tissue damage during reperfusion.
- **Edaravone**: A potent free radical scavenger, edaravone is used clinically to treat acute ischemic stroke by reducing oxidative stress and neuronal damage.

8.1.5 Oxidative Stress and Cancer

Oxidative stress plays a dual role in cancer, contributing to both the initiation and progression of the disease. While free radicals can cause DNA damage and mutations that lead to cancer development, they also play a role in tumor progression by promoting angiogenesis, metastasis, and the adaptation of cancer cells to their microenvironment. This section explores the role of free radicals in carcinogenesis, tumor progression, and the potential of antioxidants in cancer prevention and therapy.

8.1.5.1 Role of Free Radicals in Carcinogenesis

1. **DNA Damage and Mutagenesis**:

   - Free radicals, particularly hydroxyl radicals ($\cdot$OH), cause oxidative damage to DNA bases, leading to mutations. For example, the oxidation of guanine produces 8-oxo-7,8-dihydroguanine (8-oxoG), which can mispair with adenine during DNA replication, causing G:C to T:A transversion mutations.
   - DNA damage can also result in single-strand breaks (SSBs) and double-strand breaks (DSBs), which, if not properly repaired, lead to genomic instability and cancer initiation.

2. **Activation of Oncogenes and Suppression of Tumor Suppressor Genes**:

   - Oxidative stress can activate oncogenes, such as RAS and MYC, by introducing mutations that enhance their expression or activity.

- It can also inactivate tumor suppressor genes, such as TP53 and BRCA1, by introducing mutations that disrupt their function. For example, oxidative damage to TP53 impairs its ability to induce apoptosis and DNA repair, promoting cancer development.

8.1.5.2 Free Radicals in Tumor Progression

1. **Role in Angiogenesis and Metastasis:**

   - ROS promote angiogenesis (the formation of new blood vessels) by upregulating the expression of vascular endothelial growth factor (VEGF) and other pro-angiogenic factors. This provides tumors with the nutrients and oxygen needed for growth and survival.
   - ROS also facilitate metastasis by promoting the epithelial-mesenchymal transition (EMT), a process in which cancer cells acquire migratory and invasive properties. ROS activate signaling pathways, such as NF-κB and HIF-1α, that regulate EMT and metastasis.

2. **ROS-Mediated Regulation of Tumor Microenvironment:**

   - ROS modulate the tumor microenvironment by influencing the behavior of cancer-associated fibroblasts (CAFs), immune cells, and extracellular matrix (ECM) components.
   - For example, ROS can suppress anti-tumor immune responses by promoting the differentiation of regulatory T cells (Tregs) and myeloid-derived suppressor cells (MDSCs), which create an immunosuppressive microenvironment.

8.1.5.3 Antioxidants in Cancer Prevention and Therapy

1. **Dietary Polyphenols and Flavonoids:**

- Polyphenols and flavonoids, found in fruits, vegetables, tea, and cocoa, have potent antioxidant and anti-cancer properties. They neutralize ROS, reduce oxidative stress, and inhibit cancer cell proliferation, angiogenesis, and metastasis.
- Examples include resveratrol (found in grapes), curcumin (found in turmeric), and epigallocatechin gallate (EGCG) (found in green tea). These compounds have been shown to inhibit cancer cell growth and induce apoptosis in preclinical studies.

2. **Controversies on Antioxidant Supplementation in Cancer Patients**:

- While antioxidants are beneficial in cancer prevention by reducing oxidative stress and DNA damage, their role in cancer therapy is controversial. Some studies suggest that antioxidant supplementation during cancer treatment may interfere with the efficacy of chemotherapy and radiation therapy, which rely on ROS to kill cancer cells.
- For example, high-dose vitamin C has been shown to reduce the effectiveness of certain chemotherapeutic agents, such as doxorubicin, by neutralizing ROS.
- However, other studies suggest that antioxidants may protect normal cells from the side effects of cancer treatment without compromising its efficacy. Further research is needed to clarify the role of antioxidants in cancer therapy.

8.1.6 Oxidative Stress and Atherosclerosis

Oxidative stress plays a central role in the development and progression of atherosclerosis, a chronic inflammatory disease characterized by the buildup of plaque in arterial walls. Reactive oxygen species (ROS) contribute to endothelial dysfunction, the oxidation of low-density lipoprotein (LDL), and the inflammatory response that drives plaque formation. This section explores the mechanisms of ROS in atherosclerosis, the consequences of oxidative stress in cardiovascular health, and the role of antioxidants in cardiovascular protection.

8.1.6.1 Mechanism of ROS in Atherosclerosis Development

1. **Oxidation of Low-Density Lipoprotein (LDL):**

   - LDL particles are susceptible to oxidation by ROS, particularly hydroxyl radicals ($\cdot$OH) and peroxynitrite ($ONOO^-$). Oxidized LDL (ox-LDL) is a key contributor to atherosclerosis.
   - Ox-LDL is taken up by macrophages through scavenger receptors, leading to the formation of foam cells, which are the hallmark of early atherosclerotic lesions.
   - Ox-LDL also promotes inflammation by activating endothelial cells and smooth muscle cells, leading to the release of pro-inflammatory cytokines and adhesion molecules.

2. **Endothelial Dysfunction and Plaque Formation:**

   - ROS impair endothelial function by reducing the bioavailability of nitric oxide (NO), a potent vasodilator that maintains vascular homeostasis. ROS react with NO to form peroxynitrite ($ONOO^-$), which further damages endothelial cells.
   - Endothelial dysfunction increases vascular permeability, promotes the adhesion of monocytes and T cells to the arterial wall, and enhances the proliferation of smooth muscle cells, all of which contribute to plaque formation.
   - ROS also activate pro-inflammatory pathways, such as NF-κB, leading to the expression of cytokines (e.g., TNF-α, IL-6) and adhesion molecules (e.g., VCAM-1, ICAM-1) that drive the inflammatory response in atherosclerosis.

8.1.6.2 Consequences of Oxidative Stress in Cardiovascular Health

1. **Increased Risk of Heart Attack and Stroke:**

- Oxidative stress promotes the progression of atherosclerotic plaques, making them more vulnerable to rupture. Plaque rupture exposes the underlying thrombogenic material, leading to the formation of blood clots that can cause heart attacks or strokes.
- ROS also contribute to thrombosis by activating platelets and promoting the expression of tissue factor, a key initiator of the coagulation cascade.

2. **Inflammatory Response in Blood Vessels**:

- Oxidative stress amplifies the inflammatory response in blood vessels by activating immune cells and promoting the release of pro-inflammatory mediators.
- Chronic inflammation in the arterial wall leads to the formation of unstable plaques, which are more likely to rupture and cause cardiovascular events.

8.1.6.3 Role of Antioxidants in Cardiovascular Protection

1. **Clinical Evidence on Antioxidant-Rich Diets**:

- Diets rich in antioxidants, such as the Mediterranean diet, have been shown to reduce the risk of cardiovascular diseases. These diets are high in fruits, vegetables, nuts, and whole grains, which provide a wide range of antioxidants, including polyphenols, flavonoids, and vitamins.
- For example, the PREDIMED study demonstrated that a Mediterranean diet supplemented with extra virgin olive oil or nuts reduced the incidence of major cardiovascular events by 30% compared to a low-fat diet.

2. **Impact of Vitamins C and E on Cardiovascular Health**:

- **Vitamin C**: A water-soluble antioxidant, vitamin C scavenges ROS and regenerates vitamin E, enhancing its antioxidant activity. Clinical studies have shown that vitamin C supplementation improves endothelial function and reduces oxidative stress in patients with cardiovascular diseases.

- **Vitamin E**: A lipid-soluble antioxidant, vitamin E protects cell membranes from lipid peroxidation and reduces the oxidation of LDL. While some clinical trials have shown that vitamin E supplementation reduces the risk of cardiovascular events, others have reported no significant benefits, highlighting the need for further research.

8.2 Free Radicals in Brain Metabolism and Neurodegeneration

The brain is particularly vulnerable to oxidative stress due to its high oxygen consumption, abundant lipid content, and relatively low antioxidant defenses. Free radicals play a significant role in both normal brain function and the pathogenesis of neurodegenerative diseases. This section explores the role of free radicals in brain metabolism, their contribution to neurodegenerative diseases, and potential therapeutic strategies to mitigate oxidative damage in the brain.

8.2.1 Role of Free Radicals in Brain Function

1. **High Oxygen Consumption and Oxidative Vulnerability**:

   - The brain accounts for approximately 20% of the body's total oxygen consumption, despite representing only 2% of its weight. This high metabolic rate generates significant amounts of reactive oxygen species (ROS) as byproducts.
   - Neurons are particularly vulnerable to oxidative damage due to their high lipid content, which is susceptible to lipid peroxidation, and their reliance on mitochondrial energy production, which is a major source of ROS.

2. **Role of Mitochondria in Brain Oxidative Metabolism**:

- Mitochondria are the primary source of ROS in the brain, particularly during oxidative phosphorylation. Leakage of electrons from the electron transport chain (ETC) generates superoxide radicals (O_2^-), which can be converted into other ROS, such as hydrogen peroxide (H_2O_2) and hydroxyl radicals ($\cdot OH$).
- Mitochondrial dysfunction, often observed in aging and neurodegenerative diseases, exacerbates ROS production and contributes to neuronal damage.

8.2.2 Oxidative Stress in Neurodegenerative Diseases

1. **Role of ROS in Alzheimer's Disease:**

   - Oxidative stress is a key feature of Alzheimer's disease (AD), contributing to the formation of amyloid-beta (Aβ) plaques and neurofibrillary tangles. ROS promote the aggregation of Aβ and tau proteins, which are hallmarks of AD pathology.
   - ROS also damage neuronal membranes, proteins, and DNA, leading to synaptic dysfunction and neuronal death.

2. **Parkinson's Disease and Oxidative Neuronal Damage:**

   - In Parkinson's disease (PD), oxidative stress plays a central role in the degeneration of dopaminergic neurons in the substantia nigra. ROS damage mitochondrial DNA, proteins, and lipids, impairing energy production and promoting cell death.
   - The accumulation of alpha-synuclein aggregates, a hallmark of PD, is also driven by oxidative stress, which promotes the misfolding and aggregation of this protein.

8.2.3 Mechanisms of Free Radical Damage in the Brain

1. **Lipid Peroxidation in Neuronal Membranes:**

- Neuronal membranes are rich in polyunsaturated fatty acids (PUFAs), which are highly susceptible to lipid peroxidation. ROS attack PUFAs, leading to the formation of reactive aldehydes, such as malondialdehyde (MDA) and 4-hydroxynonenal (4-HNE), which damage cellular components and impair membrane function.
- Lipid peroxidation disrupts the integrity of neuronal membranes, leading to increased permeability, impaired ion transport, and ultimately cell death.

2. **Protein Oxidation and Neurofibrillary Tangles**:

- ROS oxidize amino acid residues in proteins, leading to the formation of protein carbonyls and the loss of protein function. In neurodegenerative diseases, oxidized proteins often misfold and aggregate, forming toxic deposits such as neurofibrillary tangles in AD and Lewy bodies in PD.
- Protein oxidation also impairs the function of enzymes and signaling molecules, disrupting cellular processes and contributing to neuronal dysfunction.

8.2.4 Potential Therapies Targeting Brain Oxidative Stress

1. **Role of Neuroprotective Antioxidants (Resveratrol, Curcumin)**:

- **Resveratrol**: A polyphenol found in grapes and red wine, resveratrol has potent antioxidant and anti-inflammatory properties. It activates sirtuins, a family of proteins involved in cellular health and longevity, and reduces oxidative stress in the brain. Preclinical studies have shown that resveratrol protects against Aβ-induced toxicity and improves cognitive function in animal models of AD.
- **Curcumin**: A compound found in turmeric, curcumin has antioxidant, anti-inflammatory, and anti-amyloid properties. It inhibits the aggregation of Aβ and tau proteins and reduces oxidative stress in the brain. Clinical trials are ongoing to evaluate the efficacy of curcumin in AD and PD.

2. **Clinical Trials on Antioxidant Therapy in Neurodegeneration:**

- **Vitamin E**: Clinical trials have shown that vitamin E supplementation can slow the progression of AD in patients with mild to moderate disease. However, its efficacy in preventing AD remains unclear.
- **Coenzyme Q10 (CoQ10)**: CoQ10 is a mitochondrial antioxidant that improves energy production and reduces oxidative stress. Clinical trials in PD have shown mixed results, with some studies reporting improvements in motor function and others showing no significant benefits.
- **N-Acetylcysteine (NAC)**: NAC is a precursor of glutathione, a key antioxidant in the brain. Clinical trials are investigating its potential to reduce oxidative stress and improve cognitive function in AD and PD.

8.3 Oxidative Stress in Kidney Damage and Muscle Disorders

Oxidative stress plays a significant role in the development and progression of kidney damage and muscle disorders. In the kidneys, reactive oxygen species (ROS) contribute to inflammation, fibrosis, and dysfunction, while in muscle tissues, oxidative stress is implicated in conditions such as sarcopenia and muscular dystrophy. This section explores the role of oxidative stress in kidney dysfunction and therapeutic strategies to mitigate its effects.

8.3.1 Free Radicals and Kidney Dysfunction

8.3.1.1 Oxidative Stress in Chronic Kidney Disease (CKD)

1. **Role of ROS in Renal Inflammation:**

- ROS are key mediators of inflammation in CKD. They activate pro-inflammatory pathways, such as NF-κB and MAPK, leading to the production of cytokines (e.g., TNF-α, IL-6) and chemokines that recruit immune cells to the kidneys.

- ○ ROS also promote the expression of adhesion molecules (e.g., ICAM-1, VCAM-1) on endothelial cells, facilitating the infiltration of inflammatory cells into renal tissues.

2. **Protein Oxidation and Fibrosis in Kidney Tissues**:

- ○ ROS oxidize proteins in renal cells, leading to the formation of protein carbonyls and advanced oxidation protein products (AOPPs). These oxidized proteins impair cellular function and promote fibrosis by activating fibroblasts and increasing the production of extracellular matrix (ECM) components.
- ○ Oxidative stress also contributes to the activation of TGF-β, a key profibrotic cytokine that drives the deposition of collagen and other ECM proteins, leading to renal scarring and loss of function.

8.3.1.2 *Therapeutic Strategies for Reducing Oxidative Damage in Kidney Disease*

1. **Use of Antioxidant-Rich Diets**:

- ○ Diets rich in antioxidants, such as fruits, vegetables, nuts, and whole grains, can help reduce oxidative stress in CKD. These foods provide a wide range of antioxidants, including vitamins C and E, polyphenols, and flavonoids, which neutralize ROS and protect renal tissues.
- ○ For example, the Mediterranean diet, which is high in antioxidants and anti-inflammatory compounds, has been shown to improve kidney function and reduce the risk of CKD progression.

2. **Pharmacological Approaches**:

- ○ **N-Acetylcysteine (NAC)**: NAC is a precursor of glutathione, a key antioxidant that neutralizes ROS. It has been shown to reduce oxidative stress and inflammation in CKD patients, improving renal function and slowing disease progression.
- ○ **Alpha-Lipoic Acid (ALA)**: ALA is a potent antioxidant that scavenges ROS and regenerates other antioxidants, such as vitamins C and E.

Clinical studies have shown that ALA supplementation reduces oxidative stress and improves kidney function in patients with CKD.

- **Bardoxolone Methyl**: This synthetic triterpenoid activates the Nrf2 pathway, which upregulates the expression of antioxidant enzymes. Clinical trials have shown that bardoxolone methyl improves kidney function in CKD patients, although its long-term safety and efficacy are still under investigation.

8.3.2 Role of Free Radicals in Muscle Disorders

Oxidative stress plays a significant role in muscle disorders, including muscle fatigue, sarcopenia (age-related muscle loss), and inflammatory muscle diseases. Free radicals generated during muscle activity or due to aging can damage muscle proteins, lipids, and DNA, leading to impaired muscle function and degeneration. This section explores the mechanisms of muscle oxidative stress, its impact on muscle health, and antioxidant strategies for muscle protection.

8.3.2.1 Mechanisms of Muscle Oxidative Stress

1. **ROS Production During Intense Exercise**:

   - During intense or prolonged exercise, the demand for oxygen increases, leading to elevated ROS production in muscle mitochondria. Electron leakage from the electron transport chain (ETC) generates superoxide radicals (O_2^-), which are converted into other ROS, such as hydrogen peroxide (H_2O_2) and hydroxyl radicals ($\cdot OH$).

   - ROS are also produced by NADPH oxidase and xanthine oxidase in muscle cells during exercise. While moderate ROS levels are essential for muscle adaptation and signaling, excessive ROS production can cause oxidative damage.

2. **Oxidation of Muscle Proteins and Loss of Function**:

- ROS oxidize amino acid residues in muscle proteins, leading to the formation of protein carbonyls and the loss of protein function. Key proteins involved in muscle contraction, such as actin, myosin, and troponin, are particularly susceptible to oxidative damage.
- Oxidized proteins often misfold and aggregate, impairing muscle contraction and leading to muscle weakness and fatigue.

8.3.2.2 Free Radical Damage in Muscle Fatigue and Sarcopenia

1. **Impact of Oxidative Stress on Aging Muscles**:

   - Sarcopenia, the age-related loss of muscle mass and strength, is closely linked to oxidative stress. With aging, the production of ROS increases, while the body's antioxidant defenses decline, leading to the accumulation of oxidative damage in muscle tissues.
   - Oxidative stress promotes the activation of proteolytic pathways, such as the ubiquitin-proteasome system, which degrades muscle proteins and contributes to muscle atrophy.
   - ROS also impair mitochondrial function in aging muscles, reducing energy production and further exacerbating muscle weakness.

2. **Role in Inflammatory Muscle Disorders**:

   - Inflammatory muscle disorders, such as myositis and muscular dystrophy, are characterized by chronic inflammation and oxidative stress. ROS activate pro-inflammatory pathways, such as NF-κB, leading to the production of cytokines (e.g., TNF-α, IL-6) that promote muscle inflammation and damage.
   - ROS also contribute to muscle fibrosis by activating fibroblasts and increasing the production of extracellular matrix (ECM) components, leading to muscle stiffness and impaired function.

8.3.2.3 Antioxidant Strategies for Muscle Protection

1. **Dietary Antioxidants in Muscle Recovery**:

   - Diets rich in antioxidants, such as fruits, vegetables, nuts, and whole grains, can help reduce oxidative stress and promote muscle recovery after exercise. These foods provide a wide range of antioxidants, including vitamins C and E, polyphenols, and flavonoids, which neutralize ROS and protect muscle tissues.
   - For example, blueberries, which are rich in anthocyanins, have been shown to reduce oxidative stress and inflammation in muscles after intense exercise.

2. **Role of Vitamin E and Coenzyme Q10 in Muscle Health**:

   - **Vitamin E**: A lipid-soluble antioxidant, vitamin E protects muscle cell membranes from lipid peroxidation and reduces oxidative damage during exercise. Studies have shown that vitamin E supplementation can improve muscle recovery and reduce markers of oxidative stress in athletes.
   - **Coenzyme Q10 (CoQ10)**: CoQ10 is a mitochondrial antioxidant that improves energy production and reduces oxidative stress in muscle cells. Clinical studies have shown that CoQ10 supplementation can improve muscle strength and reduce fatigue in patients with muscle disorders and aging individuals.

8.4 Free Radical Theory of Aging

The free radical theory of aging, first proposed by Denham Harman in the 1950s, posits that the accumulation of oxidative damage caused by free radicals is a primary driver of aging and age-related diseases. Over time, this theory has evolved and gained substantial support from scientific research. This section explores the historical background, mechanisms, and impact of oxidative stress on aging, as well as strategies to mitigate its effects.

8.4.1 Historical Background and Evolution of the Free Radical Theory

1. **Introduction of the Theory by Denham Harman:**

   - In 1956, Denham Harman proposed that free radicals, generated as byproducts of normal cellular metabolism, cause cumulative damage to cells and tissues over time, leading to aging and age-related diseases.
   - Harman suggested that free radicals attack cellular components such as DNA, proteins, and lipids, impairing their function and contributing to the aging process.

2. **Evidence Supporting Oxidative Stress as a Key Factor in Aging:**

   - Over the decades, extensive research has provided evidence supporting the free radical theory of aging. Studies have shown that oxidative damage accumulates with age and is associated with the decline in cellular function and the development of age-related diseases.
   - For example, increased levels of oxidative damage markers, such as 8-hydroxydeoxyguanosine (8-OHdG) in DNA and protein carbonyls, have been observed in aged tissues.

8.4.2 Mechanisms Linking Free Radicals to Aging

1. **Accumulation of Oxidative Damage Over Time:**

   - Free radicals, particularly reactive oxygen species (ROS), cause oxidative damage to DNA, proteins, and lipids, leading to the accumulation of damaged molecules over time.
   - This damage impairs cellular function, disrupts signaling pathways, and promotes cell death, contributing to the aging process.

2. **Role of Mitochondrial Dysfunction in Aging:**

   - Mitochondria are both a major source and a target of ROS. With age, mitochondrial function declines, leading to increased ROS production and further oxidative damage.

- Mitochondrial DNA (mtDNA) is particularly vulnerable to oxidative damage due to its proximity to the electron transport chain (ETC) and lack of protective histones. Damage to mtDNA impairs energy production and exacerbates oxidative stress, creating a vicious cycle of mitochondrial dysfunction and aging.

8.4.3 Impact of Oxidative Stress on Age-Related Diseases

1. **Neurodegenerative Diseases (Alzheimer's, Parkinson's):**

   - Oxidative stress plays a central role in the pathogenesis of neurodegenerative diseases, such as Alzheimer's disease (AD) and Parkinson's disease (PD). ROS damage neuronal proteins, lipids, and DNA, leading to the formation of toxic aggregates, such as amyloid-beta plaques in AD and alpha-synuclein aggregates in PD.
   - Oxidative stress also impairs mitochondrial function and promotes inflammation, contributing to neuronal death and cognitive decline.

2. **Cardiovascular Aging and Endothelial Dysfunction:**

   - Oxidative stress contributes to cardiovascular aging by promoting endothelial dysfunction, atherosclerosis, and hypertension. ROS damage endothelial cells, reduce the bioavailability of nitric oxide (NO), and promote inflammation, leading to impaired vascular function and increased risk of cardiovascular events.

8.4.4 Strategies to Slow Down Oxidative Aging

1. **Role of Caloric Restriction and Longevity-Promoting Diets:**

   - Caloric restriction (CR) has been shown to extend lifespan and reduce oxidative stress in various model organisms, from yeast to mammals. CR reduces ROS production, enhances antioxidant defenses, and improves mitochondrial function.

- Longevity-promoting diets, such as the Mediterranean diet, are rich in antioxidants and anti-inflammatory compounds, which help reduce oxidative stress and protect against age-related diseases.

2. **Antioxidant-Based Interventions in Aging Research**:

- **Dietary Antioxidants**: Antioxidants such as vitamins C and E, polyphenols, and flavonoids neutralize ROS and reduce oxidative damage. For example, resveratrol, a polyphenol found in grapes, has been shown to activate sirtuins, a family of proteins involved in cellular health and longevity.
- **Pharmacological Antioxidants**: Compounds such as N-acetylcysteine (NAC) and coenzyme Q10 (CoQ10) have been investigated for their potential to reduce oxidative stress and improve healthspan. Clinical trials are ongoing to evaluate the efficacy of these interventions in aging and age-related diseases.

NINE

ANTIOXIDANT DEFENSE SYSTEMS IN THE BODY

The human body has evolved a sophisticated antioxidant defense system to neutralize reactive oxygen species (ROS) and maintain redox balance. These defenses include both enzymatic and non-enzymatic antioxidants, which work together to protect cells from oxidative damage. This section introduces the concept of antioxidant defense systems, their importance in maintaining redox balance, and their classification.

9.1 Endogenous Antioxidants: Enzymatic and Non-Enzymatic Defense

9.1.1 Introduction to Antioxidant Defense Systems

1. **Definition of Antioxidants and Their Role in Oxidative Stress Regulation:**

   - Antioxidants are molecules that neutralize ROS and prevent oxidative damage to cellular components such as DNA, proteins, and lipids. They do this by donating electrons to free radicals, thereby stabilizing them and breaking the chain reaction of oxidative damage.
   - Antioxidants play a critical role in regulating oxidative stress, ensuring that ROS levels remain within a physiological range that

supports cellular signaling and function without causing harm.

2. **Importance of Maintaining Redox Balance in Biological Systems**:

- Redox balance refers to the equilibrium between the production of ROS and the body's ability to neutralize them through antioxidants. Maintaining this balance is essential for cellular health and function.
- Disruption of redox balance, either due to excessive ROS production or insufficient antioxidant defenses, leads to oxidative stress, which is implicated in aging and various diseases, including cancer, cardiovascular diseases, and neurodegenerative disorders.

3. **Classification of Antioxidants: Enzymatic and Non-Enzymatic**:

- **Enzymatic Antioxidants**: These are proteins that catalyze the breakdown of ROS into less reactive or harmless molecules. Examples include superoxide dismutase (SOD), catalase (CAT), and glutathione peroxidase (GPx).
- **Non-Enzymatic Antioxidants**: These are small molecules that directly scavenge ROS or regenerate other antioxidants. Examples include glutathione, vitamin C, vitamin E, and polyphenols.

9.1.2 Enzymatic Antioxidant Defense System

Enzymatic antioxidants are proteins that play a critical role in neutralizing reactive oxygen species (ROS) and maintaining redox balance. These enzymes catalyze the conversion of ROS into less reactive or harmless molecules, protecting cells from oxidative damage. This section explores the mechanism of action of enzymatic antioxidants, their regulation, and the specific role of superoxide dismutase (SOD) as the first line of defense against free radicals.

1. **Mechanism of Action of Enzymatic Antioxidants**:

- Enzymatic antioxidants neutralize ROS through specific biochemical reactions. For example, superoxide dismutase (SOD) converts superoxide radicals (O_2^-) into hydrogen peroxide (H_2O_2), which is then broken down into water (H_2O) and oxygen (O_2) by catalase (CAT) or glutathione peroxidase (GPx).

- These enzymes work in concert to maintain low levels of ROS and prevent oxidative damage to cellular components.

2. **Regulation of Enzymatic Antioxidants by Genetic and Environmental Factors**:

- The expression and activity of enzymatic antioxidants are regulated by genetic factors, such as transcription factors (e.g., Nrf2) that upregulate antioxidant genes in response to oxidative stress.
- Environmental factors, such as diet, exercise, and exposure to pollutants, can also influence the levels and activity of enzymatic antioxidants. For example, caloric restriction and physical activity have been shown to enhance antioxidant defenses.

9.1.2.1 Superoxide Dismutase (SOD) – The First Line of Defense

1. **Function of SOD in Free Radical Neutralization**:

- SOD catalyzes the dismutation of superoxide radicals (O_2^-) into hydrogen peroxide (H_2O_2) and oxygen (O_2). This reaction is the first step in neutralizing superoxide radicals, which are highly reactive and can damage cellular components.

2. **Types of SOD and Their Cellular Locations**:

- **Cu/Zn-SOD (Cytosolic)**: Found in the cytoplasm, this form of SOD contains copper and zinc as cofactors. It is encoded by the SOD1 gene and is the most abundant form of SOD in mammalian cells.
- **Mn-SOD (Mitochondrial)**: Located in the mitochondria, this form of SOD contains manganese as a cofactor. It is encoded by the SOD2 gene and plays a critical role in protecting mitochondria from oxidative damage.

- **Fe-SOD (Bacterial and Plant Cells)**: Found in bacteria and plants, this form of SOD contains iron as a cofactor. It is not present in mammalian cells.

3. **Clinical Significance of SOD Activity**:

   - **Role in Neurodegenerative Diseases**:

     - **Amyotrophic Lateral Sclerosis (ALS)**: Mutations in the SOD1 gene are associated with familial ALS, a neurodegenerative disease characterized by the loss of motor neurons. These mutations lead to the accumulation of misfolded SOD1, which is toxic to neurons.
     - **Parkinson's Disease**: Reduced SOD activity has been observed in the brains of Parkinson's disease patients, contributing to oxidative stress and neuronal damage.

   - **SOD-Mimetic Drugs in Disease Management**:

     - SOD-mimetic drugs, such as tempol and MnTBAP, mimic the activity of SOD and have shown promise in preclinical studies for treating diseases associated with oxidative stress, including neurodegenerative disorders, cardiovascular diseases, and cancer.

9.1.2.2 Catalase – Hydrogen Peroxide Detoxification

Catalase is a key enzymatic antioxidant that plays a crucial role in detoxifying hydrogen peroxide (H_2O_2), a reactive oxygen species (ROS) generated during cellular metabolism. By breaking down H_2O_2 into water and oxygen, catalase protects cells from oxidative damage and maintains redox balance. This section explores the function of catalase, its tissue distribution, and its clinical significance, particularly in metabolic disorders and aging.

1. **Function of Catalase in Oxidative Stress Control**:

   - Catalase catalyzes the breakdown of hydrogen peroxide (H_2O_2) into water (H_2O) and oxygen (O_2). This reaction prevents the accumulation of H_2O_2, which can otherwise react with transition metals (e.g., iron) to form highly reactive hydroxyl radicals ($\cdot OH$) via the Fenton reaction.

2. **Tissue Distribution of Catalase**:

- Catalase is widely distributed in tissues, with the highest activity found in the liver, kidneys, and erythrocytes (red blood cells). These organs are exposed to high levels of ROS due to their metabolic activity and role in detoxification.
- In the liver, catalase plays a critical role in detoxifying H_2O_2 generated during the metabolism of drugs and xenobiotics.
- In erythrocytes, catalase protects hemoglobin and cell membranes from oxidative damage caused by H_2O_2.

3. **Clinical Significance of Catalase Deficiency**:

- **Role in Metabolic Disorders**:

  - Catalase deficiency has been linked to metabolic disorders such as type 2 diabetes and obesity. Reduced catalase activity leads to the accumulation of H_2O_2, which impairs insulin signaling and promotes insulin resistance.
  - In diabetes, oxidative stress contributes to complications such as diabetic nephropathy and retinopathy, where catalase activity is often reduced.

- **Role in Aging**:

  - Catalase activity declines with age, contributing to the accumulation of oxidative damage and the development of age-related diseases. Reduced catalase activity has been observed in aging tissues, including the brain, heart, and muscles.
  - Studies in model organisms have shown that overexpression of catalase can extend lifespan and reduce age-related oxidative damage, highlighting its importance in aging and longevity.

9.1.2.3 Glutathione Peroxidase – The Selenium-Dependent Antioxidant

Glutathione peroxidase (GPx) is a critical enzymatic antioxidant that plays a key role in reducing peroxide-induced damage by catalyzing the breakdown of hydrogen peroxide (H_2O_2) and lipid peroxides. This selenium-dependent enzyme is essential for maintaining cellular redox balance and protecting cells from oxidative stress. This section explores the function of GPx, the role of selenium as a co-factor, and the clinical implications of GPx deficiency.

1. **Role in Reducing Peroxide-Induced Damage**:

GPx catalyzes the reduction of hydrogen peroxide (H_2O_2) and lipid peroxides (LOOH) to water (H_2O) and corresponding alcohols, respectively. This reaction prevents the accumulation of peroxides, which can otherwise cause oxidative damage to cellular components.

where GSH is reduced glutathione and GSSG is oxidized glutathione.

1. **Selenium as a Co-factor in Glutathione Peroxidase Activity**:

   ◦ Selenium is an essential trace element that serves as a co-factor for GPx. It is incorporated into the active site of GPx as selenocysteine, which is critical for the enzyme's catalytic activity.
   ◦ **Dietary Sources of Selenium**: Selenium is found in foods such as Brazil nuts, seafood, eggs, and whole grains. Adequate dietary intake of selenium is essential for maintaining GPx activity and overall antioxidant defense.
   ◦ **Impact on Enzyme Function**: Selenium deficiency impairs GPx activity, leading to increased oxidative stress and susceptibility to oxidative damage. Conversely, adequate selenium levels enhance GPx activity and protect against oxidative stress-related diseases.

2. **Clinical Implications of Glutathione Peroxidase Deficiency**:

   ◦ **Association with Cardiovascular Diseases**:

     ▪ Reduced GPx activity has been linked to cardiovascular diseases, such as atherosclerosis and hypertension. Oxidative stress contributes to endothelial dysfunction, inflammation, and lipid peroxidation, all of which are key factors in the development of cardiovascular diseases.

- Studies have shown that selenium supplementation can improve GPx activity and reduce oxidative stress in patients with cardiovascular diseases.

- **Association with Cancer Progression**:

  - GPx deficiency has been associated with increased cancer risk and progression. Oxidative stress promotes DNA damage, mutations, and genomic instability, which drive cancer initiation and progression.
  - Reduced GPx activity has been observed in various cancers, including prostate, lung, and breast cancer. Enhancing GPx activity through selenium supplementation or other strategies may help reduce cancer risk and improve outcomes.

9.1.3 Non-Enzymatic Antioxidant Defense System

Non-enzymatic antioxidants are small molecules that play a crucial role in neutralizing reactive oxygen species (ROS) and maintaining cellular redox balance. Unlike enzymatic antioxidants, they do not catalyze reactions but instead directly scavenge ROS or regenerate other antioxidants. This section explores the mechanism of non-enzymatic antioxidant function, their interaction with enzymatic systems, and the specific role of glutathione as the "master antioxidant."

1. **Mechanism of Non-Enzymatic Antioxidant Function**:

   - Non-enzymatic antioxidants neutralize ROS by donating electrons or hydrogen atoms, thereby stabilizing free radicals and preventing oxidative damage.
   - They can also chelate transition metals (e.g., iron and copper), preventing the formation of highly reactive hydroxyl radicals ($\cdot$OH) via the Fenton reaction.

2. **Interaction of Non-Enzymatic Antioxidants with Enzymatic Systems**:

- Non-enzymatic antioxidants often work synergistically with enzymatic antioxidants to enhance cellular defense against oxidative stress. For example, glutathione (GSH) regenerates vitamin C and vitamin E, which in turn protect cell membranes and other cellular components from oxidative damage.
- The interplay between non-enzymatic and enzymatic antioxidants ensures a robust and efficient antioxidant defense system.

9.1.3.1 Glutathione – The Master Antioxidant

1. **Chemical Structure and Biosynthesis of Glutathione**:

- Glutathione (GSH) is a tripeptide composed of three amino acids: cysteine, glycine, and glutamate. Its chemical structure is γ-glutamyl-cysteinyl-glycine.
- **Role of Cysteine, Glycine, and Glutamate in Glutathione Formation**:

  - Cysteine provides the thiol (-SH) group, which is critical for GSH's antioxidant activity.
  - Glycine and glutamate stabilize the molecule and facilitate its synthesis.

- GSH is synthesized in the cytoplasm of cells through a two-step enzymatic process involving glutamate-cysteine ligase (GCL) and glutathione synthetase (GSS).

2. **Functions of Glutathione in Cellular Redox Balance**:

- **Detoxification of Reactive Oxygen Species (ROS)**:

  - GSH directly scavenges ROS, such as hydrogen peroxide (H_2O_2) and hydroxyl radicals ($\cdot OH$), and reduces lipid peroxides, protecting cells from oxidative damage.

- GSH also serves as a co-factor for glutathione peroxidase (GPx), which catalyzes the reduction of H_2O_2 and lipid peroxides.

- **Recycling of Other Antioxidants (Vitamin C and E):**

  - GSH regenerates oxidized vitamin C (dehydroascorbic acid) and vitamin E (tocopheroxyl radical), restoring their antioxidant activity and enhancing cellular defense.

3. **Clinical Importance of Glutathione Levels:**

- **Impact of Glutathione Depletion in Neurodegenerative Disorders:**

  - Reduced GSH levels have been observed in neurodegenerative diseases, such as Alzheimer's disease (AD) and Parkinson's disease (PD). GSH depletion contributes to oxidative stress, neuronal damage, and disease progression.
  - Enhancing GSH levels through supplementation or activation of its biosynthesis has shown promise in preclinical studies for mitigating neurodegeneration.

- **Role in Immune System Function and Detoxification:**

  - GSH is essential for the proper functioning of immune cells, such as lymphocytes and macrophages. It supports immune responses by regulating redox signaling and protecting immune cells from oxidative damage.
  - GSH also plays a critical role in detoxification by conjugating with toxins and facilitating their excretion through the liver.

9.2 Role of α-Lipoic Acid and Melatonin in Antioxidant Defense

α-Lipoic acid (ALA) and melatonin are unique antioxidants that play critical roles in cellular defense against oxidative stress. They not only directly scavenge reactive oxygen species (ROS) and reactive nitrogen species (RNS) but also enhance the activity of other antioxidants and support mitochondrial function. This section focuses on the chemical structure, biosynthesis, and mechanism of action of α-lipoic acid as a potent antioxidant.

9.2.1 α-Lipoic Acid – A Unique Antioxidant with Dual Properties

9.2.1.1 Chemical Structure and Biosynthesis

1. **Endogenous Synthesis of α-Lipoic Acid in Mitochondria:**

   - α-Lipoic acid (ALA) is a naturally occurring compound synthesized in mitochondria from octanoic acid. It contains a dithiolane ring with two sulfur atoms, which are critical for its antioxidant activity.
   - ALA is a co-factor for mitochondrial enzymes involved in energy metabolism, such as pyruvate dehydrogenase and α-ketoglutarate dehydrogenase.

2. **Dietary Sources and Absorption Efficiency:**

   - ALA is found in small amounts in foods such as spinach, broccoli, potatoes, and organ meats (e.g., liver and kidney).
   - It is efficiently absorbed from the diet and can cross cell membranes due to its amphipathic nature (both water- and fat-soluble).

9.2.1.2 Mechanism of Action as an Antioxidant

1. **Direct Scavenging of ROS and RNS:**

   - ALA directly neutralizes ROS, such as hydroxyl radicals ($\cdot$OH), superoxide radicals (O_2^-), and RNS, such as peroxynitrite ($ONOO^-$). Its dithiol group is oxidized during this process, forming dihydrolipoic acid (DHLA), which also has antioxidant properties.

2. **Regeneration of Other Antioxidants (Glutathione, Vitamin C, Vitamin E):**

   - ALA regenerates oxidized antioxidants, such as glutathione (GSSG to GSH), vitamin C (dehydroascorbic acid to ascorbic acid), and vitamin E (tocopheroxyl radical to tocopherol), enhancing the overall antioxidant capacity of cells.
   - This recycling mechanism ensures that other antioxidants remain active and effective in neutralizing ROS.

3. **Enhancement of Mitochondrial Function and Energy Metabolism:**

   - ALA improves mitochondrial function by reducing oxidative damage to mitochondrial DNA, proteins, and lipids.
   - It enhances energy metabolism by supporting the activity of mitochondrial enzymes involved in the citric acid cycle and oxidative phosphorylation.

9.2.1.3 Health Benefits of α-Lipoic Acid

α-Lipoic acid (ALA) has garnered significant attention for its wide range of health benefits, particularly in neurodegenerative diseases, cardiovascular health, and metabolic disorders. Its unique antioxidant properties and ability to enhance mitochondrial function make it a valuable therapeutic agent. This section explores the health benefits of ALA and its clinical applications.

Health Benefits of α-Lipoic Acid

1. **Neuroprotective Effects in Neurodegenerative Diseases:**

   - **Role in Alzheimer's and Parkinson's Disease Prevention:**

     - ALA reduces oxidative stress and inflammation in the brain, protecting neurons from damage. It inhibits the formation of amyloid-beta (Aβ) plaques in Alzheimer's disease (AD) and prevents the aggregation of alpha-synuclein in Parkinson's disease (PD).

- ALA also enhances mitochondrial function and energy production in neurons, improving cognitive function and motor performance in preclinical models of AD and PD.

2. **Cardioprotective Effects and Vascular Health**:

   ○ **Reduction of Oxidative Damage in Endothelial Cells**:

     - ALA protects endothelial cells from oxidative stress, improving nitric oxide (NO) bioavailability and enhancing vasodilation. This helps maintain vascular health and reduces the risk of atherosclerosis and hypertension.
     - ALA also reduces lipid peroxidation and inflammation in blood vessels, preventing plaque formation and improving cardiovascular outcomes.

3. **Metabolic Benefits in Diabetes and Insulin Sensitivity**:

   ○ **Improvement of Glucose Metabolism and Reduction of Oxidative Stress**:

     - ALA enhances insulin sensitivity and glucose uptake in skeletal muscle and adipose tissue, making it beneficial for managing type 2 diabetes.
     - It reduces oxidative stress in pancreatic beta cells, protecting them from damage and improving insulin secretion.
     - Clinical studies have shown that ALA supplementation improves glycemic control and reduces symptoms of diabetic neuropathy.

9.2.1.4 Clinical Research on α-Lipoic Acid Supplementation

1. **Clinical Trials on Diabetic Neuropathy**:

   ○ ALA has been extensively studied for its ability to alleviate symptoms of diabetic neuropathy, such as pain, numbness, and tingling. Clinical trials have shown that intravenous or oral ALA supplementation improves nerve function and reduces oxidative stress in patients with diabetic neuropathy.

2. **Studies on α-Lipoic Acid as a Therapeutic Agent for Metabolic Disorders:**

   ◦ ALA has shown promise in improving metabolic health by reducing oxidative stress, enhancing insulin sensitivity, and promoting weight loss. Clinical trials are ongoing to evaluate its efficacy in managing metabolic syndrome, obesity, and non-alcoholic fatty liver disease (NAFLD).

9.2.2 Melatonin – The Sleep Hormone with Antioxidant Properties

Melatonin is a hormone primarily known for its role in regulating sleep-wake cycles, but it also has potent antioxidant properties. It is synthesized in the pineal gland and plays a critical role in protecting cells from oxidative damage. This section explores the synthesis, regulation, and dietary sources of melatonin.

9.2.2.1 Synthesis and Regulation of Melatonin

1. **Production of Melatonin in the Pineal Gland:**

   ◦ Melatonin is synthesized from the amino acid tryptophan in the pineal gland. The synthesis process involves the conversion of tryptophan to serotonin, which is then converted to melatonin by the enzymes serotonin N-acetyltransferase (SNAT) and acetylserotonin O-methyltransferase (ASMT).
   ◦ Melatonin production is regulated by the suprachiasmatic nucleus (SCN) of the hypothalamus, which responds to light-dark cycles.

2. **Circadian Rhythm and Melatonin Secretion:**

- Melatonin secretion follows a circadian rhythm, with levels rising in the evening, peaking during the night, and declining in the morning. This rhythm helps regulate sleep-wake cycles and other physiological processes.

3. **Dietary Sources of Melatonin and Absorption:**

- Melatonin is found in small amounts in foods such as cherries, grapes, tomatoes, and nuts. It is also available as a dietary supplement.
- Melatonin is efficiently absorbed from the diet and can cross the blood-brain barrier, making it effective for both sleep regulation and antioxidant defense.

9.2.2.2 Mechanism of Antioxidant Action of Melatonin

Melatonin is a potent antioxidant that protects cells from oxidative damage through multiple mechanisms. Its ability to scavenge free radicals, enhance mitochondrial function, and modulate inflammation makes it a unique and versatile molecule in combating oxidative stress. This section explores the mechanisms by which melatonin exerts its antioxidant effects.

1. **Free Radical Scavenging and ROS Detoxification:**

- Melatonin directly scavenges reactive oxygen species (ROS) and reactive nitrogen species (RNS), including hydroxyl radicals ($\cdot$OH), superoxide radicals (O_2^-), and peroxynitrite ($ONOO^-$).
- It also upregulates the expression of antioxidant enzymes, such as superoxide dismutase (SOD), catalase (CAT), and glutathione peroxidase (GPx), enhancing the cell's ability to neutralize ROS.

2. **Enhancement of Mitochondrial Antioxidant Defense:**

- Melatonin accumulates in mitochondria, where it protects mitochondrial DNA, proteins, and lipids from oxidative damage.
- It improves mitochondrial function by enhancing electron transport chain (ETC) efficiency and reducing electron leakage, thereby

minimizing ROS production.

3. **Anti-Inflammatory and Immune-Modulating Effects**:

- Melatonin inhibits the activation of pro-inflammatory pathways, such as NF-κB and MAPK, reducing the production of cytokines (e.g., TNF-α, IL-6) and chemokines.
- It also modulates immune responses by regulating the activity of immune cells, such as T cells and macrophages, and reducing oxidative stress-induced inflammation.

9.2.2.3 Health Benefits of Melatonin

1. **Neuroprotection and Brain Aging**:

   - **Role in Cognitive Function and Prevention of Neurodegeneration**:

     - Melatonin protects neurons from oxidative damage, reduces the formation of amyloid-beta (Aβ) plaques in Alzheimer's disease (AD), and prevents the aggregation of alpha-synuclein in Parkinson's disease (PD).
     - It enhances synaptic plasticity and memory, making it beneficial for cognitive health and brain aging.

2. **Cardiovascular Protection**:

   - **Melatonin in Blood Pressure Regulation and Endothelial Function**:

     - Melatonin improves endothelial function by increasing nitric oxide (NO) bioavailability and reducing oxidative stress in blood vessels.
     - It helps regulate blood pressure and reduces the risk of hypertension, atherosclerosis, and other cardiovascular diseases.

3. **Role in Sleep Disorders and Stress Management**:

- **Use of Melatonin in Insomnia and Circadian Rhythm Disorders**:

  - Melatonin is widely used to treat sleep disorders, such as insomnia and delayed sleep phase syndrome, by regulating the sleep-wake cycle.
  - It also helps manage stress by reducing cortisol levels and promoting relaxation.

9.2.2.4 Clinical Research on Melatonin Supplementation

1. **Studies on Melatonin in Neurodegenerative Diseases**:

   - Clinical trials have shown that melatonin supplementation improves sleep quality and cognitive function in patients with Alzheimer's disease (AD) and Parkinson's disease (PD).
   - Melatonin's antioxidant and anti-inflammatory properties make it a promising therapeutic agent for slowing the progression of neurodegenerative diseases.

2. **Melatonin's Impact on Cardiovascular Health**:

   - Studies have demonstrated that melatonin supplementation reduces oxidative stress, improves endothelial function, and lowers blood pressure in patients with cardiovascular diseases.
   - It also reduces the risk of myocardial infarction and stroke by protecting the heart and blood vessels from oxidative damage.

TEN

SYNTHETIC AND NATURAL ANTIOXIDANTS

10.1 Synthetic Antioxidants and Their Uses

10.1.1 Introduction to Synthetic Antioxidants

Synthetic antioxidants are chemical compounds that are deliberately added to food, pharmaceuticals, and cosmetics to prevent or slow down the process of oxidation. Oxidation is a reaction that occurs when substances like oxygen or free radicals interact with biomolecules, leading to damage and deterioration. In food products, oxidation leads to rancidity, color changes, nutrient loss, and the formation of harmful compounds. In pharmaceuticals, oxidation can lead to the degradation of active ingredients, compromising drug efficacy and stability. Thus, synthetic antioxidants play a critical role in preserving the quality of these products and extending their shelf life.

The primary function of synthetic antioxidants is to act as free radical scavengers, stabilizers, or inhibitors of oxidative chain reactions. By preventing the formation of free radicals or neutralizing the already formed radicals, synthetic antioxidants protect the integrity of the products they are added to. The ability to act on lipid peroxidation, protein oxidation, and DNA damage makes them essential in both food preservation and medical formulations.

Comparison of Synthetic and Natural Antioxidants

While both **synthetic** and **natural antioxidants** serve the same fundamental purpose—**reducing oxidative stress**—they differ in their sources, effectiveness, and potential health implications. Here is a comparison of these two types of antioxidants:

1. **Source**:

   - Synthetic Antioxidants: These are chemically synthesized in laboratories. Some common examples include butylated hydroxy anisole (BHA), butylated hydroxy toluene (BHT), and propyl gallate (PG). They are artificially manufactured from petroleum-based products.
   - Natural Antioxidants: These are naturally found in foods like fruits, vegetables, spices, and herbs. Examples include vitamin C, vitamin E, flavonoids, and phenolic acids.

2. **Effectiveness**:

   - Synthetic Antioxidants: Some synthetic antioxidants like BHT and BHA are highly effective at preventing oxidation in food and pharmaceutical products. They work by interrupting the free radical chain reactions and are often more stable than some natural antioxidants, especially in processed foods.
   - Natural Antioxidants: Natural antioxidants generally offer broader health benefits, such as anti-inflammatory, anti-cancer, and anti-aging effects. However, they are often less stable during processing and storage, especially in heat and light, making them less suitable for certain food preservation purposes.

3. **Safety and Health Implications**:

   - Synthetic Antioxidants: While synthetic antioxidants have proven effective in food preservation, some of them, such as BHA and BHT, have raised concerns regarding their safety in human consumption. Research has linked these compounds to carcinogenicity and endocrine disruption, although their use in food is still permitted within regulated limits.

○ Natural Antioxidants: Natural antioxidants are often perceived as safer due to their presence in natural foods, but their concentration may vary depending on the source. Moreover, the presence of other bioactive compounds may enhance their health-promoting effects, making them a better choice for long-term health benefits.

4. **Cost and Production**:

○ Synthetic Antioxidants: Synthetic antioxidants are often more cost-effective and easier to produce on a large scale, making them a preferred choice in food processing and pharmaceuticals where cost-efficiency is crucial.

○ Natural Antioxidants: Natural antioxidants tend to be more expensive due to the need for extraction from natural sources and the lower yields in some cases. The production costs of natural antioxidants may be higher, but they are in demand due to the growing consumer preference for natural and clean-label products.

Industrial Applications of Synthetic Antioxidants in Food and Pharmaceuticals

1. Food Industry: Synthetic antioxidants are widely used in the food industry to prevent oxidative spoilage of fats and oils. In products like margarine, snack foods, baked goods, and preserved meats, BHA, BHT, and PG are used to extend shelf life and maintain product quality. They prevent rancidity, which occurs when unsaturated fats undergo oxidation, leading to unpleasant flavors, odors, and the loss of nutrients.

○ BHA and BHT: These are fat-soluble antioxidants commonly used in processed foods like chips, crackers, and oils. They stabilize fats by preventing the formation of free radicals, which would otherwise break down the fat molecules and lead to spoilage.

○ Propyl Gallate (PG): This antioxidant is primarily used in processed meats, vegetable oils, and beverages to prevent oxidation of fats and oils.

○ Ascorbyl Palmitate: A lipid-soluble form of vitamin C used in fatty foods to prevent oxidation and improve food stability.

2. Pharmaceutical Industry: In the pharmaceutical industry, synthetic antioxidants play a crucial role in stabilizing medications, especially those that are susceptible to oxidative degradation, such as lipophilic drugs and vitamins. Antioxidants like BHA, BHT, and ascorbic acid are added to pharmaceutical formulations to preserve the potency and efficacy of drugs during storage and transportation.

   ○ Preservation of Active Pharmaceutical Ingredients (APIs): Some drug compounds, especially hormonal medications, antibiotics, and chemotherapy drugs, are highly sensitive to oxidation. The incorporation of synthetic antioxidants helps maintain their stability and potency.
   ○ Cosmetics and Skincare: In the cosmetic industry, antioxidants are used in creams, lotions, and serums to prevent the oxidation of active ingredients such as retinoids, vitamin C, and essential oils, which are prone to degradation upon exposure to air and light. Antioxidants like BHT and toco**herols** are frequently included in these products to preserve their **effectiveness**.

3. Personal Care Products: Synthetic antioxidants are also present in personal care products, especially in those containing oils or emulsions. Products like anti-aging creams and serums benefit from the inclusion of antioxidants to prevent lipid oxidation and preserve the active ingredients.

10.1.2 Mechanism of Action of Synthetic Antioxidants

Free Radical Scavenging and Inhibition of Oxidation

Synthetic antioxidants act as free radical scavengers, effectively neutralizing harmful reactive molecules, such as free radicals and reactive oxygen species (ROS). Free radicals are unstable molecules that have unpaired electrons, making them highly reactive. They can initiate a chain reaction of oxidation, leading to damage of biological molecules, such as lipids, proteins, and DNA. This damage plays a key role in the development of chronic diseases, aging, and inflammation.

Synthetic antioxidants prevent this damage by donating electrons to free radicals, effectively neutralizing them without becoming reactive themselves. The most commonly used synthetic antioxidants, such as butylated hydroxy toluene (BHT), butylated hydroxy anisole (BHA), and propyl gallate (PG), interrupt the free radical chain reaction, preventing the propagation of oxidative damage. By stabilizing free radicals, these antioxidants inhibit the oxidative processes that would otherwise lead to the deterioration of food products and the degradation of pharmaceutical compounds.

In food products, the reactive oxygen species (ROS) produced during oxidative stress attack the unsaturated fatty acids, leading to lipid peroxidation. Synthetic antioxidants inhibit this process by interrupting the formation of lipid peroxides, thus protecting food from rancidity. Similarly, in biological systems, they help reduce oxidative damage to cellular structures, maintaining cellular integrity and function.

Prevention of Lipid Peroxidation in Food and Biological Systems

One of the primary roles of synthetic antioxidants is to prevent lipid peroxidation. Lipid peroxidation occurs when free radicals attack polyunsaturated fatty acids (PUFAs) in cellular membranes or in food products, leading to the formation of lipid peroxides. These peroxides can then break down into aldehydes, ketones, and other toxic products. The accumulation of these products not only leads to loss of nutritional value in food, but it can also contribute to cellular damage in living organisms.

Synthetic antioxidants, such as BHT, BHA, and vitamin E analogs, effectively inhibit lipid peroxidation by intercepting free radicals before they can attack fatty acids. These antioxidants neutralize the free radicals by donating electrons, which disrupts the oxidation cycle. In addition to inhibiting the initial stages of lipid oxidation, synthetic antioxidants also prevent the formation of toxic byproducts, such as malondialdehyde (MDA) and 4-hydroxy-2-nonenal (HNE), which are harmful to both food quality and human health.

- In Food: Synthetic antioxidants, such as BHA and BHT, are frequently used to prevent rancidity in oils, margarine, snacks, and preserved meats. These antioxidants protect the lipid matrix in these products, ensuring the retention of taste, texture, and nutritional value. This is particularly important in processed foods with high-fat content, where oxidation would otherwise lead to off-flavors, odor, and nutrient loss.

- In Biological Systems: In the human body, synthetic antioxidants help protect cell membranes, lipoproteins, and other fat-soluble components from oxidative damage. Oxidized lipids can impair the fluidity of cell membranes, disrupt cell signaling, and even contribute to the development of diseases such as atherosclerosis. By preventing lipid peroxidation, synthetic antioxidants help **maintain cellular integrity** and **prevent tissue damage.**

Impact on Shelf Life and Stability of Food Products

The addition of synthetic antioxidants to food products is a critical strategy in extending the shelf life and preserving the quality of foods. As oxidative processes lead to rancidity, color changes, and loss of flavor, antioxidants provide a protective effect by mitigating these changes and ensuring that food remains fresh and nutritious for a longer period. In food storage, especially for products that contain fats, oils, or nutrients prone to oxidation (such as vitamins), the use of antioxidants helps to maintain the stability of the product under normal storage conditions (light, air, and temperature fluctuations).

For example, BHT and BHA are lipid-soluble antioxidants that are widely used in fats and oils to prevent rancidity caused by oxidative degradation of unsaturated fats. These antioxidants work by interfering with the initiation and propagation of the free radical chain reactions that drive the oxidation of fats, thus preserving the taste, texture, and nutritional value of the product for longer.

In addition to preserving the quality of lipid-rich food products, synthetic antioxidants are also used in the preservation of vitamins and nutrients in food products. For instance, ascorbic acid (vitamin C) and vitamin E are vulnerable to oxidation, leading to their loss in processed foods. Synthetic antioxidants can help stabilize these vitamins, maintaining their potency and effectiveness in food products.

In Pharmaceuticals:

The stability of active pharmaceutical ingredients (APIs) is crucial for maintaining the efficacy and safety of drugs. Many drugs, especially lipophilic drugs, are prone to oxidation, which can alter their potency and even cause toxic byproducts. The incorporation of synthetic antioxidants into pharmaceutical formulations helps prevent oxidative degradation, ensuring that drugs remain stable, safe, and effective for longer periods.

For example, vitamin C, often used in formulations for immunity boosting, is highly susceptible to oxidative breakdown. BHT or ascorbic acid derivatives are often included in pharmaceutical formulations to protect against oxidative degradation and preserve the drug's effectiveness.

10.1.3 Butylated Hydroxy Toluene (BHT)

10.1.3.1 Chemical Structure and Properties

Butylated Hydroxy Toluene (BHT) is a widely used synthetic antioxidant in the food, pharmaceutical, and cosmetic industries. Its molecular formula is $C_{15}H_{22}O$, and it consists of a toluene (methylbenzene) structure with two butyl groups attached to the hydroxyl group at the para position. BHT is a fat-soluble compound, making it particularly effective in preventing oxidation in lipid-rich products.

- Solubility: BHT is soluble in lipids and alcohol, but it has low solubility in water, which makes it effective in oil-based formulations and fatty foods.
- Stability: BHT is stable under normal storage conditions, with a high melting point of approximately 69°C and boiling point of 265°C. However, its stability can be influenced by environmental conditions such as temperature, light exposure, and pH. While BHT is relatively stable in neutral to slightly alkaline environments, prolonged exposure to high temperatures and light may degrade its antioxidant properties.
- Chemical Activity: BHT acts as a free radical scavenger, interrupting the oxidation of lipids by donating electrons to free radicals, thus neutralizing them and preventing lipid peroxidation. This makes it useful for stabilizing fats and oils in food products and pharmaceutical formulations.

10.1.3.2 Uses of BHT in Food and Pharmaceuticals

BHT is used extensively in food, cosmetic, and pharmaceutical industries due to its antioxidant properties, which help extend shelf life and maintain product quality. Here are some of the primary uses of BHT:

Role in Preventing Oxidation of Fats and Oils

BHT is primarily used as a preservative to prevent the oxidation of unsaturated fats and oils. Lipid peroxidation, which occurs when free radicals attack polyunsaturated fatty acids in food, leads to rancidity, unpleasant odors, and the loss of nutritional value. BHT inhibits this process by neutralizing free radicals, thereby protecting the taste, texture, and nutritional content of oils in food products such as margarine, fried snacks, and baked goods. BHT is particularly effective in processed or packaged foods that contain high levels of fats and oils, such as chips, butter, instant noodles, and dips.

Application in Food Preservation and Cosmetics

In the food industry, BHT helps preserve lipid-rich products from oxidative spoilage, extending their shelf life and improving product stability. Besides food, BHT is also used in cosmetic products, including creams, lotions, and shampoos, to protect oils and active ingredients from oxidative damage caused by air exposure and light. It is especially beneficial in formulations that contain essential oils and lipophilic active compounds, ensuring their stability over time.

Use in Pharmaceutical Formulations

BHT plays a crucial role in the pharmaceutical industry, where it is used to stabilize lipophilic drugs and prevent their oxidation. For example, in formulations such as capsules, oral tablets, and topical creams, BHT is added to preserve the integrity and potency of active pharmaceutical ingredients (APIs) that are sensitive to oxidative degradation. It is also employed in injectable medications, where oxidation can reduce the effectiveness of the drug. Additionally, BHT is included in vitamin preparations, particularly vitamin A and vitamin E, to maintain their stability and prevent degradation.

10.1.3.3 Health Effects and Safety Concerns of BHT

While BHT has been extensively used for its **antioxidant** properties, concerns regarding its **safety** have been raised, particularly in relation to **long-term consumption** and **high doses.**

Studies on BHT Toxicity and Potential Carcinogenicity

Research on BHT toxicity has shown that it is relatively safe when used in low concentrations in food and pharmaceuticals. However, high doses of BHT in animal studies have raised concerns about its carcinogenic and toxic potential. In rodent studies, some evidence has been found linking BHT to liver and kidney toxicity when consumed in large quantities over extended periods. Additionally, BHT has been classified as a possible human carcinogen (Group 2B) by the International Agency for Research on Cancer (IARC) based on animal studies. However, studies in humans have not conclusively proven that BHT is carcinogenic.

To mitigate health risks, regulatory bodies such as the FDA and European Food Safety Authority (EFSA) have set acceptable daily intake limits for BHT in food and pharmaceuticals. Permissible limits for BHT in food products generally range from 0.02% to 0.1%, depending on the type of product. In pharmaceuticals, the concentration is tightly regulated to ensure safety during administration. Despite some concerns, moderate consumption of BHT in regulated quantities is generally considered safe for human health.

Regulatory Guidelines and Permissible Limits in Food and Medicine

Regulatory agencies, such as the FDA, EFSA, and the World Health Organization (WHO), have established guidelines for the use of BHT in food and medicine. According to the FDA, BHT is generally recognized as safe (GRAS) when used within the established acceptable daily intake levels. However, its use is regulated, and it is only approved for specific applications, such as in fats, oils, and processed foods. For pharmaceuticals, BHT is considered a stabilizing agent and is used within strict concentration limits to prevent oxidation without compromising safety.

10.1.3.4 Clinical and Experimental Research on BHT

BHT has been the subject of several **clinical studies** and **experimental research** focusing on its potential benefits and risks in relation to **oxidative stress** and **immune modulation.**

Research on BHT's Effects on Oxidative Stress

Experimental studies have explored BHT's role in mitigating oxidative stress in human cells and animal models. It has been shown to reduce the production of reactive oxygen species (ROS) and inhibit lipid peroxidation, which are essential mechanisms of oxidative damage in diseases like cardiovascular diseases, diabetes, and neurodegenerative conditions. Clinical trials have indicated that BHT supplementation may offer protection against oxidative DNA damage, which is often associated with aging and the development of chronic diseases.

Additionally, BHT has been evaluated for its potential role in enhancing antioxidant defenses in the body. It is believed to upregulate endogenous antioxidant enzymes such as superoxide dismutase (SOD) and glutathione peroxidase (GPx), which help mitigate oxidative damage and support cellular health. Further research is needed to fully understand BHT's therapeutic potential in combating oxidative stress-related diseases.

Studies on BHT and Immune Modulation

BHT has also been studied for its potential role in immune modulation. In experimental settings, BHT has been shown to enhance immune responses, including the activation of natural killer (NK) cells, which play a key role in viral defense and tumor surveillance. Additionally, BHT has been observed to modulate inflammatory pathways, potentially offering therapeutic effects in autoimmune disorders and chronic inflammation.

However, the use of BHT in clinical immune modulation is still under investigation, with more studies required to assess the long-term effects of BHT on immune function and overall health.

10.1.4 Butylated Hydroxy Anisole (BHA)

10.1.4.1 Chemical Structure and Properties

Butylated Hydroxy Anisole (BHA) is a widely used synthetic antioxidant, particularly in the food industry, to prevent oxidative spoilage in fat-containing products. Its molecular structure consists of a hydroxy group (OH) attached to an anisole structure, with two butyl groups attached to the phenolic ring at the para position. The general chemical formula for BHA is $C_{10}H_{14}O$. BHA is a fat-soluble antioxidant and exhibits significant free radical scavenging properties.

- Antioxidant Potential: The antioxidant activity of BHA is attributed to its ability to donate hydrogen atoms or electrons to free radicals, thereby neutralizing them. This prevents the oxidation of lipids and fat-soluble compounds in food, cosmetics, and pharmaceuticals. Its phenolic structure is key to this mechanism, as it provides a stable, non-radical form once the antioxidant process is completed.

- Solubility and Stability: BHA is soluble in lipid-based systems, making it especially effective in fatty foods and oily formulations. It also shows good solubility in organic solvents like ethanol. BHA's stability is relatively high under moderate heat conditions, making it suitable for high-temperature food processing. However, its effectiveness might be reduced under extreme heat or extended light exposure, similar to other antioxidants. The stability of BHA in food and pharmaceutical formulations is critical for maintaining product quality during storage.

10.1.4.2 Applications of BHA in Food and Medicine

BHA has been widely used in several sectors due to its **antioxidant properties**, especially in **food preservation** and **pharmaceutical formulations.**

Role in Preventing Oxidative Deterioration in Processed Foods

BHA is commonly used in processed foods, especially those containing fats and oils. In these food products, lipid oxidation leads to rancidity, unpleasant odors, and the loss of nutritional value. BHA prevents these effects by inhibiting the oxidation of unsaturated fatty acids in margarine, snack foods, baked goods, and meat products. Its primary function is to preserve flavor, texture, and nutritional quality, ensuring that products remain fresh for extended periods. BHA is particularly effective in packaged foods and products exposed to high heat or light during storage.

Pharmaceutical Uses in Stabilizing Drug Formulations

In the pharmaceutical industry, BHA is used to stabilize lipophilic drugs, which are prone to oxidation. Many drugs, particularly fat-soluble vitamins (such as vitamin A, vitamin E) and hormonal drugs, are vulnerable to degradation when exposed to oxygen and light. BHA is added to drug formulations to prevent oxidative degradation and preserve the potency and efficacy of the active pharmaceutical ingredients (APIs). BHA is commonly used in capsules, tablets, and topical preparations, particularly those containing oils or lipid-based excipients.

Use in Cosmetics and Industrial Applications

In **cosmetics**, BHA serves as an **antioxidant** to prevent **oxidative damage** to products containing **oils** or **active compounds** susceptible to degradation. BHA is commonly used in **creams, lotions, shampoos,** and **serums** to **preserve the stability** of **fatty acids** and other **lipophilic ingredients**. It also protects **essential oils** and **vitamins** from oxidation, which can degrade the **texture** and **efficacy** of the cosmetic product.

In **industrial applications**, BHA is used as an **antioxidant stabilizer** in **rubber products**, **plastics**, and **paints** to prevent **oxidation-induced degradation** and maintain the **integrity** and **longevity** of materials exposed to **air** and **environmental stressors**.

10.1.4.3 Health Effects and Safety Considerations of BHA

While BHA has shown effectiveness in preserving **food products** and **pharmaceuticals**, its **health effects** and **safety concerns** have been a topic of ongoing research and debate.

Studies on BHA Metabolism and Toxicity

BHA is metabolized in the body to produce **phenolic metabolites**, and it is generally **rapidly absorbed** and **excreted**. Studies have shown that BHA has **low acute toxicity**, but long-term exposure at high concentrations has raised concerns about its potential to cause **toxicity** in liver and kidney tissues. Some studies in rodents have suggested that high doses of BHA may induce **liver tumors** or lead to **chronic toxicity**, particularly when administered at **high concentrations** over long periods. However, the relevance of these animal studies to human health is still debated, as **human exposure levels** are typically much lower than those used in experimental settings.

Potential Risks and Controversies Surrounding BHA Consumption

BHA has been classified by the International Agency for Research on Cancer (IARC) as a Group 2B carcinogen, which means it is classified as a possible human carcinogen based on animal studies. However, this classification is based on high-dose animal studies, and human epidemiological data on BHA's potential carcinogenicity is limited. The U.S. Food and Drug Administration (FDA) has recognized BHA as generally recognized as safe (GRAS) when used in accordance with acceptable daily intake limits, which are set to minimize potential risks. The EFSA has also set safe limits for BHA in food products, acknowledging its potential risks at high concentrations but deeming it safe for use within established limits.

Regulatory Guidelines on BHA Usage

In the United States, the FDA allows BHA to be used as a food additive under GRAS status (Generally Recognized As Safe) when used within regulated limits. The maximum allowable concentration of BHA in foods typically ranges from 0.02% to 0.1%, depending on the food type. In pharmaceuticals and cosmetics, the concentration of BHA is also regulated to ensure its safe usage and minimal health risks.

The European Food Safety Authority (EFSA) and other regulatory agencies across the globe have similarly set safe limits for BHA, emphasizing its safe application in food products within those limits. Ongoing studies are evaluating the potential cumulative effects of BHA when consumed as part of a dietary regimen over extended periods.

10.1.4.4 Comparative Analysis of BHT and BHA

Both **BHT (Butylated Hydroxy Toluene)** and **BHA (Butylated Hydroxy Anisole)** are **synthetic antioxidants** used to prevent **oxidative spoilage** in **food, pharmaceuticals**, and **cosmetics**. While they serve similar purposes, there are important differences in their **chemical properties, effectiveness**, and **safety profiles.**

Differences in Efficacy and Stability

- BHT and BHA are both effective lipid-soluble antioxidants, but BHT tends to be more effective at protecting oils and fats from oxidation, especially in high-fat foods. BHT has greater stability under high temperature conditions, making it more suitable for cooking and baking applications.
- BHA, on the other hand, is generally considered more effective in preserving light-sensitive products and low-fat foods. Its antioxidant activity is somewhat milder than BHT, but it still plays a significant role in preserving food quality and stability.

Comparative Toxicological Studies

When it comes to **toxicity**, both **BHT** and **BHA** have been shown to exhibit **low toxicity** at typical levels used in foods. However, **BHA** has raised more concerns in **toxicological studies** due to its potential **carcinogenic effects** at high doses, particularly in rodents. Both compounds have been **classified** as **possible carcinogens** based on animal studies, but human studies have not conclusively shown a **link** between **BHA** or **BHT** and **cancer.**

Consumer Safety and Risk Assessment

Both **BHT** and **BHA** are **generally recognized as safe (GRAS)** by **regulatory agencies** when used within prescribed limits. However, **consumer safety** concerns persist due to the **long-term consumption** of these **synthetic antioxidants**. **BHA** has a slightly **more controversial reputation** due to its **potential risks**, including its possible **carcinogenicity** at high doses, leading to calls for **alternative antioxidants** in food products. **BHT**, on the other hand, is considered somewhat **safer** in terms of health risks but is still subject to **regulatory scrutiny.**.

10.2 Vitamin Antioxidants in Free Radical Neutralization

10.2.1 Introduction to Vitamin-Based Antioxidants

Vitamins are essential micronutrients required by the body in small amounts for proper metabolism, growth, and overall health. In addition to their primary functions, certain vitamins also act as **antioxidants**, playing a crucial role in neutralizing free radicals and mitigating **oxidative stress**. Oxidative stress occurs when there is an imbalance between free radicals (reactive oxygen species, ROS) and the body's ability to neutralize them using antioxidants. Prolonged oxidative stress can lead to cellular damage, contributing to the development of several **chronic diseases**, **aging**, and **inflammation**.

The antioxidant activity of vitamins involves the donation of electrons to free radicals, thereby neutralizing their reactivity. By doing so, these vitamins protect cells from oxidative damage and support various physiological processes, including immune function, DNA repair, and tissue regeneration. Vitamins that exhibit antioxidant properties are either water-soluble (such as vitamin C) or fat-soluble (such as vitamin E), each of which works within specific environments in the body.

- Water-soluble antioxidants are typically found in the cytoplasm and extracellular fluids, where they primarily combat hydrophilic free radicals and oxidative damage to water-soluble molecules.
- Fat-soluble antioxidants are predominantly found in cell membranes and lipid-rich environments, where they are particularly effective in protecting lipid structures (like phospholipid bilayers) from lipid peroxidation caused by oxidative stress.

The importance of vitamins in oxidative stress management is highlighted by their ability to protect cells from damage, which can prevent chronic diseases such as cardiovascular diseases, cancer, neurodegenerative disorders, and diabetes. Antioxidant vitamins also support the body's natural defense systems, including enzymatic antioxidants like superoxide dismutase and catalase, which work in concert with these vitamins to reduce free radical damage.

10.2.2 Vitamin C (Ascorbic Acid) – A Water-Soluble Antioxidant

10.2.2.1 Chemical Structure and Properties

Vitamin C, also known as **ascorbic acid**, is a **water-soluble vitamin** and one of the most potent **antioxidants** in the human body. It plays a central role in protecting **cells** from oxidative damage by **neutralizing free radicals**, particularly **reactive oxygen species (ROS)**. The chemical structure of vitamin C consists of a **six-membered lactone ring** with a **hydroxyl group (-OH)** at the **C-3 position** and an **enediol group** at **C-2 and C-3**, which gives the compound its reducing properties.

- Molecular Structure: The molecular formula of ascorbic acid is $C_6H_8O_6$. The compound has a hydroxyl group (-OH), which makes it a reducing agent, capable of donating electrons to neutralize reactive free radicals. The double bond structure between C-2 and C-3 allows the molecule to act as a proton donor in the antioxidant mechanism.
- Solubility: Vitamin C is highly soluble in water and is easily absorbed into the bloodstream from the gastrointestinal tract. Because it is water-soluble, vitamin C is distributed throughout the extracellular fluid, blood plasma, and the cytoplasm of cells, where it protects soluble cellular structures from oxidative damage.
- Role as a Reducing Agent in Oxidative Reactions: The key feature of vitamin C's antioxidant activity is its ability to act as a reducing agent. In this capacity, it donates electrons to neutralize reactive oxygen species (ROS), such as the hydroxyl radical (OH·), superoxide anion (O2·–), and singlet oxygen (1O2). By reducing these radicals, vitamin C prevents them from causing oxidative damage to proteins, lipids, and nucleic acids. The reducing properties of vitamin C help maintain the integrity of cell membranes, DNA, and proteins from oxidative stress, particularly in

tissues that are exposed to high levels of free radicals, such as the skin and eyes.

Vitamin C also plays a crucial role in the **regeneration of other antioxidants**, such as **vitamin E**, by **reducing** the **oxidized form** of vitamin E back to its active antioxidant state. This **recycling effect** helps prolong the antioxidant action of vitamin E and other antioxidants, providing further **protection** against oxidative damage.

Additional Properties:

- **Absorption**: Vitamin C is **absorbed** in the **small intestine**, with the highest absorption occurring when intake is low to moderate. **Saturation** levels are reached when the intake exceeds the body's needs, after which the excess is **excreted in urine**.
- **Metabolism**: Once absorbed, vitamin C is metabolized primarily in the **liver**, where it is oxidized to **dehydroascorbic acid (DHA)**, which is then converted back to its active form in tissues. The body can store limited amounts of vitamin C, and daily intake is required to maintain optimal levels.

10.2.2.2 Health Benefits of Vitamin C

Vitamin C, as a potent antioxidant, is linked to numerous **health benefits**, including **immune support**, **cardiovascular protection**, **skin health**, and **wound healing**.

1. **Immune Support**:

   - Vitamin C is known for its ability to enhance **immune function** by stimulating the **production of white blood cells (WBCs)** and enhancing **phagocytosis** (the process by which white blood cells engulf pathogens). It also helps **prevent infections** by **neutralizing pathogens** and **boosting the body's resistance** to diseases such as the **common cold** and **flu**.

2. **Cardiovascular Protection**:

   - Vitamin C supports **cardiovascular health** by **reducing oxidative stress** in the **blood vessels** and **heart tissue**. It is involved in **collagen**

synthesis, which is essential for maintaining **blood vessel integrity** and **elasticity**. Vitamin C also **prevents LDL cholesterol oxidation**, which is a key factor in the development of **atherosclerosis**, and may **lower blood pressure** by improving the **function** of **endothelial cells** that line blood vessels.

3. **Skin Health**:

   ◦ As a powerful antioxidant, vitamin C protects the skin from **UV-induced oxidative damage**, which accelerates the **aging process** and contributes to **wrinkles** and **sunburn**. It also promotes **collagen production**, which is necessary for **skin elasticity** and **wound healing**. Regular intake of vitamin C can reduce the appearance of **fine lines** and **age spots**.

4. **Anti-Cancer Effects**:

   ◦ Research suggests that vitamin C may have **anti-cancer properties** by **modulating oxidative stress** and **inhibiting cancer cell growth**. Some studies indicate that vitamin C can prevent **cancer cell metastasis** and **tumor angiogenesis**, thereby inhibiting the spread of cancer cells in the body.

5. **Wound Healing**:

   ◦ Vitamin C plays a vital role in **wound healing**, as it is essential for **collagen synthesis**. This makes it an important nutrient for **post-surgery recovery**, **burn victims**, and individuals with **chronic wounds**. It also helps **accelerate tissue repair** by supporting the **formation of new blood vessels** at wound sites.

10.2.2.2 *Mechanism of Action in Free Radical Scavenging*

Vitamin C, or **ascorbic acid**, acts as a **potent antioxidant**, primarily by **neutralizing reactive oxygen species (ROS)** and other **free radicals** that can cause cellular damage. Its **mechanism of action** involves **electron donation**, which neutralizes these highly reactive molecules, preventing them from interacting with important cellular components such as **lipids**, **proteins**, and **nucleic acids.**

- Neutralization of Reactive Oxygen Species (ROS): Vitamin C directly scavenges free radicals such as superoxide anion (O2·−), hydroxyl radicals (OH·), and peroxyl radicals (ROO·). The hydroxyl group (-OH) present in vitamin C donates an electron or a hydrogen atom to these radicals, neutralizing their reactivity and converting them into harmless molecules. This reduces the damaging effects of oxidative stress within the body, which has been linked to the development of chronic diseases such as cardiovascular diseases, diabetes, and cancer.
- Regeneration of Other Antioxidants (Vitamin E and Glutathione): Vitamin C also plays a critical role in regenerating other antioxidants in the body, such as vitamin E and glutathione, which are also essential for combating oxidative stress. Vitamin C can reduce oxidized vitamin E (α-tocopherol) back to its active antioxidant form by donating electrons to neutralize lipid peroxyl radicals in cell membranes. This regeneration effect helps extend the antioxidant capacity of vitamin E and glutathione, creating a synergistic defense against oxidative damage. Glutathione, which is another important intracellular antioxidant, can also be regenerated by vitamin C through the reduction of its oxidized form (GSSG) to its active reduced form (GSH), ensuring that it remains functional in protecting cells from oxidative injury.

10.2.2.3 Dietary Sources of Vitamin C

Vitamin C is a **water-soluble vitamin** that is abundantly present in a wide variety of **fruits** and **vegetables.** Since the body cannot produce **vitamin C** on its own, it must be **obtained** through **dietary sources.** Some of the best sources of **vitamin C** include:

- Citrus Fruits (Oranges, Lemons): Citrus fruits, including oranges, lemons, limes, and grapefruits, are among the richest sources of vitamin C. Oranges, for example, provide about 70 mg of vitamin C per 100 grams, which is more than the daily requirement for most adults. These fruits are commonly consumed fresh or in juice form, making them a convenient source of this essential nutrient.

- Leafy Green Vegetables: Vegetables like spinach, kale, and broccoli are excellent sources of vitamin C, offering high concentrations of the nutrient along with other antioxidants, minerals, and fiber. A cup of cooked spinach contains about 17 mg of vitamin C, while broccoli can provide up to 90 mg per cup when cooked.
- Berries and Tropical Fruits: Strawberries, blackberries, and raspberries are rich in vitamin C, with one cup of strawberries containing around 85 mg of the vitamin. Other tropical fruits like kiwi, papaya, and pineapple are also excellent sources of vitamin C, with kiwi offering more than 90 mg per fruit. These fruits are not only delicious but also offer other bioactive compounds that contribute to overall health.

10.2.2.4 Health Benefits of Vitamin C

Vitamin C is involved in various **physiological processes** and plays an important role in **maintaining health** and **preventing diseases**. Here are some of the key **health benefits** of vitamin C:

1. Role in Immune Function and Infection Resistance:

   - Vitamin C is crucial for maintaining a healthy immune system. It enhances the production of white blood cells (WBCs), particularly T-cells and B-cells, which are responsible for detecting and combating pathogens. Vitamin C also plays a role in phagocytosis, the process by which immune cells engulf and destroy harmful microbes. In addition, vitamin C supports the functionality of the skin, which acts as the body's first defense against pathogens.
   - Research has shown that adequate vitamin C levels can help reduce the severity and duration of common colds and upper respiratory infections by boosting immune function and enhancing the body's defense mechanisms.

2. Prevention of Cardiovascular Diseases:

   - Vitamin C plays a significant role in cardiovascular health by protecting the endothelium (inner lining of blood vessels) and preventing oxidative damage to lipoproteins, such as LDL cholesterol.

This helps reduce the risk of atherosclerosis, a condition where fatty deposits build up in the arteries, leading to heart disease.

- Studies have shown that vitamin C can lower blood pressure by improving vascular function and promoting nitric oxide production, which helps relax blood vessels and improve circulation.

3. Enhancement of Collagen Synthesis and Skin Health:

- Vitamin C is essential for the synthesis of collagen, the structural protein that forms the foundation for skin, blood vessels, bones, and cartilage. Adequate levels of vitamin C help maintain skin elasticity and strength, preventing wrinkles and skin aging. It is also crucial for wound healing, as collagen is necessary for the repair of tissues and skin regeneration.
- Vitamin C's antioxidant properties also protect the skin from UV-induced oxidative damage, which accelerates skin aging and increases the risk of skin cancer.

4. Neuroprotective Effects and Cognitive Health:

- Vitamin C has been shown to have neuroprotective properties, especially in aging populations. It helps protect the brain from oxidative damage caused by free radicals, which contribute to neurodegenerative diseases like Alzheimer's and Parkinson's.
- Additionally, vitamin C supports cognitive function by promoting neurotransmitter synthesis and reducing inflammation in the brain. Studies have suggested that vitamin C supplementation may help in the prevention of cognitive decline and enhance mental clarity and focus.

10.2.2.5 Clinical Research on Vitamin C Supplementation

Research into the effects of **vitamin C supplementation** has shown promising results in several areas of **health maintenance** and **disease prevention**.

1. **Meta-Analysis on Vitamin C in Immune Support:**

- Several **meta-analyses** have demonstrated that **vitamin C supplementation** can reduce the **severity and duration** of the **common cold**, especially in individuals with **low vitamin C levels.** A study found that vitamin C could reduce **cold duration** by **8%** in adults and **14%** in children. **Higher doses of vitamin C** (e.g., **1000 mg daily**) appear to have a **greater effect** on reducing **cold symptoms** in people under physical stress, such as **athletes** or those exposed to extreme **cold weather.**

2. **Role in Reducing Oxidative Stress in Chronic Diseases:**

- Clinical studies have shown that **vitamin C supplementation** helps reduce **oxidative stress** and **inflammation** in chronic diseases like **diabetes, cardiovascular diseases**, and **cancer.** Research suggests that vitamin C may lower **blood sugar levels** in diabetic patients and **improve insulin sensitivity.** It also protects against **vascular oxidative damage** in patients with **hypertension** and **heart disease** by reducing the **oxidation of LDL cholesterol** and **inhibiting endothelial dysfunction.**

10.2.3 Vitamin E – Tocopherols and Tocotrienols

10.2.3.1 Chemical Structure and Classification of Vitamin E

Vitamin E refers to a group of **fat-soluble compounds** that exhibit **antioxidant properties.** It is primarily classified into two main subgroups: **tocopherols** and **tocotrienols**, each with **four distinct forms—alpha (α), beta (β), gamma (γ), and delta (δ).** These forms differ slightly in their **chemical structures** and biological activities.

- **Tocopherols vs. Tocotrienols:** The major difference between **tocopherols** and **tocotrienols** lies in their **chemical structure.** Both contain a **chromanol ring** with a **hydrophobic side chain**, but the side chains differ between tocopherols and tocotrienols. **Tocopherols** have a **saturated phytyl side chain**, while **tocotrienols** have an **unsaturated isoprenoid side chain.** This slight difference makes tocotrienols more

mobile within the **cell membrane** compared to tocopherols, influencing their activity and bioavailability.

- **Alpha, Beta, Gamma, and Delta Forms**: Each subgroup of **tocopherols** and **tocotrienols** is classified based on the position of the **methyl groups** attached to the chromanol ring. The **alpha (α)-tocopherol** form is the most **bioactive** in humans, with the highest **antioxidant activity**. The other forms (**beta, gamma, and delta**) possess some antioxidant activity but are considered less potent than **alpha-tocopherol**. However, **gamma-tocopherol** has shown **unique benefits**, especially in **cardiovascular health** and **inflammation**.
- **Fat-soluble Properties and Bioavailability**: Vitamin E is **lipophilic**, meaning it is **soluble in fats** and can be absorbed by the intestines in the presence of **dietary fat**. Due to this, its absorption efficiency can vary based on dietary intake. **Bioavailability** of vitamin E can be influenced by **dietary fat, age**, and **intestinal health**. After absorption, vitamin E is incorporated into **lipoproteins** and transported through the bloodstream to various tissues, including the **liver** and **muscles**, where it exerts its **antioxidant effects**.

10.2.3.2 Mechanism of Antioxidant Action of Vitamin E

Vitamin E acts primarily as a **fat-soluble antioxidant**, protecting **cell membranes, lipids**, and **lipid-rich structures** from oxidative damage.

- **Prevention of Lipid Peroxidation in Cell Membranes**: Vitamin E **neutralizes free radicals** in the **phospholipid bilayer** of **cell membranes**. Free radicals attack **polyunsaturated fatty acids** (PUFAs) within the cell membrane, leading to **lipid peroxidation**. Vitamin E prevents this damage by **donating hydrogen atoms** to free radicals, converting them into **stable, non-reactive molecules**. By preventing lipid peroxidation, vitamin E helps **maintain membrane integrity**, supports **cellular functions**, and **prevents tissue damage**.
- **Synergistic Action with Vitamin C and Selenium**: Vitamin E works synergistically with other antioxidants like **Vitamin C** and **selenium**. Vitamin C, as a **water-soluble antioxidant**, recycles vitamin E by reducing the **oxidized form of vitamin E**, allowing it to continue its antioxidant activity. Selenium, as part of the enzyme **glutathione**

peroxidase, helps further **detoxify peroxides** in the cell, preventing **lipid peroxidation**. This **collaborative antioxidant system** enhances the overall defense against **oxidative damage** in **cellular membranes**.

10.2.3.3 Dietary Sources of Vitamin E

Vitamin E is present in various **plant-based** and **animal-based** food sources. As a **fat-soluble vitamin**, the absorption and bioavailability of vitamin E depend on the presence of **dietary fat**. Some of the primary sources include:

- **Nuts and Seeds**: **Almonds, sunflower seeds, hazelnuts**, and **pumpkin seeds** are among the best sources of **vitamin E**, particularly **alpha-tocopherol**. A single ounce of **almonds** can provide approximately **7.3 mg** of vitamin E, which constitutes about **50% of the recommended daily intake**.
- **Vegetable Oils**: **Wheat germ oil, sunflower oil**, and **olive oil** are excellent sources of **vitamin E. Wheat germ oil** contains the highest concentration of vitamin E among oils, with around **20 mg per tablespoon. Olive oil** and **sunflower oil** also provide significant amounts of **tocopherols** and **tocotrienols**.
- **Green Leafy Vegetables**: Vegetables such as **spinach, kale**, and **Swiss chard** contain moderate amounts of vitamin E, contributing to daily intake, especially when consumed in larger quantities. These vegetables are also rich in other nutrients, including **vitamin A, vitamin K**, and **fiber**.

10.2.3.4 Health Benefits of Vitamin E

Vitamin E plays a crucial role in several health functions, ranging from **cardiovascular health** to **neuroprotection** and **skin health**.

1. **Cardiovascular Protection and Cholesterol Regulation:**

   - Vitamin E helps protect the **heart** by preventing **oxidation of LDL cholesterol**. Oxidized LDL cholesterol is a key contributor to **atherosclerosis**, a condition where **plaque** builds up in the arteries, leading to **heart disease**. Vitamin E inhibits this process, thereby reducing the risk of **coronary artery disease** and promoting **cardiovascular health**.

○ It also has a **blood-thinning effect**, potentially lowering the risk of **blood clot formation** and **stroke**. Additionally, vitamin E supports **endothelial function**, which improves **blood flow** and **vascular health**.

2. **Neuroprotection Against Age-Related Cognitive Decline:**

○ Vitamin E is essential for protecting **brain cells** from oxidative damage caused by **free radicals**. This helps prevent neurodegenerative diseases such as **Alzheimer's disease** and **Parkinson's disease**, both of which involve significant oxidative stress. Vitamin E has been shown to improve **memory, cognitive function**, and **brain health** in aging populations.

3. **Skin Protection and Anti-Aging Properties:**

○ Vitamin E acts as a **protective barrier** against **UV radiation** and **skin damage** caused by **free radicals**. It helps prevent **sunburn, wrinkles,** and **skin aging** by neutralizing **oxidative stress**. Vitamin E also supports the **healing of scars** and **wounds**, making it an important ingredient in **cosmetics** and **topical treatments**.

4. **Potential Role in Cancer Prevention:**

○ Vitamin E's antioxidant properties also contribute to **cancer prevention**. It has been shown to **modulate tumor growth** by inhibiting **oxidative DNA damage** and preventing **tumor cell proliferation**. Additionally, vitamin E can enhance **immune system function**, supporting the body's defense against cancerous cells.

10.2.3.5 Clinical Studies on Vitamin E Supplementation

Numerous clinical studies and **meta-analyses** have investigated the effects of vitamin E supplementation, particularly its role in **cardiovascular**

health, **neurodegenerative diseases**, and **overall longevity**.

1. **Research on Vitamin E in Cardiovascular Diseases**:

   - Studies have shown that **vitamin E supplementation** may reduce the risk of **heart disease** by preventing **LDL cholesterol oxidation** and improving **vascular health**. However, some studies suggest **limited benefits** in individuals who are already **taking other heart medications**. The **HOPE** (Heart Outcomes Prevention Evaluation) study, for example, found that **high-dose vitamin E** did not significantly lower the incidence of **heart attacks** or **stroke** in high-risk patients.

2. **Role of Tocotrienols in Neurodegenerative Disorders**:

   - Emerging research highlights the potential role of **tocotrienols** (a type of vitamin E) in **neuroprotection. Tocotrienols** have been shown to have **stronger antioxidant effects** than **tocopherols**, particularly in protecting **brain cells** from oxidative damage. Clinical trials have indicated that tocotrienols can potentially reduce the progression of **Alzheimer's** and **Parkinson's disease**, supporting cognitive health in aging individuals.

ELEVEN
FOOD LAWS, REGULATIONS, AND SAFETY STANDARDS

11.1 Overview of Regulatory Frameworks

11.1.1 Introduction to Food Laws and Regulations

Food laws and regulations are essential for protecting public health and ensuring the safety, quality, and nutritional value of food products. These regulations govern all aspects of food production, from food sourcing and processing to labeling, marketing, and distribution. The primary goal is to ensure that consumers have access to safe, nutritious, and accurately represented food products, thereby reducing the risks associated with foodborne illnesses, fraud, and improper food handling.

The importance of food laws lies in their ability to maintain food safety standards that prevent contamination, mislabeling, and the sale of unsafe or substandard products. Food laws also help prevent deceptive practices in the food industry and ensure that consumers are provided with the correct information about the food they consume, including its nutritional content, ingredients, and origin.

In public health, food laws play a pivotal role by regulating the use of additives, pesticides, and other potentially harmful substances in food products. They also help monitor and control foodborne diseases and ensure that food handling, processing, and preparation meet high sanitation standards. This is particularly important in a globalized world where food products cross international borders, and foodborne pathogens can easily spread across populations.

Food laws are typically enforced by government agencies and international bodies that work together to set guidelines, conduct inspections, and issue regulations to safeguard public health. These regulatory agencies are responsible for conducting research, enforcing compliance with safety standards, and penalizing violators. Through such laws and regulations, they ensure that food products meet scientific standards for safety and quality, while also considering cultural and societal aspects of food consumption.

- Role of Regulatory Agencies in Ensuring Food Safety: Regulatory agencies, such as the Food and Drug Administration (FDA) in the United States, the European Food Safety Authority (EFSA) in Europe, and the Food Safety and Standards Authority of India (FSSAI), are responsible for overseeing the safety of food products and ensuring that they comply with established safety standards. These agencies work in tandem with national governments and international organizations to monitor food safety and address concerns related to foodborne pathogens, contaminants, and allergens.They also provide guidance on nutritional labeling, the use of food additives, and the approval of new food products or technologies. These agencies play a key role in educating the public and businesses about food safety and provide resources for managing food recalls and outbreaks of foodborne diseases.
- Global vs. National Food Regulations: There are significant differences between global and national food regulations. At the international level, organizations like the World Health Organization (WHO) and the Codex Alimentarius Commission (established by the FAO and WHO) set international food safety standards and guidelines. The Codex provides recommendations on issues such as food labeling, pesticide residues, and food contaminants, helping ensure that food products can safely cross international borders.on the other hand, national food regulations are created by each country's government and are tailored to address the specific needs of their population. These regulations take into account local customs, food culture, and dietary habits. For example, food safety standards in the United States are regulated by the FDA and the United States Department of Agriculture (USDA), while in India, the FSSAI sets

the standards for food safety and quality.

While global regulations help maintain consistency in food standards across borders, national regulations often have more specific requirements based on the local context. For instance, national regulations might address specific foodborne pathogens prevalent in certain regions or tailor food standards based on regional agricultural practices.

11.1.2 The Role of the Food and Drug Administration (FDA)

11.1.2.1 Overview of the FDA's Role in Food and Nutraceutical Regulation

The Food and Drug Administration (FDA) is a crucial regulatory agency within the United States Department of Health and Human Services (HHS). It plays a pivotal role in ensuring the safety, efficacy, and security of food products, drugs, medical devices, and dietary supplements, including nutraceuticals. The FDA's jurisdiction extends over the regulation and oversight of both conventional food products and functional foods (including nutraceuticals), making it a cornerstone of public health protection and food safety in the U.S.

- Jurisdiction and Regulatory Authority: The FDA has the authority to regulate a wide variety of products, including food, dietary supplements, nutraceuticals, pharmaceuticals, and cosmetics. Its jurisdiction covers almost every aspect of food production, from processing and labeling to importation and distribution. It also ensures that food and dietary supplements meet safety standards, free from contaminants and mislabeling.Specifically Specifically for food and nutraceutical regulation, the FDA:

  - Regulates food safety, including the use of additives, pesticides, and preservatives.
  - Ensures the accuracy of nutritional labeling and claims made on food products.
  - Oversees the approval and regulation of dietary supplements, ensuring that these products do not pose a risk to consumer health.

- ◦ Monitors foodborne illnesses and responds to outbreaks by issuing recalls and public health advisories.The FDA also has the authority to establish safety standards for food additives and other chemicals that come into contact with food products. Additionally, the FDA has the power to issue guidelines for food labeling that help consumers make informed decisions about their diet.

- FDA's Approach to Food Safety and Public Health: The FDA's approach to food safety is multifaceted and aims at preventing foodborne illnesses, ensuring accurate nutritional labeling, and providing the public with reliable information regarding food and dietary supplements. The FDA's primary focus is on minimizing public health risks associated with food products through:

  - ◦ Risk-based assessments of food hazards, such as microbial contamination and toxicological risks.
  - ◦ Establishing preventive measures for food producers, such as hygiene standards and safe food processing practices.
  - ◦ Ensuring the proper labeling of food products to guarantee that consumers have accurate information about ingredients, nutritional content, allergens, and other health claims.
  - ◦ Providing guidelines and standards for dietary supplements and nutraceuticals, ensuring they are safe for consumption and effective in providing the promised health benefits.In doing so , the FDA helps to reduce the risk of foodborne diseases and toxic exposure while promoting healthy diets and informed consumer choices. Its role in public health is also critical in the prevention of chronic diseases linked to poor nutrition, such as obesity, diabetes, and heart disease, by providing guidelines and supporting health education initiatives.

11.1.2.2 Key Regulations Enforced by the FDA

The FDA is responsible for enforcing several key regulations aimed at ensuring food safety and the safety of nutraceuticals. Two of the most significant regulations in this regard are the Food Safety Modernization Act (FSMA) and the Dietary Supplement Health and Education Act (DSHEA).

- Food Safety Modernization Act (FSMA):

  - The FSMA, signed into law in 2011, is one of the most comprehensive reforms in the history of food safety regulations in the United States. The FSMA shifts the FDA's focus from responding to foodborne illnesses to preventing them. It requires food producers to implement preventive controls to ensure the safety of the food supply and holds them accountable for the safety of their products.
  - Key provisions of the FSMA include:

    - Preventive Controls: Food producers must establish and implement a food safety plan that includes preventive measures to control potential hazards.
    - Mandatory Recall Authority: The FDA has the authority to order recalls of contaminated food products if a threat to public health is identified.
    - Enhanced Inspections: The FSMA mandates increased inspection frequency of food producers and facilities, particularly high-risk producers.
    - Supply Chain Responsibility: The law holds importers responsible for ensuring that food products imported into the U.S. meet U.S. safety standards.
    - Traceability: The FSMA requires food producers to implement traceability systems to track food products in the supply chain and to enhance quick action in case of contamination outbreaks.

FSMA is a landmark regulation that significantly strengthens food safety standards and ensures that producers take responsibility for preventing contamination, rather than simply reacting after the fact. It is a key component of the FDA's commitment to public health protection.

- Dietary Supplement Health and Education Act (DSHEA):

  - The DSHEA, enacted in 1994, provides the legal framework for the regulation of dietary supplements in the United States. This regulation defines dietary supplements and establishes guidelines for their manufacturing, labeling, and marketing. While the FDA does not approve dietary supplements before they are marketed, it does require manufacturers to ensure the safety and accuracy of their products.

◦ Key provisions of the DSHEA include:

- Definition of Dietary Supplements: DSHEA defines dietary supplements as products intended to supplement the diet and may contain one or more of the following: vitamins, minerals, herbs, amino acids, and other dietary substances.
- Good Manufacturing Practices (GMPs): Manufacturers are required to follow GMP guidelines to ensure the purity, quality, and consistency of dietary supplements.
- Labeling Requirements: DSHEA mandates that dietary supplements must be accurately labeled with a list of ingredients, serving size, and health claims that comply with FDA guidelines. Claims that the product can prevent, treat, or cure diseases are strictly prohibited unless supported by sufficient scientific evidence and approved by the FDA.
- Post-Market Surveillance: Although dietary supplements are not pre-approved by the FDA, the FDA has the authority to take action against unsafe or misbranded products after they enter the market. If a supplement is found to be unsafe, the FDA can request a recall or take legal action against the manufacturer.

The DSHEA aims to balance the growing interest in dietary supplements with the need to ensure public safety. While it allows the sale and marketing of nutraceuticals and dietary supplements, it also establishes guidelines to prevent misleading claims and ensure consumer protection.

Together, these regulations, FSMA and DSHEA, shape the FDA's comprehensive approach to food safety, nutraceutical regulation, and public health protection. They reflect the agency's role in not only regulating food safety but also overseeing the growing market of nutraceuticals and dietary supplements.

11.2.2 Principles of HACCP and Their Application

Hazard Analysis – Identifying Potential Food Safety Risks

The Hazard Analysis and Critical Control Points (HACCP) system is a widely recognized food safety management system that focuses on the identification, assessment, and control of potential hazards that may affect the safety of food products. Hazard analysis is the first and crucial step in the HACCP system, where food safety risks are systematically identified and evaluated. These risks can be categorized into three primary types of hazards:

1. Biological Hazards: These include microorganisms such as bacteria, viruses, fungi, and parasites that can contaminate food and cause foodborne illnesses. For example, Salmonella, E. coli, and Listeria are well-known biological hazards commonly associated with raw meats, dairy products, and ready-to-eat foods.
2. Chemical Hazards: Chemical hazards include pesticides, heavy metals, food additives, and contaminants like mycotoxins. These substances may unintentionally enter food through contamination during production, processing, or packaging stages.
3. Physical Hazards: Physical hazards involve foreign objects that can physically contaminate food, such as glass shards, metal fragments, stones, and plastic pieces. These contaminants can pose severe health risks to consumers, ranging from choking hazards to injury.

Hazard analysis involves identifying where hazards are likely to occur in the food production process, understanding the severity and likelihood of these hazards, and prioritizing them according to their potential impact on public health. This information forms the foundation for implementing effective control measures.

Critical Control Points (CCPs) – Determining Safety Checkpoints in Food Processing

Critical Control Points (CCPs) refer to stages in the food production process where control is necessary to prevent, eliminate, or reduce food safety hazards to an acceptable level. These points are the critical control areas where even a small deviation can result in unsafe food. CCPs are determined based on the findings from the hazard analysis.

Examples of CCPs may include:

- Cooking: The cooking temperature of food is critical to eliminating harmful pathogens. For instance, cooking meat to the correct temperature ensures that any harmful bacteria or parasites are killed.
- Cooling: After cooking, foods must be rapidly cooled to prevent bacterial growth. CCPs in cooling involve monitoring the temperature drop to ensure it occurs within a safe timeframe.
- Packaging: During packaging, ensuring that the food is sealed in a clean environment prevents contamination from biological or physical hazards.

Each CCP is associated with specific critical limits—the thresholds that must not be exceeded or fallen short of for the food to remain safe. These critical limits are often scientifically determined and set based on regulatory standards or scientific research. Monitoring these limits helps ensure that the CCPs remain under control throughout the food processing cycle.

Critical Limits and Monitoring Procedures

Critical limits are defined as the maximum or minimum values to which a food hazard must be controlled to ensure food safety. These limits may relate to time, temperature, pH, moisture content, or other measurable parameters. For example, for cooking meat at a certain temperature, the critical limit might be 75°C for 15 seconds to ensure that any bacterial pathogens are destroyed.

Monitoring procedures are essential to verify that the critical limits are being met. Monitoring involves routinely checking and recording key variables at the CCPs to ensure that they remain within acceptable ranges. It typically includes:

- Measuring temperature (using thermometers or temperature data loggers).
- Timing processes (e.g., how long a product is exposed to a certain temperature).
- Visual inspections (e.g., checking for contamination during packaging).
- Chemical testing (e.g., measuring pH or moisture content).

Effective monitoring ensures that CCPs are under control and that any deviations from critical limits are detected early, preventing unsafe food from reaching consumers.

Corrective Actions for Food Contamination

If a deviation from the critical limits occurs, corrective actions must be taken immediately to prevent unsafe food from being distributed. Corrective actions involve:

- Identifying the cause of the deviation: For example, if the cooking temperature does not reach the critical limit, determining whether the equipment malfunctioned or if the product wasn't heated long enough.
- Taking corrective measures to bring the process back under control: This could involve adjusting the process, reprocessing the affected food, or discarding unsafe food that cannot be salvaged.
- Re-assessing food safety: It's essential to assess whether any unsafe food has already reached consumers. If necessary, a recall may be initiated to remove the affected food from the market.

Corrective actions should be clearly defined in the HACCP plan and regularly reviewed to ensure their effectiveness. Regular training of personnel ensures that everyone understands how to implement corrective actions when necessary.

Verification and Documentation Processes

Verification is the process of ensuring that the HACCP system is being implemented correctly and that it is effective in ensuring food safety. This includes reviewing the overall system, monitoring records, corrective actions, and verification reports. Verification activities include:

- Internal audits of the food safety system.
- Review of monitoring data to ensure that CCPs are under control.
- Calibration of monitoring instruments (e.g., thermometers, scales) to ensure accurate readings.
- Periodic validation of critical limits based on updated scientific research or regulatory requirements.

Documentation plays a crucial role in ensuring that the entire HACCP system is well-documented and transparent. All aspects of the HACCP plan, including the hazard analysis, CCPs, critical limits, monitoring procedures, corrective actions, and verification activities, must be recorded. Proper documentation allows for traceability in case of food recalls and helps to demonstrate compliance with food safety regulations during inspections by regulatory authorities.

The documentation process should include:

- Record-keeping of monitoring data (e.g., temperature logs, pH measurements).
- Action plans for corrective actions taken when deviations occur.
- Verification reports showing that the HACCP system is being followed properly.

This documentation serves not only as proof of compliance with food safety regulations but also provides an important feedback loop for continuously improving the food safety management system..

11.2.3 Implementation of HACCP in Food Processing

HACCP Compliance in Food Manufacturing Units

The implementation of HACCP in food processing is a critical step in ensuring food safety across all stages of food production, from raw material handling to final distribution. Food manufacturing units must develop and implement a HACCP plan tailored to their specific processes, identifying potential hazards, setting up critical control points (CCPs), and monitoring parameters that ensure food products are safe for consumption.

1. Identification of Hazards: The first step involves conducting a thorough hazard analysis of the food production process. This includes identifying potential biological, chemical, and physical hazards that could occur at any point in the production chain—whether during sourcing, processing, storage, or transportation. For example, in a meat processing facility, hazards could include microbial contamination from E. coli or Salmonella, while in a bakery, risks could involve allergens or physical

contaminants such as metal shards.

2. Establishing Critical Control Points (CCPs): Once hazards are identified, the next step is to determine the CCPs, which are the stages in food production where the hazard can be prevented, eliminated, or reduced to an acceptable level. For example, in the pasteurization of dairy products, the heating stage is a CCP, as it ensures the elimination of harmful microorganisms through proper heat treatment.

3. Setting Critical Limits: Each CCP must have critical limits that define the acceptable range of operational parameters. For instance, the temperature of pasteurized milk must reach at least 72°C for 15 seconds. These limits ensure that the hazard is adequately controlled and the final product is safe for consumption.

4. Monitoring Procedures: To ensure the CCPs are under control, the food processing unit must implement continuous or periodic monitoring procedures. This could involve using thermometers to measure temperatures, checking pH levels, or observing visual cues to ensure food quality. Regular record-keeping is also necessary to document monitoring activities.

5. Corrective Actions: If a deviation from the critical limits occurs, the food manufacturing unit must take immediate corrective actions. For example, if the pasteurization temperature falls below the required limit, the affected product may need to be reheated or discarded to prevent microbial contamination.

6. Verification and Documentation: Finally, the food manufacturing unit must implement verification procedures to ensure the HACCP plan is working effectively. This includes regular audits, reviews of monitoring records, and validation of CCPs based on new research or regulatory updates. Proper documentation is also essential to demonstrate compliance with food safety regulations and facilitate traceability in case of a food safety incident.

Role in Preventing Foodborne Illnesses

HACCP plays a pivotal role in preventing foodborne illnesses, which can have serious public health consequences. The approach is focused on preventing contamination rather than simply reacting to outbreaks. By addressing potential hazards at critical points in the food production process, HACCP minimizes the likelihood of foodborne pathogens, chemicals, or physical contaminants reaching consumers. Key ways HACCP contributes to preventing foodborne illnesses include:

- Reduction of microbial contamination: By implementing CCPs that target foodborne pathogens like Salmonella, Listeria, and E. coli, HACCP ensures that foods are processed at temperatures or conditions that kill harmful microorganisms.
- Control of cross-contamination: Through effective monitoring and sanitation practices, HACCP reduces the risk of cross-contamination, particularly in high-risk food products such as raw meat or dairy.
- Management of food allergens: HACCP plans address allergen control by identifying potential allergens in ingredients and managing the risk of cross-contact with allergen-free products.
- Ensuring proper food handling: By setting critical limits for storage temperatures, food handling practices, and sanitation procedures, HACCP helps reduce the risk of foodborne illnesses caused by improper food handling at any point in the food production chain.

11.2.4 HACCP Certification and Regulatory Compliance

Process of Obtaining HACCP Certification

HACCP certification is a formal process that demonstrates a food manufacturer's compliance with international food safety standards. The process involves several steps:

1. Development of a HACCP Plan: The food manufacturing company must first develop a comprehensive HACCP plan based on a detailed hazard analysis. This includes identifying potential food safety hazards, setting up critical control points (CCPs), and implementing monitoring procedures for each CCP.
2. Training and Awareness: Food safety personnel need to be trained on the HACCP principles and be knowledgeable about the requirements of the certification process. This includes understanding how to properly implement monitoring activities, handle corrective actions, and ensure

documentary compliance.

3. Pre-Certification Audit: Before applying for official certification, the company conducts an internal audit of their HACCP plan to ensure all critical aspects are addressed. This audit also includes ensuring that the food safety systems are functioning properly in the manufacturing environment.

4. External Audit and Certification: A third-party certification body will then conduct an external audit of the HACCP system. This audit typically involves a thorough examination of the HACCP plan, onsite verification of CCPs and monitoring practices, and review of all food safety documentation. If the company passes the audit, it will receive HACCP certification.

5. Continuous Monitoring and Re-certification: Once certified, companies must continually monitor their food safety systems and undergo periodic re-certification audits to ensure ongoing compliance with HACCP standards.

How HACCP Aligns with International Food Safety Standards

HACCP is recognized globally as a standard for food safety management and aligns with several international food safety standards. The system is promoted by various organizations such as the Codex Alimentarius Commission (established by the WHO and FAO) and is a requirement for food manufacturers in many countries.

HACCP aligns with several key international standards:

- Codex Alimentarius: The Codex provides internationally recognized guidelines for food safety, and HACCP is a cornerstone of those guidelines. Codex's General Principles of Food Hygiene recommends the implementation of HACCP to manage food safety in food production.
- ISO 22000: This is an international standard for food safety management systems, and it integrates HACCP principles with other management system elements. It requires food manufacturers to implement HACCP-based systems to ensure food safety across the entire supply chain.

- EU and US Regulations: In the European Union and the United States, HACCP is incorporated into food safety regulations, especially in industries dealing with high-risk products such as meat, dairy, and seafood. HACCP compliance is often mandatory for food producers exporting products internationally.

By aligning with these international standards, HACCP ensures that food safety practices meet global expectations, promoting consumer health and facilitating international trade by ensuring food products meet safety standards worldwide.

11.3 *Good Manufacturing Practices (GMP) for Food and Nutraceuticals*

11.3.1 Introduction to Good Manufacturing Practices (GMP)

Good Manufacturing Practices (GMP) are a set of guidelines and regulations that ensure food and nutraceutical products are consistently produced and controlled to meet quality standards and are safe for consumption. These practices are essential for maintaining the integrity of food products and ensuring that they are free from contamination, safe for use, and of the highest quality. GMP is a critical part of the food and nutraceutical industries and is enforced by regulatory agencies such as the Food and Drug Administration (FDA) in the United States, European Medicines Agency (EMA) in Europe, and Food Safety and Standards Authority of India (FSSAI).

GMP guidelines encompass every aspect of food and nutraceutical production, from the initial raw material sourcing to the final distribution of the finished product. It ensures that quality control, hygiene, safety, and environmental standards are met at every stage of production. This systematic approach helps mitigate the risk of contamination, ensures product consistency, and fosters consumer trust in food products.

The scope of GMP is broad, covering a wide range of aspects:

- Personnel hygiene and training
- Facility cleanliness and maintenance
- Equipment calibration and validation
- Raw material sourcing and inspection

- Product testing and quality control

GMP also ensures that manufacturers document every stage of production. This documentation serves as proof that all processes are in compliance with regulatory standards and helps identify any areas of potential risk.

The importance of GMP in food and nutraceutical production cannot be overstated. Adhering to these practices ensures that products are safe, effective, and reliable. Compliance with GMP is required by regulatory bodies in order for products to be legally sold, and failure to comply with GMP standards can lead to product recalls, legal consequences, and damage to a brand's reputation.

11.3.2 Key Principles of GMP in Food Industry

Good Manufacturing Practices in the food industry are focused on the overall quality and safety of food products. To ensure the highest standards of quality, several principles are followed. These principles address the critical areas of personnel hygiene, raw material sourcing, production facility cleanliness, and sanitation. Below are some of the key principles of GMP in food production:

Personnel Hygiene and Training

The hygiene and training of personnel are vital in the food and nutraceutical industries, as unsanitary practices can lead to contamination and foodborne illnesses. The GMP guidelines specify that:

- All personnel involved in the production process must maintain high levels of personal cleanliness. This includes appropriate hand washing, clean uniforms, and protective clothing (such as gloves, face masks, and hairnets) to prevent contamination.
- Employees must undergo regular training in food safety, personal hygiene, and the handling of food products. Proper training ensures that workers understand their role in maintaining product safety and are familiar with HACCP procedures, foodborne pathogen risks, and GMP regulations.
- Training records must be kept for all employees to ensure that training is being provided consistently and that the workforce remains compliant with the latest standards.

By ensuring proper personnel hygiene and continuous training, GMP helps prevent contamination and ensures that food products are safe for consumption.

Raw Material Sourcing and Quality Control

The quality of raw materials is fundamental to ensuring the final product's safety and efficacy. GMP stresses that:

- Raw materials, including ingredients, additives, and packaging materials, must be sourced from approved suppliers who follow certified safety practices. The quality of these materials must be evaluated through inspections, sampling, and testing to ensure they meet required standards.
- Incoming materials should be stored properly in clean, temperature-controlled environments to prevent contamination or degradation before use.
- Supplier verification is a crucial part of raw material sourcing, where suppliers should be regularly audited to ensure their practices meet GMP standards. This ensures that any materials coming into the facility are safe for use and free of contaminants that could affect product quality.
- Documenting raw material sourcing and quality testing is essential to maintain compliance with GMP and regulatory standards. Records should indicate the source, date of receipt, testing results, and storage conditions for all raw materials used in production.

By ensuring that all raw materials meet stringent quality standards, manufacturers can minimize risks of contamination and ensure consistent product quality.

Sanitation and Maintenance of Production Facilities

Maintaining a clean and safe production environment is one of the most fundamental principles of GMP. Proper sanitation ensures that products are produced in a controlled environment free of contaminants. GMP guidelines specify:

- Cleaning protocols must be established and followed to prevent the growth and spread of pathogens. This includes daily cleaning of surfaces, machinery, and equipment that come into contact with food. All cleaning agents used must be approved for food contact and properly documented.

- Sanitation schedules should be followed for high-risk areas where contamination is more likely, such as production floors, storage areas, and food processing equipment. These areas should be cleaned and sanitized thoroughly to remove dirt, oil, and other contaminants.
- Maintenance of equipment is also critical to the safe and efficient operation of the food production process. Equipment should be kept in good working order, regularly calibrated, and tested to ensure it operates safely and effectively. Any malfunctions or deviations should be promptly addressed to avoid contamination or delays in production.
- Pest control is another important aspect of maintaining sanitary conditions. Food production areas should be regularly inspected for pests, and any infestations should be dealt with immediately to prevent contamination.

11.3.3 GMP Guidelines for Nutraceuticals and Functional Foods

Differences Between GMP for Pharmaceuticals and Nutraceuticals

While Good Manufacturing Practices (GMP) are essential for ensuring the safety and quality of both pharmaceuticals and nutraceuticals, there are notable differences in the application of GMP standards between these two sectors. The primary distinction lies in the regulatory requirements, the complexity of the manufacturing processes, and the intended use of the products.

1. Regulatory Framework:

   - Pharmaceutical GMP is governed by stringent regulations due to the potential for pharmaceuticals to have significant effects on human health. Pharmaceuticals are subject to the FDA's Drug Approval Process, which includes rigorous clinical trials, long-term testing, and safety evaluations before they reach the market. Pharmaceuticals are generally subject to higher regulatory scrutiny.

- Nutraceutical GMP, on the other hand, falls under the regulatory framework for dietary supplements, which is governed by the Dietary Supplement Health and Education Act (DSHEA) in the United States. Nutraceuticals are not subject to the same pre-market approval process as pharmaceuticals. However, they must adhere to GMP standards that ensure purity, quality, and accuracy of claims made on labels.while pharmaceuticals are closely monitored for efficacy and safety through clinical studies, nutraceuticals are primarily regulated for safety and labeling accuracy. GMP for nutraceuticals ensures that these products do not contain harmful contaminants and are accurately labeled with their ingredients.

2. Complexity of Manufacturing:

- Pharmaceutical manufacturing is highly regulated and involves more complex processes, including formulation, mixing, quality testing, sterilization, and packaging under controlled conditions. The production process often includes high-tech equipment and stringent quality control.
- Nutraceutical manufacturing is less complex but still requires stringent measures to ensure the integrity of the product. For example, the production of nutraceuticals involves obtaining ingredients from natural sources, such as herbs, vitamins, and minerals. The challenge here is to preserve the efficacy of these ingredients during processing, extraction, and packaging.

3. Intended Use and Claims:

- Pharmaceuticals are designed to diagnose, cure, treat, or prevent diseases. Therefore, they must be produced under stringent clinical trial protocols, with a focus on safety, efficacy, and dosage accuracy.
- Nutraceuticals, however, are often marketed for their general health benefits, such as immunity support, weight management, and cardiovascular health. The claims made about nutraceuticals are generally related to their preventative or supportive roles in maintaining health rather than curing or treating diseases.

Role of GMP in Ensuring Product Consistency and Quality

GMP guidelines are essential for ensuring the quality and consistency of nutraceutical products. These guidelines provide a structured approach to manufacturing that focuses on quality control, product safety, and traceability.

Key aspects of GMP in nutraceuticals include:

1. Standardized Processes:

   - GMP ensures that production processes for nutraceuticals are consistent and reproducible. Standard operating procedures (SOPs) are established for each step in the production process, from raw material sourcing to final packaging. This reduces variability and ensures that each batch of the product meets the required quality standards.

2. Quality Control and Testing:

   - Rigorous quality control measures are integrated into the manufacturing process to ensure the purity and potency of nutraceuticals. Regular testing is conducted on raw materials, in-process products, and finished products. Tests may include microbial testing, heavy metal analysis, and potency testing of active ingredients.
   - Verification of ingredients: GMP ensures that the raw materials used in nutraceutical products are tested for identity, purity, and quality. This guarantees that the final product is consistent with the claims made on the label.

3. Preventing Contamination:

   - One of the most important aspects of GMP is to prevent contamination throughout the manufacturing process. This includes cleaning procedures for equipment, proper storage conditions for raw materials, and regular inspection of production facilities. Contamination can affect the safety and quality of nutraceuticals, leading to health risks for consumers.

- ◦ GMP also includes guidelines for the handling of allergenic substances and the avoidance of cross-contamination between different products, especially if they contain potential allergens like gluten, soy, or nuts.

4. Labeling Accuracy:

- ◦ GMP ensures that nutraceutical products are labeled accurately, with clear information about their ingredients, dosage, and health claims. Labels must be truthful and non-misleading, ensuring that consumers can make informed decisions about the products they purchase.
- ◦ Nutraceutical manufacturers must comply with regulations that prohibit the inclusion of unapproved health claims. For example, claims that a product can prevent, treat, or cure diseases are prohibited unless substantiated by clinical evidence.

5. Documentation and Traceability:

- ◦ Documentation is a fundamental component of GMP. Records of each batch produced, including production dates, batch numbers, testing results, and distribution details, must be maintained for traceability. This allows manufacturers to track and trace products in case of any recall or safety issue.
- ◦ Proper documentation ensures that manufacturers can verify the quality of each batch and make corrective actions if needed..

11.3.4 Regulatory Frameworks for GMP Compliance

FDA's Current Good Manufacturing Practices (cGMP)

The U.S. Food and Drug Administration (FDA) plays a crucial role in regulating the manufacturing of both food and nutraceuticals through the enforcement of Current Good Manufacturing Practices (cGMP). The cGMP guidelines are comprehensive standards aimed at ensuring that food products, drugs, and dietary supplements are consistently produced and controlled to meet the highest safety and quality standards.

- Scope of cGMP: The cGMP regulations, outlined in the Code of Federal Regulations (CFR), are designed to prevent the contamination, mislabeling, or adulteration of food products. These regulations cover aspects such as personnel hygiene, facility cleanliness, equipment maintenance, and testing of raw materials and finished products. They ensure that food and nutraceutical manufacturers follow systematic, documented processes at every stage of production, from sourcing raw materials to distribution.
- Core Areas: Key areas of FDA cGMP regulations include:

  - Quality Control Systems: Establishing and maintaining quality control systems that involve the testing and documentation of raw materials, in-process materials, and finished products.
  - Personnel Training: Ensuring that all employees involved in the manufacturing process are trained in hygiene, safety, food safety procedures, and GMP requirements.
  - Sanitation Procedures: Requiring proper sanitation and pest control measures to prevent contamination at every stage of the manufacturing process.
  - Traceability and Documentation: Requiring detailed documentation and record-keeping of every step in the manufacturing process to ensure traceability and compliance in case of audits or recalls.

By ensuring compliance with these cGMP standards, the FDA aims to protect public health, ensuring that consumers receive safe and high-quality food products and nutraceuticals.

GMP Standards Under WHO and Codex Alimentarius

The World Health Organization (WHO) and the Codex Alimentarius Commission (jointly formed by the Food and Agriculture Organization (FAO) and WHO) also play significant roles in the development and enforcement of GMP standards globally.

- WHO GMP Guidelines: WHO has established GMP guidelines for food and nutraceuticals aimed at ensuring product safety, quality, and efficacy. These guidelines are designed to facilitate international trade while maintaining product standards that safeguard public health. The WHO's GMP guidelines focus on maintaining consistency in production, prevention of contamination, and regulatory compliance across manufacturing processes.

- Codex Alimentarius GMP Standards: Codex, an international food standards organization, provides guidelines for food safety and quality assurance practices globally. Codex's GMP standards are designed to ensure food safety and consistency in the manufacturing of food products. These standards align closely with WHO guidelines and are used as references by many countries for regulatory food safety and quality management. Codex standards also complement the HACCP system, providing a framework for managing food safety from production to distribution.

Countries around the world use WHO and Codex Alimentarius GMP standards as a benchmark to align their national food safety systems. For instance, the European Union (EU) has adopted Codex Alimentarius guidelines, while the FDA uses international standards in their GMP regulations to align with global practices.

11.3.5 *Challenges in Implementing GMP in the Food Industry*

Despite the clear benefits of Good Manufacturing Practices (GMP), there are various challenges faced by food manufacturers in adopting and maintaining GMP standards. These challenges range from compliance difficulties for smaller manufacturers to the high costs associated with GMP certification.

Compliance Difficulties for Small Manufacturers

For small food manufacturers, the implementation of GMP can pose significant challenges, particularly due to their limited resources and staffing capabilities. Some of the primary difficulties include:

- Limited Resources: Smaller companies often struggle with financial constraints and lack the resources to invest in specialized equipment or qualified personnel to manage GMP compliance. For example, they may not have dedicated quality assurance teams or advanced testing facilities to ensure that products meet the required quality standards.

- Lack of Expertise: Small manufacturers may lack the in-depth knowledge or expertise needed to develop and implement a comprehensive GMP plan. This can lead to non-compliance or incomplete adherence to GMP standards, which increases the risk of contamination or product quality issues.
- Capacity Limitations: Smaller companies may also face challenges with scaling their operations to meet GMP guidelines. For instance, HACCP monitoring and critical control points (CCPs) can be difficult to implement on a smaller scale due to limitations in production capacity and oversight.

Despite these challenges, many small manufacturers can overcome them by collaborating with external consultants, investing in staff training, and streamlining processes to ensure GMP compliance without compromising on product quality.

Costs Associated with GMP Certification

The process of achieving GMP certification can be expensive for food manufacturers, especially smaller companies that may not have substantial financial resources. The costs involved include:

- Initial Setup Costs: Setting up a GMP-compliant facility often requires significant investment in infrastructure, equipment, and technology. This may include the purchase of sanitation equipment, quality control instruments, and storage or manufacturing areas designed to meet specific GMP requirements.
- Training Costs: Training staff on GMP regulations, food safety standards, and quality control systems is another significant cost. This includes hiring external trainers or enrolling employees in specialized courses, which may add up to a substantial expense for smaller businesses.
- Ongoing Operational Costs: Maintaining GMP compliance requires ongoing costs related to monitoring, documentation, auditing, and ensuring that quality control systems are operating effectively. This includes periodic audits, record keeping, and equipment calibration, all

of which incur expenses.

- Certification Fees: Obtaining GMP certification from recognized bodies such as the FDA, WHO, or Codex Alimentarius requires payment of certification fees. These fees can vary depending on the size of the company, the scope of the certification, and the certification body.

While the initial costs can be high, achieving GMP certification provides long-term benefits by ensuring product quality, consumer trust, and compliance with regulatory requirements. Moreover, GMP certification enhances a company's reputation and marketability, opening doors to global trade and increased sales.

TWELVE

LABELING, CLAIMS, AND REGULATIONS FOR NUTRACEUTICALS

12.1 Food Adulteration and Its Impact on Public Health

12.1.1 Introduction to Food Adulteration

1. **Definition and Types of Food Adulteration:**

   - **Food Adulteration** refers to the intentional or unintentional addition of inferior, harmful, or unnecessary substances to food products, which compromises their quality, safety, and nutritional value.
   - **Types of Adulteration:**

     - **Intentional Adulteration:** Deliberate addition of substances to increase quantity, enhance appearance, or reduce costs (e.g., adding water to milk, using synthetic dyes).
     - **Unintentional Adulteration:** Accidental contamination during production, processing, or storage (e.g., pesticide residues, microbial contamination).

2. **History and Prevalence of Food Adulteration Practices:**

- Food adulteration has been a concern for centuries, with historical records dating back to ancient civilizations. For example, in the 19th century, chalk was added to bread, and lead was used to sweeten wine.
- Despite modern regulations, food adulteration remains a global issue, particularly in developing countries where enforcement is weak. High-profile cases, such as the melamine scandal in infant formula, highlight the ongoing risks to public health.

12.1.2 *Common Types of Adulterants in Food and Nutraceuticals*

1. **Chemical Adulterants:**

- **Pesticide Residues:** Excessive use of pesticides in agriculture can leave harmful residues in food, posing risks to consumers.
- **Synthetic Dyes:** Unapproved or excessive use of artificial colors (e.g., Sudan dyes) to enhance the appearance of food products.
- **Preservatives:** Addition of unauthorized or excessive chemical preservatives (e.g., formaldehyde, boric acid) to extend shelf life.

2. **Biological Adulterants:**

- **Bacterial Contamination:** Pathogens such as Salmonella, E. coli, and Listeria can contaminate food during production or storage, leading to foodborne illnesses.
- **Mycotoxins:** Toxins produced by molds (e.g., aflatoxins in nuts and grains) that can cause severe health issues, including liver damage and cancer.

3. **Physical Adulterants:**

- **Dust, Stones, and Metal Fragments:** Contamination with foreign objects during harvesting, processing, or packaging.

- **Glass or Plastic Particles**: Accidental inclusion of packaging materials in food products.

12.1.3 Health Hazards of Food Adulteration

Food adulteration poses significant risks to public health, ranging from immediate illnesses to long-term chronic conditions. Understanding these health hazards is crucial for raising awareness and implementing effective prevention strategies. This section explores the short-term and long-term health effects of food adulteration and the diseases and toxic effects associated with it.

1. **Short-Term Health Effects**:

   - **Acute Foodborne Illnesses**: Consumption of adulterated food can lead to immediate health issues such as nausea, vomiting, diarrhea, abdominal pain, and fever. These symptoms are often caused by bacterial contamination (e.g., Salmonella, E. coli) or chemical adulterants (e.g., pesticides, heavy metals).
   - **Allergic Reactions**: Adulteration with undeclared allergens (e.g., nuts, gluten) can trigger severe allergic reactions, including anaphylaxis, in sensitive individuals.
   - **Gastrointestinal Distress**: Physical adulterants like stones, metal fragments, or glass can cause injuries to the digestive tract.

2. **Long-Term Health Effects**:

   - **Chronic Diseases**: Prolonged exposure to chemical adulterants, such as pesticide residues, synthetic dyes, and heavy metals, can lead to chronic conditions like cancer, kidney damage, liver failure, and neurological disorders.
   - **Nutritional Deficiencies**: Adulteration with inferior or non-nutritive substances (e.g., starch in milk, chalk in flour) can reduce the nutritional value of food, leading to deficiencies and related health issues.
   - **Developmental and Reproductive Issues**: Certain adulterants, such as mycotoxins and endocrine-disrupting chemicals, can affect fetal

development, cause birth defects, and impair reproductive health.

3. **Adulteration-Related Foodborne Diseases and Toxic Effects**:

   ○ **Bacterial Infections**: Contamination with pathogens like Listeria, Salmonella, and E. coli can cause severe infections, particularly in vulnerable populations such as children, the elderly, and immunocompromised individuals.
   ○ **Mycotoxin Poisoning**: Consumption of food contaminated with mycotoxins (e.g., aflatoxins) can lead to liver damage, immune suppression, and increased cancer risk.
   ○ **Chemical Toxicity**: Adulterants like melamine, formalin, and artificial sweeteners can cause organ damage, metabolic disorders, and even death in extreme cases.

12.1.4 Measures to Prevent and Detect Food Adulteration

1. **Government Policies and Food Safety Regulations**:

   ○ **Regulatory Frameworks**: Governments must establish and enforce strict food safety regulations, such as the Food Safety and Standards Authority of India (FSSAI) in India, the FDA in the United States, and the European Food Safety Authority (EFSA) in the EU.
   ○ **Inspections and Monitoring**: Regular inspections of food production facilities, markets, and supply chains help detect and prevent adulteration.
   ○ **Penalties and Enforcement**: Strict penalties for violators, including fines, license revocation, and legal action, deter adulteration practices.

2. **Consumer Awareness and Identification of Adulterated Foods**:

   ○ **Public Education Campaigns**: Governments and NGOs should educate consumers about the risks of food adulteration and ways to identify adulterated products.

- **Simple Detection Methods**: Teach consumers simple at-home tests to detect common adulterants, such as:

  - **Milk**: Adding a few drops of iodine to detect starch (turns blue if adulterated).
  - **Honey**: Dissolving honey in water to check for sugar syrup (pure honey will not dissolve easily).
  - **Turmeric**: Adding hydrochloric acid to detect chalk (frothing indicates adulteration).

- **Label Reading**: Encourage consumers to read food labels carefully, check for certifications, and avoid products with suspiciously low prices or unclear ingredient lists.

3. **Advanced Detection Technologies**:

   - **Laboratory Testing**: Use advanced techniques like chromatography, spectroscopy, and DNA testing to detect adulterants in food products.
   - **Blockchain Technology**: Implement blockchain for traceability in the food supply chain, ensuring transparency and accountability.

12.2 Regulatory Requirements for Nutraceutical Labeling

Nutraceutical labeling is a critical aspect of ensuring consumer safety, transparency, and informed decision-making. Proper labeling provides essential information about the product's ingredients, benefits, and usage, helping consumers make informed choices. This section introduces the importance of nutraceutical labeling and highlights the differences between pharmaceutical and nutraceutical labeling.

12.2.1 Introduction to Nutraceutical Labeling

1. **Importance of Proper Labeling for Consumer Awareness**:

   - **Transparency**: Clear and accurate labeling helps consumers understand what they are consuming, including the ingredients, nutritional content, and potential allergens.

- **Safety**: Proper labeling ensures that consumers are aware of any warnings, contraindications, or side effects associated with the product.
- **Informed Decision-Making**: Labels provide information about the product's health benefits, dosage, and usage instructions, enabling consumers to choose products that meet their needs.
- **Regulatory Compliance**: Adhering to labeling regulations helps manufacturers avoid legal issues and build trust with consumers.

2. **Differences Between Pharmaceutical and Nutraceutical Labeling**:

- **Regulatory Oversight**:

  - **Pharmaceuticals**: Strictly regulated by agencies like the FDA (U.S.) or EMA (Europe), with rigorous requirements for efficacy, safety, and labeling.
  - **Nutraceuticals**: Regulated as dietary supplements or functional foods, with less stringent requirements compared to pharmaceuticals.

- **Claims**:

  - **Pharmaceuticals**: Can make specific therapeutic claims (e.g., "treats high blood pressure") based on clinical trials and regulatory approval.
  - **Nutraceuticals**: Limited to structure/function claims (e.g., "supports heart health") and cannot claim to treat, cure, or prevent diseases.

- **Ingredients**:

  - **Pharmaceuticals**: Contain active pharmaceutical ingredients (APIs) that are strictly controlled and standardized.
  - **Nutraceuticals**: Contain bioactive compounds, vitamins, minerals, or herbal extracts, which may vary in potency and quality.

- ◦ **Labeling Requirements**:

  - ▪ **Pharmaceuticals**: Must include detailed information on dosage, side effects, contraindications, and interactions.
  - ▪ **Nutraceuticals**: Must include a supplement facts panel, list of ingredients, and disclaimers (e.g., "This product is not intended to diagnose, treat, cure, or prevent any disease").

12.2.2 Global Regulatory Guidelines for Labeling

Nutraceutical labeling regulations vary across countries and regions, but they share common goals of ensuring consumer safety, transparency, and informed decision-making. This section explores the labeling guidelines set by key regulatory bodies, including the FDA (U.S.), FSSAI (India), and Codex Alimentarius (international standards).

1. FDA (Food and Drug Administration) Regulations

- **Scope**: The FDA regulates dietary supplements and functional foods under the Dietary Supplement Health and Education Act (DSHEA) of 1994.
- **Labeling Requirements**:

  - ◦ **Supplement Facts Panel**: Must include serving size, amount per serving, and % Daily Value (%DV) of dietary ingredients.
  - ◦ **Ingredient List**: All ingredients must be listed in descending order of predominance by weight.
  - ◦ **Health Claims**: Limited to structure/function claims (e.g., "supports immune health") and must include a disclaimer: "This statement has not been evaluated by the FDA. This product is not intended to diagnose, treat, cure, or prevent any disease."
  - ◦ **Allergen Information**: Must declare the presence of major allergens (e.g., milk, eggs, peanuts).
  - ◦ **Net Quantity**: The label must state the net quantity of contents (e.g., number of capsules, weight).

- **Prohibited Claims**: Cannot make drug-like claims (e.g., "treats diabetes") without FDA approval.

2. FSSAI (Food Safety and Standards Authority of India) Guidelines

- **Scope**: FSSAI regulates nutraceuticals under the Food Safety and Standards (Health Supplements, Nutraceuticals, Food for Special Dietary Use, Food for Special Medical Purpose, Functional Food, and Novel Food) Regulations, 2016.
- **Labeling Requirements**:

  - **Product Name**: Must reflect the true nature of the product (e.g., "Herbal Supplement for Immunity").
  - **Ingredient List**: All ingredients must be listed, including additives and preservatives.
  - **Nutritional Information**: Must include energy value, protein, carbohydrates, fats, and other nutrients.
  - **Health Claims**: Must be scientifically substantiated and approved by FSSAI.
  - **Allergen Information**: Must declare allergens (e.g., gluten, soy) if present.
  - **Manufacturer Details**: Name and address of the manufacturer, packer, or distributor must be provided.
  - **Expiry Date**: The label must include the "Best Before" or "Use By" date.

- **Prohibited Claims**: Cannot make false or misleading claims about curing or preventing diseases.

3. Codex Alimentarius Standards for International Trade

- **Scope**: Codex Alimentarius, established by the FAO and WHO, provides international food standards, including guidelines for nutraceutical labeling, to facilitate global trade and ensure consumer protection.
- **Labeling Requirements**:

  - **Product Name**: Must be clear and not misleading.
  - **Ingredient List**: Ingredients must be listed in descending order of weight.
  - **Nutritional Information**: Must include energy value, macronutrients, and micronutrients.

- ○ **Health Claims**: Must be scientifically substantiated and not misleading.
- ○ **Allergen Information**: Must declare major allergens (e.g., nuts, dairy).
- ○ **Net Quantity**: Must be stated in metric units (e.g., grams, milliliters).
- ○ **Country of Origin**: Must be indicated for imported products.

- **Prohibited Claims**: Cannot make unsubstantiated or exaggerated health claims.

12.2.3 Essential Components of a Nutraceutical Label

A well-designed nutraceutical label is critical for providing consumers with accurate and comprehensive information about the product. It ensures transparency, safety, and compliance with regulatory requirements. Below are the essential components that must be included on a nutraceutical label:

1. Product Identity and Description

- **Product Name**: The name should clearly reflect the nature of the product (e.g., "Turmeric Curcumin Supplement").
- **Brand Name**: The brand or manufacturer's name should be prominently displayed.
- **Product Type**: Indicate whether the product is a dietary supplement, functional food, or other nutraceutical category.
- **Net Quantity**: State the total amount of the product (e.g., "60 capsules" or "500 grams").

2. List of Ingredients and Active Components

- **Ingredient List**: All ingredients must be listed in descending order of predominance by weight.
- **Active Components**: Highlight key bioactive ingredients (e.g., curcumin, omega-3 fatty acids) and their amounts per serving.
- **Additives and Preservatives**: Include any additives, fillers, or preservatives used in the product.
- **Allergen Information**: Clearly declare the presence of common allergens (e.g., gluten, soy, dairy).

3. Nutritional Information and Daily Values

- **Supplement Facts Panel**: Provide a detailed breakdown of the nutritional content, including:

  - Serving size and servings per container.
  - Amount per serving of key nutrients (e.g., vitamins, minerals).
  - % Daily Value (%DV) for nutrients, based on a standard 2,000-calorie diet.

- **Caloric Information**: Include total calories, fats, carbohydrates, proteins, and sugars per serving.

4. Recommended Dosage and Usage Instructions

- **Dosage**: Specify the recommended amount to be consumed per day (e.g., "Take 1 capsule daily").
- **Usage Instructions**: Provide clear instructions on how to use the product (e.g., "Take with meals" or "Do not exceed the recommended dosage").
- **Target Audience**: Indicate if the product is intended for specific groups (e.g., "For adults only" or "Consult a doctor before use if pregnant or nursing").

5. Warning Statements and Contraindications

- **Warnings**: Include any potential side effects or risks associated with the product (e.g., "May cause drowsiness" or "Consult a healthcare provider if you have a medical condition").
- **Contraindications**: Specify conditions or medications that may interact with the product (e.g., "Not recommended for individuals on blood thinners").
- **Disclaimers**: Include regulatory disclaimers, such as:

  - "This statement has not been evaluated by the FDA. This product is not intended to diagnose, treat, cure, or prevent any disease."

6. Additional Information

- **Storage Instructions**: Provide guidance on how to store the product (e.g., "Store in a cool, dry place").
- **Expiry Date**: Clearly state the "Best Before" or "Use By" date.
- **Manufacturer Details**: Include the name, address, and contact information of the manufacturer, packer, or distributor.
- **Batch/Lot Number**: For traceability in case of recalls or quality issues.

12.2.4 Compliance with Nutraceutical Labeling Laws

Compliance with nutraceutical labeling laws is essential to ensure consumer safety, avoid legal consequences, and maintain the integrity of the product. Misleading claims or non-compliance with labeling regulations can result in penalties, product recalls, and damage to a brand's reputation. This section explores the importance of adhering to labeling laws and the standardized formats for presenting information.

1. Misleading Claims and Legal Consequences

- **Misleading Claims**:

  - Claims that exaggerate the benefits of a product (e.g., "Cures cancer" or "Lose 10 pounds in a week") are considered misleading and are prohibited.
  - Claims must be supported by scientific evidence and approved by regulatory authorities.

- **Legal Consequences**:

  - **Fines and Penalties**: Non-compliance with labeling laws can result in hefty fines and legal action.
  - **Product Recalls**: Misleading claims or safety issues can lead to product recalls, which are costly and damage brand reputation.
  - **Loss of Consumer Trust**: Misleading labels erode consumer confidence and can lead to a loss of market share.

2. Standardized Formats for Presenting Information

- **Supplement Facts Panel**: A standardized format for displaying nutritional information, including serving size, amount per serving, and % Daily Value (%DV).
- **Ingredient List**: Ingredients must be listed in descending order of predominance by weight.
- **Health Claims**: Must follow specific formats, such as structure/function claims (e.g., "Supports heart health") with appropriate disclaimers.
- **Allergen Information**: Must be clearly stated in a standardized format (e.g., "Contains: Milk, Soy").
- **Warning Statements**: Must be prominently displayed and follow regulatory guidelines.

12.3 Types of Claims on Nutraceutical Products

12.3.1 Introduction to Nutraceutical Claims

1. **Definition of Product Claims**:

   - **Product Claims** are statements made on the label or in advertising about the benefits, functions, or properties of a nutraceutical product.
   - Claims can relate to health benefits, nutritional content, or the absence of certain ingredients (e.g., "Gluten-free").

2. **Importance of Regulatory Approval for Claims**:

   - **Consumer Protection**: Regulatory approval ensures that claims are accurate, substantiated, and not misleading.
   - **Legal Compliance**: Approved claims help manufacturers avoid legal issues and penalties.
   - **Market Credibility**: Products with approved claims are more likely to gain consumer trust and market acceptance.

12.3.2 Label Claims

Label claims are statements made on nutraceutical products that describe their benefits, ingredients, or nutritional content. These claims play a crucial role in informing consumers and influencing purchasing decisions. However, they must comply with regulatory guidelines to ensure accuracy and prevent misleading information. This section explores the definition, purpose, types, and examples of label claims.

1. **Definition and Purpose of Label Claims**:

   ◦ **Definition**: Label claims are statements on a product's packaging or advertising that describe its benefits, ingredients, or nutritional content.
   ◦ **Purpose**:

      ▪ Inform consumers about the product's features and benefits.
      ▪ Differentiate the product from competitors.
      ▪ Encourage informed purchasing decisions.

2. **Types of Legally Permitted Label Statements**:

   ◦ **Structure/Function Claims**: Describe the role of a nutrient or ingredient in the body (e.g., "Supports immune health" or "Promotes joint flexibility").
   ◦ **Health Claims**: Describe a relationship between a nutrient or ingredient and a health condition (e.g., "Calcium may reduce the risk of osteoporosis").
   ◦ **Nutrient Content Claims**: Describe the level of a nutrient in the product (e.g., "High in fiber" or "Low in sugar").
   ◦ **Allergen-Free Claims**: Indicate the absence of specific allergens (e.g., "Gluten-free" or "Dairy-free").

3. **Examples of Misleading Label Claims**:

   ◦ **Exaggerated Benefits**: Claims like "Cures diabetes" or "Eliminates wrinkles overnight" are misleading and prohibited.
   ◦ **Unsubstantiated Claims**: Claims without scientific evidence, such as "Boosts energy instantly," are not allowed.

- ○ **Ambiguous Language**: Phrases like "Miracle cure" or "100% effective" are considered misleading.

12.3.3 Nutrient Content Claims

12.3.3.1 Definition of Nutrient Content Claims

Nutrient content claims describe the level of a specific nutrient in a product, such as "high," "low," or "free." These claims are regulated to ensure accuracy and prevent misleading information.

1. **Regulations on Nutrient Quantity Statements**:

   - ○ Nutrient content claims must comply with specific regulatory standards. For example:

     - **"High in"**: The product must contain at least 20% of the Daily Value (DV) per serving.
     - **"Low in"**: The product must contain no more than a specified amount of the nutrient (e.g., "Low sodium" means ≤140 mg per serving).
     - **"Free"**: The product must contain negligible or no amount of the nutrient (e.g., "Sugar-free" means <0.5 g per serving).

2. **Acceptable Terms for Nutrient Content Claims**:

   - ○ **"High in Vitamin C"**: The product must provide at least 20% of the DV for vitamin C per serving.
   - ○ **"Low Sodium"**: The product must contain ≤140 mg of sodium per serving.
   - ○ **"Good Source of Fiber"**: The product must provide 10-19% of the DV for fiber per serving.
   - ○ **"Fat-Free"**: The product must contain <0.5 g of fat per serving.

12.3.3.2 Nutrient Content Claim Verification

Nutrient content claims on nutraceutical products must be accurate and substantiated to ensure consumer trust and regulatory compliance. Verification of these claims involves laboratory testing and oversight by regulatory bodies. This section explores the process of verifying nutrient content claims and the role of regulatory authorities in ensuring their accuracy.

1. Laboratory Testing for Accurate Nutrient Quantification

- **Purpose**: Laboratory testing is essential to verify the accuracy of nutrient content claims, such as "high in vitamin C" or "low sodium."
- **Methods**:

  - **Chromatography**: Used to separate and quantify nutrients like vitamins, minerals, and bioactive compounds.
  - **Spectroscopy**: Measures the concentration of specific nutrients based on their interaction with light.
  - **Microbiological Assays**: Used to quantify certain vitamins and amino acids.
  - **Chemical Analysis**: Determines the levels of macronutrients (e.g., proteins, fats, carbohydrates) and micronutrients (e.g., minerals).

- **Third-Party Testing**: Independent laboratories are often used to ensure unbiased and accurate results.

2. Role of Regulatory Bodies in Claim Validation

- **Regulatory Oversight**:

  - Regulatory bodies, such as the FDA (U.S.), FSSAI (India), and EFSA (Europe), establish guidelines for nutrient content claims and ensure compliance.
  - They review scientific evidence and laboratory test results to validate claims.

- **Enforcement**:

  - Regulatory authorities conduct inspections and audits of manufacturing facilities to verify compliance with labeling laws.

- They may require manufacturers to provide documentation, including test results and certificates of analysis, to substantiate claims.

- **Penalties for Non-Compliance**:

  - Misleading or unverified claims can result in fines, product recalls, or legal action.
  - Regulatory bodies may also issue public warnings or revoke product licenses.

12.3.4 Health Claims

Health claims on nutraceutical products describe the relationship between a nutrient, ingredient, or food and its potential health benefits. These claims are strictly regulated to ensure they are accurate, scientifically substantiated, and not misleading. This section explores the definition and categories of health claims, the scientific validation process, and examples of approved and controversial claims.

12.3.4.1 Definition and Categories of Health Claims

1. **Definition of Health Claims**:

   - Health claims describe the relationship between a food or dietary supplement and its potential to reduce the risk of a disease or support a specific body function.

2. **Categories of Health Claims**:

   - **Structure-Function Claims**:

     - Describe the role of a nutrient or ingredient in supporting normal body functions (e.g., "Supports heart health" or "Promotes joint flexibility").

- Do not require pre-approval by regulatory authorities but must include a disclaimer (e.g., "This statement has not been evaluated by the FDA").

- **Disease Risk Reduction Claims**:

  - Describe the potential of a nutrient or ingredient to reduce the risk of a specific disease (e.g., "Calcium may reduce the risk of osteoporosis").
  - Require pre-approval and must be supported by significant scientific evidence.

12.3.4.2 Scientific Validation of Health Claims

5. **Clinical Studies and Evidence Requirements**:

   - **Clinical Trials**: Randomized, double-blind, placebo-controlled studies are considered the gold standard for substantiating health claims.
   - **Epidemiological Studies**: Observational studies that establish a correlation between nutrient intake and health outcomes.
   - **Mechanistic Studies**: Research that explains the biological mechanism behind the claimed health benefit.

6. **Approval Process by Regulatory Authorities**:

   - **FDA (U.S.)**:

     - Health claims must be supported by "significant scientific agreement" or authorized based on authoritative statements from scientific bodies.
     - Manufacturers must submit a petition with scientific evidence for review and approval.

   - **EFSA (Europe)**:

- The European Food Safety Authority evaluates health claims based on scientific evidence and issues a list of approved claims.

- **FSSAI (India):**

  - Health claims must be scientifically substantiated and approved by FSSAI before use on product labels.

12.3.4.3 *Examples of Approved and Controversial Health Claims*

7. **FDA-Approved Health Claims in the U.S.:**

   - **Approved Claims:**

     - "Calcium and vitamin D may reduce the risk of osteoporosis."
     - "Soluble fiber from whole oats may reduce the risk of heart disease."

   - **Controversial Claims:**

     - Claims about weight loss supplements (e.g., "Lose 10 pounds in a week") are often unsubstantiated and prohibited.

8. **FSSAI and EFSA Guidelines on Permissible Health Claims:**

   - **FSSAI (India):**

     - Approved Claims: "Omega-3 fatty acids support heart health."
     - Controversial Claims: Claims about curing diseases (e.g., "Treats diabetes") are prohibited without scientific evidence.

   - **EFSA (Europe):**

     - Approved Claims: "Plant sterols and stanols help lower cholesterol."

- Controversial Claims: Claims about unproven benefits (e.g., "Boosts immunity instantly") are not allowed.

12.3.5 Dietary Supplement Claims

Dietary supplements are a specific category of nutraceuticals that provide concentrated sources of nutrients or bioactive compounds. Unlike functional foods, which are consumed as part of a regular diet, dietary supplements are taken in addition to the diet to support health. This section explores the differences between dietary supplements and functional foods, regulatory frameworks for supplement claims, and compliance requirements for manufacturers.

12.3.5.1 Difference Between Dietary Supplements and Functional Foods

1. **Regulatory Differences in Dietary Supplement Claims**:

   - **Dietary Supplements**: Regulated as a separate category under specific laws (e.g., DSHEA in the U.S.). Claims are limited to structure/function claims and must include a disclaimer.
   - **Functional Foods**: Regulated as conventional foods with added health benefits. Claims must be supported by scientific evidence and approved by regulatory authorities.

2. **Labeling Requirements for Dietary Supplements**:

   - **Supplement Facts Panel**: Must include serving size, amount per serving, and % Daily Value (%DV) of dietary ingredients.
   - **Ingredient List**: All ingredients must be listed in descending order of predominance by weight.
   - **Health Claims**: Limited to structure/function claims (e.g., "Supports bone health") with a disclaimer: "This statement has not been evaluated by the FDA. This product is not intended to diagnose, treat, cure, or prevent any disease."

- ○ **Allergen Information**: Must declare the presence of major allergens (e.g., milk, eggs, peanuts).

12.3.5.2 Regulation of Supplement Claims by Different Authorities

1. **FDA's DSHEA (Dietary Supplement Health and Education Act)**:

   - ○ **Scope**: DSHEA regulates dietary supplements in the U.S., allowing manufacturers to make structure/function claims without pre-approval.
   - ○ **Requirements**:

     - Claims must be truthful, not misleading, and supported by scientific evidence.
     - Manufacturers must notify the FDA of new dietary ingredients and provide evidence of safety.

   - ○ **Prohibited Claims**: Cannot make drug-like claims (e.g., "treats diabetes") without FDA approval.

2. **FSSAI Guidelines on Indian Nutraceutical Supplements**:

   - ○ **Scope**: FSSAI regulates dietary supplements under the Food Safety and Standards (Health Supplements, Nutraceuticals, Food for Special Dietary Use, Food for Special Medical Purpose, Functional Food, and Novel Food) Regulations, 2016.
   - ○ **Requirements**:

     - Claims must be scientifically substantiated and approved by FSSAI.
     - Labels must include a list of ingredients, nutritional information, and health claims with disclaimers.

   - ○ **Prohibited Claims**: Cannot make false or misleading claims about curing or preventing diseases.

12.3.5.3 *Compliance Requirements for Supplement Manufacturers*

1. **Need for Scientific Substantiation of Claims**:

   - All health claims must be supported by credible scientific evidence, such as clinical studies or peer-reviewed research.
   - Manufacturers must maintain records of the evidence used to substantiate claims for regulatory review.

2. **Prohibited Misleading and Unverified Statements**:

   - **Misleading Claims**: Claims that exaggerate benefits (e.g., "Cures cancer" or "Lose weight instantly") are prohibited.
   - **Unverified Statements**: Claims without scientific evidence (e.g., "Boosts energy in seconds") are not allowed.
   - **Disclaimers**: Must include disclaimers to clarify the limitations of claims (e.g., "This product is not intended to diagnose, treat, cure, or prevent any disease").